THE MAKING OF MODERN MANAGEMENT

The Making of Modern Management

British Management in Historical Perspective

JOHN F. WILSON
and
ANDREW THOMSON

OXFORD
UNIVERSITY PRESS

OXFORD
UNIVERSITY PRESS

Great Clarendon Street, Oxford OX2 6DP

Oxford University Press is a department of the University of Oxford.
It furthers the University's objective of excellence in research, scholarship,
and education by publishing worldwide in

Oxford New York

Auckland Cape Town Dar es Salaam Hong Kong Karachi
Kuala Lumpur Madrid Melbourne Mexico City Nairobi
New Delhi Shanghai Taipei Toronto

With offices in

Argentina Austria Brazil Chile Czech Republic France Greece
Guatemala Hungary Italy Japan Poland Portugal Singapore
South Korea Switzerland Thailand Turkey Ukraine Vietnam

Oxford is a registered trade mark of Oxford University Press
in the UK and in certain other countries

Published in the United States
by Oxford University Press Inc., New York

British Library Cataloguing in Publication Data
Data available

Library of Congress Cataloging in Publication Data
Data available

Typeset by SPI Publisher Services, Pondicherry, India
Printed in Great Britain
on acid-free paper by
Biddles Ltd., King's Lynn, Norfolk

ISBN 0–19–926158–X 978–0–19–926158–1

1 3 5 7 9 10 8 6 4 2

Dedication

This book is dedicated to Edward Brech, in recognition of the inspirational role he has played in fostering the development of management history in the UK.

Contents

PART III. Managers in Context

Preface

Since there is a dearth of literature in the specific area of management history, this book has been primarily created from tomes, articles, and monographs in a range of related fields. It would be pleasant to say that this has been complemented by a modicum of primary research based on the stories of managers, but regretfully, even if management is one of the most common and critical activities in the world, there are few of these available other than the occasional autobiography or biography of a (chief executive officer) CEO. By far the best of the books available, Sidney Pollard's *The Genesis of Modern Management* (1965), only takes us up to 1830, considerably earlier than the period on which we focus. As Gospel (1983: 102), writing in a related field, has noted: 'Unfortunately we know little about the recruitment, numbers, and activities of these managers.' This lack of information is a key reason for the several limitations of the book which are acknowledged below.

While we would like to claim that this approach will provide an unprecedented coverage of British management history, it is unfortunately impossible to do full justice to its multidimensional nature in a book of this length. This is why we have chosen to limit our coverage to just three functional roles, while at the same time looking at the issues of production and the strategy requirements derived from it in Chapters 3 to 5. A second caveat is that the book focuses primarily on the manufacturing sector, in spite of the fact that the service sector has now become the dominant contributor to the modern economy. Moreover, in some respects the British service sector, perhaps especially retailing and the utilities, developed more advanced managerial systems at various periods of time than did their manufacturing counterparts. Yet manufacturing is where the main debates have been concentrated and where history has the greatest resonance. This is in large part because of the dominance of production issues in the development of thinking about management, starting with production and moving on to strategy and structure.

A third caveat is that the book concentrates on management in large companies, on the grounds that small business does not justify the use of complex management structures. As the owner-manager is still the dominant force in the small business sector, it is evident that small businesses can operate effectively in many parts of the economy, as indeed Chandler recognized (1977: 605–28). Moreover, there are obviously firms in the economy at various stages of complexity, ranging from the single-person operation through to the multidivisional multinational; each stage has different requirements of management structure, as well as the separation between ownership and control, which we cannot take fully into account.

A fourth limitation is our inability to deal in detail with all aspects of the external environment, especially such important issues as the relationships between industry and the state, between industry and financial institutions, as well as market size and structure, and the role of labour. While all of these need to be taken into account, most notably the significant impact trade unionism has had on British management, its rich history must be sought elsewhere (Clegg, Fox, and Thompson 1964; Gospel 1993). Conversely, an attempt is made to recognize that the 'institutional rigidities' which have been seen as affecting the evolution of British management (Lazonick 1991; Langlois and Robertson 1995) consist of external forces as well as those internal to the firm.

A final caveat is that while the book purports to be about management, it needs to be accepted that many of the arguments made are general and inductive rather than detailed and deductive. While there are many business histories about the development of strategies and structures in organizations, there is virtually nothing which examines the role of management as we have defined it in any single business, never mind in the general way that broad historical surveys might have provided. Incredibly, even now in the twenty-first century we know relatively little about what managers actually do; thus, to expect this information to have been available historically would have been expecting far too much. On a slightly different slant, management is concerned with the strategy, structure, and process of the organization. We are concerned with all three, but would like to concentrate on process. However, we must confess that there is less available information on this historical aspect of management than there is on the others, even though most dimensions of the modern teaching of management are concerned primarily with process issues.

All these caveats lead us to hope that this will not be the last word on a topic which has taken long enough to reach fruition in publication. Indeed, we hope that it will encourage others to take up the pen and add to the perspectives on what deserves to become an important component of how we understand management.

The framework of the book is composed of five groups of chapters: scene-setting, organizationally focused, contextually focused, and functionally focused, before bringing the threads together in the Conclusions and Reflections. To expand on this categorization, Chapter 1 is an introduction which sets the scene by providing a number of parameters to management history. Following this, Chapter 2 concentrates on an exposition of the theory and themes of the book. Chapter 3 examines management in Britain up to the Second World War, with Chapter 4 performing the same role for the United States, Germany, and Japan. Chapter 5 then brings the history of management in Britain up to the present. These three chapters essentially deal with management in its organizational, structural, and strategic role, while the following three are concerned with the context within which managers have operated. Chapter 6 provides an analysis of the sociocultural context of attitudes towards industry and managers as well as insights into the managerial labour market. Chapter 7 is concerned with management education and training, while Chapter 8 deals with managerial thought and professional institutions, both of them reflecting on one of the themes of the book, the slow transition towards professionalism. The following three chapters provide a detailed treatment of developments in the principal functional dimensions of management other than production, namely, personnel, marketing, and accounting. Finally, there is a concluding chapter that attempts to draw together the principal themes and arguments.

It remains to thank those who have assisted and wished us well on this considerable undertaking, and especially to our mentor, Edward Brech, who inspired our interest in this new subject, which he has done more than anyone else to create. We are proud to dedicate the book to him. We would also like to mention the support of our colleagues in the Management History Research Group, while in presenting papers at several institutions (York, Queen Mary, the Open University) and conferences (ABH, EBHA, EGOS, and BAM) we have benefited enormously from the advice and expertise of those who patiently listened. In particular, Michael Rowlinson, Alfred Kieser, Howard Gospel, Chris Grey, John Quail, Linda Perriton, Trevor Boyns, Dick Edwards, and Steven Toms have been important influences. Gerry Alcock also provided some useful insights into the field of marketing. There has also been practical assistance with our research from librarians, notably at the Open University, The Chartered Management Institute, and the National Library of New Zealand. And we must pay tribute to our editor, David Musson, for his patient steering of the project through the processes of acceptance and development. But the final word must be given to our wives, Barbara and Angela, who have patiently borne the pressures incumbent on sharing a life and a house with a writer.

John F. Wilson and Andrew W. Thomson, September 2005

List of Figures

List of Tables

Abbreviations

AACP	Anglo-American Council on Productivity
ACCA	Association of Certified and Corporate Accountants
AGM	annual general meeting
BIM	British Institute of Management
BMC	British Motor Corporation
CAA	Central Association of Accountants
CCPMO	Coordinating Committee of Professional Management Organisations
CIMA	Chartered Institute of Management Accountants
CEML	Council for Excellence in Management and Leadership
CEO	chief executive officer
CIM	Chartered Institute of Marketing
CIOS	International Committee on Scientific Management (Confederation Internationale des Organisations Scientifique)
CIPD	Chartered Institute of Personnel and Development
CMA	Confederation of Management Associations
CMI	Chartered Management Institute
CPD	Continuing Professional Development
CTC	Central Training Council
DoI	Department of Industry
EEF	Engineering Employers' Federation
FBI	Federation of British Industries
FMCG	fast-moving consumer goods
GATT	General Agreement on Tariffs and Trade
GDP	gross domestic product
H-form	holding company form
HPWO	high performance work organizations
HR	human resource
ICAEW	Institute of Chartered Accountants in England and Wales
ICI	Imperial Chemical Industries
ICWA	Institute of Cost and Works Accountants
IIA	Institute of Industrial Administration
IM	Institute of Management
IRC	Industrial Reorganisation Corporation
ISMA	Incorporated Sales Managers' Association

IT	information technology
ITB	Industrial Training Board
LSE	London School of Economics
MBA	Master of Business Administration
MCI	Management Charter Initiative
M-form	multidivisional form
MRG	Management Research Group
NEDO	National Economic Development Office
NIIP	National Institute of Industrial Psychology
PEP	Political and Economic Planning
P&G	Procter & Gamble
RB	resource base
RBV	resource-based view
R&D	research and development
RD	resource-dependency
SAA	Society of Accountants and Auditors
S-form	specialized form
SIAA	Society of Incorporated Accountants and Auditors
SMA	Sales Managers Association
SMEs	small and medium-sized enterprises
U-form	unitary form
UCMDS	Unilever Companies Management Development Scheme
USP	unique selling proposition

Part I
Introduction

1

An Introduction to British Management History

INTRODUCTION

In this first chapter, we have several objectives, beginning with the aims of the book and a justification for the subject area of management history. After this we need to recognize that management has always been part of human organization throughout history, although only for the last two centuries or so has it been primarily associated with the economic and industrial contexts that dominate the use of the term now. The heart of the chapter is, however, to present the main components of management history in respect of the three ways in which the term management is commonly used, namely, as a process or activity, as a structure in an organization, and as a group or class of people carrying out managerial roles within the workforce. Each of these occupies a substantial section. There are then two other issues to consider, both providing a context for what will follow in later chapters. One is to offer a periodization of the development of the three main components of management in Britain, in order to provide a chronological framework within which other chapters are organized. The other is to provide an economic context against which our story can be told, since an inevitable part of the history of management is to evaluate it against economic outcomes, especially in relation to other countries. Indeed, although the topic is British, it would be inappropriate to talk of Britain only, without setting it in a context of what was happening in other countries. We have chosen the United States, Germany, and Japan for our main comparators. In fact, the 'big' question of the book is essentially a comparative one, namely, 'attempting to understand why corporate management structures developed so impressively in countries like the USA, Germany and Japan, while in Britain relatively little progress was made in this respect' (Wilson 1995: 134). Putting this rather more simplistically, why did what is often called 'The Managerial Revolution' not take place with the same intensity in Britain? Why was the rise of managerial capitalism, which we define as the supplanting of owners in the control of organizations by employed managers, so slow compared to other countries? While it will be necessary over the course of this book to elaborate further on these definitions, it is clear that we are, therefore, concerned with not only chronological developments but also the underlying causal considerations, creating the frame of reference by which we investigate these issues in the following chapters.

THE AIMS OF THE BOOK

It remains a curious British paradox that while since the 1970s studying management has become one of the most popular subjects at university level, relatively few resources have been devoted to understanding how and why this vital factor of production evolved into its current shape and character. This paradox is reinforced by the knowledge that in explaining Britain's historically poor economic performance, managers and management have frequently been accorded a significant share of the blame. We do have a magisterial study of early management, up to about 1830, in Pollard's *The Genesis of Modern Management* (1965: 11); he himself complained that 'one of the most glaring gaps is the story of the genesis of modern industrial management'. Shortly afterwards we had Child's major survey (1969) of British management thought, and his helpful taxonomy of perspectives on management is taken up again in a later section (Modern Management). But since then there has been little analysis to pursue the implications for management and managers into the era of big business organizations and systems, even though as Grey (2005: 53–5) outlines, management and managers have moved from relative obscurity on to centre stage in the industrialized world. Nor did economists spend much time on the inductive side of their subject; of those who did, Coase (1937) with his identification of the importance of transaction costs, and Penrose (1959) with her recognition that managerial competence was a key constraint in the growth of firms, were both only welcomed into the mainstream of economics several decades after their original contributions.

This is not to say that there has been no relevant work. Chandler (1990) has provided a starting point in his comparative analysis of structural developments in the United States, Britain, and Germany with different descriptive designations of personal capitalism for Britain, competitive managerial capitalism for the United States and cooperative managerial capitalism for Germany (although we would prefer professional proprietorial capitalism for Germany and would suggest collective managerial capitalism for Japan). Similarly, there are valuable studies of individual aspects of the overall history of management, not least in the works of Urwick and Brech (1945, 1946, 1947), Child (1969), Guillén (1994), and notably Brech's five magisterial volumes (2002*a–e*). Business, accounting, and labour historians have also offered tantalizing insights into management issues (Gospel 1992; Wilson 1995; Boyns 2005), while occasionally management writers indulge in historical perspectives as a prelude to their assessments of contemporary and future issues (Daft 1997: 41–63; Thomson et al. 2001: 35–51). Witzel (2002) has written a broadly based and long-term history of management, focusing on the *Builders and Dreamers* who are the title of his book; Donkin (2001) has produced a history of work in which management inevitably plays a significant role. Organizational theorists have also offered insights into the place of managers in organizations, bringing some dynamic perspectives to the theoretical issues (Grey 2005). But there is little or nothing specific about the history of British management in the modern era, providing us with an incentive to fill the gap. This book has consequently been planned and written as a means of both coordinating a disparate range of sources and providing an overview of British management history from the nineteenth century to the present.

So, why study management history (Thomson 2001)? One reason is that management is widely accepted as the factor of production most able to provide competitive advantage. As Guillén (1994: 304) argues: 'The successful operation of the firm under capitalism and democratic government derives in large part from the way in which the social group of economic directors [the managers] understands its function and by the adequacy of its technical knowledge and training to the demands of the situation.' Second, while there is a massive literature on management, some of which is paraded on airport bookshelves and attracts considerable attention for a short period, a more considered view of this crucial subject must surely require the longer time span of consideration which only history can provide. Sadly, the vast majority of authorities on management, often referred to as 'gurus', provide mere instructional lessons that offer a deeply flawed historical perspective based on self-interest and simplistic generalizations. Understanding management involves studying how it can work best, which requires an examination of how it has operated in the past, and this in turn involves appreciating the institutions, values, and relationships in the wider society. Above all, it is a contested terrain, especially when linked to legitimacy and authority. Third, the need to understand the role of management and managers in the development of the industrial and economic world. There is a sense in which the 'theory of the firm' leads inexorably towards managerial theory, and all managerial theories towards growth theory—with the implication that in the context of corporate capitalism the only theory worth looking at is a dynamic managerial theory. But management needs to be studied in practice as well as in theory. And as we shall see shortly, managers are now a very substantial part of the workforce. In both role and numbers, they deserve consideration. While Burnham's apocalyptic views (1941) on managers as a dominant social elite may not have proved relevant to Britain, others, such as Enteman (1993), have argued more recently that the ideology of managerialism is a major force in the modern world.

Fourth, and more specifically, every organization should understand and learn from its own past if it is to appreciate its own capabilities and weaknesses. Recent developments in strategic management thinking, including resource-based (RB) management and knowledge management (Penrose 1959; Teece, Pisano, and Sheun 1997), have emphasized the importance of organizational memory in maintaining and developing the tacit knowledge which is a key to organizational capability (Hamel and Prahalad 1994; Grant 1998; Kransdorff 1998). As the chairman of Unilever noted (Jones 2005: 15) at the company's 1972 annual general meeting (AGM), 'much of the knowledge which is important to a firm like Unilever cannot be found in books. It has to be acquired often expensively, sometimes painfully, by experience and deliberate enquiry.' The chairman also recognized that 'this knowledge was the result of cumulative learning, and multifaceted and tacit', with roots in the past, having been accumulated experientially over a period of time. Indeed, management is still largely an experientially based occupation, focused upon time and place, even though we do firmly believe that an intellectual framework is important for understanding, and, in the vast majority of cases, for success. In the light of the above quotation, it is possibly not without significance that Unilever has one of the most comprehensive and best company histories in the industrial world (Wilson 1954, 1968; Jones 2005).

THE ORIGINS OF MANAGEMENT

In one sense, management is as old as human civilization and is represented by the series of activities that were initiated at various points throughout history. Administering an empire or a church, building a pyramid or a cathedral, or leading an army, all required managerial skills involving techniques on the one hand and vision and leadership on the other; all date back long before the term 'management' was first coined. The term itself is derived from the French word 'menager', used in the context of household management. An alternative etymological origin is the Italian word 'maneggiare', or horse-handler, indicating the essentially humble and mundane meaning of management, the sense that it is something dispersed, done by everyone (Grey 2005: 53). These techniques must be seen as parts, but not the whole, of modern management, since as we see in the following section, in another sense management was barely recognized as the integrated concept it is now until the very end of the nineteenth century, resulting from the growth of large-scale industry after the 1870s.

The origins of management can be broken into three broad chronological periods, with the dating of the innovations in a highly condensed form taken from George (1968). The first is the period of recorded history up to the middle of the fourteenth century. By about 1500 BC, the Egyptians were using a number of management techniques, including: planning, organizing, and controlling; centralization and decentralization in organization; record keeping; the need for honesty and fair play in management; and the use of staff advice. The minimum wage also dates from this early period. Not long afterwards, the Chinese had recognized many of these principles, and had added that of specialization. By the time of the birth of Christ, the Greeks and Romans had added others: an element of scientific method in the way work was organized; job descriptions; staff functions; and aspects of human relations. In AD 284, Diocletian identified the principle of delegation of authority, while around AD 1000, the Arabs listed the traits of a leader and a manager. But during this long period, management techniques were used in support of political, religious, or military activities, rather than industrial or even commercial ones. Work in these spheres was not fashionable for people of high status; in the Greek and Roman civilizations, it was preferably left to slaves. Even as late as the era (the thirteenth century AD) of St Thomas Aquinas, commercial activity was rated lower by him in ranking the trades or professions than agriculture or crafts (Donkin 2001).

Nevertheless, trading flourished and the second pre-modern period might be said to have begun with the 'Commercial Revolution', involving the development of trading corporations in the Italian city states and more specifically for posterity the discovery of double-entry bookkeeping by Paccioli in 1340, an issue covered in Chapter 11. Aspects of cost accounting soon followed, including work in process accounts, while the Arsenal of Venice in 1436 is recorded as using some very 'modern' methods such as the standardization and interchangeability of parts, numbering of inventoried parts, assembly-line techniques and inventory, and cost control. Almost a century later, Machiavelli was enunciating the principle of reliance on mass consent, the need for cohesiveness in organizations, and the qualities of leadership.

Our third and final pre-modern period, leading us into Chapter 3, started with the First Industrial Revolution from around 1770, in which new methods of production became available in industry (and agriculture) and novel organizational forms and economic roles were required, including that of the manager. This is the period identified by Pollard in the title of his book *The Genesis of Modern Management* (1965), the era of the owner-manager based on little or no separation of ownership and control and a general unwillingness to delegate responsibility to salaried managers. As a consequence, by the middle of the nineteenth century, Britain had a well developed system of what Chandler (1990) has labelled personal capitalism, based upon structures that failed to encourage the rise of professional management.

In terms of techniques, Adam Smith in *The Wealth of Nations* (1776) applied the principle of specialization to manufacturing workers and noted payback computations and concepts of control. By 1800, Boulton & Watt in the Soho Works were well ahead of their contemporaries in many of their procedures, including: standard operating procedures; specifications; work methods; planning; incentive wages; standard times; standard data; employee Christmas parties; bonuses announced at Christmas; mutual employees' insurance society; and the use of audits. At much the same time, the American Eli Whitney was introducing a different range of techniques: scientific method; use of cost accounting and quality control; applied interchangeable parts concept; the span of management control. By 1810, Robert Owen had also introduced personnel practices, assumed responsibility for training workers, and built clean workers' houses. This theme of worker efficiency was pursued by James Mill, who in 1820 analysed and synthesized human motions, while in 1832 Charles Babbage wrote of the effect of various colours on employee efficiency. Soon after mid century, the early concept of organizational analysis had come into existence on the American railroads, with Henry Poor introducing principles of organization, communication, and information and Daniel McCallum making use of an organization chart to show management structure and how 'scientific' management could be applied to the sector.

MODERN MANAGEMENT

We now turn to the first of what we regard as the three components of 'modern management', namely, the further development of management as a key process or activity in the industrial context and the primary subject of this book. This component involved the integration of activities in a context of modern, large-scale industrial and commercial enterprises, namely, the trend for decision-making through managerial systems to take over from the market mechanism. This process can be seen to have begun around 1870 with the onset of the 'Second Industrial Revolution', accelerating ever faster from the turn of the nineteenth century. This is the period that saw an emerging requirement for a more professional manager, given the combination of internal and external pressures that were imposed on business. This also involved the beginnings of the separation of ownership and control and a move towards managerial capitalism, issues that are further analysed in Chapters 3 and 4. But it is not a process that can easily be provided with a specific date of change, especially since practices in British industry were more associated with continuity than radical change, at least up to the 1960s.

Moreover, prior to this period few people recognized how the series of activities which contributed to the elaboration of management were linked. While in Chapters 2 and 8 we examine the history of management thought in greater detail, it is useful at this stage to offer some insights into the development of a theoretical perspective. Litterer (1986: 74) suggests that a paper by the American Henry Towne (1885), 'The Engineer as an Economist', was the first well-presented statement of the separate identity and place of management, but accepted that Towne's conception of the identity of management was more a collection of parts than a unified whole. After Towne, although work continued on various aspects of management, it was not until almost the end of the century that one can detect the next major development in elaborating management as a unified concept. This came from a British source, J. S. Lewis (1899*a*), a practising engineer-manager in a series of articles entitled *Works Management for the Maximum of Production*. Lewis used the term 'organization'—or the management group, in modern parlance—to encompass the relationship between the various managers involved in conducting an organized activity. As such, it was an activity that required recognition and study. He also acknowledged the importance of size, using a military analogy to say that a corporal in charge of a squad could lead his group effectively without much thought about the factors or relationships involved, that is, almost by instinct. But at higher levels, with more people involved, he felt that the need for understanding relationships becomes more acute. According to Lewis, no longer could management be left to one man, because, taking a military analogy, the objectives and situations involved in a battalion were so different to those involved with a squad that a whole new set of factors were introduced. Finally, as well as stressing the need for clear definitions of authority and responsibility within an organization, Lewis argued that managers, in addition to abstract relationships, must understand how to use the people subordinate to them. It was, however, noteworthy that Lewis was expounding these views in the American journal *Engineering Magazine*, rather than in a British publication.

Lewis's protégé, Alexander Hamilton Church, who worked for Lewis before emigrating to the United States, took these ideas a stage further by emphasizing the importance of change (Litterer 1986). He was especially keen to note that change was necessary in a firm; in particular, that the solutions suitable for one context, or in one firm, would not necessarily be appropriate in another, creating the key role for management. Another important feature of management picked up by Church was the need for coordination, because no one person could hold all the details in the emerging factory. This in turn required a system for obtaining and providing information. Crucially, both Lewis and Church used the word 'organization' in the same sense as management, that is, a process not an entity. By 1900, there was therefore a concept of management as a separate function in the operation of a firm, including the distinctiveness of the work of the manager. One must also note that these ideas were being developed outside the framework of what was widely known as 'scientific management', a movement that has received much of the credit for developing the concept of management at that time.

We take an eclectic view of both management, as a broadly based process, and managers, as those who are defined within the occupational structure as carrying out this process. While management has many dimensions which must be considered, at its core there are a range of definitions (but still much disagreement) about the activities which comprise this function. An early starting point for disaggregating the term was provided by Henri Fayol, who in his book entitled *Administration Industrielle et Generale* (1916) attempted to clarify the range of tasks performed by managers. Fayol argued that every managerial role contained the same five elements: forecasting and planning; organizing; commanding; coordinating; and controlling. Mintzberg (1973), however, would argue that Fayol's overwhelming concern with function ignores the crucial issue: management is not about function, it is concerned with what managers actually *do*. This approach is based on the view that is perhaps best described as 'muddling with a purpose', given the lack of systematization, intense pressure, frequent oral communication with peers and subordinates, and an orientation towards action (Mintzberg 1996: 18–33). Nevertheless, Fayol's basic framework is still generally accepted today.

A key characteristic of modern management is its diversity, even within organizations, functionally, vertically, and laterally, which also provide dimensions of the growth of management. Few, if any managers perform the whole range of potential managerial processes—while there are many different functional roles within management which tend to be specific and not overlap—of which production, marketing, personnel, and finance are the most important, but far from the only, categories. The notion of hierarchy is also important here; there are in most organizations various levels of managers who perform quite different tasks, from goal-setting at one end of the hierarchy to operational delivery at the other, with integration of activities somewhere in the middle, and all three corresponding roughly to familiar conceptions of senior, middle, and junior management. To distinguish from hierarchy, where power and authority flow down from the top, we should also introduce the term heterarchy, where power and authority cross organizational boundaries, as in networks (Hedlund 1986). In addition to function and hierarchy, a third source of diversity and growth is that of scope across geography or industries, resulting in managers in different centres, either nationally or internationally. It is the process of this growth in function, hierarchy, and scope which was central to Chandler's arguments (1962, 1977, 1990) about the growth of managerial capitalism, and with which we will also be heavily involved.

As the twentieth century wore on and turned into the twenty-first, management became increasingly institutionalized both as a concept and as a part of society, although any public debate about management only really began in Britain after the Second World War. By the end of the century, the issue of leadership became increasingly important within the management role as the momentum of change increased. Even so, the inherent ambiguity of management in relation to roles and activities remains largely unclarified, while at the same time it has been subject to new pressures and trends. Scarbrough (1998) has identified these latter as: diffusion, in which at least some of the managerial function is redistributed to other groups; polarization, in which there is a growing division in power and identity between senior managers on the one hand and middle and junior managers on the other; and intensification, involving increased managerial workloads and extended systems of surveillance. And while there has also been a debate on the extent of convergence of management systems, it is very much part of the argument of this book not just that British management had its own unique evolution, but that there is no single historical trajectory by which management evolves and that even now universalistic theories of management are vitiated by the different meanings attached to management in different societies (Hofstede 1980; Hickson and Pugh 1995).

But before concluding this section, we also need to recognize that Fayol's technical and bureaucratic managerial role is not the only perspective from which management can be viewed; there are other standpoints to which we need to refer to throughout the book. As Child (1969: 13) notes:

Management may be regarded from at least three different perspectives: first as an economic resource performing a series of technical functions which comprise the organizing and administering of other resources; secondly as a system of authority through which policy is translated into the execution of acts; and thirdly as an elite social grouping which acts as an economic resource and maintains the associated system of authority.

But only the first of these relates to Fayol's definition, even though the other two have been vital in contributing to the history of management. Indeed, the second and third dimensions identified by Child (1969) have arguably been more important within the national social and political nexus; far from having an assured position in society, weaknesses in managers' authority and status in Britain have contributed to a lack of recognition and identity as compared to some other countries.

Another way of looking at this issue is to adopt the ideas expressed by organizational theorists like Grey (1999; 2005: 55–61), who has argued that managers' roles can be justified from three different perspectives: in a 'technical' sense, because they solve organizational problems; as an 'elite' to defend specific interests; and on the 'political' level, as a means of controlling and disciplining workers. This approach highlights how management must be seen as an expression of a particular point in time, given the way that on all three levels the context is in constant flux, justifying further the need to delve into the longitudinal perspective that this book offers.

THE EVOLUTION OF STRUCTURE

The second dimension of management to be considered relates to its key role as a part of the structure in an organization, or in other words the hierarchy to which we have just referred. In this context, it is important to provide a clear typology of organizational evolution to indicate the various structures which business has utilized during the nineteenth and twentieth centuries. While the theoretical background to these structures are assessed in more detail in Chapter 2, it is vital at this early stage to track the principal forms. Inevitably, given the enormous variety of forms adopted by firms over such a long period, our typology represents five general categories rather than explicit representations of the stages through which all businesses have passed. In broad terms, they also represent stages of evolution, although again one must stress that such stages only provide either choices available to firms or general indications of change, since on the one hand many organizations never progress beyond any particular structural type, while on the other, others have moved from one to another in response to both external and internal challenges. Moreover, and it is one of our main points, the development of structure varied considerably between countries. As we see in Chapters 3–5, British business management and organization until the last few decades was characterized by a highly personalized approach, which resulted in less sophisticated structural developments than its main competitors for any given point in time from about the 1890s to the 1970s.

The first type represents the era of the family firm, the form where in all countries owners managed and managers owned the vast majority of business enterprises. Known widely as the Specialized form (S-form), it is illustrated in Figure 1.1. It is vital to stress, though, that even where partners had been brought in to provide additional funds, it was the owning family that took all the major decisions, relying mostly on clerks and assistants to perform the more menial aspects of management. Although at works manager level people might be recruited to run the operational side of the business, rarely did their

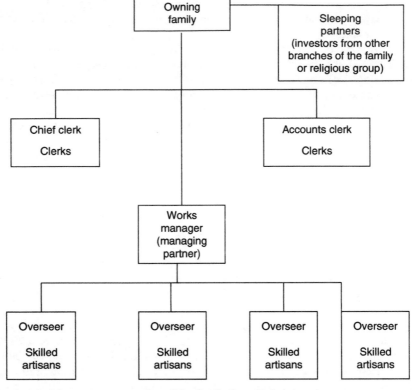

Figure 1.1. Management structure of the family firm (S-form)

responsibilities extend outside this limited scope, indicating how the organizational architecture was dominated by the owning family. Moreover, in the British
case, as we also see in Chapter 3, both labour recruitment and management, as
well as marketing and sales, were often highly externalized, indicating how in
some senses family owner-managers were willing to capture the external economies of scale available if the firm operated within one of the many industrial
districts that flourished up to the mid twentieth century (Wilson and Popp 2003).

Our second structural type is the unitary form (U-form), illustrated in Figure
1.2, reflecting the development of a range and hierarchy of functional managers as
the organization grew. It is, however, a type that although common in the United
States and Germany before the First World War, did not flourish in Britain.
Again, the reasons behind this trend are examined in Chapter 3, but one can
see from Figure 1.2 that as the U-form requires far more specialized managers to
run the various functional departments, not to mention those involved in
production or distribution lower down the hierarchy, its relatively slow development in the UK reveals weaknesses that were inherent to the business system.
Chapter 3 also illustrates how in the UK what Quail (2000) has labelled the

proprietorial form of capitalism often undermined the effectiveness of any U-form systems, given the reluctance of directors to delegate real responsibility to any managers appointed to functional and production posts.

Our third type reflects the situation where a number of companies, usually S-form companies (Figure 1.1), were brought together as a result of the merger and acquisition strategies pursued so extensively in the 1890s and again in the 1920s

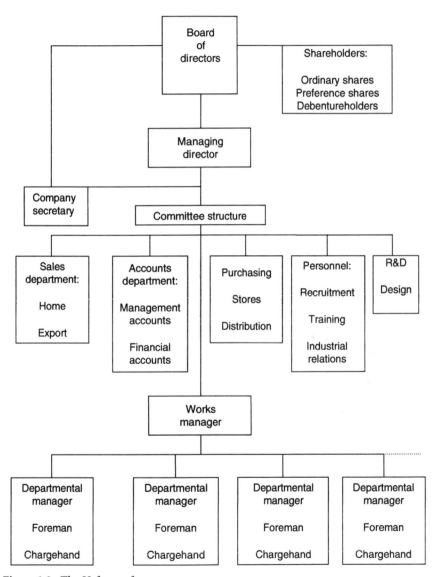

Figure 1.2. The U-form of management structure

(Hannah 1983), to form a holding company form (H-form). As Figure 1.3 illustrates, the H-form was based on a highly devolved form of organization, whereby the central headquarters rarely interfered in management at the operational levels and the production units were almost entirely self-contained businesses. While as Fitzgerald (2000) has argued, H-forms in Japan would appear to have worked in a highly effective manner, on the other hand those that appeared in the UK were often ineffectively organized federations of family firms that resented outside interference, limiting the impact of any attempt to achieve synergy and capture economies of scale.

Our fourth structural form (Figure 1.4) is the multidivisional form (M-form). This originated in the United States in the 1920s, combining centralized control with decentralized delegation of responsibility, with professional managers running the operating divisions. It is often regarded as the most effective vehicle for controlling large-scale, diversified firms, a point apparently substantiated by the ubiquitous spread of the M-form across the United States and Western Europe over the course of the late twentieth century (Whittington and Mayer 2000). On the other hand, not only was the spread of the M-form extremely slow, even in the United States (Fligstein 1991), but also its emphasis on delegated responsibility provided such enormous pressures on the quality of management that the nature of the M-form differed in the countries covered in this book.

Bringing the story up to the present, our fifth structural form is the network form (N-form) that has evolved out of recent trends associated with the

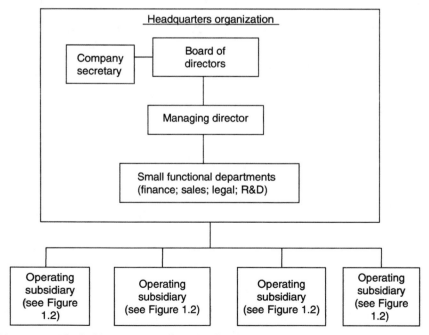

Figure 1.3. The holding company form (H-form)

emergence of the learning organization and global supply chains (Hedlund 1986). As Figure 1.5 illustrates, while many of the features of the N-form resemble those of the M-form, and especially the highly devolved nature of decision-making at the divisional level, its key feature is the extent to which external relationships feature. In particular, the N-form has become extremely popular amongst the multinational corporations that range across countries building up alliances and joint ventures as a means of either capturing external economies of scale or securing links into new markets (Dunning 1997*a*). This form of organization also imposes even more managerial strains on a firm, given the need not only to run these geographically dispersed operations, but also to monitor relations with partners that might be prone to opportunistic behaviour. It is a highly challenging form, yet one that has become highly popular amongst those firms that

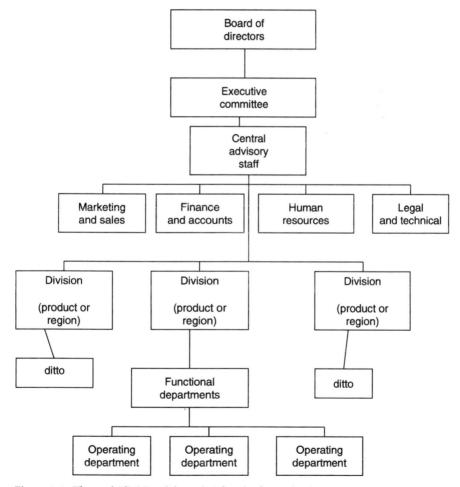

Figure 1.4. The multidivisional form (M-form) of organization

operate globally, given the advantages it provides in spreading the risks associated with such strategies.

Having identified the principal organizational forms that have dominated British business over the course of the last 200 years, it is again important to remember that not only were there many variants but also there was considerable chronological overlap across all types. While much more is said about the reasons behind this variety in Chapters 3 and 5, linking Figures 1.1–1.5 much more carefully into the contextual analysis, at this stage it is sufficient to note that they should never be mistaken for stages along some preordained path of

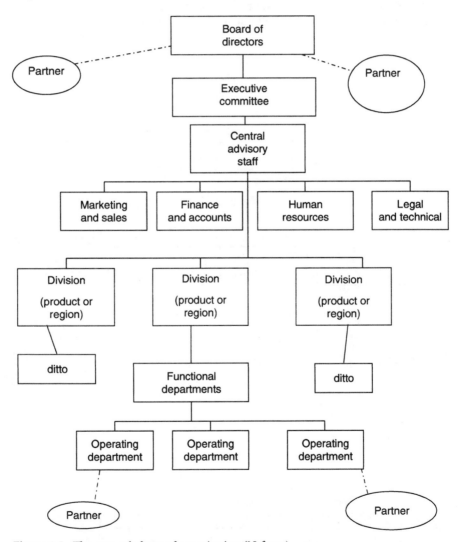

Figure 1.5. The network form of organization (N-form)

organizational evolution. Moreover, as we see in Chapter 4, there were significant differences between the British experience and those of our comparators (the United States, Germany, and Japan), demonstrating further the need to be cautious about the nature of organizational change over such a long period.

THE MANAGERS

Our third major perspective on management is concerned with the managers themselves, with a particular interest in their numbers within the labour force, and also their diversity as expressed through different categories such as function, gender, and remuneration. But these apparently simple issues throw up various problems, starting with which people and what roles are covered by the terms management and managing, both in the past and now. As we saw earlier, before the twentieth century there was no clear definition of manager or management; nor was there any recognition of such a role in the census. As a result, it is difficult to define the number of managers in the early period while their role was still emerging and vague. Even prior to the Second World War, the word 'management' was not actually in common usage, while well into the post-Second World War period the term 'administration' was frequently used as a synonym.

Another problem has been the tendency to view management as manifested in the employer, or in more recent times the chief executive officer (CEO) and possibly the board of directors, namely, equating it with the field of strategic management. Most of the debates in business history are about this level, while arguably this is the way managers are seen in the City of London and the media. In this context, it is vital to stress that we shall be taking a much wider perspective, given the need to encompass the four million or so managers featuring under that label in the 2001 National Census, including tactical and operational managers as well as strategic, and ranging from those in very large companies to those in small operations. The occupation does not, however, include foremen and supervisors; neither does it incorporate members of other professions such as lawyers and doctors, or other occupational groups that arguably carry out some managerial functions as part of their jobs. Nevertheless, our figure of over four million does include many managers who carry out specialist functions, whether in marketing, personnel, production, finance, computing, quality control, and dozens of other such roles. It does therefore go beyond another grouping which is sometimes taken as being what management is all about, namely, line managers or those responsible for the control and coordination of subordinate workers. Managers defined along these lines have been a rapidly growing section of the working population, both absolutely and as a proportion (Williams 2002; Protherough and Pick 2002).

Even now, the number of managers is far from clear-cut or agreed. To quote Williams (2001: 1), in her review of the management population, because different studies use different definitions, 'estimates of current numbers of those in management occupations vary considerably (from 2.5 million to more than 6 million) but are most likely to be around 4 or 4.5 million'. We do not intend to become embroiled in this debate, but rather provide some different perspectives on who the managers are. We should, however, note that the illustrations that follow are themselves not necessarily based on a common definition, which itself is an indication of the ambiguities associated with identifying who is counted as a manager.

The first approach must of course be historical. Census returns of the number of managers have only been available since 1911; although the specific definition has not remained constant, we are interested in broad trends rather than precise figures. We have no evidence on numbers before that and would welcome research in this area. Figure 1.6 provides a bar chart of census data for managers (bracketed with senior administrators) in which the more detailed numbers in thousands is given. Even these basic figures indicate the disparate rates of growth of the managerial occupation. In the period 1911–31, the average growth per year was some 7,000, which is by no means large given the considerable consolidation that was taking place in British industry (Hannah 1983), even taking into account the high early 1930s unemployment. By contrast, the post-Second World War growth has been extraordinary. Between 1951 and 1981, the annual rate of growth accelerated to just short of 60,000 a year; in the last two decades between 1981 and 2001, it has accelerated even further to around 90,000 a year, or the equivalent of a very substantial town. Some of the recent growth is even counter-intuitive, given the widespread publicity about the flattening of hierarchies and outsourcing of functions (Sampson 1995). More generally, however, it may be explained in the context of wider economic forces such as the decline of 'traditional' industry within the total economy and the re-designation of roles and jobs as managerial. While 1966 marked the peak year for industrial employment in

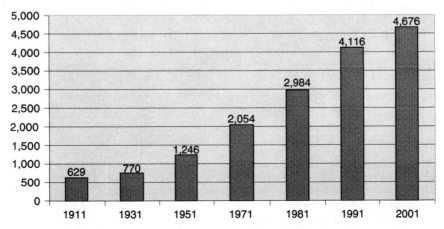

Figure 1.6. The number of managers and senior administrators listed in decennial occupational censuses, 1911–2001 (thousands)

Britain, and even if in some other respects the 1980s are arguably the watershed for the performance of the British economy and the way that people viewed the economic climate, it is clear that the tectonic plates associated with de-industrialization, globalization, and a changing work environment had begun to move well before this.

In moving to the twenty-first century management population as it disaggregates in various different ways, the enormous diversity of the management role becomes even more apparent. Manufacturing, while the primary focus of this book for historical reasons, now has a relatively small proportion of the total number of managers, with just over 20 per cent (Labour Force Survey 2001). There are also differences between industries in the number of managers as a proportion of the labour force, with education and health having less than 10 per cent, while financial intermediation, wholesale and retail, and hotels and restaurants have more than 20 per cent. Manufacturing, in contrast, has 16 per cent, against an overall average of 17.6 per cent. Another important division is by size of organization. As one would expect, numbers of managers rise with increasing size. On the other hand, as Perren et al. (2001) report, there are some 1.75 million managers in small and medium-sized enterprises (SMEs). A further related classification is by region, with London at the top with a proportion of 17.8 per cent and the South-East also high at 17.2 per cent, while at the other end the proportions for the North, Wales, and Scotland are 12.1, 12.4, and 12.9 per cent, respectively. Not surprisingly, sub-regional differences are even greater, with the City of London at 26.5 per cent and the City of Westminster at 24.2 per cent, while at the other end East Ayrshire has 10.0 per cent and Sunderland 10.3 per cent (Labour Force Survey 2005).

One of the features of the recent management population has been the considerable growth in the number of female managers, even if their proportions vary widely between industries (Marshall 1984, 1995). Table 1.1 illustrates this growth both over time and by managerial level, even if it is noticeable that while progress has been achieved at all levels, there is still significantly lower proportionate representation in the higher level positions.

Finally, in order to illustrate the considerable differences between managers in terms of status, we examine in Table 1.2 average weekly earnings in various categories of manager. What is most noticeable is the very substantial spread between different categories of managers; even then, Table 1.2 does not illustrate

Table 1.1. Female managers at different levels of responsibility

	2004	2000	1994	1983	1974
Director	13.2	9.6	3.6	0.3	0.6
Function head	17.4	15.0	6.1	1.5	0.4
Department head	26.2	19.0	8.7	1.9	2.1
Section leader	38.2	26.5	12.0	5.3	2.4
All females	31.1	22.1	9.5	3.3	1.8

Source: National Management Salary Survey, Chartered Management Institute (2004).

the large sums going into millions which are paid to some CEOs (Froud et al. 2006). One of the features of the last two decades has been the rapid rise in the multiple by which the highest paid director exceeds that of the manual worker average: in 1980, the highest paid director of the FTSE top 100 companies earned 10 times the worker pay, but by 2002 this had risen to a multiple of 75 (Froud et al. 2006). While male managers are clearly paid considerably more than females, there are also considerable differences between male managers. Perhaps most notably, the lowest decile of male managers is paid less than the average manual worker, while the lowest decile of general managers is paid less than the average of all occupations, indicating that some managers are not well paid by any conventional labour force comparisons. Within the functional management specialisms, the table notes that financial managers are paid a substantially greater amount than the other functions, with production managers paid the least.

Reviewing this section, it is clear that we need to bear in mind that management is a highly diverse occupation; indeed, we accept that there are often problems in making generalizations about this category. At the same time, total numbers are arguably not the most important dimension, because they only reflect an occupational category and say little about the identity or status of managers, both of which vary so considerably that it is difficult to argue that such a disparate grouping can be described as a cohesive body, never mind a profession. Indeed, as we argue in later chapters, although today it is often taken for granted that management is a profession, this is in fact a dubious assumption. Nevertheless, all managers do have some common characteristics and do deserve consideration as a group.

Table 1.2. Managers' and administrators' earnings

	F-T adult male	F-T adult female
All managers/administrators	668.9	468.8
General managers/administrators	952.2	544.4
Production managers	636.2	493.6
Specialist managers	825.3	585.4
Financial managers	1162.3	745.3
Marketing and sales managers	779.6	546.4
Personnel managers	730.4	589.1
Managers in transport and storing	486.8	411.3
Managers in farming, forestry, fishing	398.9	
Managers/proprietors in service industries	453.3	320.3
Other managers/administrators	633.3	472.2
All managers—lowest decile	324.9	250.0
All managers—highest decile	1109.5	748.6
General managers—lowest decile	435.1	365.9
General managers—highest decile	1821.5	764.1
All occupations	453.3	337.6
All non-manual occupations	533.9	357.5
All manual occupations	343.9	227.9

F-T: full-time. Average weekly gross earnings, with those whose pay was affected by absence excluded
Source: New Earnings Survey (2000).

A PERIODIZATION OF THE DEVELOPMENT OF MODERN MANAGEMENT IN BRITAIN

The main chronological thrust of our approach defines four stages that provide an outline periodization, an illustration of which can be found in Figure 1.7. Stage 1, up to 1870, represents the period of personal capitalism, when the dominant consideration was the development of new technologies to provide goods on an industrial rather than a handcraft scale. In this period, the nature of organizations was relatively primitive, relying mostly on family sources for most resources. In Stage 2, from 1870 to the 1940s, both personal and proprietorial capitalism prevailed, while only in Stage 3 did managerial capitalism emerge as a key influence on the nature of business operations. Finally, over the last thirty years, Stage 4 reflects the growing influence of financial considerations, leading to the establishment of the system of managerial-financial capitalism that prevails today. At the same time, as networks have become an increasingly important framework for industrial activity, this period might be called by some post-industrial capitalism, but we would prefer to use the term network capitalism.

Crucially, these stages are only intended to be a synopsis of what is inevitably a highly complex situation, with substages within them, together with inevitable

Stage One: PERSONAL
(to the 1870s)

Family-based ownership and management

Stage Two: PERSONAL-PROPRIETORIAL
(1870s to 1940s)

Clinging to family-based system with greater levels
of 'external' influence, viz., syndicates of owners
and professional managers; mergers and concentration;
holding company forms; international investment and
cartels very active; SMEs: increased dependence on
'Big' business

Stage Three: MANAGERIAL
(1940s to 1970s)

Extensive divorce between control and ownership.
Adoption of M-form by large firms owned by
professional investors; business schools appearing;
merger and international investment at record levels;
SMEs tied in to a cycle of dependence

Stage Four: MANAGERIAL-FINANCIAL
(since 1980s)

Dominance of City interests; rise of international
combines in global networks; heterarchic systems
of management; bring SMEs into loops as 'stakeholders' in the chain; 'professionalization' of management

Figure 1.7. The organizational stages of British business evolution

overlaps between periods. While this is brought out in much greater detail over the course of Chapters 3 and 5, we would like to claim that the following (linked closely to Figure 1.7) represent the most significant managerial stages in British management history.

Stage 1—Up to 1870: Personal

Britain had effective (and to a large extent appropriate) manufacturing, merchanting, and to some extent managerial systems in the period up to about 1870. As the 'First Industrial Nation', Britain enjoyed a long period of economic domination, during which the established managerial systems became embedded within a system based around externalized economic relations and dispersed production.

Stage 2—1870–1945: Personal-Proprietorial

These systems proved increasingly inadequate to the needs of both the much-increased scale of First Industrial Revolution industries like engineering, iron and steel, and those linked to the Second Industrial Revolution (often associated with the mass production of standardized commodities). While there had been significant intellectual advances in Britain in the emerging subject area of management by the end of the nineteenth century, these were rarely either operationalized or circulated beyond a narrow group, since Britain was weak in knowledge transfer mechanisms. The insularity of business organization and the lack of external checks and balances on decision-makers accounted to a significant extent for this resistance to change.

Stage 3—1945–1985: Managerial

Even when structural change across the economy did occur after 1945, there was still no adequate management cadre to make it work properly. The emergence of this cadre had to await the creation of effective supply-side institutions (business schools, management consultancy, external monitoring systems, etc.), each of which was dependent on emerging demand.

Stage 4—Since 1985: Managerial-Financial

In the last twenty years, the quantity and quality of supply of managers has improved, providing grounds for reasonable optimism. At the same time, as a series of reports have argued, deficiencies persist across British business, not least in terms of quality and the skills base of a much-expanded management cadre.

THE ECONOMIC BACKGROUND

The final component of this background to management history is to provide an economic context. As much of the debate about Britain's economic performance, and therefore about the success or otherwise of its management, has been related to comparative economic statistics, this is a convenient point at which to provide a macroeconomic background to illustrate the British position with statistics from the four main countries considered in the book over the period of industrialization up to the recent past.

Table 1.3 shows annual rates of growth in gross domestic product (GDP) per capita, indicating how the rates of growth in the century preceding the First World War were nothing special by modern standards. Moreover, Britain, even in her period of economic hegemony up to 1870, did not have a noticeably higher rate of growth than either the United States or Germany (Japan at this time was not industrializing), and in the period 1870–1913 grew substantially less fast than its comparators. It was the period 1870–1950 which enabled the United States to pull ahead of the rest of the world, while Germany and Japan had their times of rapid growth in the post-Second World War period. The impact of these rates of growth is illustrated in Table 1.4, where one can see how relatively small differences in the annual growth rate can cumulatively produce significant differences over time. Britain started in 1820 with a somewhat higher per capita GDP, extended its lead by 1870, but then fell back absolutely by 1913 compared to the United States and relatively compared to Germany and Japan. In 1950, Britain still had a higher per capita GDP than either Germany or Japan, but lost this advantage in the period up to 1973, even though this was by some margin Britain's best period in terms of cumulative growth rates. It should also be noted that Britain's performance against these three countries was also broadly paralleled against several others, such as France, Sweden, Switzerland, and Holland, so that it is not just a question of explaining the particular performance of the three countries (although we do that in Chapter 4), but of recognizing that a wide range of countries were overtaking Britain.

While we show in Chapter 5 that Britain's relative growth record has improved in the recent past, the main points to be borne in mind when evaluating the performance of British management are that over the longer period Britain did

Table 1.3. Economic growth 1820–1992

	1820–70	1870–1913	1913–50	1950–73	1973–92
Britain	1.2	1.0	0.8	2.5	1.4
USA	1.3	1.8	1.6	2.4	1.4
Germany	1.1	1.6	0.3	5.0	2.1
Japan	0.1	1.4	0.9	8.0	3.0

Average compound annual GDP growth per capita in 1990 dollars, per cent
Source: Chandler, Amatori, and Hikino (2004: 7).

Table 1.4. Economic growth 1820–1992

	1820	1870	1913	1950	1973	1992
Britain	1,756	3,263	5,032	6,847	11,992	15,738
USA	1,287	2,457	5,307	9,573	16,607	21,558
Germany	1,112	1,913	3,833	4,281	13,152	19,351
Japan	704	741	1,334	1,873	11,017	17,165

GDP per capita in 1990 dollars
Source: Chandler, Amatori, and Hikino (2004: 6).

continue to grow, but at a rate which was cumulatively slower than its main competitors. It is this that has led to an ongoing debate about performance, starting in the period 1870–1913 when Britain lost her economic leadership, although in fact her relative performance was worse in the post-Second World War period, when, paradoxically, she was growing faster than at any other time.

CONCLUSIONS

The purpose of this chapter has been, first, to provide a general background for management history, and second, to offer some important specific elements of the British context. The broad perspective we take is that while Britain had first-mover advantages as an industrial economy, the success achieved to the mid nineteenth century tended to make change more difficult, given a widespread resistance to altering what to contemporaries appeared to be a winning framework, creating a situation of path dependency. Moreover, it is also easy to make too much out of Britain's leadership in the Industrial Revolution and the first-mover advantages that this ought to have given. As Supple notes (1974: 77), 'it seems very likely that the growth rate during Britain's heroic Industrial Revolution was in fact lower than that enjoyed by most other developed countries during their initial period of economic development'. Moreover, in spite of the relative retardation against competitors like the United States and Germany, there have always been certain types of product and industry at any given period of time where Britain still had a competitive positioning as a result of a mixture of certain technological and demand factors. Indeed, Britain's relative renaissance in the last two decades reflects in part the increased importance of these industries, mainly in the service sector. But the rationale behind these developments takes us to the underlying drivers and themes of British management history, issues to which we now turn in the Chapter 2.

2

A Theoretical and Thematic Framework

INTRODUCTION

After having provided both the rationale and background for this book, it is now necessary to move on to discuss its conceptual, theoretical, and thematic framework, breaking the chapter into two rather unequal parts. The first part reviews some important conceptual dimensions of the way in which management has been viewed by different groups: the way in which economists portray management in the theory of the firm; the main schools into which writers on management thought can be broken down; and the way in which managers themselves have approached problems. The task of the second and more substantial part is to provide our own theoretical base, which consists of two frames of reference, relating to organizational development and management growth, out of which emerge the main themes of the book. Initially, we review three separate models of the development of organizational structures: that of Chandler (1990), still the most influential; the resource dependency-based cluster model pursued by Popp, Toms, and Wilson (2003); and finally, the Fligstein model (1993), which is a socially constructed approach. The second set of considerations, based on the view that the growth of management has been a complex issue based on many sources, is to identify the main drivers of change. We have broken these drivers into three categories: market-cum-technological drivers, institutional and cultural drivers, and finally those drivers internal to the organization concerned with business policy and practice. The third main purpose of this part of the chapter is to introduce four themes of the book: the persistence of personal and proprietorial capitalism; management, organizational structure, and transaction costs; attitudes towards industry and management; and the slow transition to professionalism. In total, the chapter represents a novel exercise in model building that is intended to stimulate debate about all these issues, thereby deepening our understanding of how management has evolved over time and in different contexts. This exercise also distinguishes our approach from those of other scholars, emphasizing how we are keen to link the empirical with essentially theoretical approaches to understanding longitudinal trends.

MANAGEMENT IN THE THEORY OF THE FIRM

Until the 1930s, economic theory was dominated by the neoclassical school of thought, in which the basic units were regarded as processes of production of commodities. This general equilibrium theory was based on notions of perfect competition and perfect knowledge, with the invisible hand of market forces acting as the prime determinant of activity (Devine 1976: 108–17). There were, nevertheless, some champions of inductive economics such as Marshall (1890, 1919) at Cambridge and Commons (1909) at Wisconsin. Over the course of the twentieth century, however, not only was general equilibrium theory challenged and refuted (Sraffa 1926) but also new schools of thought emerged as a result of extensive empirical investigations into the operation of the market. Indeed, during the 1930s a theory of the firm was emerging, to a large extent established by Robinson (1933) and her work on the actual decisions made by entrepreneurs and managers on prices. This strongly empirical analysis switched the emphasis away from allegedly automatic market forces to a situation in which firms influenced prices through their profit-maximizing behaviour. Dramatic changes in both industrial structure and business behaviour also persuaded economists that a change of approach was essential if the discipline was going to provide an understanding of new trends. In particular, as we see in the next chapter, the prevalence of oligopolistic trading practices (Hannah 1983), the rise of big business (Wardley 1991), and a growing divorce between control and ownership (Berle and Means 1932) required much more sophisticated tools than those provided by neoclassical economics.

Neoclassical economics started from the assumption that the economic system was coordinated by the price mechanism within a market framework, but said little about the organization of firms, and in particular their boundaries. Coase (1937) added a second coordinating principle, that of managerial hierarchy, whereby authority is used to carry through resource allocation. Moreover, he argued that the firm and the market were alternative mechanisms for carrying out the same transactions, with the firm deciding whether to make or do internally, or to buy externally. Williamson (1975), amongst others, built further upon the concept to make transaction costs a central feature of modern economics. In consequence, just as Chandler used this concept in explaining the emergence of managerial capitalism, offering the title *The Visible Hand* (1977) to distinguish this system from the 'invisible hand' of the market, we intend to employ transaction costs economics as one of the principal themes of the book. As we see later in this chapter (see The Themes of the Book), decisions concerning the degree of externalization were a vital element in the rise of large-scale organizations in British business, highlighting the importance of Coasian insights to our analysis.

Having made this break with the deductive neoclassical approach in the 1930s, another decisive move was the emergence of the theory of the growth of the firm. The pioneering work on this school of thought was conducted by Penrose (1959), who was the first to give major emphasis to management resources as a key factor in determining the pace and nature of change in the firm. She argued that entrepreneurship and the quality and amount of management talent are key factors that affect the direction and rate of growth of the firm. According to Penrose, growth (and change) requires special managerial talents, the limits to which create the 'Penrose effect', namely, that there were serious limits to the growth of the firm due to managerial constraints. Two other important contributions by her were highlighting the importance of management as a team, and her use of the concept of path-dependency, in which once on a particular trajectory created out of an evolutionary process, it becomes difficult to make radical changes. This not only infers that history matters but also suggests that each firm or indeed country has unique opportunities and corresponding limitations. Penrose also initiated the growth-oriented school (Marris 1964, 1998), in which the main objective of the firm becomes sustainable growth in size (of assets, employment, or real output).

This work sparked off a whole new branch of economic theory which today is labelled the resource-based view (RBV) of the firm. Starting from Penrose and moving forward to Hamel and Prahalad (1994), this view has become especially dominant in strategic management theory, with management as the most important capability. The RBV of the firm pays particular attention to the past through the development of capabilities and the importance of organizational memory (Kransdorff 1998). The work of Nelson and Winter (1982) on the balanced scorecard was also seminal in developing the RBV theory further, with other contributions from Teece, Pisano, and Sheun (1997) providing extensive insights into what is essentially a managerialist view of economic development.

There are other managerialist theories of the firm based on the behaviour of managers, such as the discretionary (Baumol 1959; Williamson 1964, 1970), in which managerial choice rather than maximizing profitability is central to decision-making, and the bureaucratic (Monsen and Downs 1965), in which the pyramidal structure and the desire of subordinates to please their superiors results in biased information and inherent inefficiency. The latter links closely with the behaviouralist school of decision-making, starting from Simon (1960), who substituted a concept of 'administrative man' for the economists' concept of 'economic man' which results in satisfying rather than maximizing behaviour. Similarly, Cyert and March (1963) argued that decision-making under uncertainty must take account of the internal operation of the firm, which they liken to a political system with bargaining over goals.

As managerial capitalism became widespread, the theory of the firm needed to be reviewed to reflect changing business behaviour. One such debate has been about the implications of the separation of ownership and control. Marris (1964, 1998), who was incidentally the first to coin the term managerial capitalism, argued that while shareholders might want to maximize the return on their capital, with a strong discount to the short term, managers could be more interested in maximizing growth and personal security. In other words, they would want to take a longer-term view of the enterprise than the shareholders (and their financial advisers looking to their next bonus). In this sense, managerial

capitalism might be better for the operation of the economy, although managements could always be disciplined by the threat of the takeover. However, the rise
of the stock option system for rewarding senior executives has also tended to put
a greater emphasis on managers' short-term interests, indicating how theory has
struggled to keep pace with the vagaries of managerial practice. On the other
hand, one can see from this brief overview that over the last seventy-five years
economic theory has been adapted to accommodate what has been happening
within the firm, overcoming the inherent ignorance of the neoclassical approach
and providing management with a more prominent position in explanatory
analysis.

SCHOOLS OF MANAGEMENT THOUGHT

Having demonstrated how economic theory has evolved over the course of the
twentieth century, it is also essential to review the main schools of management
thought. While in this section we are taking a worldwide perspective, one should
note that a more specifically British perspective is provided in Chapter 8, where
we see how British patterns of thought did not always coincide with those
emerging elsewhere. Nor is this the place for a complete historiography of
management thought, others having performed this task much more effectively
(Child 1969; Guillén 1994; Wren 1994). As we can see in Figure 2.1, four main
groupings] by period have fashioned management thought, the Pre-classical (up
to the 1870s), the Classical (1880s to the 1960s), the Humanistic (1930s to the
1980s), and Management science (1950s to the present). Self-evidently, there is
considerable overlap across these perspectives; some authors (Barnard and
Luthans, for example) even feature in more than one grouping. One should
also stress the reductionist nature of Figure 2.1, given the tendency to generalize
about schools of thought that operated over long time periods. Nevertheless,
in providing a framework for the study of management history, Figure 2.1
features the most significant authorities who have been responsible for fashioning
elements of the four main groupings and influencing contemporaneous practice.

   In reviewing various features of this diagram, the process starts with the highly
authoritative works of Adam Smith (1776), Charles Babbage (1832), and Andrew
Ure (1835), all of whom wrote about technical aspects of industry. As we see
in Chapter 3, however, in an era when families owned and managed their own
firms and a 'cult of the amateur' prevailed (Coleman 1973), their impact on
practice was marginal. While Babbage apparently sold over 10,000 copies of a
book that elaborated on Smith's ideas relating to the division of labour, and in the
process 'launched the fields of time-and-motion study and operations research',
there is very little evidence that manufacturers applied his ideas (Guillén 1994:
207–8).

Knowledge management

(Nonaka and Takeuchi)

The learning organization

(Mintzberg; Luthans; Peters and
Waterman; Starkey)

<u>Management science</u>
<u>perspective</u>
(1950s to present)

Total quality management

(Deming; Ouchi; McKee)

Systems theory

(Boulding; Hempel; Kast; Luthans)

Structural analysis

(Drucker; Burns; Woodward; Chandler;
Lawrence; Lorsch; Scott)

Behavioural sciences

(Cyert; March; Simon)

<u>Humanistic</u>
<u>perspective</u>
(1930s to 1980s)

Human resources perspective

(Maslow; McGregor; Likert)

Human relations movement

(Barnard; Mayo; Roethlisberger)

Administrative principles

(Fayol; Follett; Barnard; Urwick)

<u>Classical perspective</u>
(1880s to 1960s)   **Bureaucratic organizations**

(Weber; Parsons)

Scientific management

(Towne; Taylor; Gantt; Bedaux)

<u>Pre-classical perspective</u>
(up to 1870s)

Functional approach

(Smith; Babbage; Ure)

-------- // ---
1780   1900   1950   2000

Figure 2.1. Four perspectives in management thought

The first influential perspective was the Classical school, initially consisting of scientific management, in which the objective was to improve efficiency, and which itself was an outgrowth of an interest in systematic management. The model, known mostly as 'Taylorism', after its most noted advocate, F. W. Taylor (1903), assumed everyone to be rational, and that the increased surplus from higher efficiencies would benefit all in the organization; workers were assumed only to seek monetary rewards. The task of management was to specify in every detail the worker's job, with centralized management and supervisory power severely curtailed, following the principle of unity of command (Grey 2005: 34–42). This was complemented by a rising literature on administration and the nature of bureaucracy up into the 1960s (Witzel 2002: 65–76), the initiator of which was the German sociologist, Max Weber (Grey 2005: 21–34).

Overlapping with the later stages of the Classical perspective was the emergence of a 'Humanistic perspective', mostly influenced by the work of Elton Mayo on human relations in the famous 'Hawthorne Studies' at the American firm Westinghouse (Roethlisberger and Dickson 1939). The rise of human relations in the 1930s was an arguably necessary antidote to the machine age and its domination of the worker, as satirized in Chaplin's film *Modern Times*. Human relations dealt with the problems arising from scientific management, including monotony, absenteeism, turnover, boredom, conflict, and morale (Grey 2005: 44–6). Workers were seen as people with group identities, driven by psycho-social norms and needs; they seek not only money but also security, stability, satisfaction, and recognition at work. The manager's role was to create conditions that fostered cooperation in the factory by balancing its social system and harmonizing relationships.

The Humanistic perspective was at its peak when what we have classified as the 'Management science perspective' emerged in the 1950s. The first main expression of management science was structural analysis, in which the analysis of technology and the firm's competitive environment was intended to guide the design of the organizational structure. Professional managers were assigned responsibility for planning, setting goals, defining problems, and making decisions. The methodological cornerstone was a contingency approach with unobtrusive control devices such as job specification, internal career ladders, and operating routines monitoring performance. Management science then spawned off a range of derivatives, some of which were not much more than short-term fads (and which we have not mentioned in Figure 2.1), a situation which exists to this day.

The history of management thought is consequently a highly complicated narrative, featuring a considerable degree of overlap that limits the ability to produce universal generalizations concerning the impact on practitioners. As we noted in Chapter 1, however, building on Grey's insights (2005: 55) into the nature of management, the role and position of managers will alter according to the context in which it operates. Moreover, as we see in Chapters 2–5, reaffirming a point already made in this section, attitudes to and preparation for management differed markedly across countries and proceeded at varying rates in contrasting circumstances. Unravelling the intricacies involved in this process provides a rationale for management historians and the search for a more sophisticated understanding of how thought and practice have been related over time.

MANAGERIAL APPROACHES TO PROBLEMS

Although the schools of management thought were important in an intellectual sense and influenced practice both directly and indirectly, this does not mean to say that the majority of managers were aware of them in a day-to-day sense. Most managers had to deal with operational as opposed to strategic issues, and how they faced up to them was not the same as utilizing the prevailing model of thought as expressed in the literature. Litterer (1986: 20–1) suggests that over time four approaches have been taken in the way that managers and their organizations relate to problems:

- *The traditional or rule-of-thumb approach,* where managers tend to consider each problem separately and either devise the best solution on the basis of past experience or apply the solution that tradition prescribes. This might also be called 'unsystematized management'.

- *The systematic approach,* where problems are viewed as falling into recurring types, for each of which a satisfactory method of handling can be developed. These solutions are sought in the experience and thinking of others, as well as one's own, that is, the exchange of information is introduced. It was primarily concerned with the managerial functions of directing and controlling, but not with others such as planning, organizing, or facilitating. The concept of system reflected attempts to provide specific and accurately defined jobs for all members of management.

- *The scientific,* which maintains that there are basic principles which can be developed to guide management, and that decisions as to which approach should be used for solving a problem should be made on the basis of measurement and experimentation.

- *The sociological,* which maintains that most business problems cannot be solved unless the people involved in them are taken into account along with technical and financial considerations.

As these approaches are listed in the order in which they emerged, in a sense they can be seen as stages. But they are not mutually exclusive; one did not eliminate its predecessor. Indeed, frequently all could be found coexisting within an organization, not to mention a particular business system. The most important distinction for our purposes was between systematic management and scientific management. As Litterer explained (1986: 259):

Scientific management focused attention on finding the best way for a worker to do his job, while systematic management sought a way to integrate the work of many people to accomplish an overall objective. To state this a little differently, scientific management was concerned with increasing the efficiency of an individual, while systematic management was concerned with producing coordination of a group of people.

These approaches to problems are important not just in the technical sense, which is where they began, but also in wider approaches to thinking about organizations. System led to rationalization, which in turn led to strategy and an orientation to further innovation. One of the great strengths of American (and German and Japanese) businessmen was their ability to think systematically and to translate this into what Dubin (1970) called a desire for perfectibility. Thus, American industry in the early twentieth century was invigorated by a desire for rationalization and progress and a willingness to explore scientific management. This could then be taken to another level; as Whittington] and Mayer (2000: 67) have put it, 'divisionalization was the scientific management of the corporation'. In contrast, returning to the question that dominates this book (see Introduction, Chapter 1), British industry did not think as systematically and tended to be dominated by rule-of-thumb approaches.

MODELS OF ORGANIZATIONAL GROWTH

Having outlined the perspectives on management by the four groups, we now move to setting out our own underpinning frames of reference or models, building on what we said (see A Periodization of the Development of Modern Management in Britain, Chapter 1) about the chronological staging of developments. The first of these introduces three separate, yet related, models of organizational development, moving through a series of alternatives. In addition, we attempt to synthesize them, as a means of stimulating debate concerning the applicability of these ideas.

Chandler and the Market-cum-Technological Model

Chandler's model was predicated on the widening of the market and the means of reaching it as prerequisites. Then, as he described in *Scale and Scope* (1990), the new transportation systems created the potential for increased volumes of goods to be distributed, leading to new production processes that permitted increased economies of scale and scope. To take advantage of these production economies, entrepreneurs needed to make three types of investment: in high-volume production facilities; in a marketing and distribution network; and in management to administer and coordinate these functional activities. Crucially, he noted (1990: 8): 'It was this three-pronged investment in production, distribution and management that brought the modern industrial enterprise into being.'

At a second stage, when internal economies of scale had been exhausted within the initial market, firms looked to economies of scope, predominantly involving diversification into related product markets. This in turn required new organizational forms, with more managers, and an extension of the concept of hierarchy; more specifically, in Chandler's model, there was a move towards divisionalization and the use of M-form structures.

The logic underlying the actions of the entrepreneurs was that the internalization of transaction costs was cheaper and more efficient than the previous market mechanism, resulting in the 'visible hand' of management replacing the 'invisible hand' of the market. This demonstrates how Chandler's work provided the first cohesive model of the development of modern enterprises, even if his model was very much based on American experience, an issue that many critics have used to diminish his general applicability (Wilson 1995: 4–9). The model also has an element of determinism about it, which suggests a series of conscious and rational choices, casting further doubt on its relevance as an insight into the reality of decision-making. In addition, as Scranton (1991: 1103) noted: 'The usual Chandler bracketings apply. Labour, culture, state policies and all industrial activity outside the top 200 are set aside as secondary or irrelevant.' Nevertheless, Chandler's work has been extremely influential in modern resource-based theory as the basis of corporate strategy, by focusing on the internal RB for identifying unique, firm-specific assets as capabilities. Our own argument, though, is that management in Britain failed to develop in a way that would have prevented Britain's relative decline, with one important starting point in this analysis being Chandler's argument that British industry largely failed to make the three-pronged investment that was so important in the United States. In our case, of course, we are particularly interested in why there was the lack of investment in management, and the consequent impact on management up to the present.

Popp, Toms, and Wilson and the Industrial Clusters Model

If Chandler's argument is predicated on the internalization of transaction costs, there is an alternative model, which focuses on external as opposed to internal economies of scale and the concept of heterarchy rather than hierarchy. In his classic 1890 work, *Principles of Economics*, Marshall was the first to point out how external economies can be derived from cheaper inputs that can be purchased on the market, where there are local pools of skilled labour or knowledge or services. Such economies have been seen as relatively more important for SMEs, giving them an opportunity to engage in flexible specialization as part of a mutually complementary cluster of organizations and institutions (Piore and Sabel 1984). This creates external resource dependency (RD) as the opposite and alternative to the internal RB approach to strategy. As Popp, Toms, and Wilson (2003: 9) have argued, personal capitalism of the type prevalent in Britain could well be more appropriate to a system based on exploiting externalities, while managerial capitalism is more effective in utilizing internalities. Moreover, 'the general tendency to rely on the dynamic advantages of clustering and working within an intricately connected industrial district model provided many British industries with significant economies of scale and scope that underpinned their competitiveness well into the twentieth century.' Such a hypothesis helps to offset the argument that the continuation of personal capitalism was a quirky dimension of British culture and provides an underpinning logic for it.

In the context of this book, we need to be aware of the quite different implications for management structures and systems that emerged from this cluster or district-based model. (see Evolution of Structure, Chapter 1, regarding the preference for S-form.) Basically, it encouraged heterarchy and the continuation of personal capitalism, while at the same time discouraging the development of the hierarchy of bureaucratic management typical of managerial capitalism. Moreover, there was also potential for negative rather than positive externalities to emerge, if not immediately, then over time; such problems might be issues of governance of the cluster, price-fixing or other anti-competitive activities, difficulties in achieving change, lack of managerial skills, costs of information, or an inability to take decisions (Popp, Toms, and Wilson 2003). A key issue is, therefore, how far such externalities could be sustained indefinitely, or whether at least some of the three-pronged investment that Chandler emphasized was necessary. The evidence of the British economy suggests the latter.

But it is also important to note that external economies were not just relevant in Britain in the distant past; they have become important again in the last two decades or so with the emergence of network organizations, joint venture projects, the culling of management hierarchies, and the rise of outsourcing for all sizes of organization. In other words, the balance between internalization and externalization, or between hierarchy and heterarchy, has shifted again as we have moved out of the stage of what we have called organizational capitalism and into network capitalism (Pettigrew and Fenton 2000).

Fligstein and the Environmental Control Model

Fligstein's objective (1993) was to understand how large US firms, mainly in the manufacturing sector, had tried to control their environment and especially the extent of competition. In the late nineteenth century, as there were frequent booms and busts as rapid expansion was followed by market saturation, downward pressure on prices, and retrenchment or bankruptcies, firms decried the cut-throat competition and sought stability. This stability was achieved by whichever group, or 'conception of control', dominated the organization, leading over time to some fundamental re-orientations of control. He suggests that since 1880 there have been only four conceptions of control, which emerged from the interaction between leaders of large companies and have been conditioned by the state:

• Direct control of one's competitors, based on three main strategies: predatory trade practices, cartelization, and monopolization, in an era when there were few laws or rules governing behaviour. Predatory trade practices included price competition, patents, and disruption of competitors through legal and illegal means. Cartels often included elaborate written agreements to control the product market through quotas, setting prices, or division of territory. Monopolization was the ultimate objective of the great merger movement at the turn of the nineteenth century, in order to stabilize production and prices. Such practices attracted the attention of the state and resulted in anti-trust legislation.

- Manufacturing control was based on stable and cost-effective production. Strategies for control were effected through establishing control of the production process, through backwards and forwards integration and a move to oligopolistic pricing systems.

- The sales and marketing conception of the firm began in the 1920s and dominated the largest firms into the post-Second World War period. This approach was based on the assumption that the key problem was selling goods, therefore the solution was to expand sales by finding, creating, and keeping markets, thus achieving growth by non-predatory competition. Strategies included diversification, differentiation, market segmentation, advertising and promotions, and expanding overseas.

- The finance conception of control, which is currently the dominant paradigm but emerged as early as the 1950s in the United States, emphasizes control through financial tools which evaluate performance according to profitability. Firms are viewed as 'collections of assets earning different rates of return, not as producers of different goods' (Fligstein 1993: 15), with the objective being to maximize short-run rates of return by altering various factors in the product mix, increasing shareholder equity and keeping the share price high. The key strategies are financial ploys to increase the share price, diversification or retrenchment through mergers and acquisitions on the one hand and divestment on the other (rather than internal growth). This approach has also tended to be associated with corporate restructuring, usually with the aim of cutting costs.

Fligstein (1993) also notes that these successive conceptions of control contain elements of their predecessors. In organizational terms, he identifies the five key structures as the trust, the holding company, and the unitary, functional, and multi-divisional forms of firm. Not surprisingly, though, just like Chandler, he is only talking of the large firm.

Given that in the Fligstein model the business environment becomes a social construction between the actions of managers and the state, the Fligstein approach is thus more flexible and less deterministic than that of Chandler. Moreover, Fligstein argued that managers rarely know what is economically efficient. As he concluded (1993: 302): 'They have a sense of controlling a market or market share and to some degree can control costs. But the driving force for managers, just as it is for any kind of social actor, is to preserve their organizations and further their individual and collective interests.' In this context, rationality of action is by no means a prerequisite for progress, nor is there one most efficient mode of organization; everything is contingent upon circumstances and priorities.

Whereas the RB and RD approaches are about trade-offs between different cost structures, Fligstein (1993) concentrates on control of the environment. Although some of the costs involved in the RB and RD trade-offs are associated with the environment, Fligstein adds the important dimensions of the social construction of the context in which firms operate, and also reminds us of the uncertainties in decision-making. We regard his approach as a highly valuable counterweight to what might otherwise be unduly economic perspectives.

Towards a Synthesis of the Models

Having reviewed these differing approaches, it is now necessary to bring together the internalization–externalization transaction costs debate, the former associated with the model of Chandler (1990), the latter with that of Popp, Toms, and Wilson (2003). One obvious point of reconciliation is to note that the internalization approach is only appropriate for large firms, while externalization is suitable mainly for small ones; the two types can therefore coexist within an economy. But there are two additional dimensions which help to relate the two approaches. One is the modern strategic consideration of focusing either on the internal RB for identifying unique, firm-specific assets as capabilities, or the recognition of external RD, which can provide mutual externalities for a cluster (Popp, Toms, and Wilson 2003). A weakness of the resource-based view is that it ignores resources that are non-firm-specific. However, only in relatively competitive and geographically proximate industries are there likely to be external economies of scale benefits from clustering. Moreover, there is also potential for negative externalities to emerge, if not immediately, then over time; such problems might be issues of governance of the cluster, price-fixing or other anti-competitive activities, difficulties in achieving change, lack of managerial skills, costs of information, or an inability to take decisions. The other dimension differentiating the two models is that instead of the concept of hierarchy as an organizing principle there is the concept of heterarchy (Hedlund 1986). Heterarchy here is used in contrast to the hierarchy that is promoted by resource internalization within a single firm or ownership structure in Chandler's model. It has become a powerful force, especially within global supply chains, as firms seek to enhance their competitive advantage by linking with partners, even rivals, as a means of spreading the costs associated with a specific venture.

The relationship between the dimensions of RB and RD on the one hand and heterarchy and hierarchy on the other is provided in Figure 2.2, which identifies characteristics and Figure 2.3, which suggests empirical possibilities. In Figures 2.2 and 2.3, the RB refers to the RBs of the individual firms that comprise the cluster. As the RB is centralized, a single firm takes over an increasing number of

		Resource dependency	
		High	Low
Resource base	Internal	Hierarchical, centralized	Hierarchical, decentralized
	External	Heterarchical, centralized	Heterarchical, decentralized

Figure 2.2. Resources, governance, and industry characteristics (*Source:* Popp, Toms, and Wilson 2003)

		Resource dependency	
		High	Low
Resource base	Extensive	Conglomerates, M-forms, etc.	Transnationals, family firms, loose holding companies
	Narrow	Hub-based industrial district, putting out systems, etc.	Associations of firms, price-fixing cartels

Figure 2.3. Resources, governance, and industry characteristics: empirical examples (*Source:* Popp, Toms, and Wilson 2003)

functions, for example, by buying up other members of the cluster, thereby internalizing the resource bases of the constituent firm(s). Movement may also occur in the opposite direction through spin-offs, spin-outs, and demergers. Resource dependency meanwhile refers to the degree of dependence of all cluster members in the aggregate upon external resource providers. These resources include finance, labour, and raw materials.

Whereas the RB and RD approaches are about trade-offs between different cost structures, Fligstein (1993) concentrates on control of the environment. Although some of the costs involved in the RB and RD trade-offs are associated with the environment, Fligstein (1993) adds the important dimensions of the social construction of the context in which firms operate, and also reminds us of the uncertainties in decision-making.

THE 'DRIVERS' OF MANAGEMENT GROWTH

In spite of our focus on management as a central player in the economic arena, management is still a derivative of other drivers, not an independent factor in its own right, beyond certain minimal functions within the organization. Moreover, just as different countries have different pathways to economic growth (Rostow 1960), the drivers are likely to be present in greater or lesser degree in different countries and even different regions or sectors of the economy. They can also act in a positive or negative way in influencing change. Figure 2.4 identifies the range of drivers we consider to be significant, split into three groupings that are further examined in this section. We argue that this mix of drivers determined how management evolved in different countries, linking us closely to the national-institutionalist school of thought headed by Whitley (1999). Porter (1990) also noted in identifying the preconditions for competitive advancement that a range of factors can create a virtuous circle and reinforce each other, while management is a necessary further precondition in operationalizing the processes. We use the drivers in two ways. The first is to create force-field diagrams for each of our comparative countries, illustrating which drivers encouraged movement towards managerial capitalism and which tended to act as restraining forces against such a movement, at a key period in each country's development. Although the concept of a force-field diagram was created by Lewin (1951) to analyse change situations, there is as much reason to apply it to countries as to organizations. A diagram is provided for Britain in Chapter 3, while in Chapter 4 we do the same for the other three countries, the United States, Germany, and Japan, to provide a basis for comparison on an international basis. Of course, diagrams of this kind must inevitably be impressionistic in deciding which drivers encourage change, which restrain it, and which might be considered neutral. Elsewhere, we have expanded on the concepts underlying the drivers and provided a brief comparative analysis for each driver for the four countries in 1950 (Thomson and Wilson 2006).

A second way of using the drivers is to represent them as groupings, because as one can see from Figure 2.4, the drivers come under three headings: Market-cum-technological; Institutional-cultural; and Business policy and practice, with the first two sets providing the external dynamic context within the firm, or industry, and the third the internal dynamics. Again, this approach has been developed further in Thomson and Wilson (2006)], providing readers with a much more elaborate insight into how this technique can be applied to historical situations.

EXTERNAL   INTERNAL

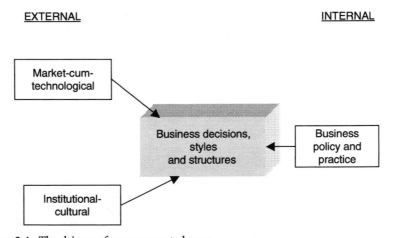

Figure 2.4. The drivers of management change

Market-cum-Technological Drivers

Markets consist of the interaction of buyers and sellers within a context of supply and demand, with the impersonal coordinating instrument being the price mechanism. In classical economics, these competitive forces operated as an 'invisible hand', to use Adam Smith's famous phrase. Under managerial capitalism, however, as Chandler (1977) demonstrated, many (but not all) of the decisions previously made in the market were taken over by managers. This transition is a central one in all economies, and why and how it occurs depends in considerable part on a wide range of market factors. Linked to this process is the transformation in production made available by changes in technology, enabling either new products to be made, or existing products to be made much more efficiently through the exploitation of economies of scale. These are also in large part the factors taken account of by Chandler (1962, 1977, 1990) in his analysis.

Our group of drivers in this category includes:

- Industrial structure
- Market structure
- Product market competition
- National innovation system
- General labour market
- Management labour market
- Impact of war

Institutional-Cultural Drivers

Langlois and Robertson (1995: 118) saw the importance of external institutions, especially those relating to the labour market and education, in explaining why 'late Victorian and Edwardian Britain did not possess the right capabilities to capture the benefits of wholly new innovations'. Similarly, Elbaum and Lazonick (1986: 2) noted that British business became trapped in a framework of 'rigid institutional structures that obstructed individualistic as well as collective efforts at renovation in industrial relations, enterprise and market organization, education, finance, international trade, and state-enterprise relations'. While we do accept that these institutional issues are of considerable importance, it is noticeable that in the discussion of British industrial history, there has been a major debate about the role of culture, but based primarily on the issue of gentrification and the loss of industrial values (Wiener 1981). While these were of some importance, we are more concerned with other cultural perspectives, especially attitudes towards industry and management as a career in a context where non-industrial elites and values tended to be dominant and managerial legitimacy questioned. It is also important to consider the attitudes of industrialists towards managers, given the belief current for most of the nineteenth and early twentieth century that as managers were 'born not made' they should recruit as far as possible from their own family or social group rather than in a meritocratic manner.

Our listing of significant drivers in this category includes:

- Physical infrastructure
- Political institutions
- Educational institutions
- Financial institutions
- Legal institutions
- Role of unions
- Public attitudes to industry
- State attitudes to industry
- Role of elites

Business Policy and Practice

Although exogenous drivers were important, so were those within the firm, especially those comprising aspects of both strategy and structure. Those strategic decisions bearing on the balance between externalization and internalization, or investment in Chandler's three-pronged areas of technology, marketing, and management (1990), were clearly important at the highest level of the firm. Equally important were lower level strategic issues affecting management techniques and the extent of training. But structural issues were also significant, from ownership patterns and governance arrangements at the top level, organizational typologies affecting middle management, and methods of planning and control at all levels.

Our final group of drivers includes:

- Organizational strategy and theory
- Predominant organizational structure
- Orientation to change (including promotion and succession)
- Role of consultants
- Internal legitimacy of management
- Investment sourcing
- Marketing strategy
- Labour strategy
- Nexus of power
- Managerial techniques

While we have identified a wide range of drivers, it is clearly not possible to ascribe weightings to each of them; rather, most situations were likely to be a complex mixture of many of the drivers. These issues are addressed in Chapters 3–5, when force-field diagrams are offered as a means of distinguishing between restraining and positive drivers. While again we must stress that this exercise is more indicative of trends, rather than a definitive statement of the balance across our drivers, it provides a reasonably accurate assessment of their relative importance at different points in time.

THE THEMES OF THE BOOK

Bringing together what we have described as the models and the drivers outlined in this chapter, and specifically how they apply to Britain, our themes provide the main explanatory framework within each chapter. Each theme itself needs further explanation and unpacking, which will later help us identify the main dimensions of management in Britain. For the present, however, it is sufficient to lay them out as propositions, noting specifically that Themes 1 and 2 relate predominantly to the structure and operation of organizations, while Themes 3 and 4 are more concerned with the external context within which organizations operated. It also follows that Themes 1 and 2 are not only central to Chapters 3 and 5 but also feature strongly in Chapters 9 to 11, while Themes 3 and 4 are predominantly the subject of Chapters 6–8.

Theme 1—The Persistence of Personal and Proprietorial Capitalism

Personal capitalism performed extremely well in Britain in the First Industrial Revolution, when risks were high, there was no alternative form of organizational start-up, and vast numbers of firms failed. The problems arose with a changing context, new technological requirements, capital needs, and the coordinating and control skills of the larger scale of industry needed to obtain maximum efficiencies which emerged with the Second Industrial Revolution after 1880. Given the centrality of the role of management in Chandler's schema, he was convinced that British competitiveness was undermined by a failure to make the three-pronged interdependent investments in production, marketing, and management (1990: 235). While Wardley (1991) has produced evidence to indicate that by 1900 a significant number of British firms were as large as their American and European counterparts, as Gourvish (1987: 20) concluded, 'corporate change in Britain before 1914 was more legal and financial than managerial, with an emphasis on the retention of control by founding family groups'. This view is confirmed by Wilson's review (1995: 132) of the business scene up to the First World War, indicating that 'the reluctance of family owner-managers in Britain to delegate responsibility to professionally-trained managers would help to explain the lack of depth to which Chandler refers when assessing managerial hierarchies in this country'. Furthermore, there were still echoes of this after the Second World War, as Channon (1973) found in his survey. It is thus not so much a question of size, or indeed personal capitalism per se, since family capitalism has always been important in all countries and is still dominant in many, but one of an unwillingness to delegate authority that made the British situation different.

Moreover, as families lost control when size increased, non-family firms did not behave much differently. As Quail (2002: 7) notes

in the UK the reservation to the directors of overall coordination combined with a strong sense of the board's role and prerogatives led to a fixity of structure and management style which had two broad consequences at the level of the firm. Firstly, firms did not evolve managerial hierarchies much beyond the departmental or functional level, top management being sparse or non-existent, with management technique in consequence generally being under-developed. Secondly, firms could not easily grow beyond a certain size or complexity of operation or respond dynamically to changing business conditions.

While the directors were seen as representatives of the owners and there was usually a requirement of being a substantial shareholder to become a director, there was no complementary requirement of knowledge of the business, leading to the prevalence of what can only be described as a highly amateurish approach to business. Quail (2002: 8) argued that 'the legal fiction was that the directors represented and were accountable to the shareholders', leading him to coin the phrase 'proprietorial capitalism' as an extension of personal capitalism, wherein there was some separation of ownership and control in the UK, yet tremendous continuity in the nature of intra-organizational relationships. Basically, the argument is founded on the notion that as personal capitalists acting on behalf of shareholders did not want to cede control to salaried managers, they were unwilling to initiate the structures and take on the managers which could lead to this happening. Hence, it provides a primary explanation as to why a cadre of British managers did not emerge as rapidly as in some other countries.

Theme 2—Management, Organizational Structure, and Transaction Costs

The focus of this theme is the tendency for British firms to use external rather than internal mechanisms of decision-making at times when firms in other countries were using internal mechanisms. We have already noted in an earlier section (Management in the Theory of the Firm) how Coase's recognition (1937) that the firm and the market were alternative mechanisms for carrying out the same transactions, while (see Chandler and the Market-cum-Technological Model and Fligstein and the Environmental Control Model), two different models of organizational development were offered, discriminating between firms that follow a policy of internalization (Chandler 1990) or externalization. This theme builds on these distinctions, based on Coase's concept of transaction costs, which he summed up as follows in the final paragraph of his 1937 article:

When we are considering how large a firm will be the principle of marginalism works smoothly. The question always is, will it pay to bring an extra exchange transaction under the organising authority? At the margin, the costs of organising within the firm will be equal either to the costs of organising in another firm or to the costs involved leaving the transaction to be 'organised' by the price mechanism. Business men will be constantly experimenting, controlling more or less, and in this way, equilibrium will be maintained.

What we will be arguing is that different market and institutional conditions in different countries resulted in and helped to explain the balance and cost framework of these choices taken by firms. This had a major impact on the emergence and utilization of management as the main internal mechanism of operationalizing these activities or transactions. Where the cost framework favours using the external market, firms will not need a sophisticated management hierarchy, especially in the service and support areas, although they will need some managers to carry out the basic production once the firm is above the size where it can be operated by a single owner-manager. But where the balance is in favour of internalizing transactions, for example, where a rapidly growing market enables the capture of economies of scale in marketing, or where a shortage of labour requires the substitution of capital and technology for labour, resulting in a more complex production system, the need for a more sophisticated managerial cadre arises. There is in other words a spectrum along which companies exist, or choose to place themselves, although this might be different for different types of decisions.

At one level, the boundaries of the firm are determined by technology, which defines the production function and helps determine economies of scale. But that is only a starting point, since the relationships with the labour, financial, and product markets as well as a wide range of functional service markets require a series of choices as to whether to perform the activity internally or use the external market. Crucially, though, these choices need not be conscious at any point in time; they will almost certainly be influenced by social, political and economic institutions, and the state of existing and indeed past markets. In effect, they are subject to a trend towards path dependency.

The cost balances can and do change over time, a point that is illustrated by the widespread move at the end of the twentieth century to outsource many of the activities that firms had previously carried out internally. Thus, the study of management history needs to take account not only of different market structures and conditions but also the social, political, and economic institutions associated with them, since the choice is determined by the conditions on the supply side as well as by the latent demand.

It is important to add that part of the choice relates to the market for management itself. If there is a substantial availability of educated and 'professional' managers to carry out the additional tasks, that will help tip the balance of choice towards internalizing many of the other transactions. But if there is little interest in a managerial career in the country, and if there is no educational or training system to produce the necessary managers, then there will be a tendency to use the external market and to continue using it even after other factors begin to indicate the need for change, because the firm will rationalize that the activity cannot be efficiently organized internally. As a result, management does not develop as a central activity-coordinating role within the firm, except in the limited area of production.

We also need to note here Quail's rather different approach to the issue of transaction costs. He argues (2002: 9–10) that

it is not at all clear in Chandler's work that any case is made for the primacy of the internalization of transactions as the motor of managerialism. It appears, in fact, that a more general point may be inferred: that the US economy, culture and society enabled management capacity to grow quickly to an extent where the market, understood in the neo-classical sense, was pre-empted or superseded.

As an alternative, Quail (2002: 10–12) suggests another factor in the development of managerialism, namely, managerial capacity, which already existed in the form of administrative innovations and an ideological mindset. Thus, the innovations in processes and managerial techniques on the American railroads can be traced back to managers trained at West Point, while the ideology and techniques of labour control pioneered by Taylor (1903) are provided as other evidence where 'inventiveness preceded utility'. Moreover, 'a considerable number of US businessmen were clearly prepared to invest in significant levels of managerial/technical excess capacity', commitments that were to pay off in the longer run because of the human capital they created.

As this concept of managerial capacity is highly useful, we return to it later when assessing the British context. At the same time, it does not overrule the importance of transaction costs as a means of conceptualizing the balance between internal and external arrangements, especially in light of the late-twentieth century move to review this balance yet again.

Theme 3—Attitudes Towards Industry and Management

It would be impossible to examine the emergence of modern management without reference to those institutional and cultural issues identified in Figure 2.4 which are linked to the status of and attitudes towards management and industry as a whole, as reflected both in the views of the public and the policies of the state. At one level, these reflected the balance in the economy as a whole. In spite of the significance of the 'First Industrial Revolution' in Britain, industry was not the dominant force in the economy (Cain and Hopkins 1993a; Rubinstein 1994). Finance and commerce were not only more established in the economic sphere by 1870 but also far better placed in the social and political spheres. This in part reflected a geographical dimension, with industry focused above a line from the Severn to the Wash, and finance and commerce below it, with London as the hub of Empire, policy, and power. Moreover, from the early days of industry, a considerable section of public opinion and opinion formers saw industry as described in evocative writings, such as Blake's 'dark satanic mills' and Dickens' *Bleak House* as exploitative, dirty, and associated with lower-class activities. As a result, industry in Britain did not acquire the support of elites and the state that it did in other countries, producing at best a neutral, laissez-faire posture and at worst one of outright hostility.

Such attitudes had a secondary effect, inducing generally negative social attitudes towards management as a role and as a career, reflecting the more enhanced status of the professions, and especially the 'learned' professions, law and medicine, finance and commerce, and the civil service in Britain and the Empire as a suitable career for middle-class Britain. Thus, industrial management did not attract the calibre of entrant that was true of other countries where the status of the occupation was higher and at key times, such as after the First World War, there was a distinct shortage of managers. Even into the final quarter of the twentieth century, a government report was bemoaning the poor status of management (Department of Industry 1977).

A third dimension is related to the legitimacy of management, in both the political and industrial spheres. There has been a political party structure which for a long period divided the country over the acceptability of private enterprise, at least in the 'commanding heights of the economy', as well as an industrial system, which was permeated with a tradition of amateurism.

A fourth dimension involves the major debate about the role of culture that has taken place in Britain. On the one hand, in a much-discussed and much-criticized book Wiener (1981) argues that the industrial middle class had aspirations to enter what was a highly elitist and anti-industrial aristocracy, thereby diminishing their effectiveness as businessmen. On the other hand, Rubinstein (1993) argues that other countries also had aspects of an anti-industrial culture, while the British economy was in any case less industrial and more dependent on the financial and commercial sectors. Thompson (2001) also argues within the cultural debate that the so-called 'gentrification' argument was not as important as the issue that entrepreneurs were paternalistic, hierarchical, conservative, and inward looking—these were the real straightjackets. These are all issues that we develop further in Chapters 6 and 7, illustrating their vital importance in providing a long-term perspective on British managerial development.

Theme 4—The Slow Transition Towards Professionalism in Management

The definition of professionalism is one which has been hotly debated over a long period without coming to generally accepted conclusions (Perkin 1989; Abbott 1988). Yet without wishing to become too embroiled in that literature, we accept that managers have certain professional attributes, some much more so than others. The distinction is sometimes drawn between family-based management that recruited only family members or a particular social circle, and 'professional' managers, using the term merely to mean those who have no such connections and are paid employees. However, we see a significant difference between, on the one hand, those salaried managers who moved into narrow functional roles from lower level positions and whose knowledge base for management was experiential or instinctive, and, on the other hand, those managers whose generic knowledge base as managers was explicitly developed in a way similar to those in the accepted professions, and hence are more deserving of the term professional. Another dimension of this distinction is that the salaried manager usually had a primary role in a functional position and was dependent on functional skills for the identity as a manager, whereas the professional manager can be seen as a manager first and not dependent on functional skills, even though that would be a significant part of the job. Equally important was the tendency for the salaried manager to have low status and low authority, while the professional manager has much higher status and more authority. The trend in the development of more sophisticated industrial systems and structures has been away from dependence on the salaried manager towards the emergence of professional managers, although even today there will be a balance between the two. The main argument underlying this final theme is that other countries, in different ways, achieved a transition from salaried to professional management well before Britain. Moreover, this was not a short-term problem, but rather one that underlay British economic development, or the lack of it, for well over a century (Handy 1987). Indeed, it is still a cause for concern in the early twenty-first century, providing a solid justification for this book.

This theme is concerned with two further points. One is that while the attributes of a professional manager are essentially individual, a professional is also linked with more general aspects of public and organizational recognition, concerned with power, status, legitimacy, and authority. While some earlier managers may have had the personal attributes of professionalism, it was much more difficult than it is now for them to enjoy these additional dimensions of esteem. By contrast, it is now much easier to achieve professional status, mainly through better supply-side institutions, even though by no means all managers do so. The other point is that professionalism is not only concerned with the individual manager's suitability to take decisions involving change, the application of technology, and strategic considerations involving marketing, labour, and financial issues, but also a cadre of managers acting in an integrated way in an organization. Crucially, though, in contrast to other professions there is no need to secure a state licence to manage, even if as we see in Chapter 11 some elements of management have been colonized by accountants who had been granted this privilege well over a century ago (Grey 1998). This raises the issue of whether management can be regarded as either a profession or an occupation, providing Chapters 6–8 and 12 with a considerable challenge.

CONCLUSIONS

As the purpose of theory is to help in the understanding of practice, we shall be referring to strands of theory throughout the book, whose absence some writers have bemoaned in the closely related field of business history (Lee 1990). At the same time, while theory provides insights, it cannot always cover every circumstance. We should especially bear in mind what Payne (1988: 58) noted in his authoritative survey:

The one certain conclusion that can be drawn ... is that there is much more to be discovered about the British entrepreneur in the nineteenth century ... It is still dangerous to speak of '*the British entrepreneur*'. No such person exists. Over the century there were countless entrepreneurs in a remarkable variety of trades and industries.

The same is true, and indeed more so, of the British manager, about whom we know even less than we do about entrepreneurs, while a similar argument of appropriate caution concerning broad generalizations can be made of our other components, the drivers, the models and themes, which we have laid out in this framework-developing chapter. They provide a means of drawing together the empirical developments in the management of organizations which are the subject of Chapters 3–5, offering a British and comparative analysis and bringing the British developments up to the present.

Part II

Management and Organizations

3

British Management and Organization up to the 1940s

INTRODUCTION

In moving from the general foundations on which this book is based to a detailed assessment of how in Britain the management and organization of business evolved, we begin to offer some empirical backing for the principal constructions—stages, themes, and drivers—offered in the first two chapters. As we also noted (see Modern Management, Chapter 1), in identifying the three main ways that management grows in organizations, through scale, scope, and the addition of new functions, this can act as a guide to tracking the dynamics of British management over the first two stages identified in Chapter 1 (up to 1870; and 1870–1945), when both the scale and nature of business activities underwent some striking changes.

At the same time, we provide further detail to support the four themes outlined (see The Themes of the Book, Chapter 2), especially the persistence of personal (Chandler 1990) and proprietorial (Quail 2000) capitalism, as well as the extent to which firms operated in dense industrial districts that afforded extensive opportunities to externalize a wide range of activities. Even though this period witnessed the emergence of big business (Wardley 1991) and intense merger activity affected many sectors (Hannah 1983), as Brech (2001: 1, 16) argues at least up to the 1930s an 'in-born ethos' dominated British management, indicating that there was 'neither call nor case for professional focus'. This will also be illustrated through an analysis of the drivers identified (see The 'Drivers' of Management Growth, Chapter 2), using a force-field diagram to demonstrate how the environment did not prove conducive to the development of managerial capitalism. While there might well have been some differences between the manufacturing and service sectors, with some of the latter displaying a greater propensity to internalize processes and develop organizational hierarchies, it remains debatable whether in Britain the management and organization of British business advanced at an appropriate pace.

INDUSTRIALIZATION AND MANAGEMENT TO THE 1870s

Although we are principally concerned with tracing the rise of modern management from the 1870s, it would be impossible to relate the full story without briefly discussing the dramatic changes that occurred across the British economy from the 1770s, when the old system of mercantile capitalism steadily gave way to modern industrial capitalism. In an organizational sense, mercantile capitalism was based on the avoidance of management by passing responsibility for production to domestic workers, with little fixed investment in buildings and machinery by the merchants who ran the system. Starting in the iron and textiles industries, progressively from the late eighteenth century an embryonic form of modern industrial capitalism emerged that was characterized by the concentration of production, posing much greater organizational challenges and placing a stronger emphasis on management, with entrepreneurs having to take on the vital task of organization building. Crucially, though, the patterns of behaviour and organizational traditions established in the era when Britain was regarded as the 'First Industrial Nation' became so entrenched by the 1870s that in spite of severe internal and external pressures it was difficult to change direction. This highlights the path-dependent nature of British management history, given the strength of the embedded processes that persisted for so long.

One of the most obvious problems facing this first generation of modern businessmen was the steep learning curve on which they had embarked. Although some standard treatises on the subject of business organization had been written (see, Schools of Management Thought, Chapter 2), little of this was accessible to the vast majority of practitioners as they struggled to cope with the learning curve. Furthermore, this was very much the personal stage of industrial capitalism, with families taking responsibility for creating, financing, and running the vast majority of firms. Nepotism also dominated recruitment patterns, with family members featuring at all levels of the organization. In this context, the central issue was trust (Casson 1993), especially as professional managers were regarded as highly unreliable. As the great Scottish economist Adam Smith noted, professional managers 'cannot well be expected that they should watch over [other people's money] with the same anxious vigilance with which the partners in a private copartnery frequently watch over their own' (quoted in Pollard 1965: 24). Pollard (1965: 21) has also noted that in the eighteenth century there were many 'examples of dishonest, absconding or alcoholic managers who did much damage to their firms', indicating why contemporaries were reluctant to devolve control to this group.

In spite of these constraints, however, it is apparent that a cadre of managers was emerging from the late eighteenth century. Guillén (1994: 208) has even noted that 'the leading managers of the first industrial revolution introduced methods of standardization, accounting, advanced division of labour, work study, and payment by results'. This claim is based on evidence derived from some outstanding pioneers who introduced highly novel means of solving the organizational challenges facing the first generation of industrial entrepreneurs. The Birmingham engineering firm of Boulton & Watt was perhaps one of the most innovative, employing from the 1790s a range of cost accounting techniques to control their expanding business (Roll 1930). Wedgwood was another of the pioneers who ran his highly successful pottery business in an effective manner

(McKendrick 1960), devising in the late eighteenth century both cost accounting and marketing techniques that were highly advanced for their day. The key issue here, however, is why these innovations were not more widely dispersed across British business, given that it is difficult to find evidence of many contemporaries imitating the pioneers (Pollard 1965: 186–8). Indeed, the vast majority of functionaries were recruited principally for their technical or organizational skills, indicating how this became a principal driver behind British organizational dynamics that persisted well into the twentieth century. Moreover, in view of their generally lowly social background, this revealed how managers were rarely endowed with much social status. Of course, managers were regarded as one step up from the even more humble clerk, the status of which deteriorated over this period (Wilson 1999). On the other hand, because salaried managers rarely came from the owning family, they were never absorbed into the decision-making ranks, while any skills developed were almost always specific to the sectors in which they operated (Pollard 1965: 187–8).

Externalization and Organizational Evolution

Having noted the existence of these alleged constraints, it is vital to stress that both Pollard (1965: 308) and Payne (1988: 18) have indicated how a strong degree of characterization features in these descriptions of the personal stage. Admittedly, philosophers and political economists like John Stuart Mill and Thomas Malthus, as well as the later populists like Samuel Smiles (1859), promulgated a philosophy of self-dependence as the key to improved economic and social betterment (Crouzet 1985: 37–49). On the other hand, given what Casson (1993: 42) has described as a 'high-trust culture', businesses operated in extensive local networks that freely transmitted information concerning market trends and general commercial matters, albeit keeping detailed management processes in-house. Furthermore, these regional business networks were located within the various industrial districts that dominated the economic landscape up to the 1930s (Wilson and Popp 2003), providing the economic rationale for a system of economic interdependence based on the exploitation of extensive external economies of scale. Within these industrial districts, firms frequently collaborated on a range of issues, especially those relating to wage rates and political intervention, providing a powerful degree of cohesion that is frequently ignored by those who assess the implications of personal capitalism. Of course, one must be careful not to exaggerate the degree of collaboration in the classic industrial district because intense local competition and a reluctance to abide by commonly accepted standards affected many industries (Popp 2001; Carnevali 2003). It is also fair to note that later in the century these networks proved cumbersome in diffusing new technologies or methods, indicating how they could well have atrophied and acted as a constraint on improved performance (Wilson and Singleton 2003). On the other hand, it is equally clear that the prevalence of these collaborative instincts undermines any claim that self-help was the dominant philosophy of that era.

Another key feature of these early modern business organizations as they struggled to cope with the conversion to industrial capitalism was the emergence of multi-layered partnerships that offered a solution to the management challenges of that era. Chapman (1969: 89) has described this system of managing partners as 'the empirical discovery of a solution to the problem of organization and control of the dispersed manufacturing sector'. This provided an enduring way of dealing with the need to find a compromise between individualism and economic reality, with managing partners featuring prominently in a large number of industries (Pollard 1965: 163–88). In effect, this became the organizational building block of British business until the late nineteenth century when the joint-stock company grew in popularity. While some of these managing partners were recruited for their technical or organizational skills, taking on, for example, the role of works manager, others simply provided investment capital. The latter would mostly come from an entrepreneur's extended family or religious network (Crouzet 1972: 168–75, 191; Cookson 2003), indicating how regional business networks were extensively exploited for this purpose. Conversely, many talented individuals were able to exploit these managerial opportunities as apprenticeships that would lead to the establishment of their own businesses. Whatever the case, in the process managing partners provided an effective solution to the organizational challenges associated with the advent of modern industrial capitalism (Crouzet 1985: 15–18).

Complementing this system of using managing partners was the parallel trend of hiring salaried managers to perform the functional and operational tasks for which owner-managers had neither the time nor the expertise. In spite of what Adam Smith said about the inherent dangers associated with delegating responsibility to managers, they were clearly in great demand from the 1790s, as owner-managers struggled with the steep learning curve associated with modern industrial capitalism. This trend can be confirmed by the substantial increase in salaries earned by 'typical managers': in the period prior to 1760 this would have been no more than £60 per annum; by the 1830s it had risen to between £500 and £2,000 (Pollard 1965: 165–73). Clearly, by the early nineteenth century businessmen had accepted the need to compromise their individualism; while nepotism continued to be a major feature of managerial recruitment for many decades, especially at the higher levels, salaried managers were increasingly regarded as essential features of the business scene. Indeed, Pollard (1965: 174, 185–6) argues that from the 1790s the 'replacement of nepotism by merit became one of the more significant aspects of the growing rationalization of industry'. He also goes on to conclude that 'the line between the manager, the managing partner and the moneyed partner was increasingly difficult to draw, as mobility between these categories remained high.' At the same time, it is also fair to add the caveat that these were still salaried managers, rather than a fully formed professional class, indicating how this cadre still had much to do in gaining appropriate status.

This caveat, of course, reveals a considerable amount about the nature of nineteenth century management and business organization in Britain. While the emergence of managing partners was a useful innovation, it is vital to remember that at least up to the 1870s British manufacturing businesses were characterized by highly primitive hierarchical structures in which management techniques were at best embryonic, if not entirely pragmatic solutions to immediate problems. In this context, Figure 1.1 provides merely an idealized structure that symbolizes the subtle process of specialization that was emerging from the late eighteenth century in response to the economic realities of industrial capitalism. As we see in Chapter 11, there is emerging evidence that modern tools of management accounting were in use by 1850 (Edwards and Newell 1991: 35–57), especially in industries characterized by high levels of fixed investment. On the other hand, there is relatively little evidence to show that these innovations impacted on all sectors of the economy, reinforcing the earlier point that in general up to the 1870s British business was still built on highly traditional structures and techniques. Moreover, as we have already stressed, the salaried managers were rarely given any form of training, other than what was colloquially known as 'sitting at Nelly's elbow', or in other words, practical experience, while their lowly status prevented them from making any kind of impact on strategy. Coleman (1973: 103) has also placed these trends in a wider context, indicating how British society in general extolled the virtues of gifted amateurs, revealing a distinction between 'gentlemen and players' that persisted well into the twentieth century. It is consequently clear that up to the 1870s, managers were recruited for their specific (mostly, technical) skills, indicating that while there were 'well-defined groups of managers in many industries', as yet this hardly amounted to the creation of a managerial profession (Pollard 1965: 188).

The Management of Business by 1870

Having emphasized this pervasive reluctance to delegate executive responsibility, it is nevertheless important to remember what was said earlier about the externalization of many functions by British industrial firms, especially those that operated in dense industrial clusters characterized by extensive specialization (Wilson and Popp 2003). With specific regard to labour recruitment and control, as we see in Chapter 9, while frequently the works manager (see Figure 1.1) dealt directly with the overseers and skilled artisans operating within his own domain, key roles like planning and supervision of operations, machine-manning and remuneration, as well as recruitment, discipline, and general factory conditions, were mostly the preserve of these overseers and subcontractors. Moreover, most firms joined (regional, and later national) employers' federations that were responsible for negotiating wages and conditions with full-time trade union officials, indicating how this crucial aspect of labour management was externalized. As this system proved so valuable to both industrialists and skilled workers, it is also clear that it would survive in most industries well into the twentieth century (Gospel 1983: 6–7). Crucially, this would not only significantly restrict the evolution of labour management skills, but also limit the development of planning and control techniques that in other economies came to be a decisive feature of organizational hierarchies. Furthermore, as we also see in Chapter 9, the existence of a vibrant trade union movement would severely limit the ability of management to introduce new ideas (Guillén 1994: 211–12), creating a further in-built obstacle to organizational progress.

It is consequently clear that the development of professional management in British manufacturing industry was severely hampered by four substantial constraints: first, contemporary attitudes towards proprietorial rights; second, a prevalent association that salaried managers worked on the shop floor, giving them a low social status; third, the widespread aversion to professional training for business; and fourth, the externalization of many functions, especially labour management and marketing and sales. Of course, even though some of the major iron and steel, textiles, and coal mining operations employed over 1,000 people by the 1850s, one should remember that large-scale businesses were a rarity at that time (Musson 1978: 129–33), given the predominantly localized nature of markets, not to mention the reliance upon subcontracting facilitated by the operation of vibrant industrial districts. This indicates that not only were sophisticated organizational hierarchies rarely required, but also the demand for professional managers was stymied. At the same time, such a distinct approach towards management had been adopted in the formative years of the late eighteenth and early nineteenth centuries that it became increasingly difficult to alter this system once economic conditions changed after 1870 and lively competitors started to appear, reiterating the path-dependent nature of this analysis.

THE RISE OF BIG BUSINESS

One can firmly conclude that the management of British manufacturing firms by the 1870s had ossified at a primitive stage of development. From the 1830s, however, established management practices and thinking had been assaulted by the emergence of a new industry, the railways, indicating how in Britain there were interesting organizational differences between the manufacturing and service sectors. Dwarfing the capital expenditure in any other industry, between 1830 and 1875, £650 million was raised by operating companies. Furthermore, as a significant proportion of this capital was raised from professional investors who had little interest in running the companies, there was a subsequent divorce between control and ownership which meant that railway managers were 'an executive elite, the first group of "corporation executives" to appear in British industry' (Gourvish 1973: 290). This illustrates how the railways not only became the 'pioneers of modern corporate management' (Gourvish 1972: 167–82), but also 'led the way in developing relatively advanced techniques in business management, making progress in the fields of accounting, costing, pricing, marketing and statistics' (Gourvish 1973: 290).

Of course, in the early years of railway management up to the mid-1840s, with little in the way of precedent or contemporary practice to inform railway managers, executives responded poorly to the challenges associated with running these complex organizations. By their very nature, the operations were geographically dispersed, stretching the lines of communication at a time when the telegraph and telephone were only just beginning to appear. Engineering, catering, and hotel businesses were also run alongside the transport function, significantly diversifying the portfolio of activities. In addition, because of the dual pressures associated with intensifying competition and tighter government regulations, by the mid-1840s a series of mergers resulted in the creation of much larger railway companies, leading to some experimentation with innovative management techniques (Gourvish 1972: 103–4). The leading innovator in this respect was undoubtedly Captain Mark Huish, the general manager of the London & North Western Railway Co. between 1846 and 1858. His main contributions to railway management were the development of adequate depreciation provision for rails and rolling stock, the introduction of internal controls on costing and pricing, and the extensive delegation of responsibility to divisional managers who would report regularly to senior staff at executive conferences. In essence, at a time when managers were rarely given much authority, Huish 'helped to promote the growth in stature of the salaried official within the large-scale company' by building a structure which relied to a significant extent on the role they played in running businesses (Gourvish 1972: 260–7).

While these innovations were undoubtedly significant, not least in helping to boost the status of salaried managers on the railways, it is vitally important to remember that even Huish experienced difficulties in overcoming the reluctance of directors to delegate responsibility down the line to functional managers (Gourvish 1972: 167–82). As the boards of directors in the largest companies were composed of aristocrats and prominent capitalists, they were regarded as reliable trustees of investors' proprietorial rights. This perpetuated what we described earlier as the 'gentlemen and players' structure which was so typical of British business generally (Coleman 1973), illustrating how the alleged 'pioneers of modern corporate management' suffered from the traditional social distinctions within British managerial hierarchies. Furthermore, while Chandler (1990: 253) admits that British railway companies '[created] the first managerial hierarchies with lower, middle and top levels of management', he also argues that they 'were less challenged to pioneer new methods of organization and of internal control' than their American counterparts (1990: 253). Wren (1994) is also careful to explain how in the United States the railroads acted as a source of innovation and learning in American management generally, a feature that was lacking in the British scene.

These points severely qualify any claim that railway management decisively changed the nature of British business organization. Moreover, even though railway companies constituted in 1904–5 the top ten British businesses, measured by market value (Wardley 1991: 278), it is clear that their impact on the rest of British management was marginal (Hannah 1976: 3). Not only were the senior railway managers recruited from upper middle-class backgrounds (Gourvish 1973: 297–316), but also their training was mostly in-house and practical.

Of course, by the 1890s some of the larger railway companies were beginning to recognize the limitations of this highly introverted approach towards recruitment and training for senior management. For example, the North Eastern Railway Co. established a formal link with the London School of Economics (LSE), leading to the formation in 1904 of a Railway Department at the university to provide training for managers (Keeble 1992: 98, 104). In general, though, it is apparent that one can easily exaggerate the impact of any innovations in British railway management, while the persistence of a 'gentlemen and players' structure severely limited the elevation in status of salaried managers.

The Manufacturing Sector

Of course, the insularity of railway management was a further indication of the trends outlined in the last section, where we noted that while by the 1830s salaried managers were beginning to appear in significant numbers, and each sector developed some standard techniques, there is little evidence by the 1870s that either the specific roles of a manager had been identified or the professionalization of management had become an aspiration of the business community. In this context, it is interesting to assess the extent to which the economic and social environment of the late nineteenth and early twentieth centuries stimulated change. Amongst the most significant influences on business were: the intensification of international competition; advances in new technology that amounted to a 'Second Industrial Revolution'; the rise of big business and nationally organized trade unions; increasing state intervention, especially after 1914; and industrial dislocation after 1921, with even more severe problems arising out of the 1929 Wall Street Crash.

Above all, as we see in Chapter 4, rival approaches to business organization and management appeared, especially in the United States where the leading corporations sought what Chandler (1990: 8) described as 'first-mover advantages' across a range of new and old industries by pursuing a 'three-pronged investment strategy' associated with mass production, national and international marketing and distribution networks, and professional management. Chandler (1977: 1, 6) had also earlier noted that in the United States by the early twentieth century the invisible hand of market forces was replaced by the 'visible hand of management', with a cadre of professional managers becoming 'the most influential group of economic decision makers'. This indicates how in exploiting the enormous market-cum-technological opportunities that emerged in the United States from the 1860s, by 1900 American business management became the benchmark against which other industrial economies would be measured.

In stark contrast to his progressive depiction of American management, Chandler (1990: 237) is in no doubt that the British system of personal capitalism resulted in a 'failure to make the three-pronged investment in production, distribution and management' across most key industries. Of course, many have cast doubt on the way in which Chandler links this alleged 'failure' to Britain's relatively poor economic performance between 1870 and 1914 (Wilson

1995: 7–8). It is also clear that Chandler ignores the inherent characteristics of British industrial structure at that time, and in particular the pursuit of external economies of scale through participation in industrial clustering and the system of industrial relations (Toms and Wilson 2003). On the other hand, there is clearly a case to answer here, because even though the scale of British business was increasing impressively (Wardley 1991), evidence of organizational or managerial progress is difficult to evince. As Chandler (1976: 40) concluded,

the large industrial enterprises in Britain at the end of the First World War were either integrated, centrally administered entrepreneurial companies or federations of family (or entrepreneurial) enterprises which were legally but not administratively combined within a holding company. As a result there were very few large central offices manned by professional managers and served by extensive staffs. At the top, owners managed and managers owned.

In addition, one should also stress that the scientific and technological base proved inadequate for the Second Industrial Revolution that was sweeping across the United States and other European economies from the 1890s. Of course, there were some success stories in the consumer goods sector (Lever Brothers, Pilkingtons, and Courtaulds, for example), while the service industries, especially finance, performed extremely well over this period. The overriding impression, however, is of a business system that rarely relied on the kind of managerial ethos that was coming to dominate American business.

Of course, as sweeping generalizations of this kind are always subject to challenge, it is important to differentiate between sectors. At the heart of the economy were the staple industries (textiles, coal, heavy engineering, and chemicals), most of which operated in dense industrial districts that relied mostly on the externalization of many managerial functions, but especially marketing and sales, as well as labour management. The frequently specialized nature of these firms was another constraint on the development of extensive managerial hierarchies, while strong familial control remained a feature well into the twentieth century. Although, as we see later, these industries were subject to intense merger waves after 1890, mostly stimulated by increasing domestic and overseas competition, thereby increasing the scale of their operations, this failed to extend internal organizations. Furthermore, as these firms remained both specialized and dependent upon high levels of externalization, opportunities to extend the managerial hierarchy remained limited.

Given the importance of these staple industries to the pre-1914 economy, it is clear that in many ways they set the tone for British managerial and organizational developments, especially in terms of production systems and the use of planning and control systems. Although we say much more about both labour relations and accounting systems in Chapters 9 and 11 respectively, in the staple industries it remained standard practice up to the 1930s at least for management to allow the skilled workers to control what happened on the shop floor, in terms of the pace of work and actual production practices. As we saw earlier, while works managers were often employed as intermediaries between owners and workers, these functionaries possessed such low status that they rarely influenced firm strategy or structure. Of course, the nature of market demand militated in favour of bespoke production, rather than mass production (Pollard 1989), providing some justification for the persistence of traditional practices. On the other hand, the abdication of management from the shop floor had grave implications for the development of internalized control procedures. It also explains why when prior to the First World War ideas associated with Taylor's system of scientific management were mooted (see The United States: Competitive Managerial Capitalism, Chapter 4), the vast majority of manufacturers regarded them as alien to the established practices that had stood the test of time. At the same time, given the low status of those managers who worked on the shop floor, rarely did they possess any technological or scientific skills that would have given them the ability either to spot new ideas or implement them effectively. Contemporaries were mostly dismissive of the general approach to production planning and control systems (Shadwell 1916: 375–6).

Having stressed these weaknesses in production management, it is also important to note how management accountants were employed in tiny numbers, an issue to be further developed in Chapter 11. Of course, as Boyns (2005: 120) has explained for the period leading up to the First World War, there are cases of firms in a range of industries (coal, iron and steel, engineering, and chemicals) where some advanced cost calculations were conducted—activities that certainly infiltrated management strategy. It is consequently clear that there were severe weaknesses in the micromanagement of what in large part were the S-form (see Figure 1.1) structures that dominated the staple industries. Although, to a certain extent, sticking to traditional practices might well have been justified by both the levels of externalization, not to mention the nature of product markets, as we go on to see these weaknesses were later incorporated into the H-form structures (see Figure 1.3) that emerged out of the 1890s merger movement. Judged by Fayol's analysis (1917) of the five key components of management—planning, organizing, commanding, coordinating, and controlling (see, Modern Management, Chapter 1)—British management in the staple industries was principally concerned with a certain amount of not very effective commanding, with very little of the other dimensions being covered at all. In this sense, British managers in the staple industries were more in the mould outlined by Mintzberg (1973), in that they were less concerned with the technocratic Fayolian functions.

Delving further into this issue, one should stress that over the course of the nineteenth century managers were to become substantially less homogeneous as a group, especially in the staple industries. Three main categories can be discerned. In the first place, as dynasties grew up, family members served as managers and on the board of directors. Management ability was taken as an inborn competence derived from a combination of inherited personal qualities, with the recognized entrepreneurial capabilities of the founder acting as the cohesive force. Second, there were those managers who were recruited through contacts and patronage, many of whom progressed to being managing partners and indeed went on to found companies of their own. Finally, there were those managers—by far the most numerous as companies grew in size—who came in at the bottom and carried out the main functional roles. Some, but not many of this latter group progressed up the ladder to senior management and even on to the board of directors. It is the last group with which we ought to be principally concerned, because as firm size and the number of functions grew, the social distinctions between different levels of managers were also extended. The families and their social partners consolidated their position at the top as the numbers of those recruited from manual or clerical ranks increased.

Although talking about the early nineteenth century, Pollard (1965: 162) provides an accurate description of the system as it prevailed at the time of the First World War:

The fear of delegating authority helped to prevent the rise of a middle management group. Managers could not be found by advertising in the newspapers or consulting an agency. Sales managers or chief accountants had to be trained from the ranks, and, unless they were relatives, the senior partner was unlikely to consult with them on policy.... In general, the situation tended towards undermanagement, a failure to recognise that a higher product-ivity might come from more careful planning and supervision.

This 'undermanagement' and reluctance to delegate was a pattern that continued well into the twentieth century, providing the central organizational pillar of both personal and proprietorial capitalism. Furthermore, Payne (1988: 26–7) suggests that opportunities for upward social mobility through promotion became even more circumscribed. This is substantiated by Erickson (1959: 189), who has described how in the iron and steel industry, an 'increasingly closed, exclusive and patrician' pattern emerged in the recruitment of managers. Indeed, Payne (1988: 27) effectively argues that the growth of the public company 'probably suffocated the entrepreneurial aspirations of the lower middle strata of society. Possessing few, if any, shares; names which had no attraction for the potential investor; and at best only the most tenuous connections with other firms, there was no room for them on the board'.

Another important branch of British industry was the consumer goods indus-tries, in which there is some evidence of vertical integration and aggressive brand building. Lever Brothers is perhaps the most famous example of this approach (Wilson 1954), while Church (1999: 16) has also demonstrated how from the early nineteenth century this sector demonstrated a highly ambitious approach to market development. Overall, though, as Chandler (1990: 389–90) argues, even in this sector the three-pronged investment in marketing, production, and management was limited by the desire of families to retain control combined with limited vision and cartel arrangements. For example, in 1917 Lever Brothers only had eighteen managers in its central office, whereas twenty years earlier a German rival, Stollwerck, had over 150 (Chandler 1990: 401), further demon-strating the limited nature of organizational developments in what was a growth sector of the British economy.

While the experiences of the staple industries and consumer goods sector conform to the Chandlerian view that personal capitalism restricted the nature of British business organization and management, the situation was even more serious in the third sector, the industries of the Second Industrial Revolution, given the long-term repercussions for the balance of the British economy. Here again, across high-growth industries like electrical engineering, automobiles, and synthetic chemicals, there was a widespread failure to build organizational hierarchies that would be capable of managing the expansion that could have been achieved had entrepreneurs been more ambitious (Chandler 1990: 348). Even though personal capitalism was weaker in the new industries, there remained a strong aversion both to delegating responsibility to professional managers and devising effective structures (Wilson 2000). Of course, one should stress that in Britain these industries failed to grow as rapidly as they did in the United States and Germany especially, given the limited markets for products that were often competing with well-established alternatives (Wilson 1995: 95–8). Weaknesses in the national innovation system, and especially the reluctance of higher education to cater for the new technologies, further limited the impact of the Second Industrial Revolution in Britain (Sanderson 1972). These constraints consequently provided few incentives to invest in the Chandlerian three-pronged approach. Furthermore, as American and German rivals exploited first-mover advantages in the new technologies so effectively, it became increasingly difficult for British firms to compete against these powerful rivals (Chandler 1990: 286).

Having been so critical of these three sectors, one should conclude by noting that certain features of the British scene limited the impact of stimuli that in the United States led to much more expansive organizational developments. It is all too easy to fall into the trap of believing Chandler's withering conclusion (1990: 392), that there had been a 'general failure to develop organizational capabilities'. In the first place, in ignoring the prominent adherence to securing external economies of scale through the dense industrial districts, this criticism ignores the extent to which British firms devolved the performance of key managerial tasks to outside bodies. Second, as market forces were much weaker than in the United States, the incentive to invest in mass-production facilities never existed to anything like the same extent. Third, the nature of demand also placed a premium on quality, as opposed to quantity production, minimizing the need to devise detailed planning and control procedures. It is consequently vital to understand the context in which British business operated rather than relying on comparisons that are based on American standards and criteria. On the other hand, when one considers the rise of big manufacturing business from the 1880s, one must still question the organizational results of this process and how they impacted on long-term trends.

Mergers and Business Organization

A useful way of highlighting these issues further is to examine the wave of mergers that affected British business from the 1880s, when it was apparent that conservative tendencies dominated both the motives behind increased concentration and their organizational consequences. As Table 3.1 reveals, during the 1880s and especially the 1890s, mergers became a prominent feature of the British corporate scene, indicating how the business community was accepting the notion of big business, albeit mostly as a defence against increasing competition. On the other hand, several characteristics of these mergers undermined any attempt to transform the organizational basis of large firms. In the first place, most of the mergers occurred in the older, slow-growing sectors (textiles, chemicals, mining, heavy engineering, and brewing), reflecting a strongly defensive rationale behind the activity. Second, no less than 98 per cent of the mergers were horizontal combinations, significantly limiting the vertical integration of activities (Hannah 1974a: 1–20). Third, while this created an opportunity to exploit internal economies of scale by rationalizing production capacity, the consequent combinations were organized as federations of firms, rather than wholly integrated operations. In consequence, the S-forms (see Figure 1.1) that had dominated British business up to the 1880s rarely evolved into the U-forms (see Figure 1.2) that were appearing in the United States at that time, emphasizing how the mergers proved to be a missed opportunity to revamp organizational capabilities. While Gospel (2006) claims that a significant number of U-forms had emerged by 1906 (see Table 5.2), one should stress that many of these lacked the rigour of their American or German counterparts. Furthermore, as one senior executive from English Sewing Cotton claimed at the time (quoted in Macrosty 1907: 133–4), 'it was an awful mistake to put into control of the various businesses purchased by the company the men who had got into one groove and could not get out of it'.

Inevitably, there were several exceptions to this general situation, in particular the robustly organized J. & P. Coats, Ltd. (Wallace 2003), Dudley Docker's Metropolitan Amalgamated Railway Carriage and Wagon Co. (Davenport-Hines 1984: 24–6), and the highly progressive Lever Brothers (Church, 2000). Many of the federations had also been subjected to a process of reorganization by the First World War (Wilson 1995: 106–11), indicating how contemporaries were slowly beginning to accept the need for rational business structures and rigorous

Table 3.1. Merger activity in UK manufacturing industry, 1880–1950

Decades	Number of firms disappearing	Values (at current prices) £m	Values (at 1961 prices) £m
1880–9	207	10	136
1890–9	769	42	401
1900–9	659	55	483
1910–19	750	161–73 [i]	998–1060 [i]
1920–9	1,884	360–411 [i]	1654–886 [i]
1930–9 [ii]	778	182–218 [i]	759–907 [i]

Key:
[i] There was a major break in the series at these dates, leading Hannah to offer a range of estimates.
[ii] For 1930–8 only.
Source: Hannah (1983: 178).

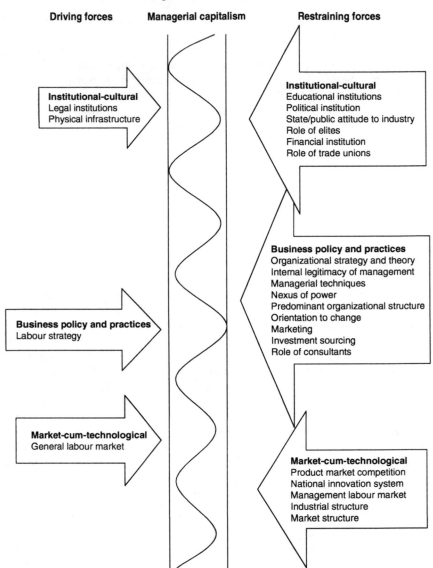

Figure 3.1. A force-field diagram illustrating the drivers at work in Britain, 1870–1900

management practices. In general, though, the attitudes towards, and development of, professional management up to the First World War at the very least continued to rely more on earlier traditions, rather than the more progressive influences disseminating from either an emerging British 'management movement' or from the United States. This substantiates our earlier claims about the limited approach towards production systems, planning and control within the staple industries, a view further supported by examining the nature of managerial appointments: as Sanderson (1972: 19–20) noted, the 'lack of a native graduate class' severely limited the pool of talent from which firms could recruit. This would result in the promotion of clerks to the post of head of department, for example at Shell in the 1890s and Dickinson's in 1903. Such a process provides yet further evidence of a dearth of appropriately trained people, in turn reflecting the failure to accept any need to change recruitment and development patterns.

While bringing all these themes together produces a severe challenge, in Figure 3.1 we provide a force-field diagram that indicates the extent to which the late nineteenth century British environment failed to prove conducive to the emergence of managerial capitalism. This diagram is based on the three groupings of drivers that we outlined (see The 'Drivers' of Management Growth), where it was stressed that it was essential to examine a range of external and internal challenges and opportunities in order better to understand the contextual issues at play in any one period. Again, we must stress that Figure 3.1 is impressionistic, providing an indicative analysis of the British scene between 1870 and 1900. It is also important to stress that Figure 3.1 must be compared to similar exercises conducted in Chapter 4 for our three comparator economies, where it will become apparent that the drivers were much more positive. Regardless of these caveats, however, one must conclude that the overwhelming impression from Figure 3.1 is negative, in that the prevalence of our drivers is heavily biased towards restraining the emergence of managerial capitalism. Moreover, we would argue that for the next fifty years the balance remained negative, with little movement across any of our three main groups of drivers.

INTERWAR PROGRESS?

Having confirmed in an earlier Section (The Rise of Big Business) Brech's view (2001) that an 'in-born ethos' dominated the British managerial scene up to the First World War, it is vitally important to examine whether after this traumatic event firms were prompted to re-evaluate their approaches. As we see in Chapter 8, this was also a period when what Child (1969: 44–105) refers to as a 'management movement' evolved into the 'Rationalization Movement', headed by pioneering management thinkers like Lyndall Urwick, John Lee, and Seebohm Rowntree. The volume of management literature (see Figure 8.1) also increased significantly at this time, while business-related degrees at the LSE, Birmingham, and Manchester generated wider interest (Keeble 1992: 96). Similarly, managerial institutes and associations of varying kinds appeared, with the specific intention of offering managers an opportunity to ape the more established professions of law, medicine, and accountancy. Judged superficially, one might look at this evidence and agree with Hannah (1983: 36) that the ideas of the Rationalization Movement were 'able to induce investment in innovating techniques of intra-firm organization and thus motivated the cheapening of management within the firm relative to transactions in the market'. Hannah (1983: 89) also provides more substantial grounds for making this claim, referring especially to merger activity and other key business developments in the interwar period as manifestations of Rationalization, concluding that these were 'an integral part of the Rationalization movement as well as a condition of its success'.

Mergers and H-forms

As one can see in Table 3.1, merger activity in the 1920s and 1930s was even more intense than the previous peak years of the 1890s. Indeed, it is vital to stress that from the end of the First World War British business indulged in an unprecedented flurry of mergers and acquisitions, resulting in the creation of much larger manufacturing firms like English Electric (1919), Imperial Chemical Industries (ICI) (1926), the Lancashire Cotton Corporation (1929), and Unilever (1929). This resulted in the emergence of an oligopolistic market structure, so that by 1930 the top 100 companies accounted for 26 per cent of net manufacturing output, compared to 15 per cent in 1907 (Hannah 1983: 180). Wardley (1991: 278–9) has also demonstrated that while in 1905 the average market value of the top fifty firms was £28.4 million, by 1935 this had almost doubled to £58.8 million, with manufacturing enterprises like Imperial Tobacco, ICI, Unilever, and Shell featuring much more prominently in the latter, as a result of which firms were faced with an even greater managerial challenge.

Having emphasized the dramatic nature of these changes, it is consequently vital to assess the extent to which business management and organization progressed over the interwar era. Bowie (1930: 8) was only one of the many commentators who noted that the business scene had been transformed so extensively that it was 'demanding of its personnel a wider knowledge, a keener specialization and ... a more intensive training'. There is also clear evidence that office practices were being changed through the introduction of new types of office machinery, from the increasingly ubiquitous telephone to duplicators, typewriters, and accounting machinery (Hannah 1983: 77–8). This is linked to an increase in the proportion of manufacturing employees classified as 'administrative, technical and clerical', from 8 per cent in 1907 to 15 per cent by 1935. While Hannah (1983: 86) claims that this largely 'represented a strengthening of centralised, functionally differentiated management', rather than a significant deepening of managerial hierarchies, it was indicative of the general process of organizational change that was affecting British business generally. At the same time, one should remember what was said (see The Managers, Chapter 1), namely, that the number of managers grew only slowly in the first four decades of the twentieth century (see Figure 1.7), undermining any claims of a 'managerial revolution' at that time.

Just how significant were the mergers? In the first place, one should stress that just like their 1890s predecessors, interwar mergers were largely defensive. Even the mighty ICI was formed in 1926 as a response to German dominance in crucial growth sectors like artificial dyestuffs and synthetic chemicals (Reader 1970). Second, in an organizational sense one can find little evidence that the new creations adopted ideas emanating from the United States. While exceptions like ICI and Unilever moved towards the kind of M-form that the American giants DuPont and General Motors had pioneered in the early 1920s, the propensity to adopt an H-form (see Figure 1.3) was much more prevalent in Britain (Hannah 1976: 198–9; 1980: 52–6). While as we noted in the last section British business had been slow to introduce the U-form of organization in the 1880s and 1890s, in the interwar period H-forms represented a ruse to avoid the kind of rigorous organizational changes that were required (see Table 5.2). As Payne (1984: 196–7) concludes, the H-form was crucial in preventing a wider acceptance of managerial capitalism by allowing family firms to shelter from competitive pressures. When combined with the persistence of externalization, these anti-competitive pressures further limited the development of sophisticated organizational hierarchies.

When trying to explain the apparent failure of many British firms to implement the new ideas about management being espoused by leading figures like Urwick and Lee (see The Interwar Management Movement, Chapter 8), one must look at both internal routines and external pressures for change. As far as the former were concerned, the 'implicit and unacknowledged obeisance to the god of continuity' dominated British business (Coleman 1987: 8–9). In simple terms, owner-managers either perpetuated the traditional organizational culture of their firm through the persistence with autocratic, centralized structures, or they sought the security of a merger as a means of preserving control in a holding company structure. Keeble (1992: 45) has also noticed how 'directors and senior managers normally involved themselves in the day-to-day running of the firm, preferring not to delegate and so create more positions with authority'. This is indicative of what we saw in the late nineteenth century, and in particular of what Coleman (1973: 92–116) has described as the traditional distinction between 'gentlemen' at the head of a business and the 'players' who performed the mundane managerial and supervisory tasks. Furthermore, the pattern of managerial recruitment underwent little change at all, with the prevalence of what Keeble (1992: 45–61) describes as 'patronage'. This must be distinguished from nepotism, because in non-family firms directors regarded the ability to find employment for friends as part of their privileges. In practice, though, as the distinguished economist J. M. Keynes argued, 'hereditary influence in higher business appointments is one of the greatest dangers to efficiency' (quoted in Keeble 1992: 47). Internal training was also 'compartmentalized', in that managers were prepared for specific tasks, rather than for the performance of a range of duties, further limiting their wider utility.

Protectionism, Trade Associations, and Externalization

Not only was the organizational culture of British business resistant to change, but also the external economic environment failed to encourage management to try much that was new. Of course, the severe depressions of the early 1920s and 1929–32 were major features of the interwar period, while the continuing threat from foreign industry materially affected the export prospects of those sectors that had traditionally relied on overseas markets. On the other hand, one should remember that in the 1930s British trading policy reverted decisively to protectionism, imposing substantial tariffs on imported goods and services. As a consequence, British trade associations were able to exert much greater control over domestic markets, guaranteeing minimum prices and market quotas for their expanding membership. With industrial districts still playing a prominent role in the elaboration of externalization strategies, this created a cosy environment based on collusion and compensation, substantially minimizing the impact of competitive market forces that might have encouraged firms to introduce new organizational ideas (Wilson 1995: 178–9).

When one combines the growing influence of trade associations with the perpetuation of an H-form in many leading firms, it is apparent that change came in the form of a retreat into defensive alliances that only served to diminish the need for extensive managerial hierarchies. As we see in Chapter 5, these features of the British market also persisted well into the 1960s, providing big business with considerable power over domestic prices and production levels. Furthermore, corporate governance pressures were so weak in Britain that managements were generally free to run their firms as they saw fit. In this context, one should also remember that even as late as 1950, 110 of the leading 200 firms still had representatives of the owning family sitting on the board of directors (Hannah 1980: 53). However, even when as a result of merger and acquisition activity a firm's equity was sold to professional investors, directors' decisions were rarely challenged. This was 'the golden age of directorial power' (Hannah 1974*b*: 65–9); it was a period when what Quail (2000) has classified as 'proprietorial capitalism' became the dominant influence, arguing that whether or not there was a division between control and ownership: 'The common factor [was] the proprietorial desire to reserve to the board the coordinating and other top management functions rather than delegate them to managers.' It would be directors who took charge of specific functions, rather than professional managers, while those who populated the lower hierarchical ranks were prevented from acquiring greater power by their subordination to a top-heavy committee structure that severely limited the devolution of influence.

If attitudes towards managers and the process of management remained stubbornly traditional up to the 1940s, it is also clear that in an organizational sense little had changed by the mid twentieth century. We have already noted how many of the large-scale mergers had resulted in a federated H-form (see Figure 1.3), with the U-form (see Figure 1.2) failing to make much of an appearance in British business. Those firms that operated within the H-form structure also continued to use the S-form of organization (see Figure 1.1), with family members managing the various departments wherever possible (Chandler 1990: 266). As we noted earlier, there were some outstanding examples of organizational innovation, including the M-forms created at ICI and Unilever, while others employed prominent accountants as a means of improving the degree of control exercised over expanding organizations (Hannah 1976: 189). Overall, though, one cannot fail to notice that there was a 'continuing failure [not only] to recruit and train the necessary managerial staffs', but also to build managerial hierarchies which would provide for long-term growth (Chandler 1990: 390).

THE BANKING SECTOR

Although as a result of examining the railways we have already stressed both the differences and similarities across the manufacturing and service sectors in Britain, it is important to sustain this exercise by looking at other parts of the economy as it evolved into a more mature stage after the 1870s. In particular, to take a particular example one ought to consider how the banking sector was organized and managed, given that this has consistently been the most successful element of the British economy from the eighteenth century to the present day.

The City, Banks, and Professionalism

By the late nineteenth century, the City of London had attained a dominant position, not only as the pivot around which the British financial system revolved but also as the world's financial capital. While one could debate at length the impact this pre-eminence had on the British economy generally (Wilson 1995: 119–32, 181–94), of much greater significance is the organization of leading financial institutions, as well as the extent to which they developed a professional approach to management. In addition, it will be important to assess the influence they had on the rest of British business, in order to contextualize the analysis and assist in drawing conclusions about the general state of British business organization and management by the mid twentieth century.

Although there had traditionally been a strong regional dimension to the British financial system (Kennedy 1987: 124–5), with provincial stock exchanges and local banks contributing significantly to the flow of both fixed and liquid capital, at the pinnacle was the City of London elite of merchant bankers. This elite, including the Rothschilds, Barings, Morgans, Grenfells, Schroeders, Hambros, and Gibbs, had emerged as the dominant force in British finance as a result of their conversion between the 1790s and 1820s from commission merchants to commission bankers (Chapman 1984). Apart from trade credit, their principal business was dominated by government funding, overseas investment, and large floatations. Above all, though, they were family-run firms that traditionally recruited from an extremely narrow social band (Cassis 1994: 202–43), cementing their elite status through nepotistic recruitment patterns that persisted until the 1980s (Scott 1997). Moreover, this elite has been described as 'gentlemanly capitalists' who operated along the lines of 'that characteristic mixture of amateurism and efficiency' which were so typical of the British establishment (Cain and Hopkins 1993*a*: 116–25). Similarly, the London Stock Exchange has been described as 'the last bastion of the British amateur', given the reluctance to insist that members should have had any training (Michie 1999: 99). Although Michie (1999: 103) points to the varied nature of Stock Exchange membership and a growing preference for training in broking and related activities, it is difficult to escape the general conclusion that well into the twentieth century the City of London continued to be dominated by the amateurism personified by the 'gentlemanly capitalists'.

Having created this image of Britain's financial capital, it is important to counter the accusations of amateurishness by emphasizing how the sources of much of the liquidity required by the system, namely, the London-based clearing (or, commercial) banks, were run along different lines. While some have criticized British banks for their alleged unwillingness to support indigenous firms, especially compared to their German and Japanese counterparts (Best and Humphries 1986: 236; Kennedy 1987: 121–3), it is apparent from the exhaustive work of Collins and Baker (2003: 255–8) that they provided abundant short- and long-term capital for industry. Moreover, Collins and Baker (2003: 250–8) have clearly demonstrated that the stability and liquidity achieved by this sector, not to mention its organizational sophistication and managerial professionalism, were considerable assets to the British economy.

While this debate will no doubt continue, especially after further research has been conducted into the demand-side in this equation, it is also vital to consider the major trends in British banking and their organizational implications. Three principal stages can be discerned in the evolution of British banking: the emergence of country banking after the 1760s, the rise of joint-stock banking from the 1820s, and finally the post-1880 bank mergers. Of course, this ignores the existence of the Bank of England (created in 1694) and a large number of London firms that operated as banks from the late seventeenth century (Ackrill and Hannah 2001: 1–3). Many of the provincial banks were also closely linked to London discount houses, the specialist institutions which dealt in credit, leading to what by the early nineteenth century was a national credit market (Cottrell 1980: 16). Moreover, from the 1860s an extensive branch network was developed by the larger joint-stock banks, allied to which in the 1880s a merger movement resulted in considerable concentration of banking under the control of City banks. By 1910, the top ten London-based banks controlled 60.7 per cent of total deposits held in England and Wales, while Barclays had 599 branches, Lloyds 673, and the Midland 846 (Cottrell 1980: 196–7; Cassis 1985: 302–5; Cassis 1994: 45–8; Newton 1998: 58–63; Ackrill and Hannah 2001: 59–66).

Apart from bringing much greater stability to the British banking system, by linking the London, Edinburgh, and provincial banking systems through an extensive national branch network (Collins 1991: 37–41), the process of concentration precipitated severe organizational challenges for the London and Edinburgh headquarters. One might also mention the continued process of concentration that continued up to 1920, by which time the 'Big Five' (Barclays,

Lloyds, National Provincial, Midland, and Westminster) accounted for 80 per cent of domestic deposits in England and Wales (Capie and Rodrik-Bali 1982: 287–8; Collins 1994: 282). They had consequently become substantial organizations in their own right, with eight featuring in the 1905 list of top fifty British firms by market value (Wardley 1991: 278). Surprisingly, though, none of these appear in the list of leading British employers of 1907 (Wardley 1999: 102–4), even though it is known that in 1914 the Midland Bank had 5,000 employees (Green 1979: 87–9), Lloyds Bank had over 2,880 and the London County and Westminster 2,032.

With extensive branch networks and rapidly rising capital deposits, it was clearly essential for these large, geographically dispersed organizations to develop an effective bureaucratic structure as a means of facilitating communication. The London-based joint-stock banks were dominated by a board of directors appointed by substantial numbers of shareholders, underneath which there were general managers working in the headquarters, who in turn controlled the branch managers. As Cassis (1994: 52–67) has demonstrated, however, while the directors were firmly in control of bank strategy, the vast majority worked part-time, devoting most of their lives to other City activities, and especially to insurance and investment. Moreover, no less than 98 per cent of the bank directors born in the period 1841–60 came from an elite background, indicating a high degree of exclusivity (Cassis 1994: 92–106). In this way, 'gentlemanly capitalists' from the acceptance houses and insurance firms were able to dictate strategy to the commercial banks, ensuring that the professional managers operating at general and branch levels implemented policies devised by the 'amateurs' at the head of the organization. It was an archetypal manifestation of proprietorial capitalism in action. As a result, the big banks evolved a 'tightly controlled, hierarchical employment regime' in which managers' activities were carefully elaborated, with internal training provided on a regular basis as a means of developing a robust internal labour market that would generate a consistent supply of trusted employees (Holmes and Green 1986: 89–119; Wardley 2000: 81; Ackrill and Hannah 2001: 76–9; Collins and Baker 2003: 151–2).

While both contemporaries and historians have criticized the emergence of the new bureaucratic structures and mechanically trained branch managers, arguing that this substantially reduced their ability to cater for local circumstances (Cassis 1985: 309–10), from the 1870s banking demonstrated a tendency towards professionalism that sets it apart from most other sectors in British business. Of course, both the provincial and early joint-stock banks were mostly run along less rigorous lines, with part-time employment common in the smaller offices that typified these operations. Similarly, the careers of those who worked in the world of private banking, including the merchant banks, were based mostly on nepotism (Cassis 1994: 106–7). On the other hand, from the 1870s a much more structured system evolved within the commercial banking sector with clearly delineated career patterns and an extensive commitment to training. Bank clerks have even been described as 'the aristocracy of the clerical profession' (Anderson 1976: 16), given both the hours of work and the possibilities for advancement into either branch or headquarter management. This status was also further enhanced when in 1875 a professional bankers' institute was established in Scotland, to be followed four years later by the formation in London of the Institute of Bankers, providing clerks with another opportunity to acquire professional qualifications and ascend the career ladder.

The principal aim that lay behind the creation of the Institute of Bankers was to provide 'a chance to obtain a professional recognition which would win security and promotion' (Green 1979: 51). Membership was achieved by passing a set of examinations, after which an individual would become an Associate of the Institute. Although Collins and Baker (2003: 156–8) stress that becoming an Associate did not guarantee promotion, the Institute served the essential purpose of setting nationally recognized standards that were the *sine qua non* of banking professionalism. On the other hand, an enormous social gulf existed between the upper-class directors and the socially subordinate managerial class, with only rare instances of the latter being elevated on to the board (Cassis 1994: 124–7). This highlights how even in a sector characterized by some elements of professionalism, proprietorial capitalism was still the abiding norm that ensured managers rarely progressed beyond a certain level. At the same time, while in setting standards and acting as a moderating influence on banking practice, the Institute of Bankers facilitated the emergence of the banking professional, one should also stress that like the railways these innovations failed to filter through into general business practice. This highlights another of the main themes of this chapter, that in allowing personal or proprietorial capitalism to persist, this restricted the opportunities for radical organizational innovations.

During the interwar decades, the 'Big Five' banks also initiated 'a managerial transformation' of considerable significance (Wardley 2000: 90–3). In particular, as a means of reaping the financial economies of scale possible in the extensive branch networks they had constructed by the 1920s, special attention was paid to developing an internal labour market based on training, Institute examinations, appraisal schemes, and recognizable career ladders (Wardley 2000: 82–9). Mechanization of basic accounting tasks was also pursued, indicating how, along with the insurance industry, banks set an example in office automation that other sectors partially imitated throughout the interwar period (Hannah 1983: 77–8). Even a family-dominated bank like Barclays proved adept in recruiting professional managers into the highest echelons of management (Ackrill and Hannah 2001: 85–9), while the Midland and Lloyds were even more progressive (Holmes and Green 1986: 171–4), leading Wardley (2000: 90–3) to conclude that 'professional management had replaced entrepreneurial enterprise in the "Big Five" by the end of the 1920s'.

Having stressed these organizational refinements, however, it is vital to add some important caveats. In the first place, one must stress how the system continued to be based on proprietorial capitalism, with the 'gentlemanly capitalists' of the City's establishment continuing to dictate strategy and structure. Furthermore, in spite of its intimate links with the manufacturing sector, there is no evidence that banking professionalism influenced attitudes outside its narrow confines. At the same time, the financial sector continued to perform effectively throughout the nineteenth and twentieth centuries. Even though the City lost its pre-eminent position to New York during the First World War, British financial institutions remained competitive both domestically and internationally. In the context of this book, however, one must wonder why proprietorial capitalism should be regarded as a restraining factor in the manufacturing sector, while in financial services it would not appear to have affected performance. The solution to this conundrum might well lie in both the degree of market power exerted by British commercial banks and the extent of internalization, with the 'Big Five' dominating the domestic market through their national branch networks, providing the 'gentlemanly capitalists' with the resources to employ in furthering their own agendas. These were characteristics that British manufacturing operations were never able to affect, with most firms operating in highly competitive environments where externalization remained viable. Banking was consequently both exceptional in the way that professionalism filtered into the organizational hierarchies, yet typical of British business in persisting with proprietorial capitalism well into the twentieth century.

CONCLUSIONS

In trying to explain the apparent dearth of organizational and managerial innovation up to the 1940s, apart from key features of the external environment like increasing levels of industrial concentration and trade association activity, one must focus on the essential elements of a business system that failed to stimulate change. As we have seen in Figure 3.1, the drivers for change were mostly negative in the British context, reflecting the durability of a traditional modus operandi that continued to operate well into the twentieth century. One of the key features of the M-form that emerged first in the United States was the delegation of responsibility down the line to professional managers, whether at functional or operational levels, something that was clearly anathema to a business community that believed in what Florence (1961: 195) described as 'leadership by inheritance'. In this context, one can hardly lay the blame for this attitude on the family firm, because as Church (1993a: 35–9) reveals family ownership and control persisted in many modern industrial economies, including the United States, Germany, and Japan. One must consequently look for different characteristics, and especially the propensity to hire large numbers of professional managers who were well trained in both general and functional management, and to whom significant responsibility could be delegated. In the British case, it is clear that the concept of 'managers are born, not made' continued to dominate business practices. Even towards the end of our second stage, buttressed by protectionism and rigorous trade associations, one can only support Quail's claim (2000) that British business was dominated by proprietorial capitalism, given the ubiquitous belief in the rights of directors to determine all aspects of a firm's activities and the negative impact this had on organization building and the recruitment of professional managers.

A second crucial factor that influenced these aspects of business was the persistence of externalization. While British business was indulging in an unprecedented level of merger activity, not to mention from the 1930s colluding on a whole range of market-rigging and price-fixing agreements, many firms relied on outside agencies for key aspects of their activities, with the continued viability of an industrial district model that had dominated British manufacturing industries since the late eighteenth century (Wilson and Popp 2003). As a consequence, it is clear that transactions-costs economics failed to encourage business to pursue a strategy associated with exploiting internal economies of scale, thereby reducing the need for both a rigorous overhaul of organizational procedures and employing larger numbers of professional managers. This confirms our earlier claim that there were limited opportunities available for the growth of management within British business; while there was clearly a considerable growth in the scale of operations, neither the scope of firms nor the extent of managerial functions were extended over the decades up to 1940. Furthermore, even where scale increased, often as a result of mergers, the strength of personal or proprietorial capitalism ensured that the demand for professional managers was restricted.

While there are strong grounds for moderating the many criticisms of British management practice that dominate the secondary literature, one must still come to the conclusion that between the 1880s and 1930s continuity would appear to have been the most prominent feature, with neither the U-form nor the M-form making much progress in a community that preferred either the S-form or H-form. This creates a highly path-dependent scenario, providing us with a theme that will be examined in several other areas of the book. Admittedly, as we see in Chapter 8, management thought had moved on to a higher plane, with the 'Rationalization Movement' offering insights into all the latest techniques and processes. On the other hand, as we noted earlier, the general impact of these pioneers was marginal, with little spin-off from the more progressive sectors, indicating how demand-side factors more than outplayed the supply-side in the years leading up to the Second World War. Indeed, one can only conclude that given the inherent characteristics of British business by the end of our second stage (1870s to the 1940s), and tying in closely with one of the book's overarching theses, a managerial constraint on the rate of growth of firms existed, severely limiting the ability of business organizations to cope with rapidly changing circumstances (Penrose 1959). In this it differed from some of its principal competitors, an issue we shall now go on to explain in much greater detail.

4

Comparative Management Systems
up to the 1940s

INTRODUCTION

Having outlined the evolution of British management up to the Second World War, it is vital that in order to benchmark the rate of progress more robustly we should conduct a comparative study of developments in other leading industrial economies. In particular, recalling the 'big' question of the book identified in Chapter 1, namely, 'attempting to understand why corporate management structures developed so impressively in countries like the USA, Germany and Japan, while in Britain relatively little progress was made in this respect' (Wilson 1995: 134), it is essential to offer some comparisons if we are going to produce useful conclusions. One must stress the generalized nature of this comparative work, given the difficulties associated with condensing an enormous amount of material into a single chapter. On the other hand, by structuring the three main sections around the drivers that we identified in Chapter 2 (see The 'Drivers' of Management Growth, Chapter 2 and especially Figure 2.2), the comparative dimension comes through much more effectively. This exercise also is supported by the provision of force-field diagrams for each country, providing a direct source of comparison with Figure 3.1 for Britain. In addition, the theoretical issues assessed in Chapter 2, and in particular the relative preferences for internalization over externalization, are also incorporated into the analysis, providing yet further evidence of the differences between the systems covered. Finally, in the concluding section it is possible to address the book's four themes in a comparative sense, producing a rich background to the British story that we take into Chapter 5.

The key theme in this chapter consequently focuses on how and why, by the early twentieth century, variants of managerial capitalism were beginning to develop a substantial presence in the American, German, and Japanese economies. As one can see from the various subsection headings, it is clear that there were subtle differences in the form that these developments took. While in the United States a fully fledged form of competitive managerial capitalism had evolved by the start of the twentieth century, in Germany one might more accurately use the term 'professional proprietorial capitalism', while for Japan we have chosen 'collective managerial capitalism'. These variants indicate how the process of change was affected by differing indigenous environments, even if in effect each country was moving decisively towards managerial capitalism. In particular, realizing that the transaction costs associated with concentrating and integrating production and distribution were much lower than those in traditional forms of industrial capitalism, entrepreneurs in these countries proved to be more enthusiastic about building large-scale firms which exploited the available economies of scale and scope. Even though family ownership and control remained prominent features of these business systems, especially in Germany and Japan, their ambitious and aggressive strategies had also resulted in the formation of extensive multi-level managerial hierarchies which were staffed by large numbers of specially trained professional managers. The crucial issue in this context is how these developments relate to what we discussed in Chapters 1 and 2, and especially in relation to the drivers outlined in Figure 2.2. This will help identify both the underlying institutional, cultural, and market-related circumstances, as well as how the pattern of business evolution differed so markedly across each economy. While the managerial pressures associated with running large-scale, geographically dispersed, vertically integrated and diversified enterprises have been similar in all three countries, it is equally important to stress the differing responses to the elaboration of strategy and structure across the three business systems. It would also be interesting to assess whether any typologies of business development can be derived from our study of business evolution in the United States, Germany, and Japan because this would be enormously helpful as a basis for later discussions. In particular, when analysing the debate surrounding British business's alleged failure to imitate its more successful rivals, we need to know whether there are any specific factors which are especially important in explaining the rise of large-scale business.

THE UNITED STATES: COMPETITIVE MANAGERIAL CAPITALISM

Introduction

As Chandler (1977, 1990) has outlined in considerable detail, while in the mid nineteenth century American business was little different to its British counterpart, over the course of the following fifty years managerial capitalism swiftly became the standard modus operandi as corporations sought to exploit the enormous market-cum-technological opportunities available to them both nationally and internationally. This Chandlerian model is clearly central to our analysis, in that it emphasizes how professional managers emerged as a distinctive elite within a business system that has often been described as the apogee of modern industrial capitalism. In addition, as we saw (see Models of Organizational Growth, Chapter 2), it is notable how Fligstein (1993: 12) has provided an alternative interpretation, focusing on what he identifies as a firm's 'conception of control', or 'how firms sought to solve their competitive problems'. This approach has led him to argue that since 1880 only four conceptions of control have dominated American business: direct control of competitors (up to 1900); manufacturing control (1900 to the 1920s); sales and marketing control (1920s to the 1950s); and finally, finance control (1950s to the present). This reveals another crucial dimension of American business evolution because in adapting so regularly to external stimuli managers were demonstrating a high level of flexibility that became a model for business systems across the world. In this respect, it is consequently vital to consider the American case first, while in the concluding section we return to this model as a means of setting up a typology of managerial evolution that can be applied to the British case.

The American move towards industrialization began in a similar way to that in Britain, with many small family firms and the utilization of an internal subcontract system of managing labour. What was different about the American economy (and indeed, those of Germany and Japan) compared to Britain was the speed with which it threw off these early structures and systems and moved towards a corporate, managerial economy. Of course, while much of American industry was based on this personal form of capitalism, there were some early harbingers of future development, notably in the transformation of arms-making at the Springfield Armoury in Massachussetts (Hounshell 1984). From its foundation in 1794, and particularly under its superintendent from 1815 to 1833, Colonel Roswell Lee, small arms manufacture was transformed from a craft pursuit to an industrial discipline. This was primarily a military development operated by ordnance officers from West Point, emerging out of lessons learned from eighteenth century French military rationalism. The key development was the interchangeability of parts through the use of machines, doing away with the handcraft skills traditionally employed in countries like Britain. This system was the forerunner of what became called the 'American system of manufactures', involving 'the sequential series of operations carried out on successive special purpose machines that produce interchangeable parts' (Black 2000). Although British ordnance developed an interest in the Springfield approach after the problems of the Crimean War in the 1850s, even sending out a delegation to inspect the facility, little progress was made in imitating the American system for many decades.

Another important antecedent emerged on the railroads, where the first stirrings of managerialism evolved out of the demands of scale and geographical dispersion that prompted firms to establish a detailed information and communication framework, comprehensive rules for the performance of roles, and a clearly defined hierarchy of authority enforced by a rigid system of discipline (Chandler 1977: 101–6; Wren 1994: 80). By 1890, the American railroad and associated telegraph and embryonic telephone networks were controlled by a small number of large managerial enterprises. In addition, the railroads precipitated a transportation and communications revolution, providing firms with the opportunity to pursue a mass-distribution strategy that would complement the parallel developments in mass-production technologies that were emerging out of the armaments industry (Wren 1994). But before proceeding with the story of the development of mass production, we need to examine what we have earlier referred to as the underlying drivers concerned with markets, institutions, and culture that influenced the nature of business evolution at that time.

The Market-cum-Technological Environment

There were several dimensions to the rapid expansion in market opportunity within the American economy in the late nineteenth century. One was the significant population growth fuelled by immigration that boosted the size of the home market to over 97 million by 1913 (compared to 45.7 million in Great Britain), justifying the investments needed for mass production and distribution. This population, moreover, was relatively homogeneous in its willingness to adopt new buying habits, unlike Europe where product markets tended to be divided according to the tastes and purchasing power of the different social classes. A second, but related dimension, was the growth in incomes and purchasing power to buy the new goods being produced; thus, by 1913 GDP per capita stood at $5,307 in the United States, an increase of 140 per cent since the 1870s, overtaking Great Britain ($5,032) as the wealthiest economy in the world (Chandler, Amatori, and Hikino 1997: 6). A third dimension was the sheer size of the country, which required multiple production and distribution facilities, branch offices, and internal communications systems well beyond what was needed in the relatively small British geographical context. Moreover, the very construction of the transportation and communications networks fuelled a substantial expansion of the geographical and labour markets, along with the agricultural machinery markets that were made much more profitable by the access to territory that the new transport system provided. In addition, at roughly the same time companies began to look at overseas markets, precipitating an internationalization process that continued unabated over the following century.

Thus, the various markets, infrastructural, agricultural, producer, and consumer, fed off each other and were further expanded by the rapid increase in population (Chandler 1977). Although the companies that supplied the markets had the same tendencies as in other countries to reduce competitive tensions, the American legal and political framework did more than in any other country to ensure that markets remained competitive, implementing from 1890 strict antitrust laws that limited the degree of collusion. Another factor keeping these product markets open and moving forward was the market for knowledge, in which there was a general willingness to discuss issues and to learn from each other, especially in the early and problematic days when managements were faced with the steep organizational learning curve (Wren 1994: 89–91).

A second important market driver was the nature of the American labour market. Waves of unskilled but highly mobile immigrants fuelled American industrialization, with most having little locational or organizational commitment. At the same time, American turnover rates were much higher than Britain; in the first detailed survey carried out, using mainly 1914 data, Slichter (1919) found that the average factory rate of turnover was 100 per cent per annum, with considerable recruitment costs to employers. There was, therefore, a strong casual culture and highly transient links with the employer. One of the effects of waves of immigrants was that the groups started by filling the lowest paid jobs and then moved to better ones as another group took its place at the bottom. This was also a reason for the optimism and social mobility in American life as well as the tendency for ethnic, religious, and language groupings to stick together with their own social institutions which often took the place of trade unions as working class institutions. One of the reasons for the creation of central personnel departments was the need to resolve these problems of recruitment, turnover, and basic training (Littler 1982: 173). Initially, though, the internal contractor was given the task of maintaining an adequate labour force, using family or immigrant group ties. By the time of the great expansion of the 1880s and 1890s, however, they could not cope in providing the necessary range of labour skills required, prompting firms to establish centralized hiring departments. While hiring was only part of the role of the contractors, it was an important part since it gave an ability to set initial wages; when that went so did the basis of the job-work system.

Another dimension to this type of labour market was that the acute shortage of skilled workers fuelled the demand for higher wages, creating pressure for an increasing division of labour and the analysis of tasks according to skill content, the wider use of technology as a substitute for labour skill and also systematic management to coordinate both the change required and the production processes. Allied to this was a widespread recognition that high wages were not antithetical to low costs if associated with mechanization and the greater division of labour, a philosophy that could bring lower unit costs than in Britain and other parts of Europe. Schoenhof's book *The Economy of High Wages* (1892) was the main statement of the high-wage–low-cost economy, helping to justify the advocates of scientific management as well as providing the mass markets for high volume producers. This contrasted sharply with Britain where international competition induced employers to try to lower wage rates further from their already low-wage convictions. The high-wage economy, of course, would also help to create a large potential market for mass-produced goods.

Technology was another key factor necessary for industrial growth. The new manufacturing technology based on the American system of manufactures spread first to the production of a new consumer durable, the sewing machine, then diffused to other equivalent durables such as typewriters, bicycles, and eventually automobiles (Hounshell 1984). It also generated the American machine tool industry; the makers of machine tools worked with manufacturers in various industries to overcome production problems relating to the planing, boring, and shaping of metal parts, generating technological knowledge that was then used to help yet other industries. Inevitably, the process was not as smooth as this may sound, with considerable production problems occurring at even the success stories of the period such as Singer and McCormick Harvesting. Both of these industry leaders initially required extensive hand-fitting and custom machining as part of the assembly process, indicating that they were less developed in using interchangeable parts than the small arms industry. Nevertheless, over time manufacturing quality and systems improved; by the early twentieth century, some industries had become so adept at producing masses of parts that a bottleneck developed at the point of assembly, for which the solution was the assembly line first exemplified at Ford's River Rouge plant. By this time, the age of mass production of low-price articles had truly arrived. The term 'mass production', rather than originating in the nineteenth century, can be traced to Henry Ford's (ghost-written) article in the 1925 edition of *Encyclopedia Britannica*. It is consequently clear that the availability of suitable product and labour markets and appropriate technology were a necessary, but not sufficient, set of conditions for economic growth.

Institutional-Cultural Drivers

Companies considering mass production required an infrastructure of two sorts. The first form was the infrastructure for physical distribution provided by the railroad networks, totalling over 240,000 miles of track by 1900, which combined with an even larger telegraph system to integrate the various regions into a more cohesive unit, facilitating the development of national marketing and sales strategies (Chandler 1990: 53–62). The other infrastructural need was access to consumer retailing, leading to the rapid emergence of mass retailers, wholesalers, and mail-order houses from the 1860s, extending distribution networks considerably and linking directly with suppliers and manufacturers to create a much more efficient system. Although Fligstein (1993: 12) claims that it was not until the 1920s that the sales and marketing conception of control took precedence in American business, over the previous sixty years firms were investing significantly in this dimension of forward vertical integration, developing an extensive network that proved capable of exploiting the expanding market opportunities available.

A second set of important institutions was financial. Here, it was the strong nature of the links between industrial and finance capital which created the capability for large-scale mergers. Although much of the finance for industrial investment had been internally generated up to the 1880s (Chandler 1977: 373), thereafter a much closer relationship with financiers was forged by American businessmen looking to reduce competition and expand capacity. Davis (1966: 255) has pointed out how American capital markets were in fact much less well-developed than Britain in the 1890s, giving prominent financiers like the Rockefellers, the Morgans, and the Mellons an opportunity to exploit their good connections to concentrate business power in the 1890s. While these big private banking houses had already risen to prominence as railway financiers, by the 1890s they had turned their attentions to industrial ventures, developing an intimate range of contacts with leading corporations (Born 1983: 92–9). Indeed, Chandler (1990: 80–1) has noted that at this time the financier-industrialist relationship was essentially personal, rather than institutional, with investment bankers, promoters, and individual entrepreneurs working closely with corporations in the pursuit of industrial concentration. Thus, in the United States, investment banks, which had come to prominence during the railroad era, played a major part in the reorganization of industry and the development of great oligopolistic corporations such as AT&T, GE, International Harvester, US Steel and the like at the turn of the century. It was this process of organization building that also prompted a growth in demand for professional managers to operate the companies, while market control enhanced the strategic planning capability of the managerial enterprises and made them more attractive for public investment (Fligstein 1993).

While the general role of the American state was neutral, only interfering through the Sherman Anti-Trust Act of 1890 to prevent the rise of monopoly, another key set of institutions of considerable importance was the educational system. At the political level there was extensive recognition of the need for an educational system to serve the needs of industry; in particular, the Morrill Land Grant Colleges Act of 1862 paved the way for a national system of state universities which were primarily intended to promote agricultural and engineering studies. In addition, American education responded quickly to the need for trained managers. First came the specialized schools and institutes to provide training in civil, mechanical, mining, electrical, and later chemical engineering. These were followed by the first business schools at Pennsylvania, Chicago, Harvard and elsewhere, offering courses in finance, production, marketing, and general management, with the Master of Business Administration (MBA) first emerging in 1920 (Locke 1989). As Lazonick (1990: 229) has argued:

The widespread success of US industrial enterprises in planning and coordinating this highly skilled division of labour would not have been possible without a massive transformation in the system of higher education between the 1890s and the 1920s. An educational system that had barely been integrated into the manufacturing sector towards the end of the nineteenth century was supplying it with tens of thousands of graduates by the third decade of this century.

With specific regard to the pursuit of professionalism, by the 1880s in railroads and the 1900s in manufacturing, specialists in different functional areas had set up professional associations (Chandler 1976: 32). The most important of these groups were the engineers, given that they assumed managerial as well as technical responsibilities. As Littler (1982: 178) concludes: 'The ability of American engineers to move out of a technical enclave meant that they were the group which captured and dominated systematic management ideas rather than the accountants, as occurred in Britain at a later date.' The engineers were also active in the development of management consultancy, diffusing new ideas much more widely as well as providing a justification for structural change. Indeed, engineers and consultants (who were often the same people) were the main promoters of systematic management. As a result, Shenlav (1999: 3) argues for the primacy of the engineer in the development of American management, even above the entrepreneur. In addition to their technical role, he argues that they made a 'political' contribution, in that the engineers enabled the application of management to be justified scientifically.

Taking this issue further, it is also important to stress that the United States did not have an established elite at the onset of industrialization; the industrial and financial elites which emerged out of this process rapidly became the dominant social groups. From this it followed that working in industry as a manager was seen almost immediately as an acceptable career, with few equivalent roles except possibly that of lawyer. The social status of management was enhanced for most of the period by the pro-business attitudes of the American public, as part of a generally conservative bent. But although conservative in a political sense, the American people were generally progressive and optimistic in welcoming change. On the other hand, the new system of large-scale capitalism arising out of the late nineteenth and early twentieth centuries was not universally welcomed. Rather, it was regarded with suspicion by many Americans, prompting widespread debates about the 'robber barons' by the 'muckrakers' and their political allies (Wren 1994: 94). Opposition was often led by small business, which was being rapidly overtaken by the new goliaths. But there were also other rather later concerns expressed about managerial capitalism, notably by Berle and Means (1932), who like many in the twenty-first century were worried about the separation of ownership from control. Later, Burnham (1941) wrote in scathing terms, regarding managers as a social elite which dominated society in a potentially negative manner. Overall, though, as one can detect from the growing popularity of management education and an increase in membership of proliferating professional associations, management became an established career in itself, reflecting the surge in demand for personnel in the organizational hierarchies that many firms were building at that time (Locke 1996: 20–4).

Business Policy and Practice

We have seen that American businessmen were faced with a highly attractive environment in the late nineteenth century; even the only weakness, the inadequate nature of existing distribution and sales mechanisms, could be turned to advantage by companies creating their own networks through vertical integration. Chandler (1977) identified two early periods of major structural change: horizontal growth, where producers in a sector combined together through mergers or trusts to gain economies of scale in manufacturing, mostly between 1879 and 1893; and vertical growth, where producers moved backwards or forwards in the production process, over the period 1898–1904. As the latter, much more than the former, required a rapidly developing management hierarchy, the ability of the system to generate these skills would become the key to success. At the same time, as Chandler (1990: 140–5) also noted, not all firms and sectors exploited this situation in similar ways, with three main groups of industries emerging from the process. The first group (furniture, leather, shoes, and textiles) did not invest substantially in new production and distribution facilities, preferring to rely on existing methods which had been developed over the previous century. Those in the second group, however, including consumer foodstuffs like meat, canned goods as well as soap and cigarettes, and light machinery producers in the agricultural and business machine sectors, integrated forwards into mass distribution and backwards into purchasing networks. In the third group (petroleum, non-ferrous metals, chemicals, rubber, and electrical machinery), corporations were highly capital-intensive in terms of both production and distribution, integrating the two functions so extensively that they were soon converted into highly advanced forms of business enterprise. This integration process allowed producers the opportunity to impose more standardized goods on consumers, while at the same time a much more astute ability to gauge market trends was possible with dedicated sales and marketing teams.

As we saw in Chapter 2, Chandler (1990: 47–8) claims that only those making the three-pronged investment in production, distribution, and management were equipped to exploit the market-cum-technological opportunities. Indeed, the three-pronged investment was mutually interlinked because without an extensive marketing and distribution system mass production facilities were a risky investment, and vice versa, while without a management structure capable of scheduling the flow of goods and information, the whole strategy could collapse. Chandler (1990: 34–5) was also at pains to emphasize that those making the initial three-pronged investments—the 'first-movers'—were able to acquire a powerful competitive advantage over their rivals, putting them 'well down the learning curve in each of the industry's functional activities before challengers went into full operation'. Among such first-movers were some of the most famous names in business history, including Duke (cigarettes), Heinz and Campbell (canned foods), Pillsbury (grain-processing), Procter and Gamble (consumer chemicals), Swift and Armour (meat-packing), Remington (business machinery), Singer (sewing machines), Eastman Kodak (photographic film), General Electric and Westinghouse (electrical engineering), DuPont (gunpowder and chemicals), and Carnegie (steel). Their activities are extensively described by Chandler (1977: 287–314, 1990: 62–71), illustrating how first-movers were able to dominate markets, nationally and internationally, exploiting their competitive advantage to such good effect that their control survived for many decades.

The assumption of mass production was that it would reduce both costs and prices, but while this might have been generally true, there is a paradox in that as Kim (1999) argues, the early success of American engineering-based manufactures was based as much on marketing achievements as on manufacturing. Fligstein (1993: 116) has also stressed how after the extensive mergers of the 1890s a manufacturing conception of control (defined as the way firms sought to solve their competitive problems) gave way in the 1920s to a sales and marketing orientation that reflected the general desire to exploit the enormous potential in the American economic scene. Both Singer and McCormick achieved their success with high prices; indeed, they were at the top of the range for their industries throughout the nineteenth century. Singer, under the leadership of Edward Clark, used a marketing strategy based on advertising, retail dealerships, service centres, and an instalment purchasing plan, allowing the company to sell more machines at the same price. This reveals the primacy of sales and marketing, an approach that was by the 1930s the dominant conception of control across American corporations (Fligstein 1993: 116).

At the same time, of course, the key to mass production was control, and that meant management, indicating a need to develop effective structures through which to ensure that large-scale investments were protected and returns generated. In this respect, American business would appear to have responded even more energetically, Lazonick (1990: 229) noting that:

> The advent of management-controlled mass production required that the enterprise employ supervisors, engineers, scientists, accountants and lawyers, among other staff deemed to be worthy of salaried status. As the firm expanded through multi-plant and multi-regional operations, as it integrated production and distribution, and as it committed resources to in-house research and development facilities, the managerial ranks grew.

The most important areas where management skills were required were production and personnel management, in particular possessing appropriate skills to deal with trade unionism in the context of changing production processes. Indeed, it would be wrong to underestimate the importance of unionism in American industrial history, as Chandler has tended to do, especially with regard to the role and extent of craft unionism. In the late-nineteenth century United States, as in Britain, craft control of shop-floor work organization obstructed the achievement of technological change and economies of scale. Craft unions, which controlled a relatively narrow activity, sought to demarcate the tasks that belonged to their particular trade and were not prepared to see the division of labour amalgamated even within a single workplace. American firms solved this problem by the time of the First World War by exerting managerial control and undermining unionism within the factory; indeed, thereafter it did not have any significant unionization in manufacturing until the mid-1930s. As Lazonick (1990: 214) has argued: 'A key feature of managerial capitalism was a shift in control over shop-floor work organization from craftsmen on the shop floor to line and staff personnel within the managerial hierarchy.' This was especially the case in industries characterized by high fixed investments, where planning and control and coordination of work were at a premium. The difference with Britain lay in the nature of the labour market; given the mobility and transience of American workers, American employers could not expect the local pools of skilled labour that were so important for British manufacturers. In addition, American industry was also highly mobile, moving westwards away from the influence of union resistance to new methods.

This was not to say that exerting control was easy. Mechanization was particularly difficult in the metal-working industries, where the machine shops gave birth to the scientific management techniques initiated by Frederick W. Taylor. As Taylor was seeking to ensure high utilization rates of the existing plant at Midvale Steel, he was challenging the long tradition of worker control over shop-floor activities. Corporate America as a whole experienced the resistance of workers to speed-up, both through shop-floor action and high rates of turnover. In effect, though, the full extent of the overcoming of craft control and the problem of turnover was not found until Ford's investments in automobile manufacturing. Ford in 1914 introduced a profit-sharing scheme that also offered five dollars a day, which was almost double the going rate in Detroit. The intention of the offer was to reduce turnover, discourage unionism, and impose work discipline on the shop floor. Ford attracted a high level of interest and desire for employment, permitting the weeding out of those who could not stand the pace. This was the point at which management took control of the shop floor. Moreover, the company introduced a more advanced system of personnel management, creating internal job ladders that could provide a means of promotion and higher wages. In 1919, in response to increased turnover and higher militancy, Ford increased the pay to six dollars a day, resulting in a doubling of output in 1921 by pushing the workforce ever harder.

In spite of some limitations, though, what Ford had achieved in its golden period following the five-dollar-day was in large part replicated across American manufacturing industry in the 1920s, resulting in a sharp increase in labour productivity. While in none of the decades since the 1880s had labour productivity in manufacturing grown faster than an annual average of 1.5 per cent, between 1919 and 1929 it leapt to an annual rate of 5.6 per cent, consolidating American leadership in mass production sectors. As Lazonick (1990: 241) has noted,

the phenomenal growth of labour productivity would not have been possible if corporate management had not taken substantially more control over the quality and quantity of work on the shop floor than they had in the previous decades, and done so with the reasonable cooperation of the workforce.

As a result mostly of merger activity, many of the large mass-production firms had acquired substantial or dominant positions in their industrial markets, providing the resources for progressive personnel policies. These dominant firms achieved economies of speed that were the basis for the simultaneous lowering of product prices, rising wages, and increasing the returns to capital and management because they were able to create value through their control over market forces, especially those of the labour market. Labour law also helped in the anti-union process, while the American Federation of Labour sought to make itself respectable by hiring its own experts to bargain over the scientific output standards, rather than insist on craft controls. Although even this was not enough for the mass-production industries, it reflected the balance of power on the shop floor as management sought to impose its own agenda on the workforce.

One can consequently see how structural change in organizations arose out of the changing nature of production and the emergence of a managerial cadre capable of running increasingly complex operations. In operational terms, systematic management arose in part out of increasing specialization in American industry (Litterer 1986). This specialization was of two types—product specialization and process specialization. After the end of the Civil War, product specialization, whereby a firm sharply reduced the range and variety of its products, proceeded rapidly in the United States. In parallel with this went increasing labour specialization and fragmentation, combined with the use of specialized machinery and technology. The increasing division of labour was also linked to systematic management in two ways. First, in order to accomplish an extensive division of labour, sophisticated job analysis was necessary. Second, the increasing division of labour created intensified problems of integration and coordination. Both of these in turn meant a need for more management.

Finally, systematic management involved the creation of specialized, central staff departments that took over many of the powers of the old traditional foremen and the internal contractors. Frequently, the foremen were initially responsible for the operation of new administrative systems, either because they insisted on retaining control or because management felt it was easier and cheaper to do this. But after a period of time, the responsibilities and decision-making were shifted to administrative staff such as production control clerks. Overall, systematic management and the development of production control systems linked to new cost accounting procedures and the creation of centralized staff departments can be regarded as the beginning of the bureaucratization of the managerial function.

While all these decisive organizational changes were occurring, underpinning them was the key development in structural change in American industry, namely, the transition from family capitalism to managerial capitalism. By the First World War, most large corporations had become vertically integrated, in that besides manufacturing, they did their own marketing, purchasing, and even controlled supplies of raw and semi-finished materials. The vast majority used the centralized, functionally departmentalized structure that is generally classified as the U-form of organization (see The Evolution of Structure, Chapter 1). Crucially, as the administration of all these large manufacturing companies required the services of a corps of lower level managers to run their many plants, offices, mines and other units as well as a sizeable number of middle managers to supervise the functional departments or subsidiaries and staff offices, the U-form created the breeding ground for professional management. Furthermore, it was the growth of this hierarchy and its accompanying bureaucracy that brought about the separation of ownership and management. Given this structure, Chandler (1962: 381) noted that 'nothing is more crucial to the later history of the firm than the way in which its founders or their families make their terms with the administrative imperatives of large-scale enterprise'. In describing the transfer of power to managers, he noted (1990: 48) that in this new structure most families did not attempt to manage the operations of the firm by themselves, given the proliferation of operating units. Even if family groups continued to play a role in strategic decision-making, professional managers were not only assisting in the process, but also implementing and developing the policies devised at the board level.

It is consequently clear that while family ownership remained an important feature of American business up to the 1940s, professional managers were

contributing substantially to the elaboration of extensive organizational hierarchies and taking on ever greater responsibility for all aspects of management.
The centralized functionally departmentalized U-form organizations that emerged
from this process were running large-scale, vertically integrated operations,
indicating how American business was adapting structure to strategy in an
effective manner. Nowhere is this point better demonstrated than at DuPont in
the early 1920s, when the eponymous owning family introduced the M-form (see
Figure 1.4) on to the business scene. Described by Williamson (1975: 382) as
'American capitalism's most important single innovation of the twentieth century', the M-form has come to be regarded as the most effective vehicle for
organizing large-scale, diversified firms.

The rise of the M-form, however, must be qualified. In the first place, we
should remember that by the 1940s less than one-third of the leading diversified
American corporations had become M-forms (Fligstein 1993: 275). Similarly,
Toms and Wright (2005: 267) have also successfully highlighted the extent of
differences between American and European corporations, undermining some of
the claims made by Whittington and Mayer (2000). Moreover, as Freeland (2001)
has illustrated so graphically with regard to General Motors and its chief
executive officer, Alfred P. Sloan, even the most innovative organizations
struggled with the M-form, frequently adapting the structure to individual
requirements. It is consequently clear that one can exaggerate both the speed at
which American firms switched to the M-form structure as well as the nature of
this innovation's diffusion across the Atlantic. At the same time, it is still
nevertheless fair to conclude that by the 1920s American business had become
distinctly managerial in form and orientation, providing professional managers
with a position of significant status and influence within the world's largest
economy.

Conclusions

By the 1920s, American business was dominated by managerial capitalism,
providing a model for other economies that was imitated in different ways and
at different times. As Figure 4.1 reveals, the ascendancy of managerial capitalism had been made possible by the formation of an environment in the period
1890–1918 that proved extremely conducive to this modus operandi, with a
heavy preponderance of drivers featuring on the left-hand side of the diagram.
These years have been chosen because they approximate to the era during which
managerial capitalism rose to prominence across American business, by which
time all the drivers were in place to prompt this move. Moreover, the extensive
pursuit of a Chandlerian three-pronged strategy based on mass production,
aggressive marketing and sales, and professional management became the
hallmark of especially the Second Industrial Revolution industries, as well
as those associated with consumer goods and metalworking, providing
these 'first-movers' with a significant competitive advantage over their European

rivals. Admittedly, the vast and relatively affluent domestic market provided the stimuli for these changes, as well as the reform of competition law in 1890, emphasizing how demand and institutional factors played key roles in this process. At the same time, both the educational establishment and corporations placed a significant emphasis on training, giving rise to the formation of a management class that was increasingly regarded as an exemplar of best practice.

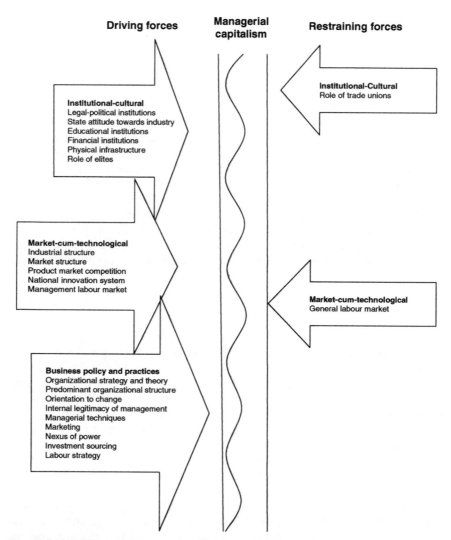

Driving forces   **Managerial capitalism**   **Restraining forces**

Institutional-cultural
Legal-political institutions
State attitude towards industry
Educational institutions
Financial institutions
Physical infrastructure
Role of elites

Institutional-Cultural
Role of trade unions

Market-cum-technological
Industrial structure
Market structure
Product market competition
National innovation system
Management labour market

Market-cum-technological
General labour market

Business policy and practices
Organizational strategy and theory
Predominant organizational structure
Orientation to change
Internal legitimacy of management
Managerial techniques
Marketing
Nexus of power
Investment sourcing
Labour strategy

Figure 4.1. The force-fields at work in the USA, 1890–1918

GERMANY: PROFESSIONAL PROPRIETORIAL CAPITALISM

Introduction

Although a late starter as an industrial economy, not to mention its belated unification in 1870, by the early twentieth century Germany had become one of the world's leading industrial nations (Fear 1995; Wengenroth 1997). This rapid pace of development was built partly on focused national policies that nurtured German industry, including a heavy investment in education and training, as well as protectionist policies to keep foreign competitors at bay. Above all, though, the rise of large-scale, vertically integrated corporations provided the dynamic for Germany's rapid economic development (Tilly 1974: 145), stimulating the creation of professional management and sophisticated organizational structures. At the same time, a paradoxical feature of the German business scene was the continued importance of both cartelization and family business, providing a proprietorial dimension that was superficially similar to the UK. Family business was especially prominent in the *Mittelstand*, the small and medium-sized operations characterized by high levels of skill and specialized technologies. These firms also worked in harmony with the larger corporations, while expressing general distaste for the latter's tendency to cartelize markets and control key industries, characteristics that prevailed up to the 1940s (Fear 1995: 147–8).

Just as in the UK and the United States, one of the key early influences on German industrialization was the railways. It was in the railway sector that professional managers first came to the fore, developing controls and operating procedures over what increasingly became not just a national but also an international railway system (Fear 1995: 138–9). Since German railway engineers and managers created a unified network for much of continental Europe, this was a major boost to the industrialization that was to follow. Much the same happened with telegraph systems. In addition, Germany already possessed a reservoir of educated personnel, as well as financial capabilities, that were superior to those in the surrounding countries, providing solid foundations for the process of industrialization that occurred in the late nineteenth century.

The Market-cum-Technological Environment

Although Germany had a substantial population of 41 million in 1871, when the country was finally united, it was much more rural than Britain, with almost two-thirds of the population living in the countryside. This was to change dramatically over the next forty years, with the population increasing to 65 million by 1910, by which time three-fifths lived in urban areas, creating a substantial market for manufactured goods. On the other hand, as Germany was not as affluent as either Britain or the United States—GDP per capita in 1913 was $3,833, compared to $5,032 in the UK and $5,307 in the United States (Chandler, Amatori, and Hikino

1997: 6)—the domestic market for consumer goods remained small. It was consequently in producer goods that Germany developed its strongest competitive advantage, building on the technological and scientific strengths that were already available. At the same time, as the merchanting system was not well developed, German firms were pushed into forward integration, which assisted in developing Chandler's three-pronged investment in technology and management, as well as in distribution. Moreover, they needed to look externally to other countries in close proximity in continental Europe, while because these other countries were themselves beginning the journey to industrialization and had different languages, customs, and institutions, German exporters required more competencies than was true for the captive domestic market in the United States or in the case of the British Empire. This also helped to promote cooperation between German firms in export markets. German corporations were consequently able to exploit first-mover advantages in the burgeoning European markets, especially for producer goods, chemicals, steel, and coal. Even though the packaged consumer goods sector was slower to develop in general, the prevailing environment facilitated the adoption of mass-production and mass-distribution methods as essential features of industrial strategy (Chandler 1990: 409–15).

Having noted these positive features of the German product market, one must also note how its principal characteristic was not competition but cooperation in the form of cartels, with over 350 having been formed by 1905. Although they only accounted for 25 per cent of total industrial output, their influence was all-pervasive in those industries—engineering, coal, chemicals, and steel—where the greatest competitive advantages had been secured (Kocka 1980: 88–9). The cartels had first emerged as a response to the depression in prices lasting between 1873 and 1896, but soon developed a range of functions, from regulation of output to arranging joint marketing organizations, impinging directly on management strategy in an attempt to create a more secure trading environment. This collusive activity was also supported by the state, not only in granting cartels a specific legal status in 1897 but also by protecting the economy from extensive import penetration, indicating how in Germany industrial interests were given a high priority. While firms that operated in the *Mittelstand* system felt threatened by these increasingly powerful cartels, it is apparent that up to 1914 cartelization did not appear to place any substantial barriers in the way of either relatively rapid growth or the exploitation of first-mover advantages in a range of industries. Indeed, in contrast to the UK, cartelization was seen as a positive asset to German economic development, particularly as a means of creating greater trading stability, in conjunction with the protective umbrella of import duties and the encouragement it gave to marketing through the distribution syndicates which emerged from the 1890s (MacGregor 1906: 191–216; Carter 1913: 46).

While German corporations were developing in this fashion up to the 1920s, it is also clear that management faced little threat from organized labour. Indeed, in comparison with either Britain or the United States, the German labour market was relatively quiescent in the late nineteenth century, even though a strong craft tradition featured prominently within the expanding industrial workforce. A key factor in this context was the suppression of trade unions between 1878 and 1890, while the progressive introduction of social insurance, worker compensation and protection legislation, and health benefits at the corporate level, undermined anything that workers' groups might be able to offer (Fear 1995: 151–3).

Institutional-Cultural Drivers

For much of the period between the 1870s and 1940s, the role of the state was important in several respects to German economic development, even if this role was indirect at times. The unification of Germany in 1871 created a sense of nationalism, while under Bismarck's leadership there developed a widespread desire to catch up with the dominant industrial power of the time—Britain. Bismarck provided strong leadership and was willing to take on the existing elites, for example, in freeing the serfs from control by the powerful landed classes. Germany's status as a late-industrializer also prompted the complete re-evaluation of priorities as the country's leaders came to terms with the requirements of keeping pace with countries like Great Britain.

One of the key reasons why management had been able to pursue strategies of integration and diversification, and one which continues to play a central role in the economy's success in the late twentieth century (Porter 1990: 356–69), was the influence exercised over German economic development at this time by the banking sector. As in many other economies, the German financial system had developed rapidly as a result of railway construction, in this case during the 1840s and 1850s, but once an extensive network had been completed and the state then nationalized most of the mileage in 1879, attention turned to the expanding industrial sector. The role of the banks was distinctive in Germany in that they not only provided funds for the considerable initial investments in capital-intensive industries but also sat on the boards, participating in top-level decisions. The banks themselves were large-scale organizations, with substantial management structures and systems that they encouraged industrialists to imitate (Fear 1995: 142–3). The banks also encouraged moves towards cooperation, since they naturally invested in more than one firm and did not like to see competition destroy profits. The dominating feature of German financial activities was a banking system that from an early stage performed two key roles: provision of long-term loans to corporate customers, as well as acting as the vital medium of communication between investors and capital-hungry firms by organizing industrial capital issues on the stock exchanges (Born 1983: 82–92). Banking was also highly concentrated, with seven large joint-stock banks dominating the Berlin Stock Exchange. Clearly, though, because of their extensive contribution to business financing, the banks also extended their influence directly into industrial management, featuring prominently at the highest levels of decision-making (Kocka 1980: 89–91).

In order better to understand how this relationship was operationalized, it is important to understand that the reform of German company law introduced in

1870 stipulated that two boards of directors should be established in each corporation. At the top was a supervisory board (*aufsichtsrat*), elected by shareholders and primarily responsible for strategic decisions on investment and product range, while below was an executive board (*vorstand*) which performed the more mundane tasks associated with functional and operational management. As the representatives of shareholders, the banks were consequently able to populate the supervisory board (Born 1983: 89–91), leading the trends towards concentration, integration, and diversification, as well as providing the finance for such strategies as a means of minimizing the impact of market forces on prices and profits. Although it is easy to exaggerate the role played by bankers in dictating strategy to German corporations, in reflecting and strengthening existing trends the industrial banks were pivotal in financing the processes (Kocka 1980: 91–2).

Having noted the role played by bank finance in the development of German business, one should not forget the continued importance of family enterprise on supervisory boards that reflected the proprietorial nature of German business. In fact, as Kocka (1978: 569) reveals, owner-managers reasserted themselves in the 1890s, displacing bankers as the principal influences on business strategy. It is also apparent that up to the First World War at least, large-scale German business was dominated by the entrepreneurial form of organization. This characteristic has been further reinforced by Church (1993: 28–9), who has demonstrated that up to the 1930s family firms were just as prevalent in Germany as they were in Britain, with ownership still concentrated in the hands of a few members of the supervisory board. Powerful industrial dynasties like Siemens, Thyssens, and Krupps were regarded as *unternehmer*, a separate social elite whose authority was accepted as being totally dominant (Dyas and Thanheiser 1976: 102–7). At the same time, functional and operational management had been extensively delegated to managers, providing substantial opportunities for those who had passed through the educational facilities provided by both the state and large-scale business. While it is important to stress that up to the 1940s German business was not as bureaucratized as the large-scale American corporations (Fear 1995: 144), with *unternehmer* operating within a loose senior management structure, the typical corporate structure was both autocratic and flexible, with the U-form (see Figure 1.2) playing a dominant role across the large-scale, diversified, and vertically integrated corporations that drove forward German industrialization.

As we have already implied, one cannot assess the German scene fully without examining the role of education, and especially tertiary education, which became the strongest in the world in the second half of the nineteenth century. German tertiary education did not just come into existence at the behest of industry, of course; it had a long history and many of its early graduates had to emigrate to find jobs, not least in Britain. The universities and the government-sponsored research institutes were serious centres of scholarship and research, especially in chemistry and physics, while the *technischehochschule* were specifically created to provide the skilled personnel required by industry. Graduate programmes in engineering led to the prestigious title of *Herr Doktor Ingenieur,* a title which is still important in the twenty-first century, giving engineering an intellectual status it never achieved in Britain. Moreover, around the turn of the nineteenth century, the *handelshochschulen,* or schools for managers, began to appear, with a curriculum based on business economics, accounting, and law (Locke 1984). These institutions together provided a stronger link between industry and education than even in the United States, while considerably outdistancing their British equivalents. German industry was especially competitive where these links were most needed, and less so in areas such as the fast-moving consumer goods (FMCG) sector where they were less important. It was consequently no coincidence that by 1913 Germany had become the world's largest exporter of the products of the Second Industrial Revolution, especially chemicals and electrical equipment and other industrial machinery, including textile and metal-working machinery (Chandler 1990: 411).

As in America, science and engineering graduates were the first to be hired on any significant scale, to staff the workshops and research departments which became the hallmarks of German industrial strategy. By the 1890s, recruits from the commercial schools were brought in to staff the expanding bureaucracies armed with the lessons taught by business economics and other applied disciplines (Keeble 1992: 17–23). As Figure 7.1 also illustrates, up to the 1930s Germany had the highest proportion of university graduates amongst its business elite, indicating how business was not only keen to recruit educated people but also real career opportunities were offered to the group. While a significant majority of the German managers with degrees would have received a technical or engineering education, compared to the business-oriented education of the American cohort, it is clear that from an early stage the business elite was highly qualified and committed.

In developing this highly educated workforce, it is also important to stress how this has gelled closely with the authoritarian nature of German society and its commitment to a clear bureaucratic order which had become part of the national heritage (Dyas and Thanheiser 1976: 103–8). This involved the acceptance of strong, centralized, hierarchical power in organizations from an early stage. Two further keys to German industrial culture were professionalism, in the sense of respect for learning, expertise, achievement, and status, along with the concept of *technik,* or the creation of useful objects. Crucially, *technik* has a much higher standing than engineering has had in Britain. It is also necessary to recognize that Germany does not have the broadly based concept of 'manager' that the Anglo-Saxon countries do; rather, there are terms which cross-cut the English word. On the one hand, there are terms for functional aspects of management, such as *techniker* (technical man) and *kaufmann* (commercial man), on the other hand, *fuhrung* represents the top level or entrepreneurial dimension of management, while *leitung* stands for line management below the board level. At the very top of the organization, as we noted earlier, there is also the *unternehmer,* or chief executive officer who in German business has been endowed with an almost divine right to rule over the business and make all the key decisions (Dyas and

Thanheiser 1976: 103–8). To describe this phenomenon another way, while the British self-concept is of *being* a manager rather than *doing* a particular kind of work, the German approach is the converse. In consequence, Germans have been hesitant to use the word management and it is not easy to conceive of management as a profession in Germany, even if many of its exponents conform to the Anglo-Saxon notion of professionalism. In spite of this, there has always been a high status in Germany associated with making things, giving engineering careers a status that is highly valued.

A cooperative spirit is regarded by Porter (1990: 356–69) as another of the main reasons why Germany has achieved considerable success as an industrial power, particularly with regard to the clustering of firms, banks, and training institutions as a means of raising standards across an entire sector. As we noted earlier, a particular characteristic of the early phase of industrialization was the operation of cartels (or trade associations, and hereafter referred to as cartels), but it also featured prominently in the relationship between industry on the one hand and both the state and the financial institutions on the other. Notwithstanding these points, German business showed a tendency towards large-scale and vertical integration, prompting an extensive demand for professional managers. The First World War and the aftermath of defeat were further factors in generating a highly cooperative approach towards economic and corporate development (Wengenroth 1997: 151–3), especially externally as German firms sought to win back markets that they had lost, linking into a 'Rationalization Movement' that advocated modernization and radical change as an essential means of overcoming the legacy of a devastating wartime experience.

Business Policy and Practice

While as we have just noted that German company strategy was based on cooperation with potential competitors in cartels, at the same time strong internal growth and vertical integration featured prominently across many sectors. With extensive protective duties sheltering key industries against the ravages of import penetration, the cartels were able to reinforce this tendency towards stability through extensive collusion on prices and marketing. German corporations were consequently obliged to develop sophisticated management structures which, while still dominated by family dynasties in 1914, exhibited all the advantages of functional departmentalization so common in their American counterparts. It was this environment which allowed the first-movers in a wide range of industries (steel, chemicals, and electrical engineering especially) to exploit their competitive advantage domestically and internationally, employing U-forms of organization to considerable effect. At the same time, although this could lead us to conclude that German firms had arrived at the same destination as the American corporations, it is important to remember that the route taken had undoubtedly been different. For example, cartelization inhibited horizontal merger activity as a means of concentrating production, largely because the security afforded by cartels provided little incentive to acquire competitors. On the other hand, mergers associated with vertical integration and diversification were common, reflecting the desire of German managers to exploit economies of scope in the development of their role as leading European progenitors of the modern industrial enterprise.

It was above all in heavy industrial machinery, chemicals, and metals sectors that Germany excelled. Indeed, of heavy machinery Chandler (1990: 457) notes that

the German machinery makers recruited extensive managerial hierarchies to supervise and integrate their processes of production and distribution, hierarchies that were probably even larger than those of the American machinery companies. Indeed almost no American or British producer of heavy machinery could match these German enterprises in size, systematic layout of works, and number of lines produced.

Moreover, the extensive range of sales offices provided information about customers and their needs to the research, design, and production departments, while the financial sides helped customers to finance their purchases. Chandler (1990: 469) even claims that by 1913 the Siemens factory and offices in Berlin 'had become the world's most intricate and extensive industrial complex under a single management'. Indeed, it is possible to claim that 'the Siemens enterprises were operating through a single administrative structure which, with a corporate office of senior executives and with several autonomous product divisions, was the forerunner of the multidivisional structure which DuPont and General Motors began to fashion in the United States shortly after the war' (Chandler 1990: 471). While the Siemens family later modified this structure, as a means of curbing the degree of power that managers had come to exert over the firm, it is clear that German business organization was adapting successfully to the challenges associated with running these large-scale diversified operations.

By the First World War, many of Germany's large companies had already taken on a modern organizational and managerial form, making the necessary investments that provided them with the capabilities to exploit the economies of scale and scope as first-movers in the markets they had established for themselves. In all this, while families were still extremely important, they were families which were willing to devolve responsibilities for operations to salaried managers and concentrate on strategic issues. It was not yet managerial capitalism in the sense of the separation of ownership and control, but the structures were ready for this next step. While the First World War obviously created massive disarray and loss of markets, it is a measure of the solidity of the underlying structures that by the mid-1920s they were able to compete again successfully in foreign markets. It was a scenario which was repeated after the Second World War.

The willingness to hire managers and give them responsibility was clearly different to what was happening in Britain at the same time. Indeed, this is considered by Chandler (1990: 500) to be the main difference in the development of the two economies. The main reason behind this could well lie in German respect for traditions of bureaucracy, rationalism, and hierarchy based on the civil service, together with respect for educational standing, especially of engineers, as compared to entrepreneurial individualism in Britain. In effect, three main features of German industrial structure had emerged by the end of the nineteenth century: large organizations with extensive management structures; strong small and medium-sized private companies, the *Mittelstand,* which still represents a source of strength in the German economy; and cartelization, built on the prevailing industrial and legal attitudes encouraging cooperation. Crucially, in the German case the cartels did not appear to act as a deterrent to increased efficiency or growth. While they may have inhibited horizontal integration, this did not affect vertical integration and diversification as a means of obtaining economies of scope. Kocka (1980: 79–88) demonstrates how by 1907 only five of the leading hundred German industrial corporations remained undiversified, while eighty-eight had indulged in some form of vertical integration (forward into sales and distribution, or backward into securing supplies of raw materials), with merger activity contributing significantly in fashioning this integrated structure.

Conclusions

Perhaps the most significant feature about rapid German industrialization and the move towards complex company organization with large management cadres was the way in which German institutions both developed themselves and strongly supported the growth of large-scale industry, with extensive, if often implicit, state support. The banking and educational systems were particularly notable in this respect; it was a symbiosis which was even stronger than in the United States, and very much more so than in Britain. The state also played an important part. At the same time, Chandler's use of the term 'co-operative managerial capitalism' to describe German business is misleading. While collusion was undoubtedly a prominent characteristic of the system, the continued dominance of family dynasties exerting proprietorial control undermines any claim that the managerial stage had been reached by the 1940s. Chandler (1990: 500–1) himself recognizes as much by noting that 'German firms differed from the American in that the family often continued to have a powerful, even decisive, say in management'. This is why we have chosen the term 'professional proprietorial capitalism' to describe German business by the 1920s. Of course, there is no doubt that German business employed large numbers of professional managers in a multi-level hierarchy, from the supervisory board down to departmental level, superficially resembling American corporations. On the other hand, one must remember how *unternehmer* continued to dominate strategic decision-making for many decades, indicating how 'entrepreneurial-managerial capitalism' would be a more appropriate label for the German business system. Nevertheless, as Figure 4.2 reveals, the drivers were very much in favour of stimulating the rise of a distinctive German form of managerial capitalism, with a significant majority featuring on the left-hand side of the diagram. In terms of scale, scope, and the addition of new functions, German business proved to be a highly conducive environment for the rise of professional management and the elaboration of sophisticated organizational hierarchies that were at least a match for their American counterparts, if not superior in terms of the depth and focus on training and professionalism.

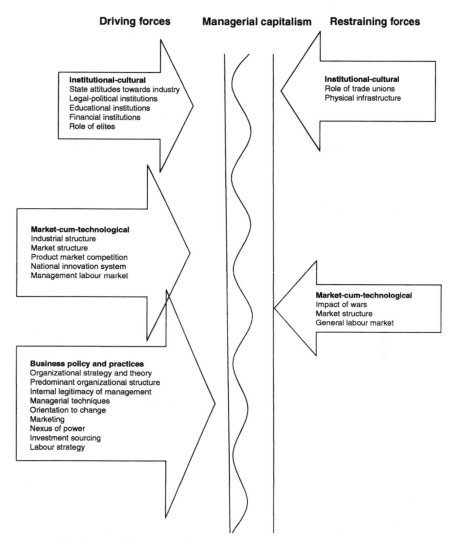

Driving forces   **Managerial capitalism**   **Restraining forces**

Institutional-cultural
State attitudes towards industry
Legal-political institutions
Educational institutions
Financial institutions
Role of elites

Institutional-cultural
Role of trade unions
Physical infrastructure

Market-cum-technological
Industrial structure
Market structure
Product market competition
National innovation system
Management labour market

Market-cum-technological
Impact of wars
Market structure
General labour market

Business policy and practices
Organizational strategy and theory
Predominant organizational structure
Internal legitimacy of management
Managerial techniques
Orientation to change
Marketing
Nexus of power
Investment sourcing
Labour strategy

Figure 4.2. The force-fields at work in Germany, 1890–1918

JAPAN: COLLECTIVE MANAGERIAL CAPITALISM

Introduction

Japan was not only another late industrializing country but also the speed with which it was transformed, in spite of its unhelpful cultural and geographical context, makes this case exceptional (Bernstein 1995: 439). Japan's transition to a modern state began with the Meiji restoration in 1868, after which a policy of pursuing industrialization to create national strength was enacted. Of course, as Miyamoto (1986: 291–309) has emphasized, Japan was by no means backward in the (Tokugawa) period leading up to 1868, when a market economy revolving around Edo (Tokyo), Osaka, and Kyoto had already emerged. During the nineteenth century, the old order was also beginning to break down, because the previously inferior merchants were beginning to ascend the social ladder and match the samurai for status and wealth in the new market economy. This provided the latter with economic and social incentives to participate in the modernization process, especially those of a highly marginal nature who had purchased their titles, giving rise to a vibrant bourgeoisie that drove Japanese business forward after 1868 (Morikawa 1992).

When Emperor Meiji ascended the throne in 1868, his regime instituted a series of fundamental changes to the political, religious, and economic spheres which dramatically altered the country's destiny. It is important to stress that as an individual's loyalty to the Emperor was paramount, society was unified around the modernization goal (Hirschmeier and Yui 1975: 70–5), even if the Meiji family was still faced with the considerable challenge of convincing the more influential conservative elements in Japan that modernization was a viable national priority. The first measure was to institute the policy of *yunyuboatsu* (import-substitution) as well as establishing pilot plants to demonstrate to private entrepreneurs the advantages of Western technology in areas like cotton spinning, shipbuilding, mining, and engineering. Over 2,400 foreign technicians and managers were brought from abroad to advise on Western methods, providing technological and business expertise that proved crucial to the success of modernization (Bernstein 1995: 447–8). Railways were also constructed, while after three important Acts (1872, 1876, and 1882), a banking system emerged that was modelled on the American system, with the (private) Bank of Japan acting as central bank to an increasing number of joint-stock operations (Hirschmeier and Yui 1975: 86–91).

Although the government set up pilot plants to provide encouragement, apart from some strategic industries, notably steel and the main trunk railway lines that remained in government hands, many were soon sold to private investors. This has prompted a debate concerning the extent to which Japan's emergence as an industrial power was primarily powered by either the state or private enterprise, because while the Meiji policies were undoubtedly significant in initiating this process, it was only when the business community came to the fore in the 1880s that success was achieved. In particular, a small number of individuals, known as the *zaibatsu* (or financial cliques) came to dominate the larger enterprises, creating extensive business empires such as Mitsui and Mitsubishi which still exist. Indeed, as businessmen soon came to control the emerging political parties, strong links between industry and the state were forged that have remained a hallmark of the Japanese system. Furthermore, heavy industry was encouraged by government-regulated banks, which provided the necessary capital for investment in Western technology. Although modernization was not achieved as swiftly as the ruling family would have liked, over the course of the period 1868–1914 an environment was created that proved extremely conducive to the development of a dynamic business community.

Market-cum-Technological Environment

One of the most significant obstacles to the rapid industrialization of Japan was its domestic market, and especially the preference of Japanese consumers for traditional tastes in consumer goods that prevented the emergence of mass-production industries for many decades (Nakagawa 1975: 200). As Yui (1988: 63–4) concludes, 'in terms of strategy, [firms] were not oriented towards mass production and mass marketing but were instead positively pursuing a strategy of extending their product lines in order to meet the requirement of fine-tuned markets'. Similarly, marketing and distribution were also controlled by the *zaibatsu* trading houses, known as *soga shosha*, giving them almost total control of Japan's import-export transactions. 'It was often more efficient for large industrial enterprises to use this external sales network than to employ a large in-house sales force' (Yui 1988: 78). *Soga shosha* were not only central to the development of *zaibatsu* but also during the twentieth century they became the main agents of Japanese trade across the world (Young 1979: 1–9).

Having noted the strength of these organizations, it is also vital to remember that it was not until the 1960s and 1970s that the Japanese domestic market provided the incentives for indigenous firms to make the three-pronged investments in manufacturing, distribution, and management which had characterized much of American business. Fruin (1992: 16–36) has also emphasized how interdependence became a hallmark of the Japanese enterprise system, reflecting a general acceptance of the need for cooperation as an essential tool in the struggle for competitiveness. It was this extensive degree of cooperation and collusion between firms and their subsidiaries that provided the basis for a successful industrial economy. Even though initially Japan was forced to utilize imported technologies, as a result of heavy investments in education and training firms rapidly became adept at adapting foreign ideas to indigenous needs, laying the foundations for a highly competitive economy that by the 1930s had become sufficiently confident to confront British and American interests.

While one of the emerging assets of this developing economy was its investment in technical and managerial skills, until the post-1945 era Japanese industrial relations were essentially hierarchical (Gordon 1985). Of course, after 1945 what we now categorize as the Japanese Employment System came to be regarded as one of the key reasons why this economy developed so rapidly, especially in terms of mass-production strategies and the use of teamwork. Up to the 1930s, however, employers were more concerned with controlling the labour force along disciplinary lines, albeit with a view to creating a strong internal labour market that would satisfy their growing need for skilled workers and managers. Paternalistic strategies were pursued in some sectors, especially cotton textiles (Brown and Tamai 2000), but only as a means of ensuring a steady supply of female operatives. The increasingly militaristic regime that came to dominate Japan by the 1930s also reinforced employer controls, leading to the arrest and imprisonment of many trade union leaders. Only after 1945 did employers recognize the need to work more constructively with their employees, forging a powerful alliance that substantially boosted Japanese competitiveness.

Having stressed these hierarchical features of the pre-1945 Japanese industrial relations system, it is nevertheless important to point out that some aspects of the post-1950 Japanese employment system did emerge in the early decades of the twentieth century. In particular, in-house training became an important feature of Japanese business as early as the 1890s, starting in shipbuilding and spreading to the rest of industry over the following two decades (Bernstein 1995: 459). The main aim behind this innovation, apart from creating an internal labour market that ensured a reliable supply of appropriately skilled workers, was to undermine the control of shop-floor activities from the previously all-powerful foremen. Employers were also keen to offer permanent employment contracts to essential workers, while a seniority-based wage scheme was introduced in those sectors where the competition for labour was especially acute. While these systems were neither as fully developed nor as extensive as they became after 1950, they provided management with total control of work practice and moulded a labour force that proved to be compliant and flexible, as well as proficient and well-trained.

Institutional-Cultural Drivers

While in Germany's case it was important to emphasize the crucial role of indigenous banks in funding a considerable proportion of corporate investment, as well as providing liquidity, in the Japanese case these institutions were even more central to the development of a modern industrial economy. Indeed, each *zaibatsu* had its own banking arm, channelling funds around the group as a means of funding both short- and long-term requirements. While the state had provided some solidity to the banking system by establishing in 1872 the (privately owned) Bank of Japan to act as a central bank, and a large number of joint-stock banks were formed over the course of the next fifty years, it was the *zaibatsu* banks that played a key role in funding modernization programmes. When some concerns about the fragility of joint-stock banking were expressed in the 1920s, the state imposed much more stringent regulations on this sector, resulting in the acquisition of many smaller operations by the *zaibatzu* banks. By 1928, the *zaibatsu* banks consequently accounted for 34 per cent of bank deposits, while the number of banks fell from approximately 1,700 in 1924 to 651 in 1932 (Rubinstein 1995: 458), emphasizing how the big groups came to play an increasingly important role in the economy overall.

While as we have already discussed, the state since 1868 had acted as an important catalyst behind Japan's industrialization, in another respect this role proved central in equipping the economy with the necessary skills to support this process. Indeed, the national education system performed the dual role of imbuing strong national loyalties into the population as well as developing a highly trained workforce, both of which were seen as critical for catching up with the West. A system of universal education was introduced in 1872, based on a French model of centralist control and a state-determined curriculum, which produced universal literacy by end of the Meiji period in 1912 and has continued to provide some of the highest standards in the world. The system also produced a highly skilled workforce that would become one of the economy's most important assets. Within higher education, the leading universities soon became the main source of the business elite (Wilson and Nishizawa 1999), although companies merely sought quality educated staff and the technological links with the universities were not as strong as in Germany, most firms preferring to nurture their own talent through extensive internal training.

Another key feature of the Japanese scene which deserves special mention is the pattern of management recruitment, because while merchant-financiers and 'marginal samurai' were willing to establish conglomerate-style operations, the families would have been hard pressed to find enough talent to staff the increasing number of divisions formed from the 1890s. In this context, one must stress the deep respect for learning which had always pervaded the Confucian-based Japanese society, leading the large firms to recruit personnel for all levels of management from the educated classes (Yamamura 1978: 235). On the other hand, while three commercial colleges established in the 1890s (at Osaka, Kobe, and Hitotsubashi) had become commerce universities by the 1920s, formal management education was rarely used in Japan because companies made a 'heavy financial commitment to thoroughly educating...employees' (Locke 1984: 282). At the same time, the much-augmented college and university system was exploited extensively from the 1880s to improve the quality of management (Wilson and Nishizawa 1999).

As Figure 7.1 reveals, the proportion of senior managers and directors with university degrees rose impressively over the period 1900–30, exceeding the US levels and almost reaching those of Germany (Mannari 1974). While the Japanese data were taken from *zaibatsu* firms, ignoring the large number of small family firms, again this was indicative of the preference for those who had passed through an extensive system of education. It is also noticeable that from the 1930s Japan developed the most highly qualified business elite amongst our four economies, further substantiating the claim that firms were committed to recruiting and retaining graduates from an early stage of the country's industrialization.

Morikawa (1992: 310) also emphasizes how 'highly educated salaried managers had [been] promoted within the job hierarchy of large industrial enterprises and had come to participate in their top management'. This reveals how the expanding organizational hierarchies that emerged from the 1880s were staffed by qualified managers who were by the 1910s coming to take on much more influential positions; that in spite of the familial character of the *zaibatzu*, they were evolving into managerial organizations as they expanded and diversified.

Of central importance to our analysis of Japanese business must be the role played by sociocultural influences in fashioning a business system which Fruin (1992: 47) claims has been for many decades based on cooperation and dedicated commitment to national goals. While Japanese traditions and social relationships are often difficult to comprehend through occidental eyes, because of the strong degree of individualism inherent in American and West European value systems, above all it is essential to emphasize how Japanese citizens subsume their own aspirations under the collective belief in loyalty to the country, or in pre-1945 Japan, the Emperor. This system became in turn a source of loyalty to the organization and to hierarchy in management. It also produced a strong work ethic, conformity, and the suppression of individualism, together with a respect for education and self-development and a willingness to learn from others.

The distinctive nature of the sociocultural traditions which characterize both Japan as a whole and its enterprise system are the key features of the country's business history over the last 120 years. Indeed, continuity dominates the whole story, in that while corporations have learnt how to adapt strategy and structure according to economic circumstances (Fruin 1992: 40–7), they have also demonstrated a faith in traditional values and relationships based on family ties and interdependent loyalties. The superficial similarities with Britain's system of personal capitalism are striking, but one can only understand the Japanese business scene by remembering how group loyalties and the collective ideal determine all aspects of an individual's life. In addition, the propensity to recruit professional managers and promote them through the hierarchy to senior positions also highlights the stark differences with the British case.

Business Policy and Practice

Given the rise of the multiple involvements of the *zaibatsu*, it was inevitable businesses required managers to operate the various organizations and to complement the strategic considerations of the family. The early economy especially needed engineers to maximize the efficiencies of the technologies imported from the United States and Western Europe. It is also notable that scientific management became popular in Japan, arguably even more so than in the United States. Certainly, Taylor's *Scientific Management* (1903) sold in large numbers. Internal training, too, was seen as important, not least to inculcate employees with the values of the organization and establish an internal labour market that would supply the necessary skills. Above all, though, strategy was based on a collaborative ideal that resulted in the creation of substantial *zaibatsu* groups that possessed a wide variety of often complementary activities, from industrial operations to banking and merchanting (the *soga shosha*), thus illustrating the collective nature of Japanese enterprise. This provided a highly competitive base from which to build an economy that by the 1930s was being taken seriously by its Western rivals.

Indeed, one can claim that Japanese enterprises became even more management intensive than those in the West, especially as by the 1920s a devolved form of organization had become the norm among the leading businesses, with family control and ownership prevalent in a structure which delegated extensive responsibility to the professional managers working in distant operating divisions. At the same time, the extensive networks of inter-firm contacts among family-controlled businesses strengthened the system, providing a means by which Japan was able to overcome the disadvantages of industrializing so late (Fruin 1992: 47–9).

The scale of these *zaibatsu* is also demonstrated by examining the top fifty Japanese industrial enterprises, because while in 1896 independent textile firms dominated, by 1919 *zaibatsu* subsidiaries and affiliates in a wide range of industries controlled the scene (Nakagawa 1975: 13–17). Moreover, as Morikawa (1992: 316–18) explains, the large groups were run by a combination of family owners and professional managers. Although only forty-two of the largest 158 firms had filled more than half of their top positions with professional managers, the latter 'had long made remarkable gains in the top management of pre-war large-scale enterprises in Japan'. At the same time, one must stress the hybrid nature of Japanese business, in that not only were most of the large-scale groups still dominated by family owners, the vast majority of joint-stock companies were also personal enterprises.

By the First World War, *zaibatsu* had already become highly integrated and diversified conglomerates with interests in many unconnected industrial sectors. They had also ventured abroad, establishing many subsidiaries in Asia especially, creating the basis for what became in the late twentieth century a flood of Japanese multinational investments (Wilkins 1986: 228–9). It is important to emphasize, though, that as Yui (1988: 62–6) argues, while the trading and banking arms of these organizations were central features of both strategy and structure, the industrial operations were managed along highly functional and sophisticated lines. Merger activity featured prominently in this process of concentration, leading to a high level of cooperation and collusion among Japanese firms. Above all, though, any dynamism came from the individual firms, rather than the central bureaucracy. Nevertheless, by the 1910s a high level of coordination and integration had been achieved within *zaibatsu* and Japanese business was already beginning to take on the characteristics which proved so successful in the late twentieth century.

In principle, this system meant that the operating divisions were usually granted independent status, even though the *zaibatsu* were very much of the entrepreneurial type, because family control and ownership continued at the senior levels of management. Morikawa (1992: 244) and Yui (1988: 62–72) have also emphasized how the whole structure was only loosely coordinated from the centre. One should not be misled, however, into believing that the divisions acted independently of their parent company, because while *zaibatsu* might well resemble a federation of companies all using the parent name or owned by a single family, the importance of group identity and loyalty provided a greater degree of cohesiveness than would be normal in Western holding companies (Fitzgerald 2000). Much was made of the federal structure as a means of encouraging entrepreneurship among the professional managers, but the Japanese value systems and lines of authority, based heavily on the Confucian ethics which stressed 'dedication to duty and selfless devotion to the established order and authority', ensured that professional managers would operate in the interests of the *Ie*, or house (Yamamura 1978: 218). Above all, it is vital to remember that family ownership was a central feature of Japanese business which in the Japanese sociocultural context was a source of strength, underpinning the national drive towards modernization and improved competitiveness. The organizational precision evident in *zaibatsu* would become a hallmark of twentieth century Japanese business (Yui 1988: 66), demonstrating in graphic form the distinguishing characteristic of this economy's evolution over the last 120 years.

Conclusion

Where the United States had a powerful driving force in its large and expanding market and Germany had strongly symbiotic institutions, Japan's rapid move into large-scale industrialization was primarily driven in its crucial initial period by the strong national consciousness imposed by the Meiji regime. Although there is inevitably a strong degree of characterization in this analysis, there emerged a commitment to collaboration that was a consistent theme in Japanese industrialization, with the *zaibatsu* developing a strong relationship with the state as a means of exploiting scarce resources. This is why we have used the term 'collective managerial capitalism' to describe the Japanese modus operandi by the 1920s. Throughout this era, it is apparent that the commitment to developing high quality human resources (HR) was a high priority, especially in the fields of engineering and management. This was why the state invested heavily in the establishment of an educational system that was oriented towards the needs of business, while firms also committed substantial resources to internal training and development as a means of creating a robust internal labour market that would respond to the needs of large-scale, vertically-integrated hierarchical organizations that demanded strong levels of coordination. Japanese management structures consequently developed a robustness that proved essential to the way that the *zaibatsu* groups evolved into extremely competitive international corporations staffed by highly qualified managers at all levels and supported by a state-funded infrastructure that underpinned a dynamic private enterprise economy.

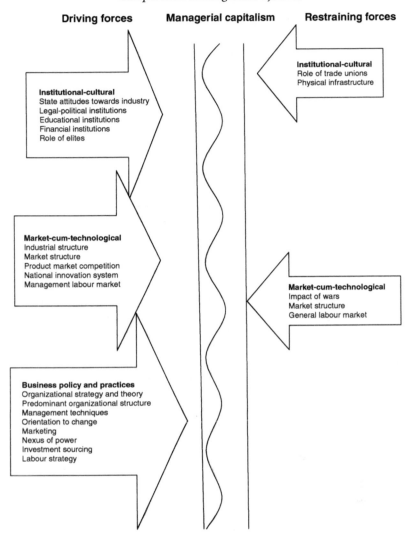

Driving forces   **Managerial capitalism**   **Restraining forces**

Institutional-cultural
Role of trade unions
Physical infrastructure

Institutional-cultural
State attitudes towards industry
Legal-political institutions
Educational institutions
Financial institutions
Role of elites

Market-cum-technological
Industrial structure
Market structure
Product market competition
National innovation system
Management labour market

Market-cum-technological
Impact of wars
Market structure
General labour market

Business policy and practices
Organizational strategy and theory
Predominant organizational structure
Management techniques
Orientation to change
Marketing
Nexus of power
Investment sourcing
Labour strategy

Figure 4.3. The force-fields at work in Japan, 1910–35

The way in which the Japanese environment encouraged the development of collective managerial capitalism can be seen in Figure 4.3, where yet another force-field diagram has been presented as a means of depicting the balance of our drivers. Just as with the United States and Germany, it is also apparent that the drivers were overwhelmingly positive, with only the product markets and general infrastructure acting as significant market-cum-technological restraints. At the same time, and again paralleling the German case, it is vital to stress that even by the 1930s Japanese large-scale business had not completely adopted the system of managerial capitalism, with family ownership and management continuing to play a highly influential role. Similarly, given the intimate relationship with the state, not to mention the distinct sociocultural environment, Japanese business operated on different levels to its German counterparts. This is why collective managerial capitalism accurately denotes the nature of the Japanese system, laying solid foundations that from the 1950s were built on to create one of the most vibrant business systems in the world.

CONCLUSIONS

While summarizing three different business systems provides an enormous challenge, it is above all vital to stress that we have been trying to understand the main factors that have precipitated the emergence of 'managerialization', as a further means of explaining why this process took so much longer in Britain. In tracking these cases, we have used the three sets of drivers that were first outlined in Chapter 2 (see especially Figure 2.2) in order to explain how a complex mixture of market-cum-technological, institutional, and cultural factors, and the nature of business policies and practices, have combined to mould particular systems. This exercise has been supported by Figures 4.1–4.3, in which it has been possible to stress how the balance of our drivers was very much on the positive side, reinforcing a point made earlier, that the environment in which firms evolve determines their characteristic pattern. This also explains why we have been obliged to use different labels to describe the respective systems, with competitive managerial capitalism proving appropriate to the United States, while professional proprietorial and collective managerial are more accurate to Germany and Japan respectively.

Having made this point, it is nevertheless possible to offer a typology of business development that provides a framework for our comparative analysis, focusing on a series of interlinked influences. These are:

- A strong willingness to change and innovate whilst at the same time maintaining continuity commensurate with a strongly identifiable indigenous culture.
- The creation of conducive market-cum-technological and institutional environments in which industrial capitalism could flourish, including the establishment of an appropriate banking system and heavy investments in education and infrastructure.
- Placing business in a central social position, thereby overcoming any bias imposed by older elites against this form of wealth-creation.
- Managerial control over shop-floor activities and the diminution of trade union influence.
- The elaboration of relatively sophisticated organizational hierarchies capable of controlling these sprawling business empires

• Recruiting staff that had been highly educated, increasingly up to university level and offering career opportunities that were based on merit, as opposed to nepotism.

In identifying these core features of our typology, it is vitally important to stress that the British case offers almost as many similarities as differences, while in the cases of the United States, Germany, and Japan the pattern of progress was markedly different. In this respect, it is reasonable to refer back to our four main themes from Chapter 2 as points of reference. In the first place, the persistence of personal or proprietorial capitalism was a feature of all four business systems, with family owner-managers featuring just as prominently in the United States, Germany, and Japan as they did in Britain. The key difference, of course, was the extent to which outside Britain real authority was delegated to the managers recruited into the expanding organizational hierarchies, not to mention the greater propensity to recruit staff from either universities or other educational and training institutes.

As our second theme refers to the nature of organizational structure and the influence of transaction costs, it is clear that the balance of indigenous transaction costs would appear to have encouraged the internalization of activities. As a consequence, American, German, and Japanese firms felt obliged to develop much greater levels of control over internal operations. This, in turn, would place much greater emphasis on the need for managerial skills, persuading owner-managers to recruit qualified staff who might be capable of handling these organizational challenges. Linking into our third theme, industry and managerial careers would also attain a social status that would further enhance their ability to effect change. And finally, managers in the United States, Germany, and Japan would consequently take on a much more professional character, acquiring both the qualifications and status required to perform their expanding range of duties.

In all these respects, it is clear from what we have seen in this chapter and the last that there were decisive differences between the British case and the experiences of American, German, and Japanese management. One need only compare the various force-field diagrams (Figure 3.1 and Figures 4.1–4.3) to demonstrate the radical differences in external and internal environments to substantiate this point. Again, it is important to accept that there were some similarities, especially with regard to the persistence of family owner-management across all four economies. On the other hand, by examining the case of the United States, Germany, and Japan in detail it is clear that a combination of indigenous influences and stimuli produced contrasting results, not least in terms of the status and social position of managers, as well as the dynamics of business organization. This further supports our use of the terms managerial capitalism (for the United States), professional proprietorial capitalism (Germany), and collective managerial capitalism (Japan), in stark contrast to the persistence of personal and proprietorial capitalism in Britain up to the 1940s. It is now important to return to the British case and assess how after the 1940s there were significant changes with respect to the four themes, leading to a metamorphosis in terms of organizational dynamics and managerial status.

5

British Management since the 1940s

INTRODUCTION

We now turn to update the longitudinal assessment of British management by looking at the nature and extent of change in the last half century. This is the period when many of the drivers and the four themes of the book changed from a negative to a positive orientation. Furthermore, by the twenty-first century management had achieved a much enhanced status and the number of managers had almost quadrupled. Of particular importance in this chapter will be the first two themes and the business policy and practice drivers, and to a limited extent the market-cum-technological drivers, leaving the second two themes and institutional and cultural drivers to the succeeding three chapters.

In broad terms, we have the persistence of pre-war characteristics up to the 1950s, significant change in the 1960s and 1970s, and the completion and consolidation of change in the 1980s and 1990s, resulting in the emergence of managerial capitalism and the substantial dominance of the M-form structure in large-scale organizations. Inevitably, this periodization is less clear-cut than the chronological divisions might suggest; many organizations continued to undergo what we have called post-war problems well into the 1960s and 1970s, while by contrast others were making structural changes earlier than the majority. Nevertheless, this gives an idea of the phasing of change, with progress towards professionalism and increasingly sophisticated management structures being the key themes of the era as a whole. These trends are encapsulated in the concluding section by two diagrams, one a force-field analysis such as we have already seen in the two preceding chapters. This time, however, it illustrates a radically different orientation of the various drivers for Britain in 2000 when compared with Figure 3.1, demonstrating how the environment was changing over this period. The other diagram provides a framework for comparing change in the different markets and the characteristics of the largest 100 companies over the twentieth century, indicating once again that the late twentieth century was a period of dramatic change that precipitated the transformation of British management into a much larger and more professional cadre.

THE 1940s AND 1950s: CONTINUING POST-WAR PROBLEMS

The post-war context was characterized by three significant areas of change. First, there was increased international competition resulting from trade liberalization through the General Agreement on Tariffs and Trade (GATT) protocol of 1947, the reduction in protective tariffs, and the rapid decline in imperial preference in Commonwealth markets. While this might have been expected to induce a restructuring of British business, after the wartime shortages there was in practice a sellers' boom market lasting well into the 1960s, combined with vigorous price-fixing across many domestic markets, discouraging organizational innovation and leading to a highly complacent attitude towards the need for change. These attitudes were also sustained by the memory of military success in the war and the continued myth of Britain as a great power (Barnett 1986). Second, a new political situation emerged that would influence various aspects of the post-war scene. After the Second World War, the Labour government's programme of nationalization and the creation of the welfare state, combined with the growth in the political power of trade unionism, resulted in less favourable public attitudes towards management. While its role and overall authority were not challenged, as they had been after the First World War, its competence was, especially as evidence of poor productivity became clear. The third, and some would say decisive, feature of the post-war scene was the creation of a full employment economy, drastically changing the labour market over the period 1945–73. With the average rate of unemployment at only 1.5 per cent, compared to an average of over 10 per cent between 1921 and 1939, management, as we see in Chapter 9, was faced with a much more formidable opponent on the shop floor, significantly determining attitudes towards innovation and change and ensuring that industrial relations issues featured prominently in the public consciousness until well into the 1980s.

Productivity and Production Management

Linking back to the discussion of economic trends in Chapter 1, in the quarter century from 1948–73 there was a rapid growth (by British historical standards) in productivity and production, with production rising at an average of 2.8 per cent per annum and productivity at 2.4 per cent. While this was impressive in itself, however, it was still well behind other countries. Indeed, there was a deficit of about 0.7 per cent per annum in productivity growth in relation to the other main European economies between 1950 and 1973, so that by the end of this period manufacturing output per head was approximately 50 per cent higher in France and Germany and 100 per cent higher in the United States (Broadberry 1997). Why did this gap emerge?

Although there was a good deal of generalized and anecdotal criticism of management, little of this analysis was either systematic or concerned with practice at all managerial levels. In discussing problems of technique, we are mainly concerned with the organization of production, and at relatively low levels of management. The most useful contemporary sources on this subject have been the Anglo-American Council on Productivity (AACP) reports, the Political and Economic Planning (PEP) survey (1966) of forty-seven companies in six indus-tries, Granick's detailed analysis (1972) of three companies as part of a survey of management in four countries, and Dunning's comparisons (1958, 1969) of the performance of indigenous plants with foreign-owned counterparts, each of which provided valuable contributions to the debate.

The fifty-eight AACP reports (1948–52), based on the visits of British teams to the United States, showed that British productivity was lower than in the United States in large part because of the slower adoption of labour-saving technologies and techniques, with an especial lag in mass-production industries. British firms had less up-to-date machinery, and it was less well laid out than in America, with a big gap between good and bad in Britain. On this latter point, Florence (1972: 360–1) showed that in a number of industries, the range of output for firms of similar size making the same product varied enormously, a difference which could only be explained by variations in management quality. One of the AACP teams, indeed, concluded that 'the greatest single factor in American industrial supremacy over British industry is the effectiveness of its management at all levels' (quoted in Gospel 1992: 118). This, however, is not to deny that some techniques were inhibited by the defensiveness of the unions or other industrial relations issues. At the same time, the government did little to see that the reports were implemented, while industry failed to respond with any enthusiasm to the AACP findings, even though they attracted considerable attention. As McGivering, Matthews, and Scott (1960: 61–2) argued:

The reluctance of British managements to delegate responsibility, in comparison with their American counterparts, is a frequently recurring theme in the various Anglo-American Council on Productivity Reports....Delegation can be achieved with greater confidence when adequate measures of the delegatee's performance exist. British management, however, is backward in the employment of techniques of work measurement, cost accounting and budgetary control, for example.... It is not that the appropriate techniques are unknown in this country; they are known but are neither appreciated nor applied sufficiently widely.

The main managerial development of early post-war Britain was, indeed, the increased focus on work study and production efficiency, or productivity, based at the level of the shop floor. While this had been routinized in America by the 1920s, Granick (1962: 253–6) claims that the use of work study as a technique in Britain was fifty years behind that in the United States. Much of this attention was also based on the extension of consultancy, rather than on internal initiatives (Granick 1962: 255). Moreover, it is arguable that consultants left problems behind them because there was rarely enough time to ensure that the managers and workers either accepted ownership of the new systems or indeed possessed the capability to operate them.

The PEP survey (1966: 13) of British management practice completed in 1964 was perhaps the most comprehensive of the period. It created fifty-nine indicators to differentiate 'thrusters' from 'sleepers' in forty-seven companies in six industries, using interviews to determine management practices. Attitudinal ratings of A (good), B (medium), and C (poor) were then apportioned according to what the indicators found, each of which in turn was compared with the firm's financial results. What the survey concluded, not surprisingly, was that while a number of firms, the 'thrusters', were progressive and using modern techniques, an equivalent number used traditional approaches and were not forward-looking. There are too many indicators to mention, but to give a flavour of the report it was clear that 'thrusters' utilized budgetary controls and long-term planning, while 'sleepers' did not; in 'thrusters' production was based on sales requirements, while in 'sleepers' production dominated sales. Industries also varied, with electronics proving to be more progressive than shipbuilding. The survey concluded that:

It became apparent that many of the firms visited did not apply even comparatively simple techniques that should contribute to high productivity. This is demonstrated so frequently in the interviews that it seems likely that indifference to modern practices for improving productivity and efficiency is widespread within certain strata of British industry.

Although the production area was not the only one where weak techniques were employed, it was the most important; Tiratsoo (1999: 109) has identified poor machine sequencing and work flow, the lack of mechanical aids for handling, and a consequent underemployment of machines and personnel and poor delivery record, together with a lack of awareness of the benefits that could come from modern methods. Some of this, he suggested, could be put down to the 'Cinderella' status of production managers, their low decision-making power in companies, and lack of support from senior management. On a related point, Tiratsoo (1999: 108) also noted that in a ranking of the Council of Engineering Institutions' fifteen member institutes, production engineers had the lowest median incomes.

American company subsidiaries located in Britain were the subject of a major study by Dunning (1958), resulting in the discovery that while they were less productive than their American parents, British-owned rivals failed to come up to their standards. Dunning (1958) concluded that if British companies were to adopt the managerial and other techniques of the US subsidiaries, they would be able to achieve three-quarters of the productivity of their American counterparts, as opposed to less than half in practice, with the rest being due to the location-specific attributes of the US economy. Obviously, these subsidiaries derived a number of different managerial attitudes and techniques from their parent companies, which in turn had a significant impact on management practice in their UK competitors, customers, and suppliers. Dunning (1958) also discovered that US subsidiaries in Britain earned substantially higher after-tax profits on net assets than did UK companies. The average figures for 1950–64 across a wide range of industries were 15.4 per cent and 8.7 per cent respectively, with the US companies ahead by a margin of 77 per cent. Furthermore, Dunning (1958) reported calculations that helped to isolate the nature of this superiority; the US subsidiaries attained a higher labour productivity in part through a higher capital to labour ratio. While they expended a smaller fraction of sales revenue on administration, more was spent on marketing and distribution, perhaps a confirmation of the frequent assertions that UK managerial shortcomings were particularly marked in assessing what the buyer wants and making the product appropriately available. Moreover, wholly owned subsidiaries did better than joint subsidiaries; those with American managing directors fared better than those with British managing directors. In addition, those subsidiaries whose methods were decisively influenced by US techniques appeared to be more successful than those whose methods were negligibly influenced. As Caves (1968: 302) noted of this survey: 'All in all, this evidence of deficient UK managerial skills seems quite compelling.'

Overall, while a lot of effort was evidently put into adopting American mass-production techniques in the post-Second World War period, this was generally unsuccessful (Broadberry 1997: 397). We would suggest that the main problem revolved around the superficial way in which American structures and systems were introduced, because few firms had a sufficiently professional management cadre to make them operate efficiently, while engineers were rarely heeded when it came to strategic decisions (Tiratsoo, Edwards, and Wilson 2003).

Planning and Control

Issues of planning and control tended to be at a rather higher level than those of technique (which is not to say that they did not exist at the shop-floor level), being essentially concerned with coordination. It was a topic that provoked Granick's survey (1972) of Britain in comparison with three other countries, the United States, France, and the Soviet Union. His main concern in investigating three British companies in considerable detail was to examine structural issues that might cause suboptimization through a lack of effective planning and control. The consequent report argued that the American advantage lay in the presence of substantial functional staffs at headquarters, whereas in Britain managerial practices did not require such staffs, leading to weak coordination and the suboptimization of resources. Three main points were used to support this contention. First, it was clear that top management did not coordinate or control the activities of the separate units or functions effectively. This was an era when decentralization characterized the attitude of top management, with very little coordination being done at any higher level. Second, while the absence of coordination was most striking at the level of top management, efforts were also made to minimize the necessity for it at middle levels. This was done through extreme decentralization and the reluctance to create middle-level jobs with wide responsibility. The third dimension was the structuring of firms as though each was composed of a number of small independent companies, namely, employing the H-form (holding company) structure that had become popular in the inter-war period (see Figure 1.3).

In short, Granick (1972) argued that British companies had accepted suboptimization and built it into the management system. All this, of course, was the reverse of managerial capitalism, with its substantial central cadres. In particular, the weakness of top management meant that there was little planning or coordination either between divisions or integration across functions, the very things that Chandler (1977) had put at the heart of the 'visible hand' which took the place of market coordination. As a result, the benefits of the divisional structure were largely lost, even if the divisions themselves were successful as entities in themselves.

Granick (1972) was not the only one to comment on the lack of planning and control systems. For example, Coleman (1987) noted that the lack of information systems, even where there was no deliberate culture of secrecy, made it difficult to arrive at properly informed decisions, providing communication problems, especially in the huge and complex newly nationalized industries that appeared in the late 1940s. Furthermore, a widespread lack of focus on research and development (R&D) and technical development generally resulted in either excessive conservatism or ill-judged investment, indicating how effective strategic planning was extremely rare in British firms.

In analysing the consequences of proprietorial structures, Quail (2000) provides a rather different, but in most respects complementary, angle on planning and control to Granick. In these systems, as the top management is limited and coordination remains the prerogative of directors, the results are a departmentalization of management in terms of role and career, as well as a failure to develop robust mechanisms of planning and control. It was a system in which there was less advantage in the reduction of transaction costs through improved coordination. Moreover, the separation of ownership and control was resisted even as firms began to move away from personal ownership through merger or floatation, exacerbating the tendency towards weaknesses in control and planning. With the proprietorial paradigm so firmly embedded within the British corporate system, even when a significant number of firms moved to adopt the M-form of organization it was impossible to effect this transition, given both the limited control exercised by top management and the lack of any internal coordination processes (Quail 2002: 7–8).

Amateur Managers

Perhaps the most frequent behavioural assertion about British management was that of amateurism, used in the sense of being the opposite to professionalism (Coleman 1973; Kempner 1984). In this sense, it meant both 'gentlemen' and 'players', to take Coleman's metaphor, since 'economics, management techniques, industrial psychology; all were frequently looked upon with grave suspicion, for they represented attempts to professionalize an activity long carried on jointly by "practical men" and gentlemanly amateurs' (Coleman 1973: 113). One dimension of amateurism was attitudinal; as Coleman (1973) indicated, most directors of proprietorial companies were amateur in this sense, as well as being only tangentially acquainted with the nature of the business they ran. Another dimension was the use of class and status, rather than merit, in judging people (Dubin

1970). A third was the lack of a trained background, resulting in a narrow perception of the role. As Caves (1980) noted, business was a second career choice, while Woodward (1965: 14) went even further, arguing that 'attitudes to professional qualifications were prejudiced, and in some firms the possession of academic or professional qualifications were regarded as a handicap'. Granick (1972) also added that the breadth of experience and training of top managers was far less than in other countries, concluding that: 'Under these circumstances it is not surprising that British top managers play a quite modest role in their companies and encourage the most extreme decentralisation found in any of the four countries.'

The implications of this form of amateurism were also outlined by Dubin (1970: 187–8):

Emulating practice and form without understanding their application spreads across the entire spectrum of business operations.... The result has been a vast proliferation of consulting services to British industry in which the consultants literally take over the managerial functions of decision-making in the guise of recommending preferred practices and policies.

While it is difficult to claim categorically that had British senior managers been better trained in business management, then they would have overcome the era's most significant problems, at least they would not have tried to cope with the challenges in such a naïve and mistaken fashion.

Linked to the issue of dealing with challenges, the strong orientation of American business towards constant change was something that impressed the AACP observers, since the converse would appear to have characterized Britain. As Coleman (1987) noted when commenting on a number of British company histories, 'one theme ... seems to recur too frequently and too widely to be ignored. It cannot be easily or precisely delineated in any of the enterprises, but it could perhaps be described as an attitude of mind antipathetic to building change into the system.' Several reasons were adduced for this attitude. One factor was the limited competition and sellers' market of the early post-war period to which we have already alluded. At the same time, more structural reasons must be considered. In particular, Caves (1968: 303) argued that patterns of management staffing

conspire to defeat industrial dynamism [because] executives who have come up through the firm lack breadth of view as well as technical training, and have often been apprenticed in the accounting tradition of 'the search for the missing shilling'. [On the other hand] the trouble with the public school and Oxbridge graduates lies not in their 'old-boy' network of recruitment, but rather in their 'amateurism' and their frequent acceptance of business as second choice when they fail to qualify for a civil service career. They tend to retain the civil service as their model and settle into a trustee role of gentlemanly responsibility that hardly conduces to rapid innovation.

Similarly, Dubin (1970) felt that British business suffered from lower levels of managerial mobility, resulting in less diffusion of ideas and practice, while the assumption of a lifetime career resulted in pressures to conformity and a lack of orientation to new ideas. This problem was also compounded by the problem of low managerial salaries in Britain, resulting in many taking compensation in the form of greater on-the-job leisure time. In addition, as Granick (1972) argued, 'precisely because industrial management is not a prestigious career in Britain as it is elsewhere, less vigor, inventiveness, and risk taking is shown by British managers'.

A final dimension of the lack of will to change was the institutional context. On the basis of his experience at British Leyland, Edwardes (1983: 163) argued that because British management's authority had been challenged and eroded in the post-war period, it had lost the will to manage. Of course, politicians, the media, the public and not least management itself blamed union negativity. In another sense, however, as we see in Chapter 9, this issue of managerial legitimacy and self-confidence was intimately related to a desire to maintain the political consensus, with the system operating in such a way as to result in a mode of resource allocation that provided both sides of the industrial divide with a fair share of accumulated wealth (Olson 1982).

Corporate Governance

Underpinning all these aspects of the British business scene was the persistence of what Quail (2004) has labelled 'proprietorial capitalism'. As we saw in Chapters 2 and 3, this was a system in which the coordination of functions was considered the prerogative of the directors, most of whom were part-time and 'amateur', resulting in an organizational style that had significant implications for management careers, the development of planning and control techniques, and not least corporate governance. As Coleman (1987) revealed, a series of characteristics was evident, including:

- managerial autocracy in large and small companies left problems of succession
- a strong culture of secrecy, especially about costs
- too many directors spent too much of their time on executive minutiae and too little on corporate policy
- a club atmosphere in the boardroom
- hidebound attitudes on industrial relations issues.

To add to these characteristics, McGivering, Matthews, and Scott (1960: 58–62) made further observations relating to a widespread unwillingness amongst family firms to raise external sources of capital if this implied a loss of control. Dominant autocrats who ran many companies also obtained considerable satisfaction from exercising power, leading to a reluctance to delegate important decisions. In any case, 'many British managements have a deep-seated prejudice against increasing the number of "staff" supervisory and managerial employees', on the grounds that as costing systems regarded them as 'non-productive' or indirect workers, this was often regarded as a sign of inefficiency. As a consequence, there were few organization builders amongst the ranks of senior British management; even fewer resembled Lord Cole of Unilever: on being asked what he did, he replied that his job was to make sure that the right managers were in the right jobs.

The other side of the coin to proprietorial attitudes was the governance of companies, which was frequently weak to the point where the shareholders had little if any influence on company policy, either directly or through the operation of the stock market. Although the post-war period saw a continuing diffusion of ownership (Florence 1961), the dispersal of shareholdings caused a considerable reduction in their effectiveness as a power source in the absence of financial institutions capable of consolidating and wielding power. Moreover, the share structure was often biased, with the frequent use of non-voting shares which often outnumbered the voting shares. This was the case at Marks and Spencer, which in 1955 had voting shares with a nominal value of £600,000 and a market value of £9.5 million, while the non-voting shares had a nominal value of £8.4 million and a market value of £108 million (Florence 1961). But even where there was no such bias in the share structure and City institutions held significant amounts of shares, governance could still be weak.

A classic example was in Britain's largest car manufacturer, BMC, which became notorious for the poor state of its industrial relations, although it also had weaknesses in other areas such as design, accounting, and management control systems. So why did the owners or the financial markets fail to bring about the needed changes? Bowden, Foreman-Peck, and Richardson (2001) suggest that while BMC was a public company in which control was divorced from ownership, neither the main board nor the lower-level managers were in danger of losing their jobs. There were no effective non-executives, while board meetings were a formality where inadequate information was presented. The owners consisted of four main groups: small shareholders who could not easily act in concert; banks which administered but had only limited powers of control over various trust and nominee share accounts; charitable trusts, mainly the various Nuffield trusts, which were the largest shareholders and were totally committed to the company, at least as long as the dividends were maintained; and finally, a small group of insurance companies, some of which, and the Prudential in particular, held large stakes in the company. In effect, though, the latter were the only group with the potential to take action. It is believed that the Prudential did discuss its concerns with the company, but not to the point of taking the 'exit' option of selling its shares. Indeed, it acquired more stock and thus helped to maintain the share price. So there was no credible 'exit' threat to put management under pressure, a scenario that prevailed across many similarly structured firms at that time. A final point with regard to BMC was that until the 1970s the British car industry was still largely insulated from foreign competition, so that the market share could be maintained. In other words, the management, from top to bottom, was not accountable for its actions, or in this case, the lack of them, and the corporate governance mechanisms, or what has now come to be called the market for corporate control, were weak and ineffective almost to the point of irrelevance.

THE 1960s AND 1970s: DIMENSIONS OF CHANGE

So far the story has been a gloomy one, emphasizing problems and weaknesses. In moving to the other key feature of the post-war period, however, namely the increase in the pace of change in the British economy, we can trace the progressive transition to managerial capitalism. This process had many dimensions, most of which affected the numbers, methods of organization, and ultimately the performance of managers. Moreover, the impact of change was not, and indeed could not be, immediate, with a time lag before the transition became effective. As we saw in Figure 1.7, there were 1,246,000 managers and administrators in the 1951 census, or 5.6 per cent of total employment, while by 1981 the respective figures were 2,984,000 and 12.4 per cent. It is difficult to allocate the increase to specific trends, but a substantial proportion was consequent on the changes in structure and size of firms, the need to improve control systems, to look outward to the consumer, all of which were linked to the transition to managerial capitalism. Other factors included the need for increased governmental returns, the pressures of labour shortages, new production technologies, and the rise of the service industries as a proportion of total employment, while the public sector also grew significantly over this period. The impact on management witnessed both the emergence of new functions such as information technology (IT) and the thickening of existing functions, trends that were further reflected in the rising membership of professional institutes, while greater mobility was created by the vesting of pensions (Keeble 1992).

An important part of the jigsaw puzzle of change lay in the progressive growth of competition in the post-war period, and in particular the move to globalization. In addition, there were important moves in the legal framework, especially the drive to eliminate anti-competitive practices and provide greater incentives to increase competitiveness. Between 1949 and 1955, the Monopolies Commission made detailed studies of the arrangements affecting the production and supply of over a dozen articles, revealing that the fixing of common prices, and often quotas, by the manufacturers was the rule, often supplemented by resale price maintenance and exclusive dealing (McGivering, Matthews, and Scott 1960: 38). As a result, the anti-restrictive practices legislation of 1948, 1956, and 1964 led to the dismantling of some 2,500 arrangements. By the latter date, public and political attitudes had moved decisively away from the interwar position supporting cartelization, although corporatist attitudes lingered on until the 1980s. This also coincided with the gradual reduction of protectionist duties over the period 1948 to 1970, while intensifying international competition was further compounded by the oil crises of 1973 and 1979 that precipitated global economic disruption.

Corporate Responses: Mergers and Diversification

One of the most significant corporate responses to these challenges was to create even larger firms that might be capable of withstanding the pressures. Figure 5.1

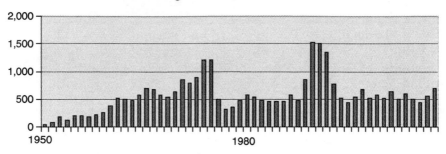

Figure 5.1. Number of companies acquired in mergers, 1950–2004

indicates that the number of mergers grew from the mid-1950s to over 500 a year in the 1960s, with another peak in the early 1970s. While this did not match the enormous expenditures on mergers of the period 1995–2004, when it averaged over £20 billion per year, the consistently high number of mergers, and especially the peak years of 1959–60, 1967–70, and 1972–3, indicate how 'Big is Beautiful' came into common business parlance.

In explaining this trend, it is apparent that most of the early post-war mergers were horizontal, having been at least partly stimulated by the compulsory termination of trade association price-fixing. In this sense, the mergers were also highly defensive, a pattern compounded by the emergence of the takeover bid during the 1950s (Hannah 1983). Indeed, the City was instrumental in much of this merger activity, resulting in the creation of a market for corporate control (Roberts 1992), while in addition the Labour Government of the 1960s was also extremely anxious to produce world-class companies that would be big enough to compete against large American multinationals (Roberts 1992). To achieve this aim, it set up the Industrial Reorganization Corporation (IRC), which acted as a kind of state merchant bank and was instrumental in some major mergers, including the creation of General Electrical Corporation (GEC) in the electrical machinery industry and British Leyland in the British motor industry (Hague 1983), an issue to which we return (see State Attitudes towards Industry, Chapter 6).

More so than in other countries, British firms grew by acquisition rather than internal growth. As various studies showed, however, the results of the mergers of the period were often disappointing, with little synergy emerging from the large-scale combinations (Newbould 1970: 113; Walshe 1991: 349–54). In most cases, acquisitions meant the addition of further units to already loose structures without much in the way of coherent structural reorganization. So the speed and size of acquisitions and mergers posed difficult coordination problems between formerly competing units and plants. These problems were further compounded in the case of diversification, because managements proved to be even less well equipped to achieve much of benefit to the firm as a whole. In fact, mergers were instrumental in increasing the amount of diversification across Britain's large-scale firms, partly as a defensive means of either limiting the impact of anti-competitive policies or the prevention of anti-competitive mergers. In a more positive sense, this strategy was also prompted by the resource-based view of the firm, in that firms were acquiring either fresh resources or skills not otherwise available. As Channon (1973: 67) noted, whereas only 25 per cent of large companies could be considered diversified in 1950, this had increased to 60 per cent by 1970. Inevitably, though, both mergers and diversification meant more complex companies, which in turn meant the need both for more managers and consideration of new forms of structure.

In considerable part as a result of the mergers, even though there had been previous waves of mergers (see, The Rise of Big Business, Chapter 3) that had resulted in the widespread formation of a holding company structure, the third quarter of the century saw substantial increases in the size of workplaces and the corporations which owned them, especially in manufacturing. Thus, the percentage of manufacturing employees working in establishments with more than 500 employees rose from 42.2 per cent in 1951 to 54.5 per cent in 1978, while those in establishments with more than 1,000 employees over the same period rose from 28.9 per cent to 41.4 per cent (Purcell and Sisson 1983: 96). Moreover, the concentration in smaller numbers of larger enterprises complemented the rise in establishment size: the proportion of employees in manufacturing enterprises with more than 5,000 employees rose from 45.8 per cent in 1958 to 56.2 per cent in 1978, while those in enterprises with more than 20,000 employees rose from 17.3 per cent to 25.1 per cent. At the same time, Utton (1982: 24–5) noted that in 1958 the 100 largest manufacturing companies had an average of twenty-seven plants; by 1972, this number had risen to seventy-two and was spread over a larger number of industries, indicating that on average British plants were smaller by the end of the period. This reflected the defensive nature of many British mergers and a failure to rationalize organization and production, given that the smaller acquired firms were allowed to continue working almost as if they had remained independent.

As in the United States, there were industries where the large enterprise was not dominant: apparel, lumber, publishing, leather, printing, and furniture. Overall, though, Hannah (1976) shows that the share of the largest 100 firms in manufacturing net output in Britain overtook that in the United States in the mid-1950s and rapidly increased to around 45 per cent by 1970, while the American proportion stayed roughly static at just over 30 per cent. This demonstrates categorically that by the 1950s and 1960s the argument voiced in Chapter 3 concerning the lack of economies due to relative size was less cogent than at the turn of the nineteenth century, even though US firms were still on average much larger. Clearly, though, it was the structure and management of firms which was of paramount importance, especially as the scale and scope of firms changed so radically over the post-war decades.

Structural Change

Although these trends provided a major organizational challenge in the period up to the 1960s, large British firms continued to rely on the holding company as an administrative and legal instrument. Increasingly, though, managements started to realize that such an unwieldy structure either did not permit them to take advantages of scale economies or enable control and planning for the subsidiaries. As a result, in the 1960s many of the leading companies turned to M-form structures (see Figure 1.4). At the same time, while Chandler (1976: 49) was able to comment that by 1970 'the structure of large business enterprise in Britain and the structure of the industries in which they operated had come to resemble their American counterparts', it is vital to differentiate between the two countries, especially in terms of the rigour with which the new structures was applied and operated.

Channon's work (1973) on the changing structure of the top 100 firms noted that in 1950 only twelve used a variation of the M-form structure, with eight of these being foreign. Of the ninety-two companies in Channon's 1950 sample, fifty-two employed some variation of the centralized, functionally departmentalized U-form structure (i.e. a structure in which each major function—manufacturing, sales, purchasing, finance, or research—was managed through its own department; see Figure 1.2). By 1960, however, only twenty-one were using the centralized form and forty the holding company structure. Of these forty, thirty-five had diversified product lines. By 1970, only eight companies in Channon's sample had a functionally departmentalized structure, fifteen used the holding company type, and seventy-two some variation of the M-form, even if many firms had only just made the transition.

While the rapid spread of the M-form was one of the principal organizational trends of that era, one of Channon's most striking findings was the different ways in which the M-form came into being in the two countries: in the United States it replaced the centralized, functionally departmentalized structure; and in Britain it evolved largely out of the loose-knit, decentralized holding company. Moreover, Channon (1973) pointed out that M-form structures used by British enterprises were less carefully defined and articulated than those of American firms. In particular, the duties and functions of the general office and the divisions were less clearly spelled out, while individual authority and responsibility were not as sharply pinpointed. British firms employed more committees and boards in managing day-to-day operations than did their American counterparts. The distinction between policy and operations was often blurred, with the heads of operating divisions working at the general office, where strategies for both current operations and the long-term policies were fabricated. Although the general service and financial staffs had increased in size, they were usually smaller and less comprehensive than those in the United States, leading to less rigour in the overall control and planning of activities in British M-forms. Indeed, by 1970 few British firms had gone beyond financial performance as the criterion used in monitoring and evaluating the performance of the divisions, although during the 1960s many introduced budgets for both control and planning. Finally, relatively few firms had formal planning offices and even fewer had offices that concentrated on management development. In both control and planning, the top executives relied more on personal contact through office visits and committee meetings than did their American counterparts.

In Britain, then, the most common organizational challenge facing those who took on the enormous task of revamping outdated structures was to convert the holding company into an M-form structure. This involved the creation of a large general office, with extensive service and financial staffs and the development of new sets and types of controls and planning techniques. In the United States, the M-form was adopted by companies that were already, and had often been for decades, managerial enterprises and administered by professional career managers. In Britain, on the other hand, many large enterprises were still holding companies composed of family firms, in which family members were still represented on the holding company board. As the transition was consequently much more difficult, it is not surprising that Channon (1973: 194–5) discovered that 'the full features of the multidivisional system were actually rare and only really found among the US subsidiary concerns. Most of the British companies still appeared to be in an intermediate phase between a holding company and a divisional system, with loose control and planning systems, and a poorly developed central office.' In other words, the resemblance with the United States perceived by Chandler (1976) was weak.

From the point of view of the international institutionalists, 'the spread of the American model of management in the post-war period is not simply an account of its technical efficiency but at least as much to do with the ideological and economic hegemony of the United States' (Whittington and Mayer 2002: 37). In part, this was operated through multinational subsidiaries and international arrangements, such as the Marshall Plan. On the other hand, it was also a function of the catalytic role of the US consultants in structural and system change. In most British companies, change was preceded by either the replacement of former leaders or declining fortunes, or both, but there was also an element of fashion. Moreover, as ICI had done earlier, management often looked to American experience for guidance, relying heavily on American management consultants. In fact, a single American consulting firm, McKinsey and Company, played a central role in the reorganization of major British companies in the food, tobacco, chemical, pharmaceutical, oil, paper, metals, metal fabricating machinery, engineering, and electrical industries. Prior to McKinsey's intrusion, the dominant area for consultants had been at a lower level and mainly in production (Ferguson 2002). After McKinsey set up an office in London in 1959, it concentrated on the organizational aspects of businesses, with their flagship service the reorganization of client firms into M-form structures. Up to the early 1970s, this firm became a dominant force for change in British industry, significantly altering the image of consultancy in general and forcing through a series of structural reorganizations that were to have a significant effect on large-scale British business. In effect, it is consequently clear that many British companies outsourced both strategy and structure to McKinsey.

Having emphasized the dominant role played by consultants, however, it is worth noting that it did not say much for the quality of internal management that they needed to rely on American firms either to initiate change or, in many cases, experienced problems in implementing what the consultants had recommended.

It was not so much a question of asking 'how do we do it', but of saying 'what shall we do'. Indeed, the adoption of the M-form could be argued in some cases to have been little more than an acceptance of fashion, with a 'McKinsey knows best' attitude prevailing in the difficult times of the 1960s. In other words, the transition in structure was improvised, rather than being a result of strategic planning.

Changing Corporate Governance

While the emergence of the M-form was a highly significant feature of the post-war era, perhaps the most notable change was the way in which firms that had been dominated by either a single owner or a small coterie of entrepreneurs sold an increasing proportion of their equity to professional investors. It was this transformation in ownership structures that led to changes in the nexus of power, a process that greatly affected the governance of organizations and the way in which managers behaved. As Florence (1961: 185–7) had concluded from his detailed study of large firms operating in the period 1936–51, a divorce between control and ownership had only become apparent among the largest firms, while few interlinking directorships connected boardrooms. By 1972, however, in only fourteen of the top 100 non-financial British firms did directors hold more than 10 per cent of the equity, while in fifty-six companies they held less than 0.5 per cent (Prais 1976: 89). This clear evidence of an apparently substantial divorce between control and ownership is further substantiated by Martin and Moores' work (1985: 14) on the leading 250 companies of 1975, indicating that the separation had also spread to the next level of company size.

The changing ownership patterns of large-scale British firms can be seen in Table 5.1, which reveals the radical changes from personal to institutional ownership. Moreover, in spite of the enormous increase in numbers of shareholders arising from the Conservative government's privatization programme in the 1980s, the distribution continued to move in favour of the institutions. As a means of exercising this growing influence, in 1973 an Institutional Shareholders Committee was formed to represent the interests of this powerful group. Later

Table 5.1. Share ownership in British businesses quoted on the London Stock Exchange, 1957–93

	1957	1975	1993
Persons	65.8	37.5	17.7
Banks	0.9	0.7	0.6
Insurance companies	8.8	15.9	17.3
Pension funds	3.4	16.8	34.2
Other financials	8.2	14.6	9.7
Public sector	3.9	3.6	1.3
Overseas	4.6	5.3	3.1

Source: Scott (1997: 86).

renamed the Investment Committee, by the late 1980s this body controlled estimated resources of £44 billion (Hilton 1987: 42), giving the fund managers who ran the investment activities of these bodies tremendous market influence. Although shareholder activism was slow to generate momentum, by the 1980s much more effort was being expended by the fund managers to extract better returns from their investments (Lazonick and O'Sullivan 1997). As both a result and a cause of these changes, the nature of ownership and control within the enterprises was considerably modified.

THE 1980s AND 1990s: MANAGERIAL CAPITALISM

By the 1980s, the impact of change was evident, with Britain appearing close to the top of the Organization for Economic Cooperation and Development (OECD) productivity league table, having been almost at the bottom in the early post-war period (Crafts 1991). Most of this was due to the 1960s and 1970s structural changes, although during the 1980s several significant innovations made an impact. One of these was the adoption of market-led policies after 1979, forcing through severe rationalization economies across the British economy. Another was the assertion of management control in the industrial relations arena, an issue we examine in Chapter 9. Indeed, within the firm there has been a move towards unitarism based on shareholder interests and away from attempts to engender consensus. In addition, as Broadberry (1997) argued, 'technological trends had moved back in Britain's favour. Given dramatic falls in the cost of information processing, technological leadership now switched back to methods that customized output using skilled workers.' Other influential characteristics of the period encouraging change were the rise of conglomerates (which were essentially about asset-stripping), privatization, globalization, the decline of manufacturing and the rise of financial services, higher rates of unemployment than hitherto in the post-war period, and a movement towards outsourcing. All this prompted the achievement of labour productivity levels that approximated to the European norm. This progress was sustained into the 1990s, with the Porter and Ketels Report (2003: 5) concluding that 'the UK has in fact achieved a remarkable success in halting the economy's protracted downward economic trajectory of the pre-1980 period'.

We thus arrive at the last of our four main stages, namely, a British recovery in which managers achieved both higher status and increased professionalism. As Quail (2000: 14) has argued, 'on a number of measures understood as diagnostic tests (the defeat of labour, organizational form, management recruitment) the managerial revolution was complete in Britain by the later 1980s'. This transformation was achieved from a position where 'not even the most "advanced" large business organizations were managerialist in 1939'. The verdict of history is difficult with such recent events, but it is clear that while much remains to be done, significant change has been achieved.

However, a further question, to be examined in more detail in Chapter 11, is whether managerial capitalism has now been transcended by financial capitalism. Further waves of mergers and acquisitions from the late 1970s and continuing up to the present (see Figure 5.1) have increased the importance of institutional investors and the growth of the market for corporate control, with important implications for senior managers who have to worry even more about the threat of hostile takeovers and pressures to produce short-term profit increases and improved share prices, rather than long-term growth and larger market shares. Risk-taking has become financial, based on the valuation of companies, rather than, as in earlier periods, considerations of technology or marketing. Consequently, as Berle and Means (1932) predicted, managers are no longer in charge of their own destiny, even if, paradoxically, the rewards for some at the top have risen astronomically as a result of stock options tied to share prices (Williams 2004). This is an issue which takes us away from the structure of organizations and the position of managers, forcing us to return to an analysis of what was really happening after 1980.

Performance and Structure

In spite of the overall improvement in economic performance, the corporate landscape has not been entirely healthy. Most large British companies operate in services or the consumer goods sector, rather than in advanced scientific and technological sectors, with some notable exceptions in pharmaceuticals and aerospace. Other high-tech companies have not survived, such as the electronics companies ICL and Ferranti, while under Lord Weinstock GEC was run as a finance-dominated company with relatively little R&D, eventually collapsing when both the profitable defence businesses were sold and under City pressure to spend the cash mountain a mistaken focus on civil telecommunications resulted in calamitous losses. British Steel, renamed Corus, is a shadow of its former self, having been absorbed into an Anglo-Dutch corporation that has significantly reduced capacity. The decline of manufacturing in comparison to other countries, and especially manufacturing with a technology dimension, must be blamed not just on poor technology but poor personnel, marketing and finance, as well as strategic management. Nevertheless, recognizing the need not just for structural but also cultural change, from the late 1970s companies began to transform themselves by changing management cultures, with ICL, British Airways, Lucas, Jaguar, and Courtaulds leading the way (Ferry 1993).

In turning to structure, Whittington and Mayer (2002: 187) have noted that their financial performance data broadly supported the M-form's economic effectiveness across countries, and 'the British have proved themselves now to be no slouches at divisionalization'. Moreover, when compared to France and Germany, Britain was the only country where the publicly held and professionally run large concerns of Chandler's divisionalized corporation dominated. Although Whittington and Mayer (2000: 188), like many other analysts, were talking of the large company group, and elsewhere the picture may not be as positive, more generally they argue that

the general principles of economic organization developed by Alfred Chandler in the 1960s have proved correct.... Although it may not do so always, it seems that the changing multidivisional still offers the most efficient, transparent and accountable means for organizing the large corporations of contemporary business life.

Of course, Whittington and Mayer do recognize that change will be both inevitable and continuous, with organizational innovations (Allred, Snow, and Miles 1996: Pettigrew and Fenton 2000) emerging in response to environmental changes. They also accepted, as indeed did Chandler (1990: 623), that 'excessive diversification' could create a 'breakdown of communication between the management at the corporate office ... and the middle managers who are responsible for maintaining the competitive capabilities of the operating divisions.... The head office becomes too easily the domain of finance specialists and industry-hopping generalists' (2002: 8). On the other hand, they argue that 'the multi-divisional can be developed to accommodate recent trends and experiments in organizations' (2002: 157). Nevertheless, as the M-form assumes a clear strategy, it is still doubtful whether most British companies have planned, as opposed to emergent, strategies, creating major problems if they attempt to link strategy to other policies in the organization, including those involving structure. On this point, Keep and Mayhew (2001: 7) argued:

It is by no means unusual to encounter organizations that have decentralized, re-centralized and then moved to another organizational form in the space of eighteen months. Coupled with this is the tendency to 'fad surf', often at the whim of an individual senior manager. The results are waves of supposedly profound, but in reality somewhat short-lived 'change programmes' centred on whatever happens to be the latest management fashion—recentralization, business process re-engineering, total quality management, or e-commerce.

The implications of this are 'to create initiative fatigue and make strategy a rapidly moving target, in turn making it difficult to gear capabilities, values and training to strategy' (Keep and Mayhew 2001: 7).

The renewed trend to externalization and heterarchy has also become a major part of corporate restructuring, mostly because in most sectors it has become possible to develop global supply chains and value chains, leading to the disintegration of vertically integrated operations and the renaissance of specialist firms that make separate contributions to the end product. By outsourcing, firms can avoid the legal obligations of employee status, as well as the fixed costs of non-core labour such as social security, health, and other forms of insurance. Moreover, lower wage costs can also be achieved if the activity can be transferred to a low-wage economy. Management of these chains is still required, however, and arguably becomes a larger part of the total process. Indeed, the Management Consultants Association noted that by the late 1990s, outsourcing had become the single biggest source of consultancy revenue (Ferguson 2002: 203).

Another related and significant trend was divestment of non-core activities, leading to significant numbers of management buyouts (Wright et al. 2000) and thus some diminution of diversification. Both of these trends indicated a higher degree of shareholder accountability than in the earlier period, with the market for corporate control having reached unprecedented levels of sophistication. At the same time, concern about the behaviour of some company directors has led to a series of examinations of codes of governance, from Cadbury to Hempel to Greenbury.

Was there a period of dominant managerial capitalism that both followed the era of proprietorial capitalism and preceded the emergence of institutional investors and the imposition of finance capitalism? Certainly, the move towards short-term performance indicators has undermined the hegemony of managerial capitalism, especially in recessions such as those in 1980–1 and 1992. By the late 1980s, there was also a strong reaction against bureaucracy, and by implication against the large-scale hierarchies associated with managerial capitalism. In a survey by Coulson-Thomas and Coe (1991), 88 per cent of respondents reported that their organizations were creating a slimmer and flatter organization, a trend which also appeared to undermine the tenets of managerial capitalism. Could it be argued that by this time the necessary managerial structures had been built and systems were no longer as necessary?

Managers

As we saw in Chapter 1, over the course of the last twenty years the numbers of managers and administrators have continued to increase, and by considerable proportions: in the 1981 census, there were 2,984,000 managers and administrators, or 12.4 per cent of total employment; by 2001, the respective figures were 4,676,000 and 17.6 per cent. This growth amounts to four times the population of Manchester, or an annual rate of growth of some 80,000 per annum, equivalent to a town the size of Carlisle or Colchester. This rapid increase in numbers, however, seems at odds with what to many managers has been the tidal wave of structural change which has swept across organizations in the last two decades, culling many managers and leading to doom-laden assertions such as 'the death of middle management'. While the renewed importance of heterarchy should enable decisions to be made by the market, rather than in managerial hierarchies, can we evaluate how far this is actually happening? Certainly, large organizations have far less employees than they used to, and probably considerably fewer managers, given the downsizing, delayering, and outsourcing that has taken place, to say nothing of the reduction in the strong central office hierarchies that Chandler saw as the key to managerial capitalism. At the same time, we must confess that none of the historical models noted in Chapter 2 seem to provide a satisfactory explanation for the continuation of the growth trend. There are a considerable number of potential explanations, which cumulatively might outweigh the organizational dimensions:

- Changes in the sectoral breakdown of the economy, with the massive expansion of the service sector, where the number of managers has proliferated over the last twenty years
- The substitution of capital for labour, resulting in a higher ratio of non-manual jobs
- The exporting of non-skilled jobs to less developed economies, again resulting in a higher ratio of non-manual jobs
- The broadening of previously non-managerial jobs to include some managerial functions
- A form of credentialism, whereby individuals seek titles to reflect their status, both within an organization and across society at large
- Nomenclature creep, which defines more jobs as managerial (for example 'train manager', as compared with the older term 'conductor'), with titles to satisfy personal aspirations almost as much as job structures and responsibilities (Grey 2005: 55)
- Status creep, partly related to the previous point
- Awareness of managerial significance which was not there in earlier decades. This might also be associated with the acceptance of management as a profession, together with the development and institutional accoutrements that professionalism implies
- The increased importance of the management and utilization of knowledge
- Management as a core, rather than a peripheral, job
- Changes in the definition of who constitutes a manager in the Census over time, with 'senior administrators' increasingly being classified as managers.

All of these issues require much more detailed research, given the lack of any detailed work on a subject that is central to an understanding of the role and status of managers.

As far as the individual manager is concerned, the flatter organization has brought additional responsibilities and less opportunity for climbing the promotional ladder at reasonably frequent intervals when compared to the traditional hierarchy. Today, links are just as likely to be lateral as vertical, with network, team, and project-based activities predominating. Accountability is also much more personalized, with rewards based on performance. While the manager's job has broadened, the detailed activities are still mixed and short-term, relying on intuition and personal contact (Mintzberg 1973). As Mabey and Ramirez (2004: 37) argue:

The impact of these changes on managers has been contradictory. There have undoubtedly been improvements in the efficiency and coordination of workplaces and there is some evidence that managers welcome the greater responsibility. But there is also evidence suggesting that the price paid for greater managerial autonomy has been longer working hours, an intensification of work and deterioration in the work-life balance relationship.

On the other hand, it is less the case that the manager's skills defy definition or analysis; management competencies and standards are moving towards a better understanding of what management involves. Nevertheless, as frequent change means problems of implementation and digestion, this seems to suggest that organizations themselves are by no means confident that they have found the right structural balance. The present certainly does not provide the stability of the golden period of the 'organization man' and the corporate career in the United States which existed for some thirty years from the 1950s (Whyte 1956), or even its British equivalent in the period of proprietorial capitalism when change was fiercely resisted.

Within management there has been a growing awareness of the extent of interprofessional competition between the main occupational groups. Management specialisms compete for resources and control over the discourse and practice of strategic management. Approaches to raise the credibility and influence of these specialisms include the creation of professional institutions and the establishment of areas of expertise which raise their importance in the organization. Both marketing (Doyle 1995) and personnel (Armstrong 1985) have apparently lost out to accounting, and sometimes (Eriksson 1999) even to production as well. Although the proportion of finance and accounting specialists is not yet as high as Fligstein (1993) found for the United States, with its 'finance' concept of the corporation, the UK appears to be heading in the same direction.

So where do the key managers come from? Certainly, in the 1970s and 1980s some of the key managers of change in difficult situations came from abroad—Ian McGregor in steel and coal, Michael Edwardes in cars, Graham Day in cars and shipbuilding. Similarly, the Japanese incursion in automobiles represented a significant move towards organizational dynamics that challenged British traditions. Sampson (2005) has even suggested that outsiders are taking over the British establishment, a point confirmed by Augur's work on the City of London (2000). It is consequently clear that British managers have provided few examples of transformational leadership, demonstrating the need for an injection of ideas from the more successful industrial economies.

On whether management is still a weakness in the British economy, the Porter-Ketels Report (2003: 38) has noted:

For the UK, there are three areas that are perceived to result in competitive disadvantages for UK companies: insufficient investment in capital assets and innovation, positioning on low input cost rather than high value, and lagging adoption of modern management techniques. Together, these areas could explain the persistent productivity gap and the low level of innovation of the UK economy relative to the United States and the leading Continental European economies.

The report went on to examine each of these three areas in turn for possible drivers, concluding that the third was the principal explanation that lay behind the first two, indicating how management weakness remains a major problem.

The issue of where managers stand today is obviously a complex one. While we return to this issue in Chapter 12, it is clear that on the one hand management has become the focus of industrial activity, virtually unchallenged internally or externally. Moreover, the end of ideological differences both at political and institutional levels has been a major step forward in raising the standing of management. On the other hand, managers have suffered increasing insecurity arising from rapid corporate change and the 'end' of the lifetime career, with delayering, outsourcing, redundancy or early retirement, and the decline, if not the destruction, of the concept of the deep hierarchy which had been central to managerial capitalism. At the same time, while there have been intimations of the death of middle management, these were premature, even if the gap between levels within management, with top managers being paid (or paying themselves) increasingly large salaries, has grown considerably over the last decade. Power, indeed, moved upwards to the top, often aided by consultants, who, as Sampson (1995: 209) pointed out, 'usually strengthened the hands of the chief executive who hired them'.

CONCLUSIONS

Having charted the dramatic post-war changes in the status and position of managers, it is clear that in comparison with Figure 3.1, by 2000 most of the drivers affecting the emergence of managerial capitalism had moved to the left-hand side of the diagram. This move is represented in Figure 5.2, indicating how apart from some infrastructure and labour market difficulties (see Chapter 9) the British environment had become much more conducive to the operation of managerial capitalism. While again we must note that these force-field diagrams are merely indicative of the total environment, at the very least they provide a clear representation of the balance of our drivers. Crucially as far as Figure 5.2 is concerned, it is almost exactly the same as Figure 4.1 for the United States, with the obvious caveat that the changes happened much later in Britain. Complementary to Figure 5.2 is Table 5.2, for which we are much indebted to Howard Gospel. Table 5.2 presents in a helpfully encapsulated form the state of markets and the industrial characteristics of the 100 largest firms at various points during the twentieth century. All the columns show very considerable change over time, even if some of the dimensions such as open product markets, concentrated financial markets, and labour market elasticity have similarities at each end of the century. But there are also linear transitions: the growth in multinationalism; towards the end of the century, the rapid decline in membership of employers' associations; and central to the Chandlerian argument about structure, the move from S-, H-, and U-form organizations to the M-form, and finally the globalization of the leading firms. While space limitations prevent us from embarking on a deeper analysis of Table 5.2, one can only conclude that the business environment in which managers operated had changed beyond all recognition over the course of the twentieth century, providing by the 1980s and 1990s especially a much more conducive environment for managerial capitalism (see Figure 5.2) and precipitating the creation of a much more professional approach towards management.

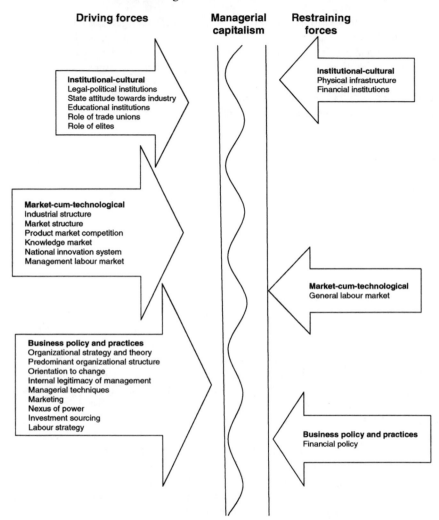

Figure 5.2. The force-fields at work in the UK in 2000

Moving on from these wider diagrammatic perspectives, the key questions at this stage of our analysis are how far Britain's post-war economic problems could be laid at the feet of management, as opposed to various structural, labour, and macroeconomic policy alternative sources of blame, and how far it can be credited with the improvements since the 1980s. On these issues, Caves (1968: 300) advised caution, arguing:

One must tread with special caution in evaluating the quality of British industrial management. Its indictment all too often rests upon a process of elimination: after more

Table 5.2. Markets and firms in Britain, 1906–98

	Markets labour	Markets product	Markets finance	Top 100 % of total labour force %	Top 100 type of large firm S, H, U, M %				Top 100 multinational	Top 100 membership of an employers' organization %
					S	H	U	M		
1906	High elasticity	Open-collusive	Concentrated family patient	8.5	37			0		
1935	Low elasticity	Closed-collusive	Dispersed	10.8	6	42	52	0	10	49
1955	Low elasticity	Closed-collusive	Dispersed	21.3	4	48	46	2	24	55
1972	Low elasticity	Open-competitive	Dispersed	22.9	0	63	24	13	44	45
1998	High elasticity	Open-competitive	Concentrated institutional impatient	17.5	0	9	2	89	67	2

Source: Gospel (2006).
Key: S-form—single-unit firm; H-form—holding-company; U-form—unitary, more centralized, and functionally organized; M-form—multi-divisional.

tangible factors have been tried and found wanting as satisfactory explanations of inferior performance, British management incurs calumny by default.

Having said this, however, he went on to provide categoric evidence of deficiencies, using Dunning's research that we have already quoted (see Productivity and Production Management, Chapter 5). A dozen years later, and expressing the same caveat, Caves (1980: 173) used regression analysis to evaluate productivity differences between industries, including some variables designed to assess the management dimension. This exercise led to the conclusion that: 'I found strong statistical evidence to support the negative influence on industrial productivity of both poor labor-management relations and deficiencies in British management.' Moreover, he found that productivity performance in Britain was relatively good in process industries in which the speed of work was machine-paced, whereas it deteriorated in assembly-type industries in which the pace of machines was not controlled and in those which required large management cadres with high levels of administrative skill. Broadberry (1997: 398) largely agrees with this, noting that

The poor performance occurred largely as a result of an unsuccessful attempt to apply American mass production techniques ... opposition by craft workers to a technology that undermined the value of their skills and took away control of the labour process from the shop floor, coupled with a hesitancy among managers to assume the responsibilities required to operate the American methods profitably, led to a serious deterioration in industrial relations.

Quail (2002: 14) for his part argues that 'there were embedded interests which structurally tended to preclude the take-up and deployment of the elements of managerial structure and technique in the UK'. As Grey (2005: 59) also notes, managers and management can be seen 'as being embedded in a particular, historically bounded and philosophically informed, view of the world', indicating how one must look at the broader context for a clearer understanding of their position and status. Clearly, the barriers to more effective operation were structural and associated with power and thought, features that proved remarkably difficult to break. In effect, then, the divorce between ownership and control was a necessary, but not a sufficient, condition for the managerial revolution: other traditions needed to be assaulted before change could be effected.

While other factors undoubtedly contributed to Britain's problems, weak management structures and poor levels of managerial skill clearly contributed. It will also have been noted that several of the weaknesses identified, those associated with coordination and control, were arguably connected with the prevalent H-form organization of the early post-war period. Governance through corporate accountability to shareholders in this period was also weak. Markets, technologies, and the legal framework all had their importance, and were stressed by Chandler (1990), but relatively little attention was given by him to the managers themselves. And yet, as Quail has argued (2002: 15) 'experience has shown that management capacity is the pre-condition for successful operation; size is not the pre-condition of management capacity'. Nevertheless, Britain did manage to make the transition from proprietorial capitalism to managerial capitalism, and then again to financial capitalism, with implications for economic welfare which are still to be resolved. These are all issues that will be further explored over the course of the following chapters, leading to a concluding analysis in Chapter 12 that attempts to provide a reasoned overview of the current state of British management.

Part III

Managers in Context

6

Managers—The Social and Cultural Environment

INTRODUCTION

This chapter is the first of three which examine the wider environmental context within which managers have operated, rather than being concerned with the internal aspects of the organization. In doing so, it is primarily focused on the third theme of the book, social attitudes towards industry, although there are also implications for the slow transition towards professionalism, as well as echoes of the first two themes. It is also strongly affected by the cultural and institutional drivers we noted in the discussion following Figure 2.4, many of which contributed to the mix of drivers which were conducive to the creation of large-scale business and the establishment of substantial management cadres in the United States, Germany, and Japan, as we saw in Chapter 4. On the other hand, as we saw in Figure 3.1, many of the restraining forces limiting the development of managerial capitalism in Britain were cultural or institutional.

The concept of a social and cultural environment embodies many complex but intangible issues such as class, history, status, tradition, and identity—all of which collectively add up to a national psyche and have a massive influence on politics, policies, and institutions, as well as our own area of interest—management development. Thus, of those who have taken a cultural perspective when addressing Britain's problems, a not uncommon assumption is that 'the UK's economic and political history had conspired to programme a lack of powerful, high level, and sustained concern for industrial prowess and technical progress into the country's psyche and into its economic, financial and social institutions' (Glover 1999: 128). The majority of the sections in this chapter take up issues that comprise this national psyche as it has affected management, namely, the role of elites, public and state attitudes towards industry, management as a career, and the psychology of industrialists.

After assessing these debates, the final section of the chapter is taken up by an examination of the managerial labour market, in order to understand who the managers were in terms of background and education and their progression within organizations, using surveys from the 1950s to provide a snapshot in historical time. As we shall see, the labour market was itself strongly influenced by cultural and institutional factors, although additionally by dimensions of our first two themes. This chapter then serves to provide a background for Chapters 7 and 8, where we examine training and education, the links between management theory and practice, and the nature of professionalism within British management.

THE ROLE OF ELITES

It is apparent that in the nineteenth century, and for at least the first half of the twentieth century, Britain had three elites: the financial and commercial elite centred on the City of London, the professional middle classes, and the landed aristocracy. In comparison with these groups, industry had low status and relatively little importance in setting policy, standards, or values. One important way of helping to explain this is to use Rubinstein's (1994: 24) insightful argument that 'Britain's was *never* fundamentally an industrial and manufacturing economy; rather, it was, *always*, even at the height of the industrial revolution, essentially a commercial, financial and service-based economy whose comparative advantage always lay with commerce and finance'. Viewed in this way, it becomes more understandable why Britain's institutions and culture did not accord to industry the primacy and support that it had elsewhere. Following on from this, many have claimed that the energies and much of the esteem that were put into industry in other countries were in Britain channelled into other activities, leading to a distinctive view of both management and being a manager that undermined the drive towards managerial capitalism. As Thompson (2001: 76) argues:

What the Victorians did have was ... an entrepreneurial culture which in general infused the conduct and definition of business affairs, but whose influence in wider spheres of government ... let alone elite society, was at best patchy and most of the time was not in serious contention with older and more powerful traditions.

Moreover, although the political and social power of industry did grow after 1880, Thompson (2001: 83) contends that business was not united in defending the enterprise culture. 'Free trade, inherited privilege, minimalist government, all these became issues in internecine disputes amongst businessmen, not battle standards in a class war.'

Of the three main elites, the financial and commercial elite has probably had the greatest influence on Britain's economic policy but since it is considered in more detail in Chapter 11, it is not further considered here. In considering the professional middle classes, we are referring to the 'higher' professions: law, medicine, the civil service, academia, the Church, the military, and emerging groups such as accountancy and journalism. The basic argument of both Rubinstein (1994) and Perkin (1987) is that the professional middle classes centred in London provided an alternative and in many respects more appealing model for values, status, and careers than did industry. As Perkin (1987: 376) concludes, in arguing against the so-called gentrification hypothesis: 'The decline of the industrial spirit, then, was in reality the retreat of the entrepreneurial ideal before the incursions of professionalism.'

Nor did industry have much in common with the other main elite of the nineteenth century, the landed aristocracy. Although the extent to which the aristocracy did help to initiate and finance industry, not to mention sitting on its boards of directors, should not be underestimated, and from the 1880s industrialists were in increasing numbers being elevated into the aristocracy (Pumphrey 1959), there remained an enormous social gulf between the two groups. At the same time, industrialists neither acted in concert as a pressure group nor did they become a significant elite in their own right, other than at the local level (Howe 1984). Certainly, some manufacturers were elected to Parliament, but this tended to happen when they were older than other new entrants. Moreover, they were mainly interested in local issues, and rarely had the rhetorical skills to make a persuasive case. Even when they were successful and rose to prominence, industrialists were too often seen as nouveau riche by the professional middle classes, minimizing their impact on society generally.

Indeed, recognition of business in comparison to other roles remained low. In the 1950s, after conducting a comparison of *Who's Who* and *The Directory of Directors*, Copeman (1955: 67–8) discovered that only one in ten of the people mentioned in the former was listed in the latter. Conversely, it was also found that about one in ten of the persons mentioned in the latter featured in the former. Moreover, some of those mentioned were likely to be in *Who's Who* not because of their role in business but because they were distinguished in some other way. By comparison, nearly a quarter of those in *Who's Who in America* held leading positions in business which appeared to involve directorships. Given that *Who's Who* is some indication of social recognition or distinction, the data indicate that business had greater public esteem in America than in Britain, while in the latter much more importance was attached to success in politics, the professions, or civil and military service.

PUBLIC ATTITUDES TOWARDS INDUSTRY

Attitudes towards industry were inevitably related to other facets of British social and economic life. One important dimension of these was the North–South divide, and particularly the position of London. More so than in almost any other country, London has been for hundreds of years dominant in almost all facets of British life, a feature that persists to this day. It is in London that one can find the country's major centres for a host of activities—the financial and commercial sectors, the professions, entertainment and the arts, politics and the civil service, the press, dominated by national rather than local newspapers, and more recently television, and, of course Society with a capital 'S'. Consequently, the middle classes were overwhelmingly in London or the nearby 'Home

Counties'. The only major feature of British life not dominated by London, at least until the twentieth century, was industry. Indeed, up to the First World War, London and industry had little in common: socially, economically, or financially. The 'dark satanic mills' image of industry portrayed by Blake's poem *Jerusalem* certainly did not help, while Dickens was in mid-century an aggressive portrayer of the 'evils' of industry, having visited Manchester and been appalled by what he saw. His *Hard Times*, with its Coketown, Gradgrind, and especially Bounderby the manufacturer, created images which many of his readers accepted as a social reality. As Thompson (2001: 79) notes, 'Bounderby is the supreme anti-industrial image of the industrialist, a caricature of mean, harsh, narrow materialism of production for production's sake and wealth for wealth's sake seized on by those who denounced industrialism and all its works.' While many handcraft activities flourished in the capital, industry was an alien world to most in the South until it began to experience its own industrial development in the new industries of the interwar period. It is, indeed, possible to conceive of two separate economies in Britain, with only limited interaction between them. Moreover, of the two the industrial sector was not the larger or the more important, in spite of the international significance of the Industrial Revolution and tags such as 'the workshop of the world'.

Yet in spite of these claims of industrial supremacy, it is still possible to note that a different perspective on the role of business in Britain has prevailed compared to other countries, a sharp reflection on which are the views of Mr P. A. Best, general manager of Selfridges, the leading retail store. In comparing British and American perspectives, he claimed that (1921: 217–18):

Britain, although a nation of shopkeepers, despises shopkeeping owing to the persistence of the feudal spirit. The employer as the equivalent of the feudal overlord does not expect a large measure of intelligence in those inferior to him. It is this which is keeping down the creative spirit in business. In the second place, the public has become the overlord inasmuch as they look to the server as inferior to those served. In this country, we consider that the person who is being served is the superior being, and that is why business is unconsciously handicapped. Therefore, since service or work is the mark of inferiority and the aristocrat is the man of leisure we have come to consider that the man of leisure is the superior being. The British businessman aspires to be a gentleman of leisure and spends no more time than is necessary for the continuance of the business .... The American attitude is very different. American aristocracy is essentially industrial; it is not the man of leisure but the man of action who is the aristocrat. In America the man who serves the community is the businessman. Since the American community is industrial, success is measured by dollars and there is a strong tendency to plutocracy ... I look to the time when our public schools and universities will realize more fully that business is amongst the noblest occupations in life.

Having pointed out these characteristics, one should also return to Rubinstein's thesis (1988: 56–7) that Britain was not so much anti-industry as pro-commerce, finance, and the services, where its comparative advantage lay. 'It was the pull of Britain's persistent comparative advantage, especially that of the supreme electromagnet, London, perfectly rational in economic terms, rather than any push given by Britain's institutions, class structure, or prevalent "spirit", which accounts for the secular shifts in Britain's economy and its manufacturing decline.' At the same time, one should also add that these favoured sectors did little if any better than manufacturing in developing the management skills required to cater for the organizational elaboration on which their futures would depend. Although as we have seen in Chapter 3 the commercial banks instilled a professional approach into its branch managers, even here proprietorial capitalism continued to dominate the hierarchy, limiting the impact of innovations at the lower level.

A second major point made by Rubinstein (1994: 25–44) is also pertinent, because in noting that there were anti-industrial elements operating in rival economies, he highlights more subtle aspects of the debate that we examine further in a later section (State Attitudes towards Industry). As an indication of how this feature worked, James (1990: 96–7) has demonstrated that nineteenth-century German culture remained 'anti-modern, pessimistic and specifically anti-industrial', with a strong family tradition dominating management recruitment patterns well into the following century. It was also certainly the case that industrialists were resented for flaunting their wealth in the United States, with a substantial anti-industrial component of the national mood represented by the 'muckrakers' that Thorstein Veblen (1899) evoked in his famous diatribe on conspicuous consumption in *The Theory of the Leisure Class*. At the same time, one should stress that the anti-industrial influences were nowhere near as vituperative as those in the UK, indicating how the institutional-cultural group of drivers were heavily negative compared to those in the United States, Germany, and Japan.

Attitudes to industry also had a rather different impact on the development of management, through the shaping of the political party system. It was the role of the unions in the creation of the Labour Party which gave Britain its political divide centring on the ownership of the means of production. In not only exacerbating the industrial divide between management and workers, but also challenging managerial legitimacy as servants of capital, this thereby reinforced negative attitudes towards both industry as a way of life and management as a career.

Furthermore, these attitudes did not disappear over time, even if they might have ameliorated a little as light industry came to the South from the 1920s. Indeed, to some extent they were reinforced by the relatively poor performance of the manufacturing industry in Britain in the 1960s and 1970s, creating something of a vicious downward spiral. In addition, the poor image was further reinforced by the tendency of parts of the national media to give undue prominence to stories that dramatized conflict and showed industry in an unfavourable light. Certainly, industrial failure was rated more newsworthy than success, with stories of major export contracts rarely meriting much space, especially compared to a significant strike or firm closure. This exposure was then reflected by the foreign media, reinforcing the downward spiral as Britain came face-to-face with the global traumas of the 1970s.

It is consequently not too surprising to find a plaintive official document like 'Industry, Education and Management' (DoI 1977: 1) bemoaning that: 'Many people seem to have too little understanding of, and respect for, the role of industry as the major creator of wealth which makes better living standards possible, including increased social provisions.' It went on to outline a litany of social problems, including the short-term profit mentality, a lack of corporate welfare, the attractiveness of careers in the professions, and generally poor standing of manufacturing industry. For a governmental document to be saying such things, and in such pessimistic terms, in the last quarter of the twentieth century indicates how deeply entrenched these attitudes had become. Indeed, they resonate even into the twenty-first century, with James Dyson, arguably Britain's most entrepreneurial manufacturer of his generation, arguing that the odds are still stacked against British manufacturing and engineering companies: 'Culturally, we are taught that manufacturing is dull, boring and rather exploit-ative' (quoted in *The New Zealand Herald*, 2 March 2005).

STATE ATTITUDES TOWARDS INDUSTRY

Apart from affecting the attitude towards business and management, the prevail-ing culture that has been discussed in the previous two sections also contributed significantly to Britain's state policy and institutions, including educational institutions which paid almost no attention to the needs of industry (see The Educational Context, Chapter 7), legal institutions which looked benignly on the emergence of inefficient anti-competitive behaviour, and a political system which until the early twentieth century espoused a laissez-faire role for the state. The latter was especially interesting, given how, as we saw in Chapter 4, the main competitor countries were making industrial growth a major feature of national policy, often accompanied by tariff protection based on the need to protect infant industries. In particular, from the mid nineteenth century the British state incorporated the component aspects of the Manchester School of Economics, namely, an emphasis on competition, free trade, and minimalist government, thereby discouraging government involvement in industry.

Although protection for British industry became an important issue at the turn of the century, and indeed split the Conservative Party (Marrison 1996), the pressure was unsuccessful. Not until the 1930s amid the depths of the Depression did Britain adopt protection, some time after British industry had been badly hurt by the debilitating impact of the First World War, followed by the return to the Gold Standard in 1925 at an unrealistic rate. The latter reflected how the Treasury was much more concerned with financial interests, with successive British governments basing their macroeconomic policies on the three major tenets of neoclassical economics, namely, restoring the pound sterling to the gold standard, balancing the annual budget, and pursuing free trade (Pollard 1992: 105–11). Even though business interests had in 1917 created the Federation of

British Industry (FBI) as a political lobbying organization, they were never able to convince politicians and civil servants of the need for a radical rethink (Roberts 1984: 93). There was some governmental tinkering on the margin, with limited protection introduced in 1921 for strategic products such as aircraft engines, optical glass, and fine chemicals, while in reorganizing the railway industry in 1921 and establishing the British Broadcasting Company (1922), Imperial Airways (1924), and the Central Electricity Board (1926), government ministers were responding to obvious weaknesses in the market, which had resulted in chaotic disorganization (Roberts 1984). It was also directly as a result of government prompting that in 1926 ICI was formed, revealing the general acceptance of a pragmatic interventionist policy at official levels for much of the interwar period. At the same time, this hardly represented the kind of interventionist strategies pursued by American, German, and Japanese governments up to the 1940s.

The decisive watershed in governmental attitudes was clearly the traumatic aftermath of the Wall Street Crash of 1929, when mass unemployment became a feature of most industrialized economies. While at no stage was a coordinated industrial strategy ever elaborated, not only did Britain become a heavily protected market, but also during the 1930s British governments intervened in a series of staple industries to attempt to limit the impact of severe market retraction (Roberts 1984: 93). Moreover, after 1935 a substantial rearmament programme was implemented, boosting activity in many industries and helping to lay the foundations of a modern corporate economy that materialized after the Second World War. One of the negative implications of these developments, however, was how protectionism provided trade associations with a powerful position, leading in 1948 to the first of a long series of Acts that attempted to limit the ability of business to control prices artificially.

While over the post-1945 era there was a decisive change in state attitudes towards restrictive practices, one should also stress that successive governments responded only weakly to the business alternative to this strategy, namely, intense merger activity (see The 1960s and 1970s: Dimensions of Change, Chapter 5). Although legislation was passed in 1965 to monitor mergers, this made hardly any impact on the creation of a much more concentrated, oligopolistic trading structure (Hannah 1983: 154). Indeed, by forming the IRC in exactly the same year, the incumbent Labour government espoused the virtues of a 'Big is Beautiful' philosophy that became the abiding business theme of that era. Having also been responsible in the late 1940s for an extensive programme of nationalizing crucial industries like transport (railways, roads, and ports), steel, and energy supply (coal, electricity, and gas), Labour had been the architects of the post-1945 corporate economy that prevailed up to 1979. Over the course of the late 1960s, the IRC was involved in ninety projects (Hague 1983: 252–306), including the creation of classic manifestations of the 'Big is Beautiful' philosophy such as British Leyland (in the automobile industry), GEC (electrical engineering), ICL (computers), and Swann-Hunter (shipbuilding). Highly ambitious industrial policies were also enacted through new ministries for industry and technology, while building on the previous Conservative government's attempt to introduce macroeconomic planning through the creation in 1962 of the National Economic Development Council, a Department of Economic Affairs was formed as a means of creating greater stability in the economy. Crucially, though, in allowing management to build up either oligopolistic or even monopolistic market positions through intensive merger activity, this provided what Walshe (1991: 379) has described as 'a cushion for managerial incompetence and induced managerial sloth, leading to general losses in industrial efficiency'.

This conclusion might well stand as an indictment of post-war competition and industrial policies in general, given that little of this activity would appear to have boosted Britain's flagging growth and productivity growth records (Crafts and Woodward 1992). It was also one of the clarion calls of a new style of government that came to power in 1979, when under Margaret Thatcher the Conservatives were elected on the promise to overhaul economic performance through the introduction of radical market-based policies that would roll back the role of the state in economic affairs. One of the key elements in this programme was the privatization of nationalized industries, resulting in the floatation of total asset sales worth almost £28,500 million by 1990. While one might argue that privatization was more oriented towards City interests, given the relatively low prices at which most of the firms were floated, and there is little evidence that former nationalized industries were more efficient after privatization, the Conservative message associated with injecting greater private enterprise into the economy was trumpeted extensively across the economy. For example, while in 1975 a Labour government was willing to nationalize Ferranti when this leading defence equipment supplier ran into liquidity difficulties, this option was closed off in 1993 after the firm ran into financial problems arising out of the acquisition of an American rival (Wilson 2006).

State attitudes towards industry had consequently reverted to the non-interventionist approach of the early twentieth century, albeit in the context of macroeconomic policies that were much more hands-on than those followed up to the 1920s. Whatever the period, though, and with the possible exception of the 1960s, it is clear that over the last hundred years business has rarely played much more than a marginal role in fashioning policies that created the kind of environment on which American, German, and Japanese firms could rely in the period up to 1970s. This contrast reflected the British cultural divide between business on the one hand and politics and the civil service on the other, a divide that severely limited the pursuit of cohesive macro- and microeconomic strategies that would have supported corporate strategy and boosted performance.

THE PSYCHOLOGY OF INDUSTRIALISTS

When considering the psychology of industrialists, there are two rather different dimensions: one looks outwards towards a personal role in society, while the other looks inwards to the industrialist's, and by extension the manager's, role in the organization. The external orientation has become associated with the 'gentrification' thesis, which is best associated with the work of Wiener (1981: 154) and the way he places the blame for many of Britain's economic woes on the 'cultural absorption of the middle classes into a quasi-aristocratic elite' after 1850. This thesis claimed that the first generations of industrialists had sent their sons to the public schools of England in order to learn how to be gentlemen, rather than to be scientists, engineers, or managers. Furthermore, he claims that a substantial proportion of industrial wealth was invested in landed estates, leading him to conclude that a process of 'gentrification' had occurred.

While generally appealing, however, this interpretation of British economic history lacks credibility. In the first place, as Rubinstein (1994: 114–15) reveals, there is an interesting paradox in Wiener's thesis, in that financial and commercial interests were the predominant users of public schools, '*yet it was industry which declined* and finance and commerce which continued to prosper'. Another phrase used in this context was the 'Buddenbrooks syndrome', denoting the tendency of firms to lose their dynamism once second- and third-generation owners took over. Yet this term was derived from a German novel written by Thomas Mann which attacks the German, not the British, business classes (Rubinstein 1994: 54). Moreover, as Thompson (2001: 97) notes: 'One need only look up the Hudson Valley at the rows of great mansions and parks of the Roosevelts, Rockefellers, and Vanderbilts, at the Hearst Castle and estate in California, or at the rural retreats of great German business dynasties like the Krupps, the Hoeschs, or the Siemens, to see that in other economies such manifestations of aristocratic tendencies have not been seen as signs of moral or economic decay'. In addition, Rubinstein (1994) has pointed out that since an aristocratic ethos extolling the virtues of landownership and gentlemanly lifestyles had dominated British society for centuries, it could not suddenly have been implanted in late-nineteenth-century Britain. In any case, industrialization was accepted and encouraged by the ruling aristocratic class prior to 1850, as Landes (1969: 8) has observed. This is a point further developed by Payne (1990: 33–4), who emphasizes how British aristocratic values were far from anti-industrial; even if society remained stratified and hierarchical, this does not necessarily mean that the middle classes suffered a net loss of talent to landownership.

Given the substantial weight of evidence undermining the claims of any secession from industry by the entrepreneurs and their families, the Wiener case is unproven. Most Lancashire cotton-textile families 'retained a lifelong interest in their firms' (Howe 1984: 43–6). This group was actually more concerned with securing social and political power as the 'cottonocracy', rather than aspiring to enter a different social grouping, establishing their own regional elite as a means of imposing political control over their localities. On a more general level, Rubinstein (1981: 178) has concluded from his survey of the wealthiest people in nineteenth-century Britain by claiming that: 'Most businessmen ... were simply carried along by their seemingly pre-ordained roles as successors to their fathers and grandfathers ... [and] had no desire to rise above their family firms and become something greater.' While some may have acquired or constructed houses in the country, this was more often a response to deteriorating urban living conditions, while such assets could be employed as collateral against bank loans or other forms of credit. It is consequently misleading to claim that British industrialists were absorbed by the aristocratic elite, a point further reinforced by the preference among the new breed of businessmen to retain control and ownership of their firms within the family and limit outside interference within the organization. It is therefore at the microlevel that one might look for a cultural explanation for backwardness, given that a business culture which placed so much emphasis on family control and ownership would have acted as a constraint on the development of organizational innovations like functional departmentalization and the professionalization of management. Thompson (2001) concludes his comprehensive review by noting that the real straightjacket was not gentrification, but that industrialists were paternalistic, hierarchical, conservative, and inward looking.

Having rejected the gentrification hypothesis, it is clear that the internal dimension of industrialists' psychology is more important for our purposes. We have seen from our definitions of personal and proprietorial capitalism that industrialists did not take easily to devolving power and authority, even at the expense of ignoring strategic considerations. One dimension of this was that they wanted the power for themselves, but two others were the belief that managers were born not made, and that managers were not to be trusted. One expression of these sentiments came from no less a person than John Stuart Mill, who wrote in his *Principles of Political Economy* (1844, quoted in Winter 1993: 182):

Management, however, by hired servants, who have no interest in the result but that of preserving their own salaries, is proverbially inefficient, unless they act under the inspecting eye, if not the controlling hand, of the person chiefly interested: and prudence almost always recommends giving to a manager not thus controlled a remuneration partly dependent on the profits; which virtually reduces the case to that of a sleeping partner.

It is a comment that reinforces the earlier points made (see Industrialization and Management to the 1870s, Chapter 3), where we noted that the lack of trust in managers acted as a significant obstacle to organizational evolution during the first industrial revolution.

Attitudinal differences also existed within British management, with stratification persisting well into the late twentieth century. Senior management were distanced from middle and lower management by class background and education, while in physical terms this was manifested in the construction of separate refectories and lavatories for the many ranks that emerged out of this delineation of status. As Child and Partridge (1982: 137) argued: 'The major break in the vertical structure of British companies today comes between shopfloor supervision and management proper, rather than between supervision and shopfloor.' This increased the gap between management and men, creating a sense of isolation that would only exacerbate tensions when they arose (Tiratsoo 1999).

While industrial management was never regarded as a highly prestigious career by the wealthier classes, equally within its ranks there existed similarly stark differences in status and privilege that mirrored wider social divisions.

MANAGEMENT AS A CAREER

In assessing the general attitudes towards management as a career, it is useful to employ Rubinstein's notion (1988) that there is a difference between a search for security and a search for status. In particular, he argues that on both grounds the drift to the professions, the military, teaching, the civil service, and the South-East of the country was quite logical in terms of bright young people looking to a career. Indeed, most of these bright young men were already in the South as sons of middle-class parents with professional backgrounds. The days of young working-class educated graduates did not arrive until well after the Second World War. An exception would have been Scotland, although even here a move to Glasgow or Edinburgh reflected similar trends. Moreover, managerial jobs were not only relatively poorly paid when compared to the professions, but also provided distinctly uncertain promotion up the hierarchy, given the attitudes of industrialists under personal and proprietorial capitalism. Companies also had competitive market situations and far from infrequent liquidations, while whole industries were subject to the swings of the trade cycle and the process of de-industrialization substantially reduced opportunities, especially in the older staple industries. So who could blame young men for settling for security, especially if it also carried higher status? Even for those from within business, which was growing as a proportion of the workforce until after the Second World War, there was an intergenerational drift away to other jobs with more security and status.

Reinforcing all this, of course, was the limited demand for managers, a point clearly elaborated in Chapter 3. On the one hand, the small size of many companies severely restricted the idea of a 'career' or even a vacancy for a manager as such, as opposed to a functional skill. And even in the larger companies that emerged from the merger movements of the 1890s and interwar decades, organizational hierarchies rarely emerged from the process, further limiting the demand for management trainees. When one combines this with the 'born not made' philosophy to be further analysed in Chapter 7, it is clear that the preference for nepotism over merit in managerial appointments would have compounded all the other problems

And there was little in the way of positive urging. The public schools primarily educated their students for professional careers because that was what the pupils' families expected. This was also largely true of the universities, with some exceptions where special technical or scientific departments were set up with support from local industry (Keeble 1992). As Perkin noted (1987: 119): 'It was the public-school masters and university tutors ... who held up the ideal of selfless public service in the professions and in government at home and in the empire, and it was the sons of middle class, both professional and business men, who most fully imbibed those values from them.' However, Hicks (2004) outlined how the universities failed to set up appointment boards; Oxford for all its other failings did so as early as 1893. And dribbles at first, and then larger numbers, made their way into industry. It is also clear that this system worked reasonably effectively for much of the twentieth century, undermining any claims that universities lacked the appropriate mechanisms to channel graduates into industry. On the other hand, there was never a thumping drum announcing that a career in industrial management was the best opportunity for graduates, reflecting general attitudes towards this track.

Given these factors, it is not surprising that management had a poor image as a career. In stark contrast, writing in 1896, C. R. Henderson (quoted by Bendix 1956: 256) was positively lyrical on American industry as a career:

In this country the great prizes are not found in Congress, in literature, in law, in medicine, but in industry. The successful man is praised and honored for his success. The social rewards of business prosperity, in power, in praise, and luxury, are so great as to entice men of the greatest intellectual faculties. Men of splendid abilities find in the career of a manufacturer or merchant an opportunity for the most intense energy. The very perils of the situation have a fascination for adventurous and inventive spirits. In this fierce, though voiceless, contest, a peculiar type of manhood is developed, characterized by vitality, energy, concentration, skill in combining numerous forces for an end, and great foresight into the consequences of social events.

On the other hand, the status of alternative careers would never appear to have been anything like as powerful as in Britain, minimizing the competition for the best talent in the United States, and indeed in many other countries.

It is important to note that what was true of management was also true of engineering, given its strong association with industry. In stressing the importance of engineers to the development of management in the United States, one of Shenlav's most telling comments (1999: 25) was that most of those who practised mechanical engineering were from the upper middle class, and that they utilized their elitist attitudes to create a meritocracy. In Britain, of course, as engineers rarely came from the upper middle class, they could never be described as an elite. Similarly, in Europe engineers were from higher-class backgrounds. As Ahlstrom (1982: 98) noted:

Like most students in higher education in nineteenth century Europe, those in higher technical education in France, Germany and Sweden were usually drawn from the middle class, but a notably large and growing proportion came from the upper classes, too ... at the turn of the century in Sweden, for example, almost 95 per cent of the total number of students at the technical universities belonged to the upper and middle social classes, the highest group contributing almost 50 per cent of the total number.

Figures such as these would have been totally unbelievable in Britain, indicating how substantial social barriers had been erected between specific groups and careers, often with detrimental effects on recruitment and quality. Indeed, in Britain the engineers' main activity, production, has been the least popular of the management functions. As the DoI (1977: 30) noted:

Arguably production management ... is the most difficult work in industry, needing greater ability than any other work in industry. It is also the least glamorous: those in production work in less pleasant physical conditions than their colleagues, they are in the front line in dealing with industrial relations ... and in Britain they tend not to carry much weight in strategic decision-taking despite their central responsibilities.

This is a view that accurately summarizes the situation right up to the present day.

THE MANAGERIAL LABOUR MARKET

Attitudes to management as a career were, of course, also based on the reality of career structures as depicted in the managerial labour market, which in part reflected the mirror of society's views about management and in part was a function of organizational policy and practice. We have touched on aspects of the nineteenth-century managerial labour market in Chapter 3, while changes in organizational structure noted in Chapter 5 and the dimensions of management development that we examine in Chapter 7 have also played a part in influencing the way in which the labour market has operated. Our aim in this particular section is to take a snapshot of the managerial labour market as it existed in the 1950s, long enough ago to have a historical perspective, but also recent enough to identify the beginnings of changes towards the present. The 1950s were also convenient in that this was the decade in which growing interest in management encouraged survey research into what was happening in the market, notably by the Acton Society Trust (1956) and Clements (1958). Clements' survey consisted of interviews with 646 managers in a wide range of company sizes in Lancashire and Cheshire, while the Acton Society survey consisted of 3,327 managers in large manufacturing companies of more than 10,000 employees.

A starting point for reviewing the managers of the 1950s is Clements' detailed allocation of his respondents to social, career, and educational categories, as shown in Table 6.1.

Judging from this evidence, more than half the managers had risen from the bottom, meaning that they started without special favours, training or opportunities in jobs that were populated by millions of others who had never risen from this level. At the same time, the group who left school after the age of 15 is only half that of those who left at 15 or earlier. Almost all of those rising from the bottom did, however, engage in part-time studies for several years, with 40 per cent of the later leavers and 25 per cent of the earlier leavers obtaining 'professional' qualifications. Moreover, while on-the-job training had proven important, especially technical apprenticeships, this part-time study seems to have been

Table 6.1. Types of managerial career by social origin

	Types of career						
	Crown prince	Managerial trainee	Pre-qualified specialist	Special entrant	From the bottom	From the bottom and left school early	Total
Social origin—father's occupation							
Professional/high administrative	25	33	38	27	8	0	131
Managerial/executive	3	16	32	28	23	5	107
Higher supervisory	0	8	22	12	15	13	70
Lower supervisory	0	6	22	9	34	74	145
Skilled manual/ routine non-manual	0	5	12	2	26	98	143
Semi-skilled manual	0	0	3	1	8	27	39
Unskilled manual	0	0	1	0	0	10	11
Total	28	68	130	79	114	227	646
Schooling							
Elementary only	0	1	4	0	0	156	161
Other secondary	0	0	6	7	17	47	77
Grammar	3	22	73	27	69	19	213
Minor public	6	24	30	30	24	2	116
Major public	19	16	9	9	0	0	53
Other	0	5	8	6	4	3	26
University education							
Graduates	9	51	87	7	10	0	164
Oxbridge	5	42	11	3	1	0	62
Science/technology	5	9	81	3	6	0	104
Number of Directors	23	7	10	7	5	8	60
Average duration of part-time study (years)	1	2	2	4	5	6	4
No. studied part-time	8	44	77	67	109	206	511

Definition of types of career:
1. 'Crown prince' are those whose progress can be ascribed to close family links with the ownership or top management of the firm.
2. 'Managerial trainee' are those recruited for schemes of training for management, open to all to apply for.
3. 'Pre-qualified specialist' are those entering after acquiring qualifications in some skill, at university or professionally such as engineering, science, or accounting. Qualifications included holders of HNC as well as university graduates and members of professional institutes.
4. 'Special entrant' refers to those who did not start at the bottom but were not in the first three categories, such as premium apprentices or trainee salesmen who were not initially marked out for management.
5. 'From the bottom' comprises the last two groups, split between those who left school before and after 15.

Source: Clements (1958), Appendix 2.

important in determining career success in rising from the ranks; indeed, it seems to have been as much a test of character as of academic ability. Nevertheless, many identified the lack of education as a stumbling block in their careers, Clements (1958: 77) concluding that 'a feeling of inferiority' was often expressed by those without formal qualifications, especially in terms of 'putting over a good case owing to a lack of command of words, and of general mind training, and in writing letters and reports'.

The table also identifies the social origins of managers. This reveals how 238, or almost 37 per cent, had fathers who were from the two top groupings, the professional and managerial. All of the others, almost two-thirds of the total, had fathers from a lower social origin than they achieved by becoming managers. Those from the top two groupings also worked disproportionately in the commercial area, while those from the lower level backgrounds did so disproportionately in production. Those who left school at 15 or earlier mainly worked on the production or maintenance sides, with relatively few in commercial, technical, or personnel jobs. Most of them spent over twenty years at work before moving even into lower management. It is these men who rose from the bottom who filled middle- and lower-management posts, albeit with some rising to the top. Thus, their value as managers depended to a large extent on their role in a particular specialist position, rather than as a manager per se, indicating a low level of transferable skills. The skills, moreover, were obtained through experience and little else. Management could thus easily become highly inbred, with much of the promotion into retired or 'dead men's' shoes. Lack of transferable skills was the inevitable result of these deficiencies. Moreover, managers, because of their use of different techniques, formed almost completely non-competing groups; in another sense, though, competition between departments might be quite acute, limiting cooperation and the exchange of complementary knowledge.

Judging from Table 6.1, it is clear that the social system had a profound influence on the lives of these managers before they joined industry, as well as the manner in which they started work, on the types of jobs they first took up and later moved to, and on the speed and extent of their promotion. As Clements (1958; 94–5) concluded: 'The dice has been loaded against those from working class homes and against those of slightly superior social origins becoming managers ... it looks as if industry has been unable to assimilate these men wholly to the social class to which their successful careers apparently lead them, and their social progress has remained incomplete.' In a related sense, Clements was also referring to the lack of adequate selection and training procedures that prepared individuals for their first posts. This adds to the general impression that in the 1950s preparation for management was not taken seriously by most British firms, with personality and background regarded more highly than qualifications as the criteria for most appointments.

As Table 6.1 contains all age categories, it hides the extent to which in the 1950s the labour market was already in transition in terms of education and social class. Younger managers were better educated than the older ones, while a surprising feature was the sharp increase in the numbers of managers from public schools. Thus, only 7 per cent of those born before 1895 were from public schools, whereas 38 per cent of those born after 1925 had a private education. It is consequently clear that some of the social constraints restricting the value of a career in industry were breaking down after the Second World War, even if this process was only happening slowly and did not affect the whole management population.

One of the features of Clements' (1958: 152) survey was the low position of production within the management structure, in terms of both the backgrounds of the managers and the attitude of senior management. Clearly, top managers felt that technical knowledge was not an essential feature of their competencies, given the preference for using the expertise of others. This issue has been further explained by Ahlstrom (1982: 100), who concluded from a comparative study of European production that three key factors were apparent in Britain: the low demand for highly qualified engineers and the engineer's limited chances of entering a career leading to a top post within business; the unsatisfactory development of the engineering profession in Britain and its internal status differences, for example, the element of snobbery in that civil engineers looked down on mechanical engineers; and the generally low status of engineering, so that it was considered a socially unsatisfactory choice of career. In consequence, senior management rarely demonstrated much interest in what was happening on the shop floor, an approach that says much about the relative British failure to develop more extensive control procedures and planning mechanisms.

A final aspect of Clements' study that deserves attention was his scepticism as to whether management possessed the homogeneity for a broadly based occupation. One aspect of this lack of cohesiveness was the diversity of roles it entailed (Clements 1958: 159):

Industrial management appears to be a host of diverse jobs, entailing diverse techniques and experience, different standards and types of education, and different attitudes and sets of principles. It seems that these differences even lead to recognisably different patterns of career, and that different social origins frequently coincide with these other differences. Has the extent to which these people form a homogeneous elite in the social body been exaggerated?

A second such dimension was the difficulty of recognizing the managerial element in a context where the functional role was usually dominant (Clements 1958: 159):

There is scope for more investigation into the nature of 'management'. This enquiry suggests that only in a very tenuous sense not yet fully explored is there much in common between these men called 'managers'.... The great significance of 'non-managerial' qualities in a manager's make-up and career, and the difficulty of identifying 'managerial' capacity account for what appears to be the comparative rarity of movement. If the 'managerial' element were more easily recognised, less difficulty would be encountered in changing firms. It looks as though managers constitute many non-competing groups.

The work of the Acton Society Trust (1956) provides complementary evidence to that of Clements, in particular by providing more detailed evidence in terms of mobility and promotion. As Table 6.2 outlines, there was an especially high correlation between social background and the chances of promotion. Commenting on this table, McGivering, Matthews, and Scott noted (1960: 68) that there

Table 6.2. Factors influencing promotion

Category	Index	Number in category
Advantageous categories		
Arts degree: Oxford or Cambridge	0.68	82
Major public school	0.64	99
Non-technical qualifications	0.56	149
First job: trainee	0.47	253
Arts degree: other university	0.46	49
Higher degree	0.43	103
Science degree; other university	0.31	255
Lesser public school	0.23	373
Grammar school	0.20	648
Technical qualifications	0.13	370
First job: technical or senior clerical	0.13	663
Disadvantageous categories		
Ordinary secondary school	−0.16	771
First job: clerical	−0.17	717
First job: manual	−0.21	529
First job: lab assistant or sales	−0.24	188
Elementary school only	−0.44	450
Has been foreman	−0.52	367

Source: Acton Society Trust (1956: 28–9).

were two barriers to promotion, the first being at foreman level, which was 'seldom regarded *in practice* as the lowest level of management; rather it is the highest rank to which a manual worker could reasonably hope to aspire'. The second barrier involved the step up from departmental manager to top manager, because this was where a public school education would appear to have been the most important recruitment criterion. Social origins would consequently appear to have been the key to promotion, with 50 per cent of the top managers having a public school background, compared to 15 per cent of middle managers.

In Chapter 5, we looked at Granick's argument (1972: 368) concerning what he called 'sub optimization' derived from 'extreme decentralization', and thus the lack of coordination in planning and control. This, in turn, followed from British managerial career systems, given the high degree of specialization exhibited by most managers and the lack of cooperation between functions. Furthermore, as Granick stresses (1972: 56): 'Both middle and upper management in large British industrial companies are recruited to a smaller degree from either a social or an educational elite than is the case in any of the other three countries'. Although Hicks (2004) has recently argued that recruitment from university graduates was from the 1950s highly developed and effective, on the other hand there is widespread agreement that in general British senior managers came from a narrow social elite. In addition, given their lack of training in general management, highly conservative attitudes towards innovation and risk-taking were followed, undermining the competitiveness of British industry (Granick 1972: 50).

Overall, then, the managerial labour market in the 1950s was disorganized and imperfect, displaying a 'silo mentality', namely, the placing of most managers within prescribed territories. Moreover, the vast majority had a poor educational background, most were provided with only narrow functional skills, barely any preparation for top management was incorporated into career planning, whilst there existed extensive social divisions and few had generic, transferable skills. The external labour market was limited by poor information, relatively low mobility, and an absence of qualifications or other indicators of merit, while the internal labour market, as well as being a function of the limited structures in most organizations, had little or no sense of career planning or of broadening perspectives, producing a highly heterogeneous occupation. As Clements (1958: 160) said, 'this sample suggests that so great are the practical differences between [the functional managers] that claims to form a "profession" of management so far have little foundation in reality or theory'. Moreover, it was not just a shared identity for the managers; each company saw itself and its problems as unique.

Change from the system of the 1950s was slow. This is best exemplified by the work of Crockett and Elias (1984) some two decades later, who found that managers were still drawn mainly from the shop floor, and that only a small proportion of the inflow into managerial occupations originated in the educational sector. Even where they did exist, managerial qualifications at the graduate or postgraduate level did not appear to raise earnings. Nevertheless, the trend towards managerial capitalism in the period of structural change from the 1960s (see The 1980s and 1990s: Managerial Capitalism, Chapter 5) brought with it a process of bureaucratization, at least in the larger organizations. Career ladders emerged and 'organization man' became a reality. The functional silos at least partly disappeared, with the rise of incomers trained in general management who nevertheless needed to spend some time within a function. Increasingly, individual managers accepted responsibility for their own careers. As proprietorial capitalism was eroding away, some degree of meritocracy began to take over. This was a slow and cumulative process that is not easy to measure, except in the broad increases identifiable from the decennial census returns, but rather like the tide coming in and filling nooks and crannies of organizational life previously unpopulated by managers.

Clearly, though, meritocracy did not succeed easily and some elements of patronage for the highest jobs continued into the later part of the twentieth century, as Stanworth and Giddens (1975) illustrated in examining the interlocking nature of an established inner circle. But no sooner had the managerial capitalism of the 'organization man' apparently become the norm than it began to be undermined by new processes derived from the impetus towards financial capitalism. In general, there has been a recent move away from internal labour markets to more flexible and externally based markets, with few 'jobs for life' and the termination of 'traditional' career paths. Indeed, Sampson (2005) notes that there has been a trend to control being taken over by outsiders to the traditional social circles, indicating how as a result of financial capitalism and the introduction of flexible labour markets in the 1980s British managers have been forced to adapt to rapidly changing circumstances.

CONCLUSIONS

For much of the period from the late eighteenth century through to the 1970s, it is apparent that the underpinning cultural framework in Britain was not as conducive to either industry or management as it was in the three comparator countries examined in Chapter 4. And these factors, in turn, influenced the political system in two ways. On the one hand, they meant that industry was given little attention by comparison to the dominant interests of the City of London, while on the other, they helped to create the political divide on industrial grounds. The first of these continues to this day; the second only became less important in the last decade. Neither was found to anything like the same extent in the other countries studied; both were antithetical to the development of management as an occupation, one for career reasons, the other for legitimacy reasons.

Following on from this broad generalization, one can also conclude that the managerial labour market was inefficient in several respects. First, it did not attract the same quality of entrants as in other countries. In large part, this was due to the social context in which industry was seen and the unattractiveness of management as a career. A second factor was that becoming a manager did not reward merit; rather, individuals were treated according to the background from which they came. A third factor was that generic management as an identifiable occupation was seen as less important than the functional roles which comprised it. This was partly due to the length of time it took individuals to become managers, but also to the lack of interaction between the functions and the lack of training to widen managers' perspectives. Viewed in these ways, it is not surprising that the labour market, as Clements (1958) noted, did not encourage the concept of management as a profession. It is to this issue of professionalism that we now turn in Chapter 7.

7

The Development of Managers

INTRODUCTION

In focusing on the system of management education, training and development, and in the process expounding on our fourth and final theme, namely, the slow transition towards professionalism, this chapter builds further on what we said about professionalism in the labour market and career sections of Chapter 6, and foreshadows two other important dimensions of professionalism, namely, the body of knowledge and professional institutes, in Chapter 8. In particular, we examine the educational context, including technical provision, followed by the four main modes through which management development has been pursued: in-company training, the use of consultants, professional institutes, and management education and the role of business schools. Finally, we examine the important dimension of the demand for development. In concentrating on predominantly formal systems, however, we recognize, but do not allocate much space to, what has been and arguably still is the most important mode of development for managers, that of experience on-the-job.

Education also reflects and reinforces some of the cultural factors underlying attitudes to management that we examined in Chapter 6, since education not only provides knowledge but also acts as both an indicator of social status and a sifting mechanism into careers. In addition, there is an important demand dimension, in that employers needed to provide training or recruit graduates, demands which were against the instincts of personal and proprietorial capitalists. Indeed, as we see, the lack of demand for professional managers was a key factor in the slow transition to professionalism.

In comparison to her main competitors, Britain has long had deficiencies in her educational and developmental institutions (Handy 1987). This highlights a paradox in Britain in respect of management: although it was the first country to industrialize, it has been the last amongst the developed nations to recognize management as a distinctive economic role, requiring a body of knowledge and standards, and, for the purposes of this chapter, a means of engendering higher efficiency. A prime reason has been a belief that 'managers are born, not made', and that teaching is irrelevant to the acquisition of experience. In 1906, a leading article in the journal *Engineering* announced that 'the success of the manager or foreman depends primarily on personal qualities, an ability to handle people and situations—on something that is inherent in men "born" to be leaders in industry' (quoted in Urwick and Brech 1946: 123). Given this belief, there was no apparent need for education and development. There were attempts, albeit sporadic and without any strong national backing, to set up education and development for managers before the rise of the business schools after 1965, but few of these achieved anything more than limited success. Nevertheless, we do want to argue that development of various kinds has greatly aided the transition towards professionalism in the last two decades.

THE EDUCATIONAL CONTEXT

Before the Industrial Revolution, education in England (Scotland was rather different) consisted of two universities, a range of grammar and public (namely, private, fee-paying) schools founded by and for the gentry, and, although by no means universal, the village school for the children of farmers and craftsmen. The Industrial Revolution created the need for new knowledge, especially for skilled artisans and white-collar workers, the main responses to which were nonconformist academies, which added to the stock of grammar schools, and the mechanics institutes, which flourished from the 1820s to the 1850s (Pollard 1965). Many of the early managers received much of their education at such institutes, which dealt mainly with technological and commercial matters. But they failed to become established in the way of the European technical institutes, partly through having no financial support other than fees, and partly because of the lack of basic education in the absence of any state system of schooling.

In line with Bismarck's dictum that the nation that has the schools has the future, it is the system of general education which provides a critical base for the later training and development of all managers. In this respect, England was extremely weak. When the state began direct provision of primary education in 1879, only 40 per cent of 10-year-olds and 2 per cent of 14-year-olds were officially receiving full-time education. Secondary education lagged still more, with a curriculum that was geared to the needs of universities, even though only a minute fraction went there, and classics predominated to the substantial exclusion of science. Even in 1926, the Hadow Committee found that only 7.5 per cent of the 11–15 age group were in secondary schools of any sort (Aldcroft 1992: 5–6), and the numbers staying on beyond the minimum leaving age of 14 were very small indeed. As a consequence, a high proportion of able children had no education beyond the elementary level, as reflected in the review of Clements' (1958) survey of managers in Chapter 6. After elementary school, there was little prospect of further education or training while in employment, except for those in the formal apprenticeship programmes (which had their own weaknesses) and part-time evening study on a voluntary basis. While after the Second World War, educational opportunities expanded considerably, aspects of quality and attitudes to education remained questionable. Towards the end of the twentieth century, Porter (1990: 497) could still argue that: 'The more serious problem is the education of the average student. British children are taught by teachers less qualified than those in many nations, receive less training in math and science, put in fewer hours, and drop out more.' Underlying these problems of both quantity and quality was that of status; the public (private, fee-paying) schools provided the basic hallmark of the British class system, while 'vocational' alternatives to the university-oriented grammar schools, such as secondary modern schools and technical colleges, had low esteem and were seen to be failures (Aldcroft 1992).

An important factor in the slow remedial action was the relative weakness of the state, compounded by the lack of support for action in the middle classes, who were complacent in their own provision through the public schools. As we saw (see State Attitudes towards Industry, Chapter 6), the Victorian state and to a large extent its successors were committed to minimal regulation, having abrogated any responsibility for industry or its educational and skill requirements. As a consequence, in spite of the warnings about a loss of competitiveness, education was never a priority until after the Second World War. Indeed, many would argue that this remained the case until much more recently. While in other countries to a greater or lesser extent the education system was developed by the state to serve national purposes (see Institutional-Cultural Drivers, Chapter 4), in Britain this has never been the case.

The situation in higher education was no better than secondary schools. The ladder to higher education was for a very small number until almost the end of the twentieth century, in spite of efforts by local merchants and manufacturers throughout the nineteenth century to establish universities, as well as the major boost provided in the 1960s. In 1900, there were just 20,000 university students (0.8 per cent of the age group); in 1924, 42,000 (1.5 per cent); in 1938, 50,000 (1.7 per cent); and in 1960, 100,000 (4 per cent). Clark (1951: 480) ranked the United States top in a sixteen-country survey for the number of university students per thousand population in 1930–2, with 7.88 per cent; England and Wales ranked bottom with 1.21 per cent, although Scotland ranked much higher. Since the 1960s, and more particularly 1980s, there has been a rapid acceleration in two key dimensions: the total numbers studying in higher education and the numbers studying management at university and other parts of tertiary education. Indeed, management and related qualifications have become the largest single group of studies. Perhaps the epitome of this new attitude was reached in 2001: when Oxford University launched the centre of humanities education, it had more applications to study the management undergraduate degree than any other subject.

Thus, until very recently a key consideration for the development of management was quantitative, in that the numbers obtaining higher education qualifications were wholly inadequate to provide an educated management cadre. Furthermore, one should add that there is a considerable time lag between graduation and becoming an effective manager. But numbers were not the only consideration; the further question of content and focus in higher education has also been a major issue, with the domination of humanities education and a disdain for vocational development acting as prevailing attitudes. While Oxford and Cambridge in particular were lost causes for vocationalism in the nineteenth century, it was not just university attitudes; student background did not prove conducive to vocational development. Taking both the ancient universities together in the period 1870–86, only 4 per cent of students had a business background, which was well below the 46 per cent at Harvard at the same time (Sanderson 1972). While the new provincial universities did develop industrial specialisms in their research and teaching which served local and national industry, these departments found it difficult to place their graduates in industry (Keeble 1992).

Even when in the early twentieth century the universities did make attempts to provide vocational training for students, industry made no reciprocal move to recognize these efforts through their recruitment policies. In consequence, by the 1930s the universities had become wary of trying to gear their policies to industry. Meanwhile, the graduates were hardly faced with strong inducements to join industry, given the prospects of starting at the bottom on low rates of pay and facing the uncertainties of the promotion system and the preference for family members. Moreover, companies seemed not to know what to do with them until they had acquired 'practical experience'; often, either they did work which a non-graduate could have done just as well or were left to make their own way. Thus, for a long period, the relationship was not a happy one. Nevertheless, numbers did increase so that by the late 1930s some 25–30 per cent of graduates went into industry, while after the Second World War, there was a rapid increase in the demand for graduates, resulting in the onset of the 'milk round' by which recruiters visited universities en masse. At the same time, as one can see from Figure 7.1, for much of the twentieth century the proportion of senior managers and directors who possessed a university degree remained small when compared to comparator countries, with the gap only closing in recent decades.

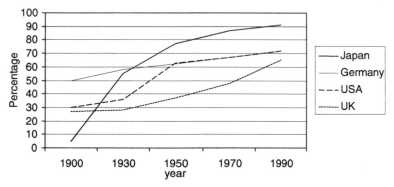

Figure 7.1. Proportion of senior managers and directors with university degrees (*Source:* Hicks 2004)

Moving to the provision of technical education, we have already noted in Chapter 3 that at least a part of the weakness of British manufacturing was attributable to the deficient level of technical skills in British management at all levels. This again contrasts sharply with American engineers (Shenlav 1999), who were at the forefront in the development of management (see Institutional-Cultural Drivers, Chapter 4), while in Germany and Japan similar trends were apparent (see Institutional-Cultural Drivers, Chapter 4). The extent of technical and scientific education was clearly not only a key factor in levering up production efficiency, but also acted as a source of managers. In non-manufacturing industry, on the other hand, it is not so important for managers to have a technical appreciation, which is arguably one reason why Britain has been relatively more successful in these areas.

Early industrial development depended very little on science. Most improvements were mechanical and the prime skills needed were an inventive turn of mind and a practical ability to design and produce machinery; skills were transmitted through apprenticeships and practical experience (Wrigley 1986). Such scientific and technical education as existed depended largely on artisan initiative through the hundreds of mechanics institutes. However, the institutes were in decline by the middle of the century and in no way equivalent to the technical university systems of the continental countries. The dominant form of engineering education well into the twentieth century was a combination of night school and apprenticeships, both of which were conducted outside the main research universities. While this provided mobility between the skilled trades and professional engineering, it also linked being an engineer with the working class and trade unionism, rather than providing social status in the sense of a middle-class profession. Furthermore, it added to the gap between higher education and industry. As late as 1964, about 55 per cent of the qualified engineers in Britain were trained outside universities, mainly in technical colleges, while even in the 1970s there was no first degree available in the key area of production management (Aldcroft 1992: 118). Not only were the technical college engineers likely to be of a lower standard in school attainment, but they were also likely to be taught by instructors with lower qualifications and less access to research themselves than would have been the case in universities. Inevitably, their qualifications were consequently seen by employers as second-rate. As late as 1980, the Finniston Committee on 'Engineering Our Future' found continuing deficiencies in both the education and employment of engineers in Britain. It is also a measure of the continuing problems in engineering that the Committee's sensible recommendations were almost entirely ignored.

Overall, the educational system failed to provide British industry, both quantitatively and qualitatively, with the source of managers, and especially technologically literate managers, that it needed to keep up with other countries. But not all of the faults lie with education; arguably, even more was due to the lack of demand from industry, a topic we return to after examining the various different routes by which managers have been developed. One might stress that while from the interwar period there was considerable growth of internal research in large companies, such as ICI, Courtaulds, Metro-Vicks, BTH, GEC, Lever Bros., and Boots, generally this was not connected to the universities. Similarly, although scientific research was conducted at extremely high levels in British universities, especially in Cambridge and London, again little of this directly addressed industrial needs. This contrasted sharply with the United States and even more so Germany, where the links between industry and the universities were strong.

CORPORATE TRAINING AND DEVELOPMENT

There was little in the way of purposeful in-house training and development for managers before the Second World War. For those managers promoted from the ranks because they had some technical knowledge and sufficient character to maintain discipline, they were obliged to gain experience where and how they could, often on their own initiative, using their wits and their backgrounds in craft activities or trading rather than any formal education or training. As well as experience, patronage through family or social ties was a feature of management recruitment and promotion. Although doubtless some experience and knowledge were transmitted through these ties, either informally or through some deliberate coaching, frequently this was limited to highly practical aspects of any job to be performed. Where specialist skills were required, from about the 1860s British industry often brought in foreign, mainly German, talent, whether technical or managerial. More generally, and in line with our second theme of externalization, the British system of training has been based on market mechanisms and occupational labour markets on which employers were able to rely, especially for skilled manual labour. It was these skilled craftsmen who became the main source of production managers and engineers. Moreover, doing the job at hand was all that mattered; there was little sense of widening managers' knowledge of other activities or developing them for future promotion, even if a few firms provided experience of different departments. In these circumstances, and because firms did not develop strong managerial and technical hierarchies, there was neither a strong need nor incentive to invest in training. Thus, the ability to develop HR within the enterprise was, and remained, weak. Firm structure also mattered; in Britain, there were many small companies and loosely organized larger companies, which lacked the ability to organize effective training systems. Some industries did involve more regulation, predominantly for reasons of safety, especially the mines and the railways, and here qualifications became important. In addition, there were some companies, Dunlop in rubber, Pilkington in glass, Courtaulds in fibres and Nobel in explosives, where Chandler (1990: 265 *passim*) accepts that there was investment in management hierarchies in emerging industries of the Second Industrial Revolution. In general, though, there were relatively few managers and little attention given to their organizational and technical development.

A central focus of development was the apprenticeship system, which was designed for shop-floor level skills, but also acted as the basis for honing higher-level skills required by engineers and managers. These latter skills, however, could only be learned on-the-job or through part-time study on a voluntary basis, since there was no framework in almost any company to provide them more directly. Moreover, the apprenticeship system was itself not a strong base for skill development; at its best, it was dependent on the willingness and abilities of the craftsmen who supervised the apprentices, while at its worst, it was only a cheap form of direct labour for employers. McKinlay (1991) has also argued that both the institutions and the process of apprenticeship experienced a slow deterioration in the fifty years before 1914—a deterioration which accelerated to virtual collapse in the interwar years. A survey in 1925 indicated that in the industry widely regarded as the most generous provider of day release, textiles, only 10 per cent of employers offered this to apprentices. It is also clear that many employers in the interwar years neglected the training of apprentices and systematically used them as a source of cheap, non-union labour.

As generations of owning families became established, the argument that managers, especially at higher levels, are born (from the established family background) and not made became more widespread. Management was seen as an inherited art honed by years of practical experience. For the family members who went into business, there was an apprenticeship which emphasized learning-by-doing. This experience was self-reinforcing; thus, when the younger family members reached director status, they too did not see the value of education. At a lower level, as management was not a recognized occupation, most managers remained close to the shop floor (Clements 1958). In the larger and more structured organizations such as the railways, army officers were common because they were amongst the few who had gained experience of organizing large numbers of staff and operating detailed plans. Indeed, Black (2000) argues that the soldier-technologist was the basis of modern management, and that the Royal Military Academy Woolwich was in effect the first British business school. Overall, though, one might conclude by arguing that the British system of training, both generally and for managers, worked well until after the middle of the nineteenth century and had the great advantage of being cheap. Thereafter, however, it became increasingly inadequate in coping with the new technologies and methods of operation associated with sectors of both the First and Second industrial revolutions.

After the First World War, there was more recognition of the need for managers; indeed, from the 1930s management trainee schemes began to emerge among the larger companies, albeit on the basis of small numbers. (Unilever, one of the largest recruiters, took only eight a year in the late 1930s.) Moreover, the schemes were not always successful. In a survey of 114 firms that took Cambridge graduates in 1936–7, only twelve had training schemes. Thus, before the Second World War, few companies took much interest in, or made much provision for, training their managers. Insofar as there was any interest in training, it was in technical and commercial areas, rather than in generic management or people skills, with the predominant onus being placed on the individual to improve skill levels.

Things began to change slowly after the Second World War, with the tradition of personal self-development declining and more companies introducing some element of in-house training for both graduates and other aspiring managers. Unilever was a leader in this area, with its Unilever Companies Management Development Scheme (UCMDS) starting in 1952, making it the responsibility of top managers to spot potential talent and utilizing psychological tests similar to those developed by the Army for officer selection. While this progressed to taking 100 graduates a year in the UK and a further 100 on the Continent, to put these figures into perspective, some thirty years later UCMDS trainees only amounted to 9 per cent of Unilever managers. There was also an expansion in the number of private training colleges, of which there were estimated to be about 60 in 1965 (Whitley, Thomas, and Marceau 1981: 34). Of these, the Administrative Staff College at Henley and Ashridge College have survived to achieve independent degree-granting status. Even so, change was slow and limited. In a highly publicized survey, PEP (1966: 260) estimated that in the mid-1960s 'of the 450,000 managers in industry today, less than 1 per cent have received any form of external management training; among larger companies it has been estimated that about a fifth have a systematic training scheme, while among the smaller ones there are hardly any'.

At the same time, the more proactive attitudes of government in the mid-1960s resulted in the passage of the Industrial Training Act in 1964 and the establishment of the Central Training Council (CTC) and Industrial Training Boards (ITBs). Two CTC reports provided guidance on the principles, policies, and practices recommended for the attainment of managerial competence, while the various industry boards took a range of actions. One should consequently conclude that these governmental initiatives undoubtedly stimulated interest in management development amongst organizations (Brech 2002a: 437), offering new hope that Britain was catching up on its rivals.

Again, while further progress was made in the 1970s as more companies came to recognize the need for management training, there was a particularly scathing criticism of the situation by Crockett and Elias (1984: 42), using the 1975–6 National Training Survey. They found that the majority of firms did not train their managers for the jobs they held, other than the usual short tour of the establishment. Indeed, a quarter of all managers had not had as much as a single day's vocational training for any job since leaving school. Their conclusion followed from these findings: 'The lack of any clear relationship between vocational, on-the-job training and the earnings of managers, together with the low priority firms place on the training of their managers represents a weak point in current "supply-side" strategies designed to improve economic performance in the UK.'

Over the last twenty years, we have seen some significant improvements in company attitudes to management development, not least as a result of three influential reports in the mid-1980s (Mangham and Silver 1986; Handy 1987; and

Constable and McCormick 1987). It was also a key finding of Thomson et al. (1997) that the higher levels of management education and training of senior managers had contributed to the general growth in manager training, resulting in a self-reinforcing momentum. In response to the target set in the 1980s that managers should receive five day's training per annum, a survey in 1996 found that the average reported by companies with more than 100 employees was 5.5 days. A similar survey in 2000 reported 6.5 days (Thomson et al. 2001). Overall, there was evidence of organizations moving along a spectrum from a 'weak' to a 'strong' management development system, in which a 'strong' system is charac-terized by a planned structure, a policy framework, and effective processes. A key factor was that the demand for training by individual managers had also in-creased substantially, leading to the inference that the rise to the leadership of companies of those who had themselves undergone various aspects of manage-ment development contributed to the willingness of organizations to provide such a service. All this is not by any means to say that an ideal situation has been reached, since the data represent averages, with many falling below. Moreover, there were still structural weaknesses: less than half the organizations with more than 100 employees had a written statement or an explicit budget for manage-ment development, while line managers had a relatively low involvement in the initiation and implementation of management development. Nevertheless, by the standards of twenty years earlier, the situation was much improved.

So far we have been primarily concerned with formal development by organ-izations, ignoring the informal aspects of a system that have always existed, yet unfairly disregarded as a form of training. Moreover, many managers have always engaged in aspects of development outside their employment, from reading to participating in seminars or activities of professional institutes to obtaining qualifications. More recently, various forms of informal development have been made more explicitly part of development policy, and some organizations now have formal systems of mentoring and coaching as part of working on the job. Crucially, these informal development exercises have been estimated to be more significant than those received through formal means (Thomson et al. 2001: 141). Nevertheless, the trend has been towards more formal systems of training; in the series of management development surveys, where in 1996, 35 per cent of respondents said there was more formal than informal development in their organization, while 40 per cent said there was more informal, in the 2004 survey, 41 per cent said there was more formal, while only 28 per cent said there was more informal (Mabey 2005).

THE ROLE OF CONSULTANTS IN DEVELOPMENT

Another route by which training has been initiated in companies was through consultants. Ferguson (2002: 145) has demanded recognition of their role, argu-ing that 'ever since management consulting first appeared as a service in support of organizations, management consulting and consultancy firms have led the way in the development of management thinking and practice'. There have been three main phases in their contribution, beginning in the nineteenth century when individual freelance consultants developed services based on their experiential-developed skills, but with no training for what they were doing, and in which developing managers was an offshoot, not a primary purpose.

In many respects it is the second phase which is of most interest to this study, an era launched by the arrival of consulting organizations, led by Charles Bedaux, a Frenchman who had made his name in the United States. Although organized consultancies were late to develop in Britain compared to the United States and even France and Germany, when they started work from the late 1920s they realized that it was necessary to train managers, supervisors, and operatives in the new methods. Bedaux also introduced the crucially important component of appreciation courses for senior management to ensure buy-in from this group. Additionally, as part of the service, specially selected individuals, commonly referred to as 'Bedaux Representatives', were trained to ensure continuation of the system after the assignment was completed. It was these 'Representatives' who became the forerunners of the training department in some large companies (Ferguson 2001: 98). Thus, ICI's influential work-study departments dated from a Bedaux consultancy. Urwick Orr, PA, PE, and Harold Whitehead were other important British consultancy companies that started in the interwar period, with the first three following Bedaux in focusing on the production area, while the latter concentrated on sales. In the absence of other training mechanisms, these were important catalysts for change in management practice, and indeed the knowledge derived from the assignments became the base of practice elsewhere, often through publishing the results in the emerging management magazines. Another key training innovation was the establishment of the Bedford Work Study School by Urwick Orr in 1941, to train both consultants and practitioners. This was not only valuable in its own right, but provided an inspiration for other consultancy companies to set up management training schools after the war, one of which, PA's Sundridge Park, survived into the twenty-first century.

Although there were only these five substantial consultancy companies until the 1960s, when both American consultancies and the large accountancy firms began to involve themselves, the total impact was not inconsiderable. A conference in 1961 was given some interesting statistics by Urwick of the contributions by members of the Management Consultancies Association (MCA), the gist of which are shown in Table 7.1. Compared with what was available or being produced elsewhere at the time, these were impressive figures. The consultants also tended to be more popular with companies than other modes of training. The major PEP (1966: 265) study of the mid-1960s reported that 'many of the courses provided by consultants, for instance, are well supported in sharp contrast to the weak attraction of the longer courses with a higher "educational" content that the colleges and universities offer'. Other important contributions by consultants were lectures, books, pamphlets, and articles. Indeed, in the absence

The Development of Managers

Table 7.1. Consultants' direct and indirect contributions 1940–60

	1940–55	1956–60
Student weeks of management training	11,858	43,194
Student throughput	2,276	7,042
Firms assisted in starting management training	99	211
Facilities		
Number of external lectures delivered	1,813	1,973
Number of books and booklets published	64	81
Articles published	257	378

Source: Ferguson (2001).

of business schools before 1965 the consultants were the main source of initiative in the management development field.

After the arrival of the American firms and the accountancy companies, which announced the third phase, the amount of training provided by the larger companies, that is, those who were members of the Management Consultancies Association, increased in the mid-1970s, but then began to decline, probably because other providers were entering the field. However, they have maintained an important and increasing role in direct consulting (Kipping 1999; McKenna 2006), without having the same emphasis on training. Nevertheless, significant numbers of individual consultants and trainers are now involved with corporate training programmes, through both in-company tailored programmes and less frequently open programmes. The 2004 Management Development Survey (Mabey 2005) found that 81 per cent of respondents used private providers, meaning consultants, for formal external management development, a higher figure than for any other organizational type.

DEVELOPMENT THROUGH THE PROFESSIONAL INSTITUTES

From their origins in the interwar period, the various professional institutes associated with management were interested in developing formal educational qualifications, with the Institute of Industrial Administration (IIA) the first to do so after its creation in 1920 (Brech 2002*a*). Indeed, education became the main focus of the IIA's existence. As other management-related institutes emerged around the same time, they too developed their own systems. In 1934, four of them: the Works Management Association, the Purchasing Officers' Association, the Office Management Association, and the Institute of Labour Management, created the Confederation of Management Associations (CMA)—one of whose key aims was the development of the common-interest aspects of educational programmes (Brech 2002*e*: 128). In 1939, the CMA drew up a four-year part-time course (with predominantly American texts in the absence of suitable British material) in which the first two years were common to the four associations and the special training required was covered in the last two.

While the War put an end to this initiative for its duration, the plan remained on the table and was taken up by the Urwick Committee on Education for Management, which was appointed in October 1945, with the terms of reference being: 'To advise the Minister of Education on the educational facilities required for management in industry and commerce ... bearing in mind the various requirements of professional organizations and the need for their coordination.' In other words, the focus of the Ministry was on the institutes, rather than the universities or in-company development. The Committee's recommendations were intended to induce the various institutes to include in their syllabuses as large a common management content as possible, confining specialized demands of the various functional fields to an essential minimum. The courses leading to qualifications should be limited to two stages, 'intermediate' and 'final', with the former having a syllabus common to all institutes, while the latter would include the specialist requirements as well as two general and common subjects of management, 'principles' and 'practice'. The common intermediate stage (Certificate) started in 1948–9, with the Diploma in Management Studies being inaugurated in 1952–3 for the general management area, in which the British Institute of Management (or BIM, founded in 1948) had a key role. Clearly, though, the programmes did not develop much momentum, because by 1961 only 810 Certificates and 640 Diplomas had been awarded—a disappointing outcome for such a promising initiative.

In its early days, the BIM did not provide management development, although it did give information and advice on other development schemes. From the late 1950s, however, arising from the demand for seminars on current management practice, the regional and branch offices started to respond. By 1963, the BIM was producing guidance on starting in-company management development schemes, while in 1974 a central BIM Management Development Unit was started (Brech 2002e: 428). This side of the Institute's activities slowly grew, resulting in a situation by the 1990s where the Institute has become much more oriented to both general development and qualifications, in part due to the merger with the Institute of Industrial Managers in 1992.

As Britain has such a wide range of professional institutes, it is not possible to do justice to all their contributions to the development of management as an outcome of their professional roles. The Consultative Council of Professional Management Organizations (CCPMO) was formed in 1966, representing many of the functional management societies which are cumulatively considerably more important and deal with larger numbers than the central institute. Even beyond the recognized management functions, most professional institutes in whatever field have a management dimension. Thus, Harvey and Press (1989), for instance, draw attention to the standards of mining engineers in the late nineteenth century, in spite of their lack of university education, and give credit to these standards to the education and regulation provided by their professional institute. Other examples could doubtless be adduced and the cumulative impact on management would be significant. Indeed, the most important professional institute for management has arguably not been the BIM, but rather the chartered accountants, a point further discussed in Chapter 11.

In retrospect, the early post-war focus on the institutes proved to be a blind alley, because (with the exception of the accountants) neither the professional institutes in the management area nor the colleges, which they used as providers had the requisite recognition or status, compared to universities. Nevertheless, the institutes are now generally healthy and well-established, playing an important part in external management development, with 67 per cent of respondents to the 2004 Management Development Survey reporting that they use professional institutes for this purpose (Mabey 2005). Importantly, a developmental component is now part of almost every professional institute's membership criteria. This is complemented by the almost universal trend to having a continuing professional development (CPD) component in institute schemes as a means of maintaining or achieving higher professional levels.

MANAGEMENT EDUCATION AND THE RISE OF THE BUSINESS SCHOOLS

While Kennedy and Payne (1976: 253) have noted that business schools appeared to have accelerated the diffusion of management techniques and practices in the United States in the first half of the twentieth century, in Britain by contrast they did not exist until after the mid-1960s and such a contribution did not happen. Although there is an understandable argument that the British universities were recalcitrant in introducing management as a subject until the 1960s, this is only part of the story, because there had been efforts to do so much earlier, which were not successful and which deterred others. There were attempts at the LSE, Birmingham, and Manchester to provide management degrees from the turn of the century (Keeble 1992; Whitley, Thomas, and Marceau 1981), but in all cases there was little support from local industry in financing the programmes, sending their own sons, or recruiting graduates. This was not due to the lack of effort on behalf of the programmes, or indeed the capabilities of their main progenitors, since Beveridge at the LSE, Ashley at Birmingham, and Bowie at Manchester were all extremely capable individuals. Rather, what Ashley called 'the remarkable conservatism and inaccessibility to ideas' of industry won the day (quoted in Keeble 1992). All tried to provide some vocational experience for the students, but this required the practical cooperation of industry that was not forthcoming. Indeed, all of the initiatives struggled for money to stay in existence.

So why was British industry so reluctant? A comment by the London Chamber of Commerce about the LSE degree may have some general relevance:

The great majority of employers are not anxious to employ University men or women. They prefer to recruit their staff at the age of sixteen or seventeen, as in most cases the actual experience of office routine is more valuable to the employer than general commercial knowledge. Any responsible posts which cannot be filled by the promotion of men or women already on the staff, are given to applicants of business experience.... While there can be no doubt that the Bachelor of Commerce has a good general background for business work, it is of little value to the employer until a man has had some practical experience (quoted in Keeble 1992: 108).

The most that employers would permit was for their staff to attend evening classes, but even then there was little evidence that those who took the courses benefited from them in boosting their careers. Moreover, such classes were confined to the technical colleges, with the Regent Street Polytechnic, where Elbourne had become Director of Studies in the Department of Administration in 1927, the most outstanding example.

There seems to have been no consideration of the MBA as a suitable degree in the early post-war period, even though it was by then well established in the USA (Locke 1989). Rather, as we have seen above, the Ministry of Education preferred development through the professional institutes. At the same time, though, there was a reasonably flourishing private sector, led by Henley and then Ashridge, and a number of universities provided non-qualification programmes (Wilson 1992). In general up to the 1960s, there was an introverted complacency in the university world about the nature of disciplines and knowledge, combined with no sense of responsibility for the world of work. As a consequence, students did not see industry as an attractive career, compared to the situation in the United States, where the top universities, such as Harvard, Chicago, and Stanford, operated business schools from very early in the century or before, and the best students saw industry as intellectually and socially acceptable. Similarly, in Germany with its *handelshochschule*, or France with the *Grandes Écoles*, attitudes were different from those in Britain. Indeed, by the mid-1960s Britain had still not reached the point achieved by these other countries at the end of the nineteenth century. The first British academic journal in management, *The Journal of Management Studies*, did not appear until 1964.

The main impetus for the spread of management education in the post-war period came not from industry or the universities but from the creation of the Foundation for Management Education (FME) in 1960. This was largely the brainchild of John Bolton, himself a Harvard MBA, but was also driven by various industrialists and MPs, most notably Sir Keith Joseph. At least the FME managed to raise the profile of the area and bring it before the Robbins Committee on Higher Education (1963). Robbins was distinctly ambivalent about teaching managers or prospective managers, but did recommend setting up 'at least two major postgraduate schools'. The Franks Report, published the following year, examined ways to activate these recommendations, with the result that the London and Manchester Business Schools were launched in 1965 (Wilson 1992). Industry did provide a considerable amount of the funding through the Council of Industry for Management Education, which actually raised £5 million against a target of £3 million, and a further appeal enabled additional funding to be provided to other universities, Warwick and Bradford in England, and Glasgow, Edinburgh, and Strathclyde in Scotland. This was a major step forward in the creation of business schools, encouraging other universities to increase their efforts in what was clearly a promising field for university expansion.

But even then the new business schools did not have an easy time, especially in relation to industry's expectations. London and Manchester essentially wanted to recreate the American model of management education, and especially the two-year MBA (Wilson 1992). Industry for its part did not want the business schools to produce young, academically qualified managers; what it wanted was practical training for existing middle managers through post-experience courses, many of which were well supported. Nevertheless, the business schools did begin to make considerable headway in the 1970s through four main routes. Perhaps the most important aspect of the move forward was that the division between the business schools and industry was at least partially resolved, largely because the schools opened up part-time and later distance-learning qualifications which could be taken by existing managers without being absent for a year, or worse, two, while existing managers for their part were becoming increasingly enthusiastic about such programmes. There was also a rapid spread of undergraduate degrees in business, initially through the polytechnics, but soon with many universities joining the scramble for students. Another important route to undergraduate management teaching was through engineering programmes, which as a result of the 1972 Dainton Report were deemed to need an input of management studies. Several of the most prestigious universities originated management programmes in this way. Finally, and very attractively for the universities, there was a rapid expansion in the number of overseas students in business, making business or management schools highly lucrative aspects of degree provision.

Of course, these developments took time to have an effect. They also occurred against a backdrop of mounting criticism of management development, culminating in the Constable–McCormick and Handy Reports of 1987. These were complementary reports, published on the same day: the former, entitled *The Making of British Managers*, was based primarily on the results of four working parties that had looked at various aspects of management development in Britain; and the latter, *The Making of Managers*, compared management development in the United States, France, Germany, and Japan, as well as Britain. Taken together, they represented the most comprehensive analysis of management development yet carried out. Both were heavily critical of many features of the British system, or, as Handy (1987) argued, the lack of a system in contrast with its main competitors. Each of these competitors had a different system: the French was elitist, operating through the *Grandes Écoles*, with a strong emphasis on mathematics; the German stressed technical studies and business economics in technological universities; the American was based primarily on the business schools and the MBA; and the Japanese focus was on in-house training after an academic education at one of the top universities. As a result, Constable–McCormick, and Handy provided numerous recommendations, most of which were subsumed into the initial objectives of a new body which arose out of the two reports, the

Council for Management Education and Development, soon to become better known by its marketing arm, the Management Charter Initiative (MCI). The MCI, however, was less influential in the 1990s than it might have been, mostly because it concentrated on National Vocational Qualifications (NVQs) rather than degrees. In 2000, it was replaced by the Council for Excellence in Management and Leadership (CEML), which carried out yet another evaluation of management education (2001) that resulted in further tinkering with the system.

The business schools are now well-established and mature, having plateaued after a major growth phase in the last quarter century, with a focus on degree-level qualifications. At the same time, one should stress that as Grey (2005: 120–1) noticed, 'the professional managers produced by business schools are professional only in a very narrow—though not altogether insignificant—sense'. While they have acquired the 'superficialities of managerial language' and been inducted into the academic literature that now abounds, it remains a moot point whether this is sufficient to qualify them either for the career on which they embark or the title of 'professional'. These are issues to which we return both later in this chapter and the next, emphasizing its importance to our overall analysis.

Having devoted some space to the business schools, it is also important to stress that there has been a substantial amount of development through non-assessed post-experience programmes; indeed, some schools have derived more revenue from this source than they have from qualifications. At the end of the twentieth century, there was an annual output of some 20,000 undergraduate degrees in management and 11,000 MBAs. While this is still modest compared with the size of the management population, it is an approximate tenfold increase over the position in 1980. From having virtually no management education, the subject is now the most popular at both undergraduate and graduate levels. It would also be wrong to ignore the importance of management education outside the business schools in the further education sector; Keep and Westwood (2003) note that the business schools, in terms of the overall need for management development, play a relatively marginal role, even if the MBA has achieved some status. Additionally, the creation of vocational qualifications (VQs) has provided a new opportunity to have management attainments assessed by verifying functional competences based on national management standards. Some 20,000 per year at Level 3 and above are now being awarded (Williams 2002: 12), indicating how one should look broadly at the general level of management education and training.

THE DEMAND FOR DEVELOPMENT

We have seen in several previous references in this chapter that demand was a key factor in expressing the lack of interest by employers in management development. In this section, we deal more specifically with the issue, because while it is one thing to examine the various supply-side approaches to develop managers, it is easy to overlook the importance of demand in these systems, and indeed in the management labour market. Demand can be manifested either by organizations or at the level of the individual manager. We have seen so far in this chapter that organizations expressed little demand for their managers to be trained; in so far as there was training, it was focused on making sure that the manager could do the job s/he was in, rather than training for the future. Consequently, bringing in consultants often meant that the managers affected had to be given some training in the new techniques. As for using the business schools or professional institutes as training facilities, there was no interest until the second half of the twentieth century, and specifically only in the last twenty years. Sometimes this negativity reached surprising levels, as Brech (2002e: 238) noted when highlighting the difficulty of filling the two annual Harvard Business School scholarships set up in 1950.

Why this lack of demand for development? Gospel and Okayama (1991: 18) suggest three main factors. First, since few entrepreneurs and senior managers themselves had a technical or managerial education, they may have failed to see its importance for others and instead placed their confidence in what Lever called the 'University of Hard Knocks'. Second, where firms needed expertise, they could look to the market and buy it in, either from other firms or abroad (including Scotland), and from consultants. Third, many British firms, relying on well-tried techniques and with access to a relatively abundant supply of skilled manual labour, could rely on their shop-floor workers and felt little need to develop their managerial and technical hierarchies.

However, at the level of the individual there has been a greater expression of interest in development, leading to the reasonable assumption that there was always a considerable latent, although by no means always fulfilled, demand. The people who set up and operated the mechanics institutes, the managers who struggled to set up professional bodies, those managers who tried to improve their knowledge and experience by taking evening classes, were all expressing demand for development. In fact, it is arguable that the recent increases in development have not been so much due to the high quality or relevant provision of the business schools or the enthusiasm of industry, compared to pressures from ordinary managers both to learn something more about the subject they were practising, as well as to have a qualification to validate their knowledge and to provide them with transferability in the labour market. It is the willingness of managers to contribute large amounts of their own time, often within the counter-pressures of job and family, which has made the growth of management education feasible. It is consequently no accident that over 80 per cent of MBA graduates are from part-time or distance-learning programmes, while the full-time programmes have a majority of overseas students.

This latent demand has both grown and become especially effective in the last quarter of a century. On the one hand, Mansfield and Poole (1991: 35) identified in their second survey of management attitudes a high perception of the value of training, concluding that:

This almost totally unanimous support for management training and corporate support for such training is the strongest set of attitudes assessed anywhere in either of the two surveys and clearly indicates the importance that the British manager now places on this.... It would be very surprising if this degree of support had been present at the beginning of the 1980s ... training clearly has an enormous intrinsic value as judged by the views of the British manager today.

On the other hand, a number of other factors have helped to reinforce these attitudes, as Thomson et al. (2001: 79) have highlighted:

- A continuing momentum towards training
- A critical mass factor
- The self-reinforcing nature of demand
- Better-defined objectives for training
- The need for transferable skills in a more fluid labour market
- Better-developed senior managers to lend support in the organization
- Managerial insecurity
- Structural change
- Better supply
- Government exhortation
- More clearly defined targets for management development
- Recognition of individual responsibility for careers
- Diminishing of the assumption that managers are born not made

Nevertheless, CEML (2002: 4) has recently noted that: 'We have found among many organizations, an unclear and unfocused demand for management and leadership development which leads to dissatisfaction with provision and with outcomes without sending clear signals as to what needs to change.' This reflects the continued level of uncertainty that surrounds this issue, even if one can conclude with some certainty that British attitudes have changed radically over the course of the last fifty years.

CONCLUSIONS

Looking back over the last fifty years, there have clearly been major changes in both the supply of, and demand for, management development. The numbers going on to higher education are now over 40 per cent of the age group, and status has become less important, although some echoes of a class-based educational system still remain. In particular, management has not only achieved status as a career, at the highest levels it is regarded as a profession, although perhaps not a higher profession. The issue is no longer the quantity of development programmes available, but there are still some concerns about quality. Nevertheless, Britain has finally made the investment in management that Chandler (1990) wanted, even if as Grey (2005: 117) argues 'the manager ... whilst not professionalized in the classical sense of the term, is possessed of techniques, language and values denied to others'.

On the supply side, the general trend has been towards the American model, with large numbers going through undergraduate or graduate business education. However, there are too many and overlapping academic qualifications, and in the case of the best-known, the MBA, there are too many different varieties of length, content, quality, and mode of delivery for it to have a single coherent image in the managerial labour market. In-company development has become more efficient by better structuring of training methods and objectives, in part due to the increased recognition of management competencies, which in turn have helped to create more transferable skills, even if tacit varieties still remain important. The role of both the professional institutes and the consultants in the development process has also been substantial. Moreover, the role of the state has increased significantly, not so much in funding, but in terms of exhortation and the creation of more active labour market institutions. Finally, changes on the demand side have been important, nowhere more so than in the recognition of the individual manager that qualifications and CPD are important dimensions of a career in which they recognize their individual responsibility.

At the same time, formal development is not and never can be the solution to all management development problems; informal methods, in particular experiential development, must always play an important part. But perceptions of the balance between the two have changed over time, just as attitudes to management have also changed markedly away from the 'born not made' philosophy of the earlier periods that made formal development seem unnecessary. A series of surveys have tracked the attitudes of senior management development executives to various potential components of making a good manager on a five-point scale of importance, with the results shown in Table 7.2. Thus, where almost two decades ago inherent ability/personality scored 4.6 out of 5, it has now fallen to second place behind job experience, while in-company training and post-experience management education have improved their rankings considerably. Nevertheless, personality and experience still rank the highest, indicating a level of consistency that harks back to Victorian attitudes.

While these are the positive sides of recent developments, there are still many negative features. For all the progress, British managers still have limited educational qualifications, with only some 30 per cent possessing a degree or degree equivalent, much less than any other 'profession'. As CEML (2002: 7) has noted,

Table 7.2. What makes a good manager?

	2004	2000	1996	1986
Inherent ability/personality	4.1	4.1	4.2	4.6
Job experience	4.2	3.9	3.9	4.1
Job-relevant qualifications	3.4	3.2	2.8	3.2
In-company training	3.7	3.6	3.7	2.9
General qualifications	2.5	2.3	2.7	2.5
Post-experience management education	3.3	3.2	3.1	2.3

Source: Mabey (2005).

at current rates of take-up of all management qualifications, the proportion of managers achieving these would not rise much above 20 per cent even in the long term. Figure 7.1 also highlights how in spite of recent progress fewer senior British managers and directors possess a university degree than in other major industrial economies. Moreover, improving the quality of management is a relative concept which must be seen in a comparative context. As a recent comparative survey of Western European countries noted, Britain spent the least on management development per manager, with Germany at the top spending 4,438 euros against Britain's 1,625 (Mabey and Ramirez 2004: 22). CEML (2002: 4) also stated that much of the latent demand is immune to supply-side interventions, especially in the small business sector, while overall there was 'a deficit in management and particularly leadership skills'.

There is still no absolute link between education and training on the one hand and performance on the other. At the same time, anyone who reads this book and still believes that the palpable amateurism and ignorance of much of British management in the past is somehow superior to the present system, whereby the education and training of managers is taken more seriously, is deluding themselves. Compared to where it had been fifty years or less previously, there has been massive advance along the road to the educational and developmental standards required to achieve professionalism, even if there is still a great deal of room for improvement both along this road and in comparative terms, issues that we continue to assess in Chapter 8.

8

Managerial Thought and Institutions

INTRODUCTION

This chapter continues our examination of the theme of the slow transition towards professionalism by discussing separately two further important dimensions of managerial professionalism. The first is the predominant framework of management thought and the emergence of a managerial knowledge base in Britain, arguing that for the most part British management lacked either a coherent system of thought or a generic knowledge base. Having identified in Chapters 3 and 5 some of the deficiencies in management techniques, which contributed to low productivity, it is clear that this was in large part due to the weakness of the technical aspects of its role, including its knowledge base, while its system of beliefs was dominated by a defensive set of attitudes concerned with legitimizing its role vis-à-vis both society at large and the workforce.

The chapter's second dimension is a review of the role of the professional institutes in management history. Britain has arguably paid more attention to professional institutes than any other country in the world. Indeed, Perkin (1989: 25) has argued that professionalism as an organizing principle has superseded class in Britain and that company management has become one of the two pivotal hierarchies of professional society. However, as we see, the manifestation of this through institutes has both taken a long time in comparison to other professions and even now remains very far from being complete.

In the conclusions, we bring together the evidence from the various dimensions of professionalism and try to decide how far 'the slow transition towards professionalism' has advanced. It is assumed, indeed taken for granted, that while some claim that Britain has a cadre of professional managers (Whittington and Mayer 2000; Porter and Ketels 2003), we are not convinced that this easy acceptance is justified.

EARLY MANAGERIAL THOUGHT

This chapter is not the place for a full review of the history of management thought, either in Britain or more generally; Child (1969) and Wren (1994) have devoted substantial books to the subject, while we have also already provided a synopsis of international intellectual developments (see Management in the

Theory of the Firm, Chapter 2) (see Figure 2.1). During the Industrial Revolution, companies such as Wedgwood and Boulton & Watt were coherently organized on essentially modern principles. Indeed, their founders might be considered to be the first systematic managers. However, the early industrial philosophy, up to the 1870s at least, was based on individualism, laissez-faire, and self-help principles (Bendix 1956; Thompson 2001). Entrepreneurs saw themselves, through having achieved a higher social standing, as possessing moral superiority and thus the right to control based not only on property rights but also their innate knowledge and ability. This essentially tacit knowledge was then (supposedly) handed on to the next generation, forming the basis of the view that 'managers are born, not made'. Since the experience of each company was seen as unique, its owners and managers had no real interest in being told how to run it by outsiders. Any technical development that happened to emerge did so as a result of practical experimentation, rather than through theory or books.

Of course, books dealing with the demands of the new industrial context were written, some of which were important both at the time and for posterity (Smith 1776; Babbage 1832; Ure 1835). Where the knowledge required was more general, as in accounting, there was a substantial number of textbooks (Pollard 1965: 140). On the other hand, the focus was predominantly on the function or the industry; there was no common body of knowledge about management as such, and indeed there was no sense of an emerging profession and little to link the groups of managers across industries.

Moreover, there was little cumulative development of management themes, even though practice was clearly evolving. Indeed, as Figure 8.1 (see also Figure 2.1) indicates, there was a gap in the production of relevant literature in Britain from the 1830s to the 1880s. One might even argue that the first important book specifically in the management area was Smith's *Workshop Management* (1878), which was in essence a manual for foremen. Smith accepted the need for technical proficiency, but also saw the need for wider skills, such as assigning workers to jobs that fully utilized their capabilities in order to make the best use of expensive labour. From the 1880s onwards, as Figure 8.1 also indicates, there was a steady stream of British books on management. While Smith's work was important, Slater Lewis (1896) was the first to write a general text in the main areas then covered by management, that is, mainly production techniques such as production planning, stock control, and costing. He also described the positions and duties in the line organization of the firm, from the board of directors to the first line supervisor, as well as the specialists who were to assist line management. However, this early, path-breaking work of Lewis about the technical nature of management did not lead to further work by others, while few British firms, with their more individualistic and family-based management, operated this sort of system.

Although the numbers of books grew from the 1890s, there were relatively few articles on management; Litterer (1986) found less than ten in the second half of the 1890s, far fewer than in the same period for the United States. The technical journals, such as *The Engineer* and *Engineering*, showed a lack of curiosity about

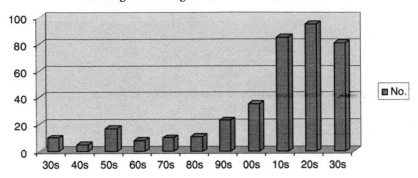

Figure 8.1. British books on management-related issues, 1830–1939 (*Source:* Brech 2002*d*)

what was happening on the organizational front, devoting little space to the debates about management issues that featured in their American equivalents, where practitioners who were primarily concerned with resolving the organizational challenges they faced at that time shared their ideas and experiences with others in a spirit of mutual development. Litterer (1986) saw these articles as an attempt to systematize management, leading to the replacement of the old rule-of-thumb approach by what in Chapter 2 we described as *systematic management.* The enthusiasm of American journals for the new must be contrasted with the equivocal attitudes of British journals towards change. Nor was there the same willingness to divulge information, as Outerbridge (1899) revealed in his study of the differences in attitudes in Britain and the United States; whereas most companies adopted an open-door policy on products and processes in the United States, in Britain there was much more secrecy, with the result that each firm had to devise its own solutions based on its own experience and 'rule of thumb'. Even then firms were never aware whether they were ahead of or behind others, which in turn tended to restrict development. Moreover, the body of knowledge gained by sharing experience was slower to develop and diffuse across industry. Thus, the president of the Institution of Mechanical Engineers complained in 1917 (quoted in Levine 1967: 60): 'Except in a few cases, workshop organization here has not received the attention given to it in America or Germany.' This difference in attitudes in the late nineteenth and early twentieth centuries meant that there was much less movement in Britain away from the rule-of-thumb approach to problem-solving and on to systematic management. In Britain, the stage of practitioner involvement in the development and exchange of knowledge did not emerge until the 1930s, with the rise of management magazines and professional institute journals.

Up to the First World War, the significant British writers, such as Slater Lewis, his protégé Alexander Church (who later emigrated to America), Edward Elbourne (1914), and amongst the industrialists Edward Cadbury, did not have the critical mass, the communication vehicles, or the momentum that was achieved in the United States. In consequence, the British management literature was more the work of individuals who had relatively little interaction, while the journals rarely contributed to the debate. In effect, at a time when both systematic and scientific management were at their zenith in the United States, and there was great interest being shown in the concept in Germany, France, and Japan, there was no intellectual framework for managing in Britain, even though the latest techniques could have been accessed if the will had been there to do so. Of course, while this backward attitude to problem-solving is a key factor in the neglect of systematic and scientific management, other factors have been offered as part of this explanation, including product market rigidities, trade union opposition, and a lack of engineering leadership to initiate the change (Levine 1967; Littler 1983; Anthony 1986; Guillén 1994). Significantly, in the most influential British book of its generation, much used in the First World War, Elbourne's *Factory Administration* (1914) saw scientific management in an unfavourable light, arguing that the 'golden rules' proclaimed by American scientific managers could never be a substitute for 'good men'. Elbourne was an industrial engineer who had visited America. As a pioneer of cost and management accounting, moreover, he might well have been expected to be sympathetic to scientific management. There were some such as Hans Renold, who did favour scientific management (Boyns and Matthews 2001), but not nearly enough to offset the more general trepidation and apathy. As a result, the new managerial methods expressed in both systematic and scientific management to a large extent passed Britain by for a generation.

At the same time, the ideas underpinning scientific management and the skills developed by facing up to the challenges of work analysis and measurement provided a large part of both the technical expertise of management and thereby, in Child's terms (1969), its legitimacy. This lack of a basis for authority and legitimacy was a serious gap. As Checkland (1983: 225) observed of this era, 'business man was still in control, but he no longer had a confident rationale of what he was doing, no confirmatory theory of economy and society, and no sustaining set of religious and moral beliefs'. It was this 'lack of an ideological underpinning' (Littler 1983: 180) which the management movement sought in part to fill in the interwar period, a goal enhanced by the traumatic experiences of the First World War and the need for new solutions. Before the First World War, however, there was no real management movement and little or no intellectual leadership, with only a few relatively isolated individuals choosing to speak out about management or put pen to paper. Nor was there the sense of optimism and progress which was so evident in the United States in the era before the First World War.

THE INTERWAR MANAGEMENT MOVEMENT

It was in this uncertain context that the group which came to be known as the management movement emerged in Britain after the First World War, following the reinforced challenges to managerial authority in the wartime shop steward movement and the wider aspects of socialism, both in Britain and Russia. As Child noted (1969: 112) of this period, 'an important part of the labour movement and many intellectuals were questioning managerial authority at its very roots; many were at that time attacking the very principle of management'. Of Child's three strands of management (1969), as a technical function, as a social group, and as a system of authority, the last of these, and to some extent the second, came to be concerned with considerations of social legitimation in wider society, particularly in relation to labour. As a result of these primary concerns, the first strand, with all its implications for efficiency and professionalism, was prejudiced by arguments about legitimation. Although not part of Coasian externalizing, this had the same effect of distracting attention away from internal technical efficiencies, not just in the labour sphere but in other areas, such as new techniques in marketing and accounting, and thus away from professionalism.

In this context, the management movement emerged with the objective of establishing a coherent body of knowledge, operating on scientific principles, with management justifying its authority through professionalism and an ethic of service. The creation of a 'science' of management was argued to be a necessary prerequisite for management to be a true profession. The main sources for these ideas (and practical manifestations) were the Quaker companies, especially Rowntree and Cadbury. Rowntree in particular produced three of the most important writers in the management movement, in Seebohm Rowntree, Oliver Sheldon, and Lyndall Urwick. It is important to note, however, that the focus was on an ethical and educational route to professionalism, to be followed later, especially by Urwick, by a concentration on administrative issues, with little attention being given to workshop organization or technical competence. Thus, Sheldon's *The Philosophy of Management* (1923) was an important explanation of the responsibilities of directors and managers in contributing to the well-being of the community, both as employees as well as owners. Sheldon also made the important distinction between the role of directors as representing the ownership of the organization, and that of managers which we have earlier used in defining the proprietorial theory of the firm (Quail 2000). This meant that if management did not have property rights to justify its authority, it needed professional status and esteem as an alternative to provide legitimacy

A related statement came in John Lee's *Management: A Study in Industrial Organization* (1921), which envisaged a means of ameliorating the industrial unrest through the substitution of a 'scientific' approach provided by 'an expert professional class' for the arbitrary role of ownership, whose technical skills would justify control of industry. Lee's second book, *Dictionary of Industrial Administration* (1928), was a major work that brought together most of the prior writings. By the late 1920s, however, the focus had moved to rationalization in 'an attempt to substitute organization for the rule-of-thumb anarchy of economic life' (Child 1969: 86). Exemplifying this, Urwick's essay in Lee's Dictionary, *Principles of Direction and Control* (1928), was the beginning of his personal search for a scientific approach to management at the level of the enterprise, rather than the workshop.

Clearly, the management movement (and its later manifestation the rationalization movement) was always small and the work of a relatively few intellectuals who were themselves involved in management, as we also noted (see Interwar Progress?, Chapter 3). As such they were well beyond the interests or even awareness of the great majority of managers, even though prominent industrialists such as Sir Alfred Mond (the first chairman of ICI) espoused their principles. Most of the writing was done by managers themselves, or consultants, since there was little academic or public writing about management in the interwar period, James Bowie (1930) being the exception. Neither did the professional institutes, as they emerged, initially add much to the writing. Thus, there was no institutional backing for the management movement, further limiting its ability to become a mass movement. Indeed, the vast majority of managers, even if they had been aware of what it was arguing, would have been dismissive, viewing themselves as 'practical' men with no need for such abstract thoughts, especially since the management movement was not providing a solution to technical problems in the way that scientific management claimed. In reality, the management movement was aspirational as much as based on the reality of management life, and having little impact on what was actually implemented. As Whitley, Thomas, and Marceau put it (1981: 32): 'The members of the management movement found themselves preaching to a largely unresponsive audience, and were sometimes driven to bitter criticism of employers for their extreme conservatism in the face of new ideas, their lack of interest in business research, and their unbending resistance to management education.'

In terms of the actual creation of a body of management knowledge, there was little in the way of an institutional framework either in industry itself, the nascent professional institutes, or the universities, although there was an interest in industrial issues amongst some well-known economists, especially at Cambridge and the LSE. Amongst them was Ronald Coase (1937), who did his important early work on the nature of the firm and transactions costs in Britain, including his seminal article 'The Nature of the Firm' (ultimately recognized through the award of a Nobel Prize), before moving to Chicago. As his work was done in an economics department, however, it was not built into the mainstream of management teaching, never mind industrial practice. Early management research was based not in universities but through consultants in research-focused institutes such as the National Institute of Industrial Psychology (NIIP, founded in 1919) and the Tavistock Clinic (founded in 1921). These added a specifically British dimension to the emerging 'science' of human relations, acting in part as consultants. Indeed, the NIIP was responsible for coming up with the idea for *Black Magic* chocolates as part of an assignment at Rowntree. The NIIP's main area of interest, however, was in more applied issues of psychology and human relations, such as the effects of fatigue, methods of selection, working conditions, time study, and the impact of various payment systems. The main published outcomes of this work came from three books by the NIIP's director for many years, Charles Myers, *Mind and Work* (1921), *Industrial Psychology in Great Britain* (1926), and *Ten Years of Industrial Psychology* (1932), the latter written jointly with the Institute's chairman, H. J. Welch. Myers was also instrumental in persuading the British Psychological Society, which had been founded in 1901, to adopt a sectional structure, with one section devoted to industrial applications. The bulk of the research in the sense of informed contribution to knowledge came from the consultants carrying out investigations and using them as a basis for further assignments, as well as in some cases writing them up for one of the industrial journals of the time. In this context, Littler (1983: 115) suggests that British management found the Bedaux system (see The Formalization of Bargaining in the Interwar Period, Chapter 9) to be more acceptable because it 'limited the restricting of management implied by classical Taylorism, and enabled the control system to be clipped onto the existing management structure'.

While there was a growth of knowledge in techniques and practices in the interwar period, this was very much based on experimental pragmatism within individual companies, with the increasing number of consultants from the late 1920s being the main catalysts for such developments (Ferguson 2002: 72). By the mid-1930s, management journals, such as *Industry Illustrated* (1933) and *The British Management Review* (1936), together with the house journals of the professional institutes, provided an outlet for managers or consultants to write about their experiences and add to the widening volume of knowledge. Such journals did not, however, have a wide circulation, limiting their impact significantly.

Within industry, the only coherent attempt to share experience came through the Management Research Groups (MRG), which were set up in 1926–7 by Seebohm Rowntree of the chocolate family and a major figure in the management movement, based on an idea he had picked up in the United States. These consisted of the confidential exchange of developments in practice among the directors of member companies. There were ten groups in Britain, centred on different cities, most with between seven and fifteen company members and each autonomous, albeit with a central office and from 1935 a chief executive, Harry Ward. Although Group 1, based in London, and therefore with most of the big companies, was larger and more significant than the rest, most were relatively small-scale operations. Moreover, in spite of their name, they were not concerned with original research or a national audience, providing more of an internal dissemination role. Frequently, they took up an issue proposed at a meeting by the host company and discussed it and/or gave it to subcommittees of specialists with a view to identifying the best practice for the benefit of the members of that group. On the other hand, they clearly had some value, since they existed until the 1990s, and their records would repay quarrying as an indicator of the issues of the time. They also had an international dimension, under the auspices of the International Management Institute. Two other focal points of activity deserve note at this time. One was the annual Oxford Conferences, initially organized by Seebohm Rowntree from 1919, at which new ideas were put forward and discussed, and later reported in *The British Management Review* after its foundation in 1936. The other was the Industrial Welfare Society, which had corporate membership and ran various programmes and a journal covering aspects of employment. The editor of the journal, Reginald Pugh, was also an important influence in organizing management forums in the interwar period.

The later part of the interwar period also saw the development of two main schools of management thought, the 'classical' school and the human relations school, as we saw (see Schools of Management Thought, Chapter 2) (and Figure 2.1). The classical school was not founded on research or even a theoretical base; rather, it was a normative model created by a relatively small number of proponents, most notably Lyndall Urwick. It began with Urwick's *Principles of Control and Direction* (1928), which was an attempt to search for a scientific approach to management. Urwick was strongly influenced by the French management thinker, Henri Fayol, and especially the assumption of being able to establish management theory on scientific foundations, that of the 'one best way'. With this and later writings, often jointly with Edward Brech, Urwick became the main exponent of the 'classical' school of management in Britain, initially proposing a 'one best way' until he and Brech took more flexible positions in the 1950s, as well as providing leadership in the development of management institutions both nationally and internationally.

As opposed to the rejection of systematic and scientific management (see The Formalization of Bargaining in the Interwar Period, Chapter 9), Britain developed early aspects of human relations. While human relations was derived from Mayo and his followers in America, it was in some respects foreshadowed in Britain by managers seeking to legitimize themselves vis-á-vis the workforce. Although the early management movement accepted the need to relate to trade unions, attention to the unions diminished in the 1930s as the importance of human relations grew, in that it pursued a more unitary view of the enterprise in which management leadership of the workforce played a key part. Such a leadership style was held to satisfy worker needs for social satisfaction, hence as Child put it (1969: 101), 'the technical process of managing labour was in essence to effect a "spontaneous" worker acceptance of managerial authority'. But even into the 1940s, the vast majority of personnel managers, never mind other managers, had probably never heard of the Hawthorne experiments. Human relations was essentially a management ideology, although surprisingly many trade union leaders and Labour party members espoused it. As Guillén (1994: 302) argued: 'British managers believed in HR theory as a result of their mentality of traditional humanism, emphasizing the community, the integration of the worker, and the avoidance of conflict, as opposed to the technocratic and empirical approach in the US.' It was also conventional wisdom amongst British managers that the human, social, and cooperative aspects of work should take precedence over the technical.

TOWARDS A BODY OF KNOWLEDGE

After the Second World War, the main focus of management thought continued to be on human relations (see Figure 2.1), with paternalist and legitimatory overtones to try to persuade the workers of common interests and the ability of management to meet workers' emotional needs. A considerable amount of attention was given to making the supervisor able to

(a) weld the group together in a harmonious whole (b) maintain authority in the democratic group (c) encourage spontaneous discipline (d) accept full responsibility for the group (e) establish firm, fair, friendly treatment of employees (f) raise morale, and create enthusiasm (g) inspire security, certainty and confidence (Burns Morton, quoted in Child 1969: 119).

In this, little explanation was given to the role of unions or how the supervisor was supposed to carry out these tasks in the context of a full employment economy and increasing shop-floor power (see the Post-War Battle to Control the Shop Floor, chapter 9). Moreover, even though managers were urged to make the supervisors feel part of management, the reality for most was that they did not feel supported (Child and Partridge 1982). At the same time, while human relations was the mainstream of thought, scientific management in the form of work measurement actually made a belated entry on to the industrial scene after the Second World War, some three or four decades after the original debates over its meaning and impact.

By the early 1960s, however, Granick (1962: 242) was arguing that British managerial theory had developed along two main strands. While a common element was a rejection of the view that there existed managerial principles which can be taught, there was an amateur theory of management and a specialist theory holding that there are no managers as such, only specialists. In addition, the view was prevalent that a university education was unnecessary for a successful business career, revealing a considerable degree of continuity with an approach that had been popular in the nineteenth century. Clearly, though, these perspectives taken together did not amount to an intellectual framework; management theory, as the basis of the new managerial professionalism, did not come into its own in Britain until the founding of the new business schools in the 1960s and after.

Indeed, early post-war developments were again outside the universities. The Tavistock Institute of Human Relations was founded in 1946 to complement the Tavistock Clinic, leading to significant work on human relations through assignments such as the Glacier Project and the long-wall mining project. Another major contribution to socio-technical systems, by Joan Woodward (1958), came from a study based on the South-West Essex Technical College, rather than any institute of higher education. J. A. C. Brown's *The Social Psychology of Industry* (1954) was another influential book of the time written by an industrial practitioner in psychiatry and psychology. The Glacier Project, in which Elliot Jacques of the Tavistock joined with the company's managing director, Wilfred Brown, was probably the outstanding exercise in applied management thought of the whole post-war period, even if what Child (1969: 203) called its 'sweeping and normative social programme' was atypical of later social science, which tended to be more pluralist and less prescriptive. The dominant discipline for several decades became sociology rather than psychology, with an emphasis on group interests and identities, and the recognition of conflict as part of organizational life.

When the universities did become involved in management issues in the 1960s, the rise of structural analysis in social science was in considerable part led from Britain by Woodward (who by this time had moved into higher education), Burns and Stalker, and the Aston Group, who were all influential in American as well as British thinking. This was the first time that the universities, or at least the educational system, had made a major contribution to management thought, with research funding support from the state. As a result of wartime innovations, Britain also contributed to the rise of operations research as an information-based discipline in management, especially in the coal industry (Kirby 2003). At the same time, although the concept of 'one best way' so beloved by the classical school was softened by Urwick and Brech from the mid-1950s, the issue of contingency versus universalist approaches continues to this day.

After the 1960s, however, British management thought lost its managerial identity and became subsumed in the growth of academic analysis and the importation of American ideas, in no small part due to the adoption of American theories and texts by the business schools. Moreover, this was also the boom period for the American consultants; British firms came to be dominated by these consultants and were apparently unable to think for themselves (see Structural Change, Chapter 5), while Charles Handy is arguably the only British management scholar to have achieved a world reputation in the last thirty years. Even while British thought had existed separately, it was not based on any research or empirical analysis, and hence was oversimplified. One of the features of the last thirty years in particular has been the succession and proliferation of management fads, each of which would appear to have had a natural lifecycle, often with its source being overseas: empowerment was fashionable in the 1970s, followed by quality circles from the late 1970s, organizational culture from the early 1980s, total quality management from the late 1980s, lean production, the learning organization, and business process re-engineering from the early 1990s, and knowledge management from the mid- to late 1990s (Huczynski 1993; Kieser 1997). Emotional intelligence is perhaps the most recent at the time of writing. Most of these, it could be argued, were dimensions of what a sensible company would have been pursuing as a matter of course. Even now, it is dubious as to whether there can be said to be a general theory of management; certainly, there is not one which is distinctively British. Rather, it is something like a changing kaleidoscope in which the pieces are the same, but the patterns differ as fashions come and go. Nevertheless, judged by the amount of literature on the subject, its easy availability and popularity on airport bookstalls, and the rapid growth in qualifications and training which we reported in the Chapter 7, it must be accepted that there is now an available body of knowledge sufficient to justify the designation of a profession.

PROFESSIONAL INSTITUTES FOR MANAGEMENT

Having noted these trends in the development of management thought, it is now necessary to change the focus of the chapter, starting with an examination of another major dimension of professionalism, that of the professional institutes. Professional institutes have long been a key symbol of professionalism, especially in Britain, where they have arguably been more important than in any other country. At the same time, while the precise membership data are uncertain, it is highly probable that members of any professional institutes do not cover more than 20 per cent of the 4.76 million managers we noted in the 2001 Census, while membership of the central institute and a wide range of management-related functional institutes probably do not cover more than 10 per cent. Moreover, most of these managers are members of institutes because of their functional rather than their managerial skills. Thus, there is only a weak link between management as an occupation and professionalism as symbolized through the institutes. Indeed, the BIM most certainly did not, and the Chartered Management Institute (CMI) to a slightly lesser extent would not, accept an argument that all managers are professionals in terms of being worthy of an institute membership. Nevertheless, the history of management needs to include the contribution, or maybe the lack of it, of the professional institutes, not least because they had perforce to take on the role of offering credentials for the labour market in the absence of any vocational education provision by the universities (DoI 1977).

The earliest professional organization was formed by the Civil Engineers in 1771, with a royal charter following in 1828. Crucially, though, in pursuing the development of technical skills, the complementary management functions were either pushed into the background or left to clients and subcontractors. This was a path which was imitated by the other institutes for engineers and accountants that followed at intervals over the course of the nineteenth century. Indeed, judged by the urge to create institutes, there was obviously a strong conception of the importance of professionalism, even if this was not yet as true of management. Perkin (1989: 439) argues that the urge to institutionalize an occupation comes from the desire to turn human capital into property capable of earning a rent similar to land or industrial capital, and that this requires its transformation into a scarce resource through the device of closure, i.e. 'the restriction of access to the profession by means of expensive or selective training, education and qualification, better still by the grant of a state monopoly'. Management has never come close to being able to restrict access in any of its functions, especially in the area of generic management, where institute membership has been at its weakest. Nevertheless, the statutory recognition of management through the chartered status of the CMI in 2002 does, of course, confer an important additional level of professional identity, since chartered status is one of the valued marks of a profession in Britain.

The 386 professional organizations in Britain identified by CEML (2001) stretch across a spectrum from legally institutionalized to semi-formal and loosely integrated bodies, with management closer to the latter end, while some of the functions which constitute management, such as accounting, may be closer to the former end. We can roughly categorize those professions which require either membership of an institute or a legal standing in order to practice as strong professions, while others, including management, must be seen as weak professions. All institutes contain some members whose role includes a managerial dimension, which many are now recognizing as part of their own professional identity. Nevertheless, management per se has never been an important part of their raison d'etre.

At the same time, there are indubitably many managers who by any reasonable standards meet the individual requirements of being designated as professionals. Clearly, therefore, managerial professionalism includes an additional issue relating to individual managers, which is how far they can claim to be professional as a result of their individual attributes, rather than their institutional membership. This again is too complex an issue to debate at length here, but it would be difficult to argue that all managers are professionals, even though they are paid for the role of being a manager. On the other hand, there is evidence that managers increasingly perceive themselves to be professionals. For example, Poole, Mansfield, and Mendes (2001), in the third of their surveys of managers (admittedly drawn from membership of the Institute of Management (IM), which is not a representative sample), note that in response to the question 'Do you regard yourself as a professional?', 59 per cent answered positively in 1980, whereas in 2000 this figure had risen to 95 per cent. Self-regard, however, would not satisfy a more stringent definition of professionalism.

THE CENTRAL INSTITUTE IN MANAGEMENT

As Brech (2002*a*) has provided a comprehensive review of the development of a central institute in Britain, what follows here is only a brief synopsis of a somewhat tortuous evolutionary path. Before the First World War, there was no concept of an institute for managers, in spite of the formation of a wide range of other professional institutes by this time. Thereafter, however, many increasingly recognized the need for a central institute in management, mainly within those linked to the 'management movement' (see Towards a Body of Knowledge, Chapter 8). It was consequently in the aftermath of the First World War, when Edward Elbourne suggested 'a society for industrial administration research', leading to the launch of the Institute of IIA (Brech 2002*a*: 793). At the first AGM of the IIA in 1921, there were 222 enrolled members. A year later, however, the membership had actually dropped, with almost no new enrolments, while its journal ceased publication in 1923 after just fifteen issues. By 1924, the organization was moribund, except as a registered name. There were several contributory reasons to the failure of the IIA, including the severe recession of the early 1920s and the lack of dynamic leadership, but most of all a lack of interest from everyday managers and employers, in spite of the support of a number of well-known people. At the same time, its educational committee had drafted a syllabus, which Elbourne took to the Regent Street Polytechnic to develop a programme to be conducted in the IIA's name from 1928. This then created an opportunity to revive the IIA in 1929, since it needed to assume formal responsibility for the award of the educational certificates which became its main focus.

In spite of this unpropitious start, by the late 1920s there was a recognized need for a central institute, if only as a counterpart to developments in other countries within the International Committee on Scientific Management (CIOS). There was a paradox, in that Urwick, in his role as Director of the International Management Institute from 1928, assisted in the establishment of similar bodies elsewhere in Europe. The FBI, which had been founded during the First World War as an employers' organization (Davenport-Hines 1984), took upon itself the formal role of hosting the London CIOS conference in 1935, with Harry Ward of the MRG Council acting as organizing secretary. Thereafter, however, the FBI again withdrew from management issues, while it should also be noted that few British managers attended, another sign of apathy concerning these issues. This gap was filled by the formation in 1937 of the British Management Council (BMC), at the instigation of the MRG Council, in order to prepare for the 1938 CIOS conference in Washington. It was a federal coordinating council consisting of some twenty-eight management-related associations, rather than a central institute in the modern sense, while its terms of reference were as an international representative rather than a national body concerned with pursuing managerial competence. The BMC was, nevertheless, the first time the various players on the management scene had been brought together. On the other hand, it was too new in creation, too diverse in composition, and too limited in its objectives to take up the lead managerial role for a nation on the verge of war. Consequently, it effectively went into abeyance at the outbreak of war, leaving management without any institutional leadership and Britain well behind many other countries in its lack of a central institute.

Preparatory steps to create a central institute began during the Second World War, resulting in the post-war Labour government announcing the formation of the Baillieu Committee to consider the situation. This body reported in 1946, laying down the basic design for the BIM as a professional body 'promoting research into management problems, cooperating in the development of training and educational schemes, and undertaking widespread propaganda on good management practice' in order to 'raise the standards of management throughout the country' (quoted in Brech 2002a: 160). As there was general support for the recommendations and the new council, composed of leading industrial and public figures, as well as government financial support for full-time staff and administration, a smooth beginning was anticipated.

On a number of fronts, however, progress was far from smooth. One aspect was relations with the existing societies, including the IIA, especially as the BIM concept of 'local management associations' seemed to undermine the local branches of the other societies and reduce them in status. Although an amalgamation of the BIM and the IIA did finally occur in 1957, relations with the other management-related institutes remained problematic, resulting in the formation in 1966 of a joint body of their own, the Coordinating Committee of Professional Management Organizations (CCPMO). Thus, while the early assumptions had been that a common body of management knowledge would develop, an aspiration accepted by the functional institutes, the institutional implications were never fully implemented. A second area of concern was in the BIM's activities; it took a considerable amount of time to develop a national network capable of initiating publications for managers, while the initial premises in Hill Street, London, soon proved to be a financial incubus. As we also noted in Chapter 7, when discussing education, only limited numbers were achieved on the key qualifications. As a result, by the late 1950s the BIM was experiencing such serious financial problems that retrenchment was enacted in various areas.

In addition to these problems, however, arguably the most difficult of BIM's challenges was the issue of membership, where there was a clash of perspectives between those who took an elitist conception of membership, namely managers who had achieved identifiable career success and status in becoming general managers, and those who followed the IIA approach of providing for a system of managerial growth through professional standards, qualifications, and education. While the BIM was not necessarily against professional standards as such, the first Chairman, Sir Charles Renold, laid down two fundamental convictions:

(1) that professional qualifications in general management are desirable only in so far as they can establish themselves with industry as significant indications of capacity to manage, i.e. to undertake general management responsibility; and (2) that an assessment of personal qualities is an indispensable element in the granting of professional qualifications in general management (quoted in Brech 2002a: 501).

These effectively meant that achievement was to be the key attribute, and that it was to be measured by industrial success, rather than through qualifications, while the term 'general management' meant the upper level of management involved in coordinating activities and reporting to the board of directors. This was inevitably a restricted concept of management, implying the existence of a senior managers' club and denying the managerial role of levels below general management, especially of younger managers. Moreover, it did not relate to three of the key concepts in most professions, namely, specialized training, a code of behaviour, and the pursuit of a body of knowledge. Unsurprisingly, it consequently attracted relatively few members. By the end of 1949, there were only some 500 of the 'founder members' it saw as its base, as opposed to some 1,500 'associate members' who did not carry voting rights. By 1957, after the amalgamation with the IIA, the BIM had a membership of around 2,500 collective subscribers (a term for company and institutional members) and 7,000 individual members in the various grades, the great majority of them having been brought in from the former IIA. These were extremely small figures by comparison with the potential membership in the wider management community and must be seen as a major missed opportunity.

Any analysis of the BIM's performance must take account of the senior personalities involved. For example, BIM's first chairman, Charles Renold, had what Brech (2002*a*: 274) describes as 'a deep-rooted personal antipathy to the notion of "professional" in the managerial context'. It is consequently surprising that he took on the role, given that the Baillieu Committee had specifically recommended that the new Institute ought to develop an individual professional management membership. It is also apparent that in different ways the early directors (Russell, Livock, and Marsh) never proved capable of exploiting the momentum established in 1948. Russell, in particular, alienated the other societies and preferred the prestige derived from large company involvement and individual membership of eminent and established industrial personalities. Thus, in summarizing the early history of the BIM, the intended impact on the world of industry was nothing like as significant as had been hoped. Crucially, the promise expressed in the Baillieu Report for improving the standards of management was not fulfilled. As Brech (2002*a*: 605) noted at its silver jubilee in 1972, 'it was exerting no influence at all on national industrial policies. Nor was it seen either by the public in general, or even by industrial opinion, as a body of significance for contemporary events.' In retrospect, the IIA would have provided a much better base for development, both in its branch structure and focus on management development, rather than mere recognition of status.

Having expressed such a negative view, it is important to note that from the late 1950s the BIM began to change to a much more broadly based organization, both geographically and in terms of membership, recognizing that a policy of focusing only on an elitist membership was not sustainable. In consequence, it has become more like other professional institutes, with an increasing focus on development both for its members and management more generally, requiring CPD of its members. Moreover, since the amalgamation with the Institute of Industrial Management in 1992 to form the IM, there has been a greater focus on operating qualifications both directly and through Institute-validated courses in more than 150 further education colleges. In addition, the Institute has put an emphasis on qualifications as a criterion for entry and movement up the grades of membership, while in common with the other professional institutes in the management area, it has become a significant player on the management training and development scene. Since 2001, its qualifications have included an MBA, although the numbers on this are small. In 2003, it became the CMI, when it finally achieved incorporation by royal charter, and since then a Chartered Manager qualification has been initiated as a new mark of professionalism.

OTHER PROFESSIONAL INSTITUTES

In numerical terms, over five million people in the UK labour market are today classified as professionals or associate professionals, or about one-fifth of the total labour force. It is not clear how many of these are in either a professional institute or an institute with functional roles in management. Of the latter, the several accounting and engineering institutes and the company secretaries date from the nineteenth century, while the main marketing and personnel institutes can trace their origins to before the First World War. The Institute of Directors was formed in 1902, mostly to relate to the legal aspects of a director's responsibilities, although it fell into virtual abeyance from about the First World War until after the Second World War. Soon after the First World War, the Institute of Cost and Works Accountants (1919) was formed, along with the Institution of Production Engineers (1921) and the Institute of Public Administration (1922). Another important period was the formation of three management associations (Works, Office, and Purchasing) in 1931–2, which launched a joint journal, *Industry Illustrated*. This was a valuable focus for expanding knowledge of good practice, since most of the published material came from management practitioners. Nevertheless, these institutes were created to recognize functional, rather than managerial, skills; indeed, the growth of functional differentiation within management tended to obscure the emergence of generic management. Although industrial concentration called for a greater degree of generic management at the top, this tended to be subsumed within the directorial role in the system of proprietorial capitalism that prevailed in Britain up to at least the first half of the twentieth century. At the same time, however, this also created a move towards lower-level functional specialization in management, precipitating the formation of institutes to cater for these groups.

The development of a range of management-related functional institutes was partly legitimized by the absence of a central management body, or indeed a managerial ideology or identity. The very existence of the management-related institutes even helped to perpetuate the view that rather than being managers, they were engineers, salesmen, buyers, and accountants who happened to run departments. It can also be argued that this intraoccupational specialization encouraged fragmentation and competitive divisions within management and discouraged mobility between functional silos. At the same time, although the great majority of functional managers did not see themselves as part of a wider profession with its own identity and standards, the development of a CMA in 1934–5 does indicate that the institutes recognized some common bonds under a generic management umbrella.

Brech (2002*a*: 110) also notes that the specialized associations were characterized by a focus on information and education, rather than on performance and standards. As a result, they did not have a significant role in creating and defining management thought, even in the absence of any real contribution from the universities, in the way that the Associated Society of Mechanical Engineers did in the United States. Thus, the engineering profession did not play an important part in the introduction of scientific management either in the first two decades of the twentieth century or indeed when it did come in the 1950s; rather, this latter move was facilitated by state agencies and external consultants, at times with the collaboration of trade unions.

In the interwar period, there had been no strong momentum to expand membership across the spectrum of management institutes. Joining was a matter of individual initiative; progressive companies might publicize meetings, but there was no expectation that their managers should join and there was little marketing to attract any latent demand. As one can see from the membership figures provided in Table 8.1, numbers were consequently low, with no individual association having any substantial number of members. Nevertheless, as we saw in Chapter 7, they were held to be of sufficient significance to be seen as the main vehicles for national management development in the post-war period, given that higher education was even weaker in the vocational area.

Since the Second World War, not only has the membership of the management-related institutes increased considerably, from hundreds to tens of thousands, but they have also been more willing to recognize the management component of their specialist role, as indeed have other professional institutes. A survey by Perren (2000) found that some three quarters of his 386 respondent associations regarded management and leadership as either moderately or very relevant to their members. On the other hand, only 10 per cent had mandatory, and 30 per cent expected, management specifications for membership. This highlights something of a paradox between the reality of a management dimension in the role and the relative lack of recognition of it in the associations' requirements of their members (Perren 2000). It is highly likely that a similar survey in the past would have found even less recognition for the managerial dimension. Moreover, there always has been a strong trend for those carrying out functional activities to join and remain in the same professional institute, even when their role changes to include a greater element of management. Thus, the organized developmental contribution to management of the professional institutes outside the business group has probably been insignificant, although experientially developed skills undoubtedly made many of these professionals into competent managers, building on their functional competence. In addition, of course, many members of professional institutes take management courses or

Table 8.1. Membership of management institutes in 1939

	Founded	Members
Industrial administration	1920	478
Works management	1931	*c.*800
Factory managers	1938	*c.*100
Labour management	1913	760
Office management	1932	600
Purchasing officers	1932	550
Sales managers	1911	2,000+
Cost and works accountants	1919	1,000
Production engineers	1921	2,015
Industrial welfare society	1918	corporate
Institute of directors	1903	*c.*250

Source: Brech (2002*a*: 109).

qualifications outside the provision of their institutes, implying that there is an element of management development that goes unrecorded, even if this has always been on the margin.

CONCLUSIONS

This chapter has helped to illustrate two of the main components of the slow growth towards professionalism. The reality of British management thought, as opposed to the aspirations of the management movement, was defensive in its objectives and not oriented to providing the self-confidence needed for professionalism based on genuine technical skills. Moreover, until well after the Second World War it was neither well developed nor effectively diffused, focusing more on the legitimatory aspects of management, rather than the technical elements which could have induced greater efficiency and expertise. Meanwhile, companies operated in a culture of secrecy, viewing problems in the light of their own experience and a rule-of-thumb approach, without the desire to share concerns and build a general body of knowledge. Underpinning these problems were a lack of intellectual leadership as far as most managers were concerned, as well as the lack of a coherent ideology which might have provided self-confidence. Nevertheless, up to the Second World War the British contribution to management thought was by no means insignificant in the writings of authorities such as Lewis, Elbourne, Sheldon, and Urwick. The problem was rather one of dissemination in the absence of any substantial university intermediation, while the professional institutes remained weak.

Although professional institutes have played an important part in structuring Britain's higher occupations, especially in the light of the lack of an educational system historically unwilling to provide vocational development, it took a long time for a professional institute for managers to emerge. Furthermore, when one did emerge, it had a policy based on recognizing success already gained, rather than developing new managers or building a recognized body of knowledge. In some respects, it was more of a club than a professional institute. While there were opportunities for institutional development as a professional body, these were missed, in no small part for reasons of personality and lack of leadership. Of course, a widespread 'silo' mentality and concentration on the functional attributes of management did not help. Moreover, none of the management institutes (with the exception of those in accounting, to be discussed in Chapter 11) had the necessary recognition within industry to enable them to make an impact on the generality of managers. So in answer to the question as to whether the institutes provided leadership in the pursuit of professionalism, the answer must be not until well after the Second World War.

We have now examined several dimensions of professionalism, starting in Chapter 6 with the discussion of the lack of status of management as a career, the inefficiency of the managerial labour market, and the limited educational and low social backgrounds of most managers. In Chapter 7 we devoted space to the inadequate provision of management education and training, combined with the very limited demand for such a facility. This chapter has also demonstrated how two additional important components, the shape of an accepted body of know-ledge and membership of professional institutes, contributed to this movement. The historical reality is that in none of these dimensions did management as an occupation demonstrate any of the credentials of professionalism, in spite of a growing public realization from the 1950s of the importance of management to the economy. Much progress has been made along the various dimensions, but even now the issue of whether management as a whole can truly be considered a profession must remain questionable, in spite of the undoubted presence in its ranks of many individuals whose personal professionalism cannot be doubted.

In a society with a wide range of interest groups, management has never been a clearly defined interest group. It would never have been feasible for Burnham (1941) to write his magnum opus about the dangers of British management becoming an uncontrollable elite. Furthermore, the pursuit of professionalism was accepted by a relatively small minority, and certainly not by those who either saw management as an art rather than a science or those who believed that managers were 'born not made'. While these latter debates have now largely disappeared, there are still many of Britain's 4.7 million managers for whom management is still an occupation rather than a profession; in other words, that it is essentially the administration of work, rather than the use of expertise, auton-omy, and initiative which is involved in the conception of professionalism. While professionalism in management has undoubtedly advanced, the transition has been slow and it is not yet fully achieved.

Part IV

Managerial Functions

9

The Practice of Management—Labour

INTRODUCTION

This chapter is the first of three dealing with important functional areas of British management, starting with arguably the most important dimension of British management over the last two centuries, the relationship between employers and their workforces. This area has been vital not just for its substantial effect within the organization, but also because it has had a major impact on Britain's wider social, political, and economic development. Furthermore, as with other aspects of the business system, the framework established in the early period of industrialization proved difficult to restructure when the economic environment changed, resulting in a legacy that remained in place at least up to the 1970s.

Throughout the nineteenth century, and indeed up to the Second World War, with the exception of the four years of the First World War, there was a high level of unemployment, which meant that there was a buyers' market for labour. Coupled with this, there was a sufficient level of skill to perform the tasks that British industry required, including skilled craftwork. This made it easy, and indeed rational, for employers to operate an external labour market policy based on hire-and-fire and low-wage costs for over a century. Moreover, product markets were fragmented, cyclical, and resistant to standardization. Investment in new production technology was dubious for the same reasons, resulting in the retention of existing technology–labour relationships and requirements. More efficient use of labour, such as might have occurred through the adoption of scientific management techniques, was not introduced by management, partly because of the nature of the product markets, but also because the inherent skills proved inadequate and the unions insisted on retaining craft systems of job control. Personnel management as a specialist function did not exist in the nineteenth century, emerging first around the time of the First World War, with a slow and limited process of internalization thereafter. When the labour market changed substantially, as it did during and after the Second World War, employers found that the institutions they had used for the earlier type of labour market were now no longer appropriate. By that time, however, powerful shop-floor groups had begun to emerge amongst semi-skilled as well as craft workers, acting as a bulwark against modernization. Moreover, the process of labour–management relations had assumed significant political overtones, with consequences for management authority and legitimacy.

To put this into a managerial context, as a result of the apparent success of the early policies based on the ready availability of labour and low wages, there was a delay in the development of appropriate systems and methods of modern management in the personnel field. Instead, in a Coaseian sense, companies delegated or externalized the responsibility for the management of labour in various ways (to subcontractors, foremen, employers' associations, and even to shop stewards), used the external labour market rather than developing an internal one, and failed to build up a structure of internal managerial control and leadership. Thus, there was little contribution to the hierarchy of managers associated with managerial capitalism; even more importantly, there was a loss of control in the workplace, resulting not only in inefficiencies but also a challenge to the legitimacy of management and indeed capitalism as a whole.

The story of this chapter is therefore primarily about the problems caused by the externalization of responsibility and the slow transition to internalization and professionalization of labour management. This slow transition is reflected in the stuttering growth of personnel departments. The rapid recent growth is closely associated with the emergence of the M-form organizational structures of managerial capitalism, as well as the increased range of legal and administrative obligations imposed on the employment relationship. This numerical growth can also be complemented by identifying various overlapping stages in the development and professionalization of the labour, personnel, and HR (to use the current parlance) management function:

1. Up to 1900: no relationship other than through the market and subcontracting;
2. 1900–30s: welfare officers introduced, initially for female workers;
3. 1920–45: labour management to administer work-related issues;
4. 1945–85: industrial relations concerned with relationships between management and trade unions;
5. 1945 to the present: emergence of personnel administration with the spread of subfunctions;
6. 1980 to present: rise of human resource management (HR).

There is a substantial literature on the history of the management–labour relationship in Britain, most of it written in terms of the two parties, the institutions created around their relationship, and the ideology according to which the relationship was conducted as the components of what was essentially an endogenous system of the type defined by Dunlop (1958). Conversely, the dominant model of organizational development, that of Chandler (1962, 1977, 1990), did not take account of labour matters as a key factor influencing change. More recently, however, Gospel (1992, 2003, 2005) and his various collaborators have stressed the importance of exogenous factors, notably product markets, wider labour markets, and organizational structure, providing a more open approach that we intend to pursue.

Before moving into the historical narrative, a caveat is needed, because what has been said above implies a universal framework. It is consequently vital to stress that our arguments relate especially to mining and manufacturing, and most specifically to the staple industries of the nineteenth century. While the overall framework was substantially similar, inevitably there were different patterns in different industries and even different companies. Most of the service sector has had a rather less turbulent relationship between management and labour over the last two centuries than our story reflects. Nevertheless, the theme of externalization is still relevant to the general analysis, providing genuine insights into the national scene.

EARLY DEPENDENCE ON SUBCONTRACTING

Even by the limited standards of management at the time, the management of labour in the early stages of industrialization scarcely existed, given that it was almost entirely delegated or externalized. Most of the early relationships were also personal, rather than administrative (Bendix 1956: 57). For example, Matthew Boulton of Boulton & Watt maintained a personal relationship with his workers, knew their names and their families, and relied upon the relationship to ensure the discipline and work performance needed in his enterprise. On the other hand, succeeding generations of industrialists were less inclined to regard their workers as individuals, even if socially inferior. Moreover, they did not believe that their work performance could be controlled on this personal basis; rather, they tended to regard the workers as factors of production, for whom the main consideration was cost, and for whom they rejected a direct relationship, preferring to delegate or externalize it to others. There were several dimensions involved in this approach:

- Due to continuing high unemployment and a relatively immobile labour force, British employers had at their disposal an abundance of labour, including skilled craftsmen, from early industrialization up to the Second World War, with the exception of the First World War. This gave employers a power advantage in the labour market.

- Wages were low and employer policy aimed at keeping them low, rather than to increase productivity through modernization via new technologies or production systems.

- The response to competition was either to seek to take wages out of the sphere of competition by ensuring that all employers paid the same through multi-employer agreements, or in the case of foreign competition to seek to lower wages further.

- Firms were happy to rely on the more experienced workers to recruit, train, supervise, and allocate shop-floor labour. On-the-job training systems, with senior operatives training their eventual replacements, permitted the renewal of a skilled labour force at little if any expense for employers. Meanwhile, the younger workers, being eager to gain entry to the 'aristocracy of labour', were kept hard at work by the promise of promotion.

- The reliance on experienced labour to perform these functions had the advantage of low fixed costs, not only for individual firms, but also for the British economy as a whole.

- The prevailing philosophy of laissez-faire and freedom of contract in the first half of the nineteenth century, whereby individuals were considered responsible for their own destiny (although with some legislative concern for women and elements of paternalism in some industries), meant that most employers felt little responsibility for their workers. Even among workers there was an acceptance of self-dependence, especially amongst craft workers and their unions as they developed.

Two important features of this system for our argument are that, first, it worked well for a long time, becoming embedded and embarking on a trajectory of path dependency, and second, it required little or no management to operate it. In the absence of a management control structure, subcontracting was prevalent as a mechanism of externalization. Littler (1983: 61) suggests that there were three main patterns of subcontracted management that emerged in the nineteenth century. One was based on the family as the basis of the workforce, with the father as 'minder' and supervisor of his family members, a situation frequently found in cotton spinning. The second was where master craftsmen had apprentices bound to them and not to the owners of the company, as in iron, shipbuilding, and to a rather lesser extent in engineering and the metal trades. The third was concerned with work organized in gangs under a gang boss or contractor, often found in building and civil engineering, railway and canal construction, and coalmining. All three systems provided a level of legitimated independence to labour, relieving the employer of responsibility.

In the open labour market context that these arrangements created, unions came into existence to try to regulate market forces by creating a 'common rule' for particular classes of labour in a particular trade, initially in local labour markets, but ultimately within national product markets. This was easiest where there were specific craft skills to defend and the price elasticity of demand for labour could be controlled through limiting the numbers in the labour market. As early as the 1790s, mule spinners in the cotton industry had organized themselves into strong unions, seeking to pressure employers to adhere to printed wage lists. At the company level, the high degree of competition in the product market persuaded employers to favour conciliation rather than confrontation; thus, in the Preston strike of 1853–4, the employers won the battle over wages with their workers, but lost badly to other districts which were not involved with the strike. In other traditional industries, such as iron and steel and mechanical engineering, the reasons for craft control were much the same as in cotton, namely, the need to preserve craft job control and jurisdiction. Subcontracting at the employer level also fitted well with collective bargaining between unions and multi-employer organizations. The outcome of this was an acceptance that labour management was effectively left in the hands of these overlapping groups, something which, as we saw in the previous paragraphs, employers were in any case disposed to do.

This was one of the defining issues for the management of British labour. It meant that companies were willing to continue with hand skills, rather than moving to machine skills. Indeed, the concept of craft was antithetical to that of machine standardization and deskilling; it meant that companies could operate with low fixed investments, while in addition few managers were required to control operations. It also meant that employers were committed to labour-intensive methods, rather than the substitution of labour for capital that mass production systems would require. On the other hand, the system created problems for generations to come. The craft system, with its start in apprenticeship, created a defensive set of attitudes in workers concerned to protect their investment in traditional skills. As the Donovan Commission was to note as late as 1968, 'the knowledge that they have virtually committed themselves to a craft for life makes men alert to guard what they consider to be their own preserve, and to oppose relaxations in practices which, however desirable and even essential for efficiency, may seem to constitute a threat to their whole way of life' (Donovan 1968: 87). The cost for employers was that they lost control over the distribution of tasks, the pace of work, apprenticeship programmes, and wage structures.

Of course, in spite of accepting the advantages of craft control, there were some significant confrontations between management and workers, often largely initiated by the employers. Examples, such as the lockout in mechanical engineering in 1852 against the newly formed Amalgamated Society of Engineers, or the conflicts in the iron industry in the late 1860s, reflect at least a partial willingness to challenge the system. On the other hand, the favourable economic conditions of the third quarter made employers more susceptible to sharing power over working conditions and pay levels, allowing the system another generation in which to embed itself as 'custom and practice'.

THE RISE OF ORGANIZED LABOUR AND THE LOSS OF MANAGERIAL CONTROL

This period from 1870 saw the beginnings of growth in size and organizational complexity, the rise of unions as a significant challenge, adverse trading conditions to replace the mid-century confidence, and more competitive product markets as other countries rapidly industrialized. While all of these had an impact on the management of labour, there was no strong willingness or indeed ability to change. The implications of the abdication of control became especially apparent in this period, but not to the point where employers were willing to take control by substantial investment in middle managers, scientific management systems, and new technologies. Their basic attitudes did not change; rather, they sought refuge in other forms of delegation, notably the foreman and the employers' association, as the role of the subcontractor declined. There were some examples from the late nineteenth century of advanced practice, especially in the utilities and in large companies with relatively favourable product market positions with restricted competition where labour cost increases could be passed on, such as the utilities, the chocolate companies, and at Lever Brothers. Such developments, mainly in training, wage structures, benefits, and welfare, involved internal managerial responsibility and administration. The substantial majority of companies, however, was in less stable markets and they were obliged to respond to demand changes and trade cycles. A further factor of considerable importance was that the pattern of demand did not lend itself to mass production in the older industries, being largely bespoke and fragmented. In these circumstances, using the external system of hire-and-fire and lay-off was the easiest approach for most employers.

In the engineering industry, while one of the main mechanisms for increasing production from the 1880s was the piecework system, there was little or no sophisticated measurement associated with it. Rather, it tended to be ad hoc and rule of thumb, resulting in management trying to reduce rates while the workers tried to restrict output. Furthermore, this unsystematic way of managing allowed labour in the form of unions or workgroups to continue to exert control over the pace of work. Nevertheless, given the availability of reasonably well-trained labour and low-wage costs held down by unemployment, the invisible hand of the market mechanism worked well for employers. The system was cheap, and indeed not just cheap, but for quite a long period it was efficient in permitting Britain to continue to dominate various markets, because production workers assumed what is now viewed as the managerial function of ensuring flow through the production process. The structure of industry also played a part, since following the industrial clusters model described in Chapter 3, companies remained small and specialized for the most part, especially in the staple industries. This system was not, however, compatible with the high-throughput, mass-production technologies that became available from the late nineteenth century, primarily from the United States, and requiring a substantial management structure for planning and control. Indeed, it was not compatible with change of any sort, with employer attempts to exert control meeting only with limited success in the staple industries, and especially engineering. As Zeitlin (1983: 35) noted, 'by 1914 it had become clear that despite important gains, engineering employers had failed, at least in the older sectors of the industry, either fully to displace skilled workers from their central position in the division of labour or to break the back of craft regulation as a significant constraint on their freedom of action in the workplace.'

In the couple of decades before the First World War, the nature of externalization changed with the substitution of foremen for the internal labour contractor and the rise of employer associations to look after the developing issues of industrial relations. In many respects, the traditional nineteenth-century foreman performed the same functions as the subcontractor: hiring and firing, promotion, discipline, payment, production planning, and the allocation of work, with the crucial differences being that he did not employ his own labour and he was himself paid a wage, rather than having an entrepreneurial interest in costs and profits (Melling 1980). Indeed, the importance of the foreman was considerable, being 'very much the master in the workplace and ... the key figure in labour management' (Gospel 1983: 98). He became, and in some contexts still is, the controller of labour and of the production process. At the same time, this did not make him the extension of managerial control to the labour process, for two main reasons: the foreman was normally recruited from the ranks of those he supervised, and was rarely promoted to the ranks of management; and his role was inadequately supported by management (Anthony 1986: 87–8). Thus, foremen were not seen as, nor did they feel, part of management.

While associations of employers dated back to the eighteenth century and were commonplace by the early nineteenth, it was the spread of unionism late in the nineteenth century which gave a new focus to employer associations. Indeed, these were to be the main institutional form of externalization for almost the following century. Employer associations performed three main functions. First, they defended managerial prerogatives and helped to curtail trade union activity at the workplace. Second, they often took the initiative in creating relationships with unions at the district or national level through disputes procedures. And third, they gradually developed a framework of substantive agreements on wages and conditions. Less explicit, but arguably even more important, was that they also helped to take labour out of the sphere of competition.

While national agreements were minimal and largely based on dispute-settling procedures, they gave employers nominal managerial control in the workplace, as well as some degree of product market control, while at the same time minimizing the need to develop internal systems. Most employers operated on the concept of voluntarism (although by the First World War there were wage boards in some low-skill industries) and exerting managerial prerogatives at the plant level, which were central to their views of the system. While in the 1890s the Engineering Employers' Federation (EEF) and the engineering unions fought over the 'right to manage' issue, with a major dispute in 1897 that the former won decisively, relatively little changed in an industry dominated by bespoke markets. Not all industries had such ongoing difficulties, with industry-wide procedures providing a framework of peace. On the other hand, national wage agreements also meant that there was less opportunity or incentive for trading increases in productivity at the plant level for increases in wages, since wage rates were set elsewhere. Indeed, the national wage structure did not provide reasonable incentives for workers. National agreements also accepted a system of multi-unionism, which could later become a source of problems over jurisdiction or membership.

By the turn of the century, there were approximately two million trade union members, or some 15 per cent of the workforce, more than in any other country at that time. Numbers also continued to grow up to and through the First World War. At the same time, industrial relations deteriorated in this period of rising prices and threats to real wages, to the point where in 1914 a general strike seemed possible. The problems for employers were further exacerbated by the ability of British unionism to exercise influence through its political partner, the Labour Party, which achieved strong union support after the Taff Vale case in 1901 had challenged the legal status of unions. Henceforth, British politics would be dominated by the industrial divide for most of the next century. The War itself provided a dramatic, if short-lived, change in the labour context, and especially in the requirements for management in this area. There was a massive increase in the demand for labour, as well as greater turnover, while many workers (especially women) joined the labour force for the first time. This period also saw the rise of shop stewards at the plant level, together with government controls over both labour and production, including the establishment of an Arbitration Board. Furthermore, the influential Whitley Committee advocated the formalization of labour–management relationships. All these required new managers and management systems in the factory, especially with regard to the supervision of labour. However, even though in many companies novel systems were adopted, few of these survived after the War, leading to a return to the status quo and all that implied for production and shop-floor management.

THE FORMALIZATION OF BARGAINING IN THE INTERWAR PERIOD

During a short-lived post-war boom, characterized by a rise in union numbers to a peak of over eight million in 1920, or 45 per cent of the workforce, widespread fears were expressed about the implications of collectivist tendencies amongst workers in the light of the 1917 Russian Revolution. After 1920, however, with unemployment returning to haunt the workforce—between 1921 and 1939, never less than 10 per cent of the insured workforce were unemployed—these fears dissipated. Indeed, as employers still thought in terms of money wages rather than efficiency wages, there were significant wage cuts in the early 1920s and 1929–33. Symptomatically, when Ford followed a high-wage–high-output approach based on its American system, the EEF even tried to persuade other firms not to follow suit. A broadly based managerial school of thought believed that unemployment was desirable, because it enabled employers to manage on a hire-and-fire basis. Nor was there a strong interest in productivity; rather, there was an intensification of work within the existing technologies, using the foreman to control labour. The net result was a widespread failure to implement the systems and structure associated with American managerial capitalism.

Having noted these generally limited responses, it is important to remember that there were some structural reappraisals as companies were forced to review their market position in the cold light of the post-First World War situation. Delegation of responsibility for labour matters could not continue indefinitely, because the growth of complexity in production systems and the requirements of new payment systems meant the need for a more structured back office. It was in this period that the works manager emerged as a key figure, with specific responsibility for labour matters, along with nascent personnel professionals, including work study engineers and management accountants in the new middle ranks of management. Moreover, more workers were directly employed by the firm and there was less subcontracting and casual work. These developments also meant that a new functional area of management was required, with recruitment becoming more organized. In addition, a concept of job property rights for workers began to emerge. On the other hand, minimal attention was paid to training and development. Apprentice development was handed over to the skilled men, with little or no central coordination from management, a system that usually amounted to 'sitting by Nellie' (Gospel 1992: 66). In practice, apprentices were used as a source of cheap labour, rather than being identified as the skilled resources for the future of the firm.

Alongside these limited internal innovations, the delegation of industrial relations issues was if anything accentuated after the Whitley Committee recommended a format of joint industrial councils essentially based on existing arrangements. By 1920, there were some 2,500 multi-employer agreements. Although in theory the system existed at three levels, workplace, district, and national, in practice most firms had only rudimentary machinery at workplace level, since employers strongly preferred to deal with trade unions outside the plant. Very few works councils were set up following the Whitley Report, while many of those did not survive the depression of the early 1920s. Similarly, not all industries operated at the national level, with the General Strike of 1926, for example, arising out of the union's desire to enforce district agreements in coal. Additionally, in the growing number of multi-plant companies, there was no provision at the company level, which would have been important for the development of integrated policies or management structures in the personnel area.

There was a further substantial shift to plant-based piecework in the interwar period, since it acted as an incentive at the individual level. However, as a safeguard against rate-cutting, the EEF was willing to allow piecework prices to be fixed by mutual agreement, something that was to cause problems after the Second World War when the employment situation changed. Moreover, piecework prices were not based on analysis, but rather for the most part on rule of thumb at the departmental level. Thus, 'easy' piecework rates set by lower-level management reflected a lack of higher-level management control. There was little concern given to job analysis and grading (leading later to job evaluation) which would have required skilled input and coordination by personnel managers. This, in turn, meant that the measurement of productivity was not a crucial factor in industrial relations, as it was under 'internal' systems operating some form of scientific management. Rather, piecework took the place of management in the control of labour. Thus, plant level managerial prerogatives were soon being threatened by the weaknesses in the system in skirmishes over 'the frontier of control'. While the militant shop steward movement of the First World War had died away by the early 1920s, workplace bargaining began to grow outside the agreed procedures. In consequence, it was estimated that half the strikes in the engineering industry were in breach of procedure.

National agreements also varied considerably according to the product market, being more comprehensive and effective either where there was shelter from foreign competition or collusion between firms. As Gospel (1992: 90) noted: 'Trade competition is a powerful factor in determining to what extent the members of an association will adhere to a common policy.' Engineering, the largest and most important industry, had a number of different sectors with variations in profitability, competition, and market stability, creating divisions for the EEF. As McKinlay and Zeitlin (1989: 33–4) observed, 'moreover, such internal divisions within the Federation left little scope for unilateral amplification of managerial prerogative into a substantive code specifying machine manning arrangements, training methods or payment systems for the industry as a whole ... the actual use of the managerial prerogative was more to intensify work within existing structures and technologies than to introduce change'.

At the same time, some firms did not participate in these agreements: small companies, firms which refused to recognize unions, and some large companies which dealt with unions outside the aegis of employers' associations, such as ICI, Unilever, Cadbury, Imperial Tobacco, and most American-owned firms. Apart from being a leader in work study, ICI had an elaborate system of works councils, whilst also recognizing and dealing with unions at the company level. It was also these companies which sought the help of management consultants, initially Bedaux, whose system has been described by Littler (1982) as 'neo-Taylorite'. The Bedaux system was intended to simplify jobs and create clearly defined job boundaries, resulting in a division between direct and indirect labour, and concentrating authority and initiative in the hands of the planning department. Additionally, it established a system of monitoring effort through the introduction of more formal effort norms. Although rapid diffusion of new ideas has never been a strong point of British industry, industry leaders such as ICI, Lucas, and Joseph Lyons employed Bedaux consultants, leading as many as 250 companies to imitate them by 1939. Bedaux thus became the most common system of management control in Britain. Nevertheless, there was considerable resistance to the introduction of Bedaux systems in Britain (Littler 1982), especially as many firms experienced severe industrial relations problems after their consultants left. While several consultancy firms were also established in the 1930s, including Urwick Orr, PA, and PE, consolidating neo-Taylorite ideas and practices in substantial parts of British industry, there was still no strongly defined managerial ideology. Nevertheless, the new systems, alongside the slow emergence of fringe benefits, such as pension and sick pay schemes, did require internalization and new labour managers to operate them, stimulating some limited investments in what we now regard as middle management (Hannah 1983).

One manifestation of this new trend, and reflecting the dawn of a new professional identity, was the creation in 1913 of the Welfare Workers' Association, most of whom were female (Niven 1967). Although they were initially appointed for the 'external' dimensions of welfare, it was not long before the more committed of them became involved in aspects of factory administration, including in some cases payment systems. After growth during the War, the postwar period proved difficult, given the changing labour market. Nevertheless, legal incorporation was granted in 1924, so that the body changed its name to the

Institution of Industrial Welfare Workers. In 1927, there were 420 members, of whom only 15 were men. There was, however, a widening of the role into areas connected with the management of labour, especially selection and training. In 1931, the Institution also decided to change its name again, this time to the Institute of Labour Management, which made it possible to recruit some high-profile labour managers, in particular Richard Lloyd-Roberts of ICI and C. H. Northcott of Rowntrees, both of whom were to play a major role in the Institute. Lloyd-Roberts, for example, insisted that while it was essential for labour policy to come from the board, labour managers should also be able to advise their boards. Another move to establish itself in the labour field was the production of an influential policy paper entitled 'Note on Industrial Relations', thus entering a hitherto delicate area.

In spite of the fact that the Institute was reasonably firmly established by 1939, the area had by no means achieved professional status. While there were a substantial number of specialized managers, one could not recognize an overall function comprising the whole of personnel. Furthermore, with very few exceptions, there was almost no representation at senior levels.

THE POST-WAR BATTLE TO CONTROL THE SHOP FLOOR

In the third quarter of the twentieth century, although there was a gradual accretion in personnel managers and their functions in the firm, the key issue of the period was industrial relations, driven by high rates of employment and a legacy of poor relationships. In the post-war period, employers did little either to confront the unions as they did in the United States and Japan or to cooperate with them, as in Germany and Sweden. Crucially, the existing system became increasingly ineffective as large gaps in the industrywide agreements became obvious and power moved decisively back to the shop floor. Managements found themselves dealing with shop stewards and groups of workers under the pressure of full employment and uncertain product markets in a system of workplace bargaining which was, in Flanders' famous phrase 'largely informal, largely fragmented, and largely autonomous' (1970: 169). Not infrequently even the shop stewards, themselves acting in quasi-defiance of the union hierarchies, were outflanked by work groups who took 'unofficial unofficial' action, thereby undermining the tenuous relationship between stewards and managers. Indeed, stewards often found themselves acting as de facto managers in decision-making and trying to enforce discipline (Gospel 1983). Multiple unionism was a further complicating factor that Broadberry and Crafts (1996) identified with poor industrial relations. Workplace bargaining was initially the responsibility of individual managers at a relatively low level, but as time went on it became a challenge to the organization as a whole, requiring consideration at the highest levels (Purcell and Sisson 1983). How to regain control became a major issue, often leading to the appointment of industrial relations specialists at board level.

Admittedly, these trends were mainly found in manufacturing and were much less prevalent in the service industries, but the overall impact was sufficient for the 'English disease' to achieve worldwide notoriety. It also had a significant effect on the authority, legitimacy, and confidence of management.

While the situation was clearly difficult, it was not as bad as the image sometimes given in the media and politics. Keenoy (1985) put the amount of time lost by strikes between 1946 and 1973 into perspective by measuring it as 0.07 per cent of working time. Nevertheless, the Royal Commission on Trade Unions and Employers' Associations (1968), chaired by Lord Donovan, was a necessary stage in bringing the nature of the problem home to employers, workers, and the public. The Commission (Donovan 1968: 261) noted that 'Britain has two systems of industrial relations. One is the formal system embodied in the official institutions. The other is the informal system created by the actual behaviour of trade unions and employers' associations, of managers, shop stewards and workers', and that 'the informal system is often at odds with the formal system'. Amongst the problems identified by Donovan were:

- Wage drift caused by payment by results systems working loose
- Fragmented structures and power, causing 'unofficial unofficial' strikes
- Poor management controls
- Restrictive practices
- Multi-union jurisdictional problems
- Domination of 'custom and practice' and precedent in the absence of detailed agreements
- Leapfrogging or parity wage claims

The Donovan Report essentially blamed the lack of a developed managerial structure for the situation. The role of employers' associations meant that there was little incentive to introduce professional management in the firm. Moreover, when the gaps in the industrywide system became apparent, the employer associations could not provide solutions. At the same time, the Commission (1968: 25) also noted the spread of personnel managers, yet asked and then answered the key rhetorical question:

If companies have their own personnel specialists, why have they not introduced effective personnel policies to control methods of negotiation and pay structures within their firms? Many firms have no such policy, and perhaps no conception of it.... Many firms had acquired disorderly pay structures and uncoordinated personnel practices before they appointed a personnel manager, and the burden of dealing with disputes and problems as they arise has absorbed his whole time and energy.

In other words, personnel managers in the 1960s were paying the price of inadequate policies stretching well back into history.

In its proposed solution, the Commission essentially tried to reform but maintain a system of voluntarism and pluralism. It saw the solution in procedures, which recognized the reality of what was happening on the shop floor, and especially in providing better management. Above all, Donovan asked why firms did not develop effective policies and looked to the boards of directors of large companies to take the initiative. Only slowly, however, did they respond. Procedures helped to legitimize the decisions made by management and could themselves take several forms, most notably to differentiate between issues of interpreting existing agreements (especially in the introduction of much more formalized grievance and disciplinary procedures) and new issues, for which revised bargaining structures with a focus at the company level were commonly introduced. But procedures were not enough by themselves. Another key area was in work definition through the improved use of work study techniques and job evaluation systems, new payment systems, notably measured day work, plantwide bonus schemes, and the reduction of individual incentive pay. In addition, there was a move to more flexible working practices across previous job boundaries. Extending from these measures was a rise in productivity bargaining, albeit often as a means of side stepping the range of incomes policies introduced by successive governments as means of overcoming inherent inflationary pressures. Another innovation was the introduction of accounting controls, with the development of M-form structures often on the advice of consultants and associated with the spread of computer programming. These enabled senior management to reconnect with what was happening on the shop floor, and although bargaining became increasingly decentralized from industrywide systems, this was in the context of budgetary frameworks within which the personnel officers had to work.

All these developments required management specialists to assume responsibility for ensuring that the policies and procedures were enforced. Crucially, this meant taking some of the power and discretion to make decisions by supervision and line management which had permitted the growth of informal bargaining in the first place. While one might argue that many of these developments should arguably have been introduced half a century earlier, at least by the late 1970s there was a strong move to internal, single-plant, employer-based collective bargaining at plant or company level and a concomitant decline in the influence of employers' associations. Moreover, these new technologies and methods of working required more sophisticated managerial competencies, including strategic understanding at the top level and technical/organizational expertise at middle and lower levels.

Of course, at times the changing situation sometimes developed in a conflictual way, notably with British Leyland under Sir Michael Edwardes and Eddie Shah in printing, both of whom reconstructed workplace industrial relations and imposed management prerogatives over recalcitrant unions. From the perspective of the late 1970s, it would not have been expected that the battle would have been won so quickly, but with mounting unemployment and significant changes in the legal status of trade unions, the odds moved decisively in favour of employers. The last great eruption of what might now be called old-style industrial relations was the national coal strike of 1984, a fiercely waged battle which saw most of the resources of the state aligned against the striking miners. After the miners' defeat, a new phase started in which the authority of management has since been unchallenged.

Another important development was that, post-Donovan, successive governments from both major parties started to introduce a wide range of legislation to cover aspects of the employment relationship, including pay, labour market structures, health and safety, equal opportunities, discipline, and dismissal. This further reduced the role of the union in being the sole champion of the workforce by creating a platform of individual rights. The law also required employers to establish a framework of employment relations. The Advisory, Conciliation, and Arbitration Service (ACAS), created in 1975, complemented the legislation and helped many companies with advice and leaflets on best employment practice, as well as providing a greatly valued conciliation and arbitration service. Workers would now have to look to the law for protection as much if not more than to unions, while in addition the law also required employers to develop professional standards and organization in the way that they managed.

The internalization of staff management not only meant a growth in professionalization of the function, but also in the growth of the Institute in the post-war period. The coming of war had again made a major difference, with widespread labour controls introduced that gave the Institute and company labour officers a much more prominent role. The role itself also expanded, as indicated in yet another change in title to the Institute of Personnel Management. Much of the last half-century has been taken up in consolidating the function as it grew within the organization. Institute membership also grew, from 2,881 at the end of the War to some 15,000 in the mid-1960s, while by the late 1970s it stood at some 50,000, coinciding with the period of structural readjustment to managerial capitalism. The upgrading of standards through the creation of qualifications for membership has been a recurring theme. Full membership was restricted from 1955 to those who took a recognized course of training in personnel management or passed the Institute's examinations or were a practising personnel manager over 35 with several years' experience. In 1975, this was changed to experience coupled with the examination, while at the turn of the century came a requirement for Continuing Professional Development (CPD), by which time membership was almost 100,000. Institutionally, in 1994 there was a merger with the Institute of Training and Development, to create the Institute of Personnel and Development, while in 2000 the ultimate accolade was achieved when chartered status was granted and it became the Chartered Institute of Personnel and Development (CIPD).

THE ASSERTION OF MANAGERIAL CONTROL: 1985–PRESENT

The move to professionalize industrial relations in the post-Donovan period was complemented by external developments: a recession in the early 1980s, resulting in higher unemployment, the reduction in wage drift, or indeed wage inflation, and the decline of manufacturing. There has also been some rationalization within the big companies in a search for external, rather than internal, economies of scale. In addition, the introduction of much tougher anti-union industrial relations legislation by the Conservative government of Margaret Thatcher gave strength to management, although this was offset to some extent by EU legislation which added a good deal of further substance and complexity to the law, requiring organizations to be much more responsible employers. The results were significant. Managements initiated offensives against union working practices, with a limited amount of derecognition occurring across many sectors. The strike record also changed markedly: from its problematic record of the 1970s, Britain became one of the most peaceful in the world. In consequence, union membership declined, from just over 11 million in the early 1970s to seven million at the turn of the century, with a particular decline in the private sector. The supremacy of industrial relations issues within the overall labour field also subsided, with the subject changing its name to 'employee relations', that is, it moved from the collective focus of industrial relations to a more individual focus.

Indeed, we are currently seeing a new and quite different phase of managing people. Managements have asserted their new-found authority, with a significant change in the rhetoric of managing people, from personnel administration to the American model of human relations management (HR), involving an integration of HR policies with strategy and seeing the human dimension as a key factor in giving a competitive edge, involving the securing of employee commitment, as opposed to mere compliance, and much more attention given to the selection and development of employees. Associated with this approach has been a change in the management frame of reference, or ideology, in the labour field. Pluralism became the dominant ideology of the post-war period, in which the enterprise is seen as consisting of a number of stakeholders, each with different interests and objectives, some of which clash and some coincide. In particular, unions are seen as the legitimate representatives of the workers and clashes of objectives are resolved by bargaining and compromise. In the unitary perspective, the emphasis is on common goals for every party connected with the enterprise, with the legitimacy and authority of management associated with setting these goals. In this perspective, unions are accepted on sufferance as interlopers, if at all. While the nineteenth-century entrepreneur had a unitarist view based on social and property rights, the new system of HR also took a similar perspective, although with a greater recognition of the needs of labour as a means of improving efficiency.

There has been much discussion about what constitutes the appropriate package of HR policies to provide a people-based competitive edge, with particular interest in the concept of high performance work organizations (HPWOs) as providing commitment, flexibility, and quality. Debate has also centred on whether such a package should be based on universalist or contingency assumptions. Nevertheless, there has been research which shows reasonably clearly that successful financial outcomes can be achieved by an HPWO package, both in the United States (Huselid 1995) and Britain (Patterson et al. 1997). All this required policy integration of the whole HR package and the management of corporate culture, as well as systems and procedures. In addition, the management of people was seen as being too important to be left to the personnel specialists; line managers needed to be involved as both deliverers and drivers of HR policy (Storey 2001).

Given the rhetoric and research in favour of people as a source of competitive advantage, the question then becomes what sorts of policies are actually being operated on the ground. It is in this respect that the evidence is not encouraging:

- Personnel is still a weak function in the UK, still relatively rarely on the board of directors, and especially weak in relation to the finance function. It tends to be administrative and reactive, rather than strategic and proactive. In a comparative survey, both HR managers and line managers in Britain rated HR as a source of competitive advantage considerably lower than did their counterparts in six other European countries. They also gave a low rating to the link between HR and strategy (Mabey and Ramirez 2004: 13).

- Keep and Mayhew (2001) suggest that the proportion of UK firms which have well-developed high-performance work systems is no more than 2 per cent of the total. But at the other extreme from the HPWO ideal there are many companies which have as little to do with the personnel function as possible.

- Training in Britain remains largely voluntaristic, with resistance by employers to attempts by government to encourage an increase in this crucial dimension of managerial professionalism. Moreover, managers in many UK organizations believe that their workers require only limited skills (Cully et al. 1999).

- A focus on the short term which Sisson (2001: 94) explains in terms of the financial orientation of the UK's business system places a premium on cost minimization, rather than investment in HR.

- Gospel (1992) argues that internal labour markets in Britain are weaker than in the United States, Germany, and Japan. One might also stress how they have tended to weaken further since he wrote.

- With the rise of HR, there has been a strong tendency to downgrade the personnel function in favour of more responsibility for line managers. At the same time, Keep and Westwood (2003: 23) argue that 'one of the largest skill gaps in UK management appears to centre on the ability of managers to handle people issues in constructive and innovative ways and to put to best use the skills of those that they employ. The problem has become more acute with the move by many organizations to devolve responsibility for large areas of people management to line managers, many of whom have been singularly ill-prepared to deal with these newfound responsibilities.'

- Fringe benefits, especially company-based pensions, are under threat.

- There tends to be a core of privileged workers and a periphery of more casual employees, with much more part-time working, especially female. In essence, risk in the product market has been transferred to employees, and especially to non-core employees.

- Employers believe that a deregulated labour market is a source of competitive strength (Keep and Mayhew 2001). The UK (together with the United States) holds bottom place in the OECD's table calculating the intensity of labour market regulation. Low levels of protection and high insecurity tend to be associated with work intensification and long hours. People in the UK work the longest hours in the EU, with a considerable amount of unpaid overtime.

- The period has seen a return to externalization through widespread outsourcing of various functions, including various personnel functions from recruitment to wage administration. Indeed, some firms have subcontracted the whole employment function for non-core staff to external agencies.

Thus, in spite of a good deal of credible research about the links between the quality of people management and organizational performance, there is little evidence that such links are being heeded in Britain. Why not? The answer seems to lie in the intensification of product market competition, including competitive pressures from abroad where labour costs are lower, forcing companies to take a short-term perspective. Alongside this is the wider product market strategy of many British companies in which deciding to compete in low specification product or service markets means competing on price, which in turn means competing on unit labour costs, Fordist work organization, and a lower need for skilled labour. Thus, the pragmatic case for an HPWO approach is weakened. Furthermore, as the success of tough stands is publicized, the shift to unitary policies based on coercion rather than cooperation becomes more frequent and less challenged. This in turn reduces the power of the specialist HR managers within the organization.

CONCLUSIONS

For most of the last 200 years, British employers have pursued a commodity approach towards labour, resulting in a degree of path dependency created by the early relationship which was not broken until the 1970s and 1980s. It is consequently ironic that just as they were moving to a more internalized approach, the domination of the financial marketplace has pushed labour back to a commodity status. Many of the arguments have been based on employer use of the external, rather than an internal, labour market in Britain, with its implications for certain types of skills and skill formation. Figure 9.1, borrowed from Littler (1982), illustrates the differences between external and internal labour markets. While these are ideal types, they can also be used to differentiate the British labour market, using A and B, with the type of labour market preferred in the United States, Germany, and Japan, focused on C and D. The craft system meant a primary loyalty to the craft and the unions which defended it, while unskilled recruitment was ineffective without a training programme to provide both general and specific skills, especially if, as in Britain, the education system was poor at providing a vocational preparation prior to entering the labour market.

	Linked to external labour market	Linked to internal labour market
Broad task range	A. Craft work based on apprenticeship system	C. Multi-talent skills based on internal promotion system
Narrow task range	B. Unskilled work	D. Semi-skilled work with on-the-job training

Figure 9.1. Types of skill formation (Source: Littler 1992)

Moreover, without a strong middle management, both types of labour would cause difficulties, whether in the pursuit of their own interests or through the requirement for supervision. These problems would have occurred without the issue of industrial relations, but the presence of unions certainly compounded the long-term difficulties of pursuing the strategy of externalization.

This is not to say that there was no logic behind externalization, but it had strong disadvantages, especially after these outweighed the advantages from the late nineteenth century. Externalization of authority in the labour–management relationship was a source of considerable weakness in any long-term consideration. It prevented clarity of objectives at the shop-floor level, made measurement and control problematic, increased the social distance between management and workers, and encouraged lack of competition in other markets. It is strange that businessmen who did not want to delegate authority to managers over many issues were willing to do so in the labour field to others over whom they had less control than their managers. It contributed to negative attitudes towards industry in those who saw mainly a battleground between management and labour interests; it also contributed to the development of a political system which was primarily based on class divisions in the industrial arena. But once the pattern was set, it became difficult to change. Indeed, it is arguable that in the third quarter of the twentieth century, as a result of the build-up of problems from earlier generations, British managements became too concerned with the human aspects of the organization.

As we have seen, a key problem until very recently has been the issue of managerial legitimacy and authority. Yet in the debate about authority, there has been little suggestion that the ultimate structural role of management was being challenged in a revolutionary way. Apart from some limited expression in and immediately after the First World War, workforces and trades unions have recognized the generic role of management. What they were interested in was the effort bargain, or as Goodrich (1920) put it, 'the frontier of control'; it was more the looseness of the detail of the effort bargain than the ultimate structure of authority that was being challenged. Certainly, management lacked self-confidence at key times, but this was in large part due to a lack of competence than the efforts of others such as the unions.

As a result, the growth of professionalization in this area was slow until after the organizational restructuring of the 1960s and 1970s. The issues of work control vis-à-vis the labour force had also existed in other countries, where scientific management had been essentially adopted as an engineering-based solution to this problem. But as engineers possessed little status and influence in Britain, employers found it easier not to face up to the problem, hence the attraction of externalization. Moreover, although management has now asserted control, it is doubtful if this outcome could have been attained merely by applying the recommendations of the Donovan Commission. It was fortuitous that British companies were at the same time engaged in substantial organizational restructuring, which enabled better control systems to be initiated and improved policy communication between senior executives and the shop floor, as well as the growth of a more structured and professional management hierarchy. It has also to be said that unemployment and industrial, political, and legal changes facilitated this process, especially in the early 1980s.

More recently, the enterprise has been seen to exist almost solely for the good of the shareholders, arguably to the detriment of the people who work for it. Management has finally asserted control over work practices and in doing so has achieved the authority and legitimacy which were lacking earlier. Moreover, personnel is now a relatively professional function within British industry. At the same time, it is one which wields little real influence. In the major mergers, takeovers, internal restructuring, and indeed overall company strategy, there is hardly any evidence that the people dimension has been of any substantial significance. What companies say about people being their major asset is rhetoric, rather than the basis of their actions.

10

The Practice of Management—Marketing

INTRODUCTION

Marketing history has not been well treated by historians or marketing academics in Britain. While Corley (1993) argued for a more systematic approach to researching the history of marketing to remedy what he described as the lack of 'all-encompassing generalisations', still today there is no overall survey of British marketing. Of course, there has been work by writers such as Church (2000*a*, 2000*b*), Popp (2001), Chapman (1992), Davenport-Hines (1986), and Nicholas (1984), but this has concentrated on the period up to the First World War. This has left an enormous gap, because there has been no serious analysis in Britain of the contribution of markets or marketing to the development of managerial capitalism, or of the growth of the marketing function in organizations, or indeed of corporate marketing strategies, in the second half of the twentieth century. Indeed, little has been written about marketing at all outside the consumer-oriented industries. Wilson (1968: 23, 91), one of the relatively few company historians to pay attention to marketing, noted that while 'the successful manufacturers had progressed through skill in distributing and selling methods as much as through skill of manufacture', market issues 'have never been examined or visited as much as the associated technological virtues'.

The boundaries of marketing have not been and still are not easy to delineate. Moreover, there have been vigorous debates, especially in America, about the various stages in its evolution (Keith 1960; Fullerton 1988; Tedlow 1993). The dominant paradigm has been Keith's breakdown into three eras, namely, domination by production, sales, and marketing. Domination by production meant focusing on the technological and human constraints on supply, while distribution was secondary and left to wholesalers and retailers. This era was held to last until the Great Depression of the 1930s, which forced companies to refocus on more aggressive methods of selling backed by advertising and market research. From the 1950s, domination by marketing meant a more sophisticated analysis of customer needs and wants as a basis for production planning, including in particular a focus on market segmentation. While Fullerton (1988) argued that this did not do justice to earlier developments, Church (1998: 83; 1999) has pointed out that 'at all times there have been enterprises which have been concerned to employ a variety of mechanisms to sell, promote, advertise, modify and improve products' in pursuit of market transactions; what changed over time were techniques and intensity, as part of broader changes in the economic and social environment. Although this debate has relevance, we intend to use our own British periodization for the section headings of this chapter, identifying the most important features of the development of marketing in a particular period. Before we move into these stages, however, we need to discuss the role of marketing and externalization in the rise of managerial capitalism.

As a preliminary point, the importance of markets needs to be noted in a more general sense than just marketing. The widening of the market, as Commons (1909) outlined in his classic article 'American Shoemakers, 1648–1895', following the transition from a personal bespoke market supplied by itinerant shoemakers to a world market supplied by mass industrialized production, was a key factor as a catalyst in moving from one economic era to another. Commons illustrates the way in which the widening of the market led to other dimensions of the industrial system well beyond marketing: entrepreneurship, organization, labour contract, and trade unions. Again, the structure of demand affected the choice of technique, and thus influenced productivity, patterns of employment, supplier relationships, and many other facets of industry (Levine 1967). Indeed, the structure of British (and international) markets in terms of issues such as growth and fragmentation is an important issue in British industrial development.

Another factor of major importance is the way in which industry responded to the markets. Marketing is one of the three key areas in which Chandler (1990: 612) argued that investment was necessary in order 'to develop the capabilities to exploit fully the economies of scale and scope'. The main thrust of our explanation lies in the Coasian argument about the nature of transaction costs, with British industry tending to look to external mechanisms rather than internalize and develop a corps of marketing managers. The nature of early British capitalism was such that it paid entrepreneurs to operate their market relationships through intermediaries in a system generally known as merchanting, rather than have a direct relationship with the market (Chapman 1992). In a second dimension of externalization, starting in the late nineteenth century and continuing up to the Second World War, the nature of product markets was such that anti-competitive practices were rife and there was no strong requirement for sophisticated competitive marketing. A third aspect was outsourcing of key marketing functions to external agencies, mainly advertising agencies. While all companies used advertising agencies for their creative inputs, some have also tended to use them, or consultants, for the strategic aspects of their marketing. These features, when combined with other components of British industry, such as the reluctance to delegate authority and the tendency for family-controlled companies within holding companies to maintain a significant operating autonomy, resulted in the failure to develop a substantial central office for coordination and resource allocation which would have been desirable for effective strategic marketing.

Understanding the role of marketing in the rise of managerial capitalism is a key part of the total picture, providing a major part of the strategy of vertical integration. In earlier stages, the consumer had been separated from the manufacturer by a set of intermediaries: brokers, jobbers, wholesalers, agents, and mercantile institutions, with marketing acting as the logistics of getting the product to the consumer. But when mass production became the norm, the manufacturer took control of the relationship with the consumer through branding and advertising in a mass market, and in the case of consumer durables by building their own direct marketing organization, including demonstration, installation, consumer credit, and after-sales service and repair. This also meant that there was a trend to concentration through marketing as both a source of competitive advantage and a barrier to entry via high advertising expenditure and the development of brands and the use of trademarks. Scale economies then provided cost advantages, and thus high profits, to enable them to carry out extensive research and development for new product development, leading on to diversification as a means of expanding from the original product base. Managerial capitalism thus appeared when firms were able to integrate the processes of mass distribution with those of mass production.

There is, indeed, a school of thought which argues that marketing, rather than technology, has been the source of the new corporate structures, and hence of managerial capitalism. Kim's analysis (1999) using census data sought to understand why some multi-plant firms in certain industries grew to dominate the American economy. He found that economies of scale in marketing were the primary determinant in explaining the rise of multi-unit organizations, thus challenging Chandler's emphasis on technical economies of scale and scope. However, we shall argue that this was never the case in Britain; nor was there an era of sales and marketing control that Fligstein (1993) saw as a key stage in American corporate development. Indeed, British marketing was highly distinctive and firmly embedded in the institutions that grew up around industries, highlighting the need to look at this subject in a much broader context.

EARLY BRITISH MARKETING—THE HEYDAY OF MERCHANTING TO 1870

The industries of the British Industrial Revolution, namely, textiles, coal, iron and steel, engineering, and smaller but still important ones such as glass and pottery, were supported by a well-established system of merchants and agents from the eighteenth century to the twentieth century (Chapman 1992). Indeed, McKendrick, Brewer, and Plumb (1982) illustrated that the Industrial Revolution succeeded because production and marketing worked in tandem. For most manufacturers the merchant was the primary or only source of orders; there were no selling or marketing activities as such. Of course, there were some exceptions, including a few early British pioneers of new production methods such as Josiah Wedgwood, who created large-scale demand by techniques such as market segmentation, product differentiation, prestige pricing, direct mail campaigns, and reference group appeals which have usually been associated with post-1950 American innovations in the new age of marketing (McKendrick 1960).

In general, though, by the early nineteenth century, marketing and distribution were controlled by an extensive and highly specialized network of wholesaling factors, commission agents, brokers, and merchants. The mercantile system performed valuable functions for small companies for whom the transaction costs of organizing their own distribution and sales operations, especially abroad, would have been uneconomic. The system provided credit and a network of agents in foreign countries which was invaluable; indeed, some of the great merchant houses, such as Jardine Matheson, still exist today (Connell 2006). How widespread was this system? Chapman's work (1992) concentrates mainly on the cotton trade, which was undoubtedly its main stronghold. It certainly existed elsewhere, but there is more debate here, with Nicholas (1984) for exports and Church (2000*a*) for domestic goods arguing that it was by no means general, and that British companies developed their own arrangements to a greater extent than had hitherto been supposed. Church (2000*a*: 9) also argues that 'a vibrant competitive process does not support the view of marketing as having been inhibited by unchanging structures during the mid-nineteenth century'. He quotes examples, such as Colman's and Reckitt's, of companies which used aggressive marketing strategies and commercial travellers well in advance of the great expansion in the consumer markets, issues that are discussed in the next section. Chapman (1992) probably exaggerates when he claims that 'it seems reasonable to conclude that in Britain merchant houses in one form or another maintained the major role in overseas activity down to the First World War and in some imperial territories beyond the Second World War'. On the other hand, it is also dangerous to argue that British marketing vigour matched that of American and German business. While there were some notable examples of this, for most companies it was a matter of necessity that forced them to rely on the established institutional framework.

While this system clearly helped firms that lacked the resources to commit to extensive marketing, there were also considerable implications for the long-term development of British business organization. These included: providing little incentive for vertical integration; favouring scope rather than scale, by creating little pressure to standardize production; hampering information flows and increasing their costs; using agents who often had multiple interests, and therefore priorities; and in the medium- to long-run, creating a system of path dependency which made it difficult to change when adaptation should have been necessary. More specifically for this chapter, by separating the producer from the consumer, it denied that relationship which is the hallmark of modern marketing. What especially needs to be explained is the gap between what Casson (1997: 98) has described as 'the evolution of regional networks of middlemen supporting the factory system in the nineteenth century and the movement towards vertical integration of mass marketing and mass production around the turn of the twentieth century'. This is the same point where Britain began to lose competitiveness and where Chandler's argument (1990) about the lack of interdependent investment in production, marketing, and management begins to have force.

1870–FIRST WORLD WAR: THE RISE OF BRANDING AND ADVERTISING IN A CONSUMER SOCIETY

This was a period when production was dominant and distribution secondary in the staple industries, with a continuation for the most part of the merchanting and agency system. But in another significant group of industries, Britain came close to the emergence of managerial capitalism and its marketing methods, namely, the newly emerging FMCG industries which were not as susceptible to fluctuations in demand and took account of the increasing incomes of the working class. As Chandler (1990: 267–8) has pointed out, 'it was in branded, packaged products—food and drink, tobacco, and consumer chemicals—that the British industrialists of the Victorian era made their mark.... British industrial fortunes came from these industries and not from oil, industrial chemicals, machinery, and metals, as they did in the United States and Germany.' He also notes that these industries required less costly facilities and less complex managerial and technical skills than the capital-intensive industries. But another dimension was that as consumer products they required marketing, leading to many new developments, from packaging to distribution to selling, and particularly to a massive growth in advertising.

Over the period 1870–1914, the consumer market grew as a result of a 50 per cent rise in purchasing power of the urban worker. This increase was in large part due to favourable terms of trade and the falling prices of imported food and raw materials (Perkin 1989). Meanwhile, the distribution sector witnessed the spread of multiple, department and Co-op shops in what Jefferys (1954: 6) called 'a transformation of the distributive trades comparable in many ways to the revolutionary changes that had taken place in the industrial structure of the country in the previous century', to the point where Britain could be called the world's first modern consumer society. These two developments provided a great opportunity for manufacturers, many of whom were not slow to take advantage. This in turn led to different aspects of marketing becoming a key factor in the intense competition in the product markets that supplied the new retailers. Advertising by the manufacturer was vital both to inform the consumer and persuade the retailer to stick to the product, while branding followed on to provide differentiation within a previously generic product and to give a guarantee of quality. Moreover, the retailer could now have a major effect through the prominence with which goods were displayed, as they had to stand out to the customer through another dimension of marketing, merchandizing. Pears' Soap was the first example of branding in the 1860s, with the use of packaging to identify the brand as well as give protection. Similarly, Lever Brothers did the same with Sunlight Soap in the 1880s. Both of these and other soap firms were amongst the earliest and most heavy users of advertising, while in insurance the Prudential had its well-known image association with the Rock of Gibraltar from the 1890s.

The capacity for entering an industry, and then rapidly expanding in the way Lever or Beecham did, depended on marketing skills and aggressive competition. Of course, while product development also played a role in success, Church and Clark (2001) argue that technology was less important than marketing skills. Advertising provided the opportunity to appeal direct to the consumer, rather than being dependent on intermediaries, while the concept of branding was the logical outcome of identifying the product in the advertising process. In 1870, few consumer goods were regularly advertised, with most advertising covering relative luxuries such as books, sheet music, and the theatre (Goodall 1986: 20). Thereafter, however, a tremendous growth of advertising occurred in the late nineteenth century, mainly in trade journals directed at retailers, and advertisements for the general public in magazines, with a concomitant growth of agencies, initially to sell space.

Advertising was followed by promotions, discounts, and various forms of 'hard' selling as producers sought to woo customers; even though, being short-term in operation, these tended to undermine the brand loyalty that advertising was intended to generate. In these early days, however, it is doubtful if brand loyalty was a consideration; rather, advertising was intended to generate product recognition through reiteration of the message. Indeed, the message was often very basic, using no more than two or three words to couple the name of the company with the product, such as Price's Candles, Colman's Mustard, or Pears' Soap (Church 2000b). Nevertheless, Pears' Soap was spending £100–130,000 a year on various forms of advertising by the mid-1870s (and close to £1 million by 1914), but other companies such as Rowntree, Beecham, and Bovril were not far behind. Indeed, the intensity of advertising growth in the consumer market in the period 1890–1914 probably indicates that supply was outrunning demand. There were also British 'experts' before First World War, especially in advertising, such as Samuel Benson, whose advertising agency remained one of the biggest in Britain into the 1960s. Thomas Russell also rose to prominence on the basis of analysing clients' businesses and emphasizing the need for research based on economic and statistical principles before recommending appropriate advertising. Russell also gave the first set of lectures on advertising at the LSE in 1919 (even if they were not to be repeated for many years). In addition, by the 1870s the FMCG firms felt the need to expand their horizons beyond dealing with wholesalers, leading to the appointment of commercial travellers to take the product to the retailer. Although they had been known for most of the century, the rate of growth from 20,000 in the 1871 census to more than double that number in the 1881 census indicated the sharply increased momentum.

Overall in the FMCG sector, British companies responded aggressively to the opportunities provided by the growth in demand. At the same time, although the mass consumer market was undoubtedly significant for FMCG, in many other markets: 'The impression remains of many small firms still producing quality goods for a limited market. There was a tendency to go for the top end of the market, with emphasis on a variety of individual specifications, rather than the standardization of the mass market' (Fraser 1981: 237). Even in the FMCG sector, marketing was still more about selling what was produced, with production dominant. Moreover, British firms had little concern for the more integrated aspects of marketing, such as competitive and market analysis of customer needs; in other words, those dimensions which required a substantial marketing department and management structure. Rather, marketing was dependent on two different sources, the personal abilities of the entrepreneur and the growth of advertising agencies. Moreover, lessons were often not learned and the momentum not maintained. Thus, Rowntree concentrated almost all its advertising expenditure on one product, Elect, for several years from 1896 because the Rowntree patriarch, Joseph, was unconvinced about advertising (Goodall 1986). Huntley and Palmer, after early developments in marketing in the 1840s, also regressed when the seven Palmer sons each took over a department and sought to maintain their own positions (Corley 1993). The Beecham experience was far from uncommon, because while Thomas and then his son Joseph exhibited great marketing skills, a leadership vacuum emerged on Joseph's death in 1916 (Corley 1993).There was also a tendency, when mergers took place, to allow all the existing brands to continue and indeed compete against each other, instead of devising a coordinated marketing strategy or rationalizing the number of brands in the interests of economies of scale and scope. Basically, companies tended to employ more aggressive selling techniques to equate demand with their own supply; in other words, they were trying to extend the concepts of the production era and maintain the management practices they knew best.

The traditional staple industries were in a different situation. As Elbaum and Lazonick (1986: 15) have noted of the late nineteenth century: 'One element impeding the adoption of mass production methods was market demand conditions. Amidst sluggish domestic growth and free international trade, British firms found it difficult to secure the requisite market outlets to justify mass production.' In many of these industries, Britain was facing strong competition, even in its domestic market, in the last two decades of the century. A further factor was the limited opportunities for standardization in Britain, especially in engineering. Levine (1967: 52) only discovered traces in sewing machines, the cycle trades, some of the newer branches of engineering, and some electrical trades. It was not until the First World War and the enormous demand for standardized products it generated that the model of variable and bespoke output in much of British metal manufacturing began to be replaced.

Meanwhile, in a third group of industries, those born of the Second Industrial Revolution and based on the more sophisticated use of technology and science, Britain had little in the way of development, and hence little in the way of marketing. Rather, foreign firms were able to set up plants which became dominant features of their locality, such as Singer (sewing machines) in Clydebank, using American techniques of selling such as producer-operated direct sales or mail-order sales to consumers. This was also the way in which typewriters, washing machines and other household goods were introduced in the United

States, employing techniques of hard selling to support the heavy fixed-capital investments.

There are different views about the quality of British overseas marketing at this time. Nicholas (1984) and Platt (1972) have suggested a positive perspective on British overseas marketing up to the First World War, with the former arguing that British manufacturers used a sensible mix of mercantile intermediaries where there was a low frequency of transaction, together with direct representatives, branch offices, and ultimately branch manufacture where volumes justified this activity. However, this perception is largely rejected by Payne (1988), Kirby (1981), and those authors marshalled by Davenport-Hines (1986). Indeed, Kirby (1981: 8), in commenting on the decline of British economic power, asserted that 'possibly the most outstanding area of neglect was in overseas marketing'. In spite of some successes such as Mather and Platt, the overall view was that Britain did not move forward in this vital respect. While German manufacturers organized themselves into highly effective export associations, British manufacturers were too individualistic and less knowledgeable about local tastes. Clearly, from our main perspective of whether a substantial managerial cadre was emerging to handle overseas marketing, the answer seems to be mostly negative. There was little strategic consideration, few visits to the markets, poor language skills, and hardly any response to such customer information as came available, principally because most companies were not structured to do such things. Davenport-Hines (1986: 14) concludes his introduction to British overseas marketing with the damning comment:

historians tempted to reject the traditional picture of British industrialists deploying amateurish marketing techniques and obsolete selling institutions should recall the fate of the British commercial attaché in Berlin who organized a large conference of furniture makers in London in 1913. He provided detailed figures on the market opportunities in Germany where there was a craze for imitation English antiques. Having besought his audience to write to him for introductions and further details, he received only one letter; and that addressed to the Commercial Ambassador, British Embassy, Berlin, France.

So where did British marketing stand in 1914? Corley (1987: 66), taking a critical line, concluded that 'from the available evidence, British marketing in 1914 must have been less skilful and effective than it had been during the industrial revolution', noting Kindleberger's explanation (1964) that the decline was due to the advancing social status of the controlling families, most of whom held salesmen— for long derogated as 'travellers'—in low esteem. As the most important directors were production-focused, the sales department existed to sell what was produced. There was little investment in marketing and distribution during this key period; while there were some individuals, both entrepreneurs and in advertising agencies, who were extremely creative, there were few if any managers who were designated as marketing managers. Thus, the approach was still too dependent on individuals, with the frequent result that the creativity died with them. While there was some development of a sales function, and new American methods such as mail-order, door-to-door selling, and hire purchase were beginning to find their way into Britain, there was little in the way of a central office concerned with marketing. To the extent that there were professionals, they tended to be external, in advertising agencies, the media, or the various types of intermediary.

THE INTERWAR PERIOD AND THE BEGINNINGS OF INSTITUTIONALIZATION

For obvious reasons, marketing of consumer goods had a very low priority in the two World Wars; indeed, many consumer goods were rationed. Thus, marketing, unlike personnel, did not move forward. Moreover, the interwar period was characterized by highly unpredictable markets, with several recessions, a long depression, and more international competition, especially for the staple industries. As a consequence, British companies rarely attempted to improve their marketing skills, but rather increasingly took shelter in various forms of market-fixing, including trade associations, trusts, and tariff protection. The merger wave of the 1920s and the adoption of protection in 1931–2 bolstered these arrangements, which had tacit and sometimes overt governmental support. Hence, this aspect of externalization provided little competitive spur to pursue aggressive marketing, so that although the interwar period witnessed the development of many new industries, there were not many new approaches to marketing. In any case, marketing was still not an integrated concept in Britain, with very few of the marketing departments that had become common in the United States. As Corley (1987: 71) notes, 'perhaps surprising[ly], the large number of consumer firm mergers, especially in the food and drink industries, seldom led to group marketing activities or to the rationalizing of product ranges; the sales departments in the merged units continued to compete against each other.' Thus, the centralization of marketing, a key part of the forward integration which was central to American managerial capitalism (Chandler 1990; Fligstein 1993), did not happen in Britain, at least to anything like the same extent, until very much later. Nor, in this period, despite some novel developments in the 1930s, was there very much in the way of market research to investigate market needs.

Nevertheless, the recognition of the consumer as the starting point for the consideration of production policy dates from this period (Church 2000a). Moreover, there were some highly successful marketing campaigns, often the work of a gifted individual, such as the launch by Rowntree of several new and still existing brands such as Black Magic, Aero, Smarties, and Kit Kat under George Harris. Another success was C. C. Wakefield's Castrol lubricating oil, based on intensive technical research and advertising which focused on auto and air races in which the oil was used. Corley (1987) also mentions Lord Perry, who appreciated the possibilities for the mass marketing of cars and became first the dealer and then the assembler of Ford cars in Britain. And there were some accidental successes; for example, Howlett and White launched a national advertising campaign for its Norvic shoes, only for the production side to be unprepared for the massive success of the campaign, leaving backlogs to be filled over a considerable time.

Overall, though, British marketing was well behind that in America, as exemplified by the Lever–Hedley competition in the soap industry. Although Lever Brothers, led by the redoubtable William Lever until his death in 1925, had established a quasi-monopoly in Britain after extensive takeovers, it was also at the forefront of marketing. At the same time, one should stress that there was no further rationalization beyond ownership and a pricing structure; by the end of the 1920s, with forty-nine soap manufacturing companies in the Lever Group, there were no less than forty-eight separate sales organizations, with brand competition rife. Indeed, Lever had insisted on rivalry between his companies to keep them on their toes. In reality, although perhaps the most outstanding British entrepreneur/marketer of his time, Lever was nowhere near as competent at creating a coherent structure or an integrated marketing strategy for the wide-ranging portfolio (Wilson 1954).

Of course, Unilever (as it became in 1929, after a merger with some Dutch margarine firms) began to discover these deficiencies when in 1930 P&G, widely acknowledged as the leading FMCG marketing company in the United States, took over Thomas Hedley, a small and local Newcastle soap company (Wilson 1954). The 1930s then saw the start of a major and still continuing competition with Unilever. Each of the main Lever products was challenged by a corresponding Hedley product, with heavy advertising on a national scale. From an annual sale of some 5,000 tons in 1930, Hedley sales by 1938 had reached 70,000 tons, with considerable capital having been put into both the original factory and new premises in Manchester. In contrast to the extreme decentralization of the Unilever soap interests, Hedley's products were concentrated under unified control and focused on a limited number of heavily advertised brands which were mainly derived from the newer sectors of the industry, namely, the powders and liquids, rather than hard soaps. Hedley also had the financial and technical resources of P&G, and not least its marketing know-how based on a century of American experience. Thus, if Unilever were to compete there had to be a rationalization and centralization of its motley empire, a process begun (but by no means completed) by Geoffrey Heyworth during the 1930s, when many factories were closed and sales forces slashed, while the marketing effort was concentrated on a more limited range of the more popular brands. Nevertheless, as Edwards (1962: 195) notes, in spite of the sheer size of the Lever companies, the conflict was 'an unequal one with the odds in favour of Hedley's'. By the outset of the Second World War, the active competitive leadership of the industry had passed to Hedley's, indicating how even the best marketing company in Britain could be challenged and lose its leadership within a decade by an American firm using state-of-the-art marketing techniques.

Turning to the topic of overseas marketing in this period, the reflections of Chance (1930: 1596–8), in his Presidential address to the British Glass Convention in 1930, provide a useful perspective on British exporting. He suggested that there are many British manufacturers, and probably not a few of them in the glass trade, who suffer from a curious type of inferiority complex in regard to the export trade, so much so, that not only do they feel a conviction that they cannot compete successfully for such business, but actually seem quite resigned to this state of affairs and will not even take the trouble to investigate the possibilities.

From this perhaps not untypical viewpoint there is little evidence that things had moved forward significantly since the nineteenth century. It is also interesting to note that at the same convention marketing was deliberately equated with salesmanship by one speaker, and advertising with publicity by another.

Having made these critical comments, it is worth pointing out that the inter-war period did see the beginnings of the institutionalization of the functions involved in marketing. We have seen that most marketing decisions were based on the entrepreneur, with continuity consequently becoming a major issue. In effect, though, there was a series of functional activities which did not add up to a coherent whole in modern marketing terms. To some extent, the progress of the field can be measured by the record of the main British marketing institute, which began life as the Sales Managers' Association (SMA) in 1911, when a meeting was called by an American, E. J. Daniells of Ingersoll Watches, to set up a body with the key aim being

To promote, encourage and co-ordinate the study and advancement of sales management in all its branches ... and to assist and further the development and improvement of sales management, market research, advertising and the conduct and handling of all sales of commodities, goods and services in the higher interests of the British people (Bellm: 1).

Putting aside the American nationality of the SMA's creator, one should stress that this statement mentions some of the component parts of marketing, but not marketing as such, and suggests domination by the sales activity.

Initially, the main activity was a monthly dinner with a speaker; in this sense, it was discursive rather than developmental. In June 1921, when the membership was reported to be around 500, the SMA became incorporated and renamed the Incorporated Sales Manager's Association (ISMA). At the same time, the committee structure was expanded to include five areas: education, membership, export, finance, and editorial. This was clearly a major move forward from what had been a monthly dinner-based society, leading in the following year to a clear formulation of how members could become Fellows of the ISMA, another step towards professional status. Over the interwar period, further developments presaged a wider perspective in which the ISMA increasingly saw itself as a professional institute. In 1927–8, the first subject examinations were held, while in 1929 a conference was held in Bristol, which then became an annual event. In 1931, the Association journal was changed from *Sales Promotion* to *Marketing*, and given a wider scope. In 1934, ISMA extended its definition of sales management, so that it covered 'the whole part of business administration known as distribution'. Finally, at the silver jubilee of the Association in 1935–6 it was decided to make an application to the Privy Council for a Royal Charter, described as 'the cherished dream of any serious and progressive institution'.

However, this was refused, and it was to be some fifty years before another application was made. Although membership on the eve of the Second World War was 1,978, with fourteen branches, it was still to be some time before the name of the institute incorporated the term marketing, indicating how ISMA still had a limited outreach, both in scope and impact.

Certainly, at this stage, there was no professionalism in the sense of the existence of a body of professional marketing managers. Crucially, no body of knowledge had been formulated, with intuition having become the hallmark of most marketing and key individuals playing lone roles in its development. Nor was there any theory or model-building from an academic perspective in Britain; this only emerged in the 1960s, or even later. In so far as there was professional expertise, it resulted from outsourcing to external agencies, especially advertising agencies, which soon became the main repositories of marketing skills, as a major extension of their core function of selling space. While Unilever set up Lintas as its own in-house advertising agency in the 1930s, this was unique, indicating how up to the 1940s marketing was heavily externalized and failed to become a major feature of British business organizations.

POST-SECOND WORLD WAR: TOWARDS STRATEGIC MARKETING

The retention of rationing for some years after the Second World War prevented active marketing. Indeed, well into the 1960s there was a seller's market which meant that marketing did not seem to be a key priority in comparison with production. Nevertheless, from the late 1950s marketing grew in significance, albeit slowly, to the point where it is now a universal consideration, if not as often effectively implemented, in organizations. By effective implementation, we mean that customer-orientation has become a key part of firm strategy, with the use, even if implicitly, of some framework such as Porter's five-forces model (1980) to analyse the external environment. Initially, though, many pre-war policies and organizational structures persisted well into the post-war period, and marketing as an important management tool in the more strategic sense did not begin for many companies until after they had restructured in the 1960s.

There were several key developments in the post-Second World War situation which affected marketing from the 1950s:

- The new medium of commercial television from 1955, capable of deploying advertisements which could be much more expressive than the static ones of press or billboard and both fascinated consumers and made retailers anxious to stock advertised goods
- The abolition in the 1960s of retail price maintenance
- The development of large supermarket chains, which rapidly extended their range from groceries to many other consumer goods

- The allocation of shelf space according to brand market share, which encouraged the use of marketing to maximize the space provided
- Associated with the previous point, merchandizing and presentation became important elements of marketing
- The introduction by the supermarkets of 'own label' products, which competed strongly with the advertised brands
- American advertising agencies became dominant in Britain, having brought with them significant marketing expertise, and effectively ran the key marketing activities of many of their clients
- The rise of convenience foods and other household support products as more women went out to work
- Rapidly rising disposable income raised the level of demand, as well as increasing competition
- The concept of branding became increasingly important both to consumer and producer, initially in the consumer goods field, but then spreading into services

In this context, a sales orientation was no longer enough; the older type of salesman selling to the shopkeeper disappeared and was replaced by negotiations at the head office of supermarket chains. Moreover, price alone was no longer the only yardstick of marketing; competitive advantage became concerned with other aspects of the marketing mix. Companies were, therefore, pushed into developing marketing policies and took on the managers to develop and implement these techniques. In particular, brand management became an accepted part of company structures, especially as they began to move to divisionalization (see The 1980s and 1990s: Managerial Capitalism, Chapter 5). It also became difficult for small manufacturers to compete with the large firms that spent huge amounts on advertising, with the result that a small number of market leaders came to dominate most sectors, a process that was further exacerbated by the era's intense merger activity.

In the post-war period, the most lively and highest expenditure marketing competition was in soaps and detergents, with Lever Brothers and P&G (operating as Thomas Hedley until the 1960s) featuring prominently. As the post-war period saw the introduction of synthetic detergents as superior clothes-washing products in hard water areas, the result was an even more competitive marketing situation than before. In particular, given that the market moved over to synthetics, Hedley's share of the aggregate washing product market more than doubled. This was not merely importing American policies; Edwards (1962) ascribes part of Hedley's momentum at this time to the leadership of Robert Craig Wood, the managing director. Price cuts, coupons, free samples, giveaways such as plastic daffodils and 'personality' promotions, known collectively as 'scheme' advertising, were intended to complement large amounts of 'theme' advertising, whose objective was the long-term development of the brand image through 'USP' (Unique Selling Proposition) messages. One of the most successful USP's was devised for Persil, introduced in 1911, which more than half a century later still accounted for one-third of the washing machine powder market, using the same simple slogan 'Persil washes whiter'. Of course, there were several relaunches, many small product improvements, and subtle updating of the message, all based on sophisticated market research. Although this frenetic activity was treated with some suspicion by large parts of British public opinion, Edwards' conclusions (1962: 241–56) indicated that the oligopolistic competition had resulted in higher consumption, higher exports, higher productivity, and higher wages. Moreover, Edwards (1962: 253) argued that the level of competition had been effective in maintaining prices at a reasonable level in relation to the cost of production. Thus, he was able to conclude (1962: 199) that 'on the whole the consumer interest would seem to have been well served [by oligopoly]'. Nevertheless, detergent advertising was referred to the Monopolies Commission, which reported in 1966 that oligopolistic trading was against the public interest because it blocked out new entrants (Jones 2005: 120).

In the 1960s and 1970s, Leonard Hardy did for Lever Brothers what Wood had done for Hedley, leading to them regaining market leadership from P&G (as they had renamed themselves in the early 1960s). By 1975, Lever had opened up a twelve percentage point gap between themselves and P&G in the important washing powder market; indeed, they had achieved market leadership in six out of the seven main product categories. As a consequence, P&G's financial position was affected, with profits before tax declining from £10.6 million in 1978 to £0.6 million in 1982 (Hardy 1987). This indicates how the overall impact of P&G was to force Unilever to become more professional and take marketing to a much higher level of strategic integration within Britain. However, the challenge was beginning to move from success in Britain to a focus on integration in the European market to achieve both economies of scale in production and 'economies of scope possible from cross-border transfers of knowledge'. Clearly, this required the central coordination of many brands which although sharing the same name had different images and even product performance in different countries. But this also reflected a past 'imprecision of central direction' (Jones 2005: 38, 52). This European challenge was shared by many multinationals, indicating how it was highly beneficial for British marketing that many American companies approached the wider European market through Britain, not only enhancing Britain's role, but also giving valuable experience to its marketing managers. Later, in 1990 Lever Europe was established to control all the European Unilever soap interests, while at the turn of the twentieth century, when the stage became global, one of the main strategic initiatives of Unilever under Niall Fitzgerald was to reduce some 1,600 brands worldwide to around 400 brands with international standing, paralleling Heyworth's coordination in the 1930s.

There were also other notable exponents of sophisticated marketing in the FMCG sector in the early post-war period, such as Mars (chocolate and pet food), Beechams (personal products and pharmaceuticals), and the chocolate companies, Cadbury and Rowntree. Marketing managers trained in companies such as these were much in demand in less advanced companies, leading to a dispersal of progressive practices through extensive recruitment campaigns, given the lack of any marketing training in higher education. All these companies adopted the system of brand management to provide an integrated marketing framework at a lower level in the producer, thus providing a basis for a professional hierarchy of marketing expertise.

Outside the FMCG sector, however, other major and relatively concentrated industries were not as advanced in marketing. As Ackrill (1993) has noted of British banking, by any modern definition few did any marketing at all by the end of the Second World War. Any advertising that was placed in the press derived from the press or information office; indeed, marketing in the sense of having a marketing department did not arrive until the late 1960s. It was only when they entered the home mortgage market in the late 1970s that marketing became an important weapon of competition with the building societies. In the 1990s, demographic changes, especially the growing importance of the 'Baby Boom' generation, stimulated the whole financial sector into more aggressive marketing. In other less concentrated and large-scale industries, marketing, although still necessary for efficient operation, had not developed by the third quarter of the twentieth century. Channon (1973: 43–4) noted that several of the reports produced by the National Economic Development Office (NEDO) found marketing to be an area of weakness in industries as widely dispersed across the economic spectrum as wool, shipbuilding, and printing. Moreover, a major NEDO (1979) study of exporting found that a lack of expertise in marketing was the single most important cause for the disappointing international performance of British companies in the previous two decades. The report suggested that too many British companies had treated exporting as a marginal activity, that they had devoted insufficient resources to increasing competitiveness in non-price terms, and that they had spread their exporting effort too widely, rather than concentrating on key markets. Overall, the report concluded that Britain's relative decline was in non-price dimensions, mainly concerned with aspects of marketing, rather than in price competitiveness. Singleton (2002) exemplifies these problems with regard to New Zealand, a country which almost more than any other was tied to the British market by heritage, goodwill, and Commonwealth preference.

Another facet of marketing has been increased professionalization, of which one dimension was the rising numbers joining the professional institute, the ISMA. Soon after the War there had been a considerable membership surge, with a continued increase in numbers over the succeeding decades, indications that the subject area was one of growing professional interest. Given the increased importance of marketing, this also stimulated debate about ISMA's title, resulting in 1962 in a change of name to the Institute of Marketing and Sales Management. By 1967, it had simply become the Institute of Marketing, denoting the final transition to marketing as the dominant activity in the range of fields concerned with the customer and the market. In 1989, a Royal Charter was finally achieved and a consequent further name change enacted, to the Chartered Institute of Marketing (CIM).

However, to focus on the CIM is to give only part of the picture. By the 1970s, there was a wide range of institutes in fields related to marketing. As well as the Institute of Marketing, there was the Advertising Association, the Institute of

Practitioners in Advertising, the Incorporated Society of British Advertisers, the Market Research Society, the Industrial Market Research Association, the Marketing Society, the Institute of Export, and the Institute of Public Relations. Not all of these had the links to the business school world of academic teaching that the CIM was to develop, but all represented attempts to create a dimension of professionalism in a particular niche of the marketing world, with some form of qualification having been introduced as an indicator of status.

Another element of professionalization was in higher education, where marketing was even slower than other business subjects to find a place in the syllabus. The leading management teaching institution of the early post-war period, the Administrative Staff College at Henley, taught no marketing. It was 1967 before the first chair in marketing was established, at Lancaster, while the pioneering business schools at London and Manchester were obliged to recruit overseas for this discipline, such was the dearth of indigenous expertise. More recently, though, marketing has become an accepted part of the syllabus in the rapid expansion of business schools, with student recruitment rising progressively in recognition of its popularity as a career.

CURRENT BRITISH MARKETING

So how has marketing changed in more recent decades? From the 1960s until the 1980s, segmentation and market positioning became the main focus of marketing strategy, followed more recently by a trend to relationship marketing and an increased amount of brand-stretching across a range of products. The growth of market research and pretesting as a means of reducing risk, given the considerable sums required to launch a new product or brand, meant that the days when a gifted entrepreneur such as Lever could gauge customer tastes by hunch and experience were no longer feasible; more systematic and 'scientific' methods which relied on the use of computers came to predominate, whilst still leaving scope for imaginative ideas. Moreover, marketing is now generally recognized as an important function, even in the public and not-for-profit sectors. On the other hand, based on a broad survey (Mercer 1996) there is little evidence of widespread active marketing in areas such as pricing, promotion, or market research. Indeed, the defining characteristic of current marketing in the UK would appear to be a firm commitment to the general philosophies of marketing, but with very little interest taken in its practical use, especially at the routine level of the activities undertaken by its marketing department.

Moreover, in spite of what Willmott (1999: 205) calls 'a widely held and ascendant belief in markets—as superior, efficient and effective allocators of resources and satisfiers of customer needs—surely presents marketers ... with a powerful rhetoric for augmenting their credibility and authority as well as extending their influence', there are indications that all is not well. It is arguable that marketing reached a high-watermark of influence in the 1980s, at a time when in line with Porter (1980) strategy was dominated by a focus on external market analysis, while the concept of professionalism and self-identity had also become important. Since then, the dominant view of strategy has become the resource-based theory of the firm, looking inwards rather than outwards. At the same time, the dominance of financial considerations driven by shareholder value has become the key focus of boards of directors. Doyle (1995) provided a trenchant review of the marketing scene, arguing that after the high point of the 1980s, the 1990s were much less promising:

- In key sectors, notably FMCG, there had been a decline in market share and profitability for manufacturers' brands, mainly in the face of private label competition from retailers
- There was widespread restructuring of marketing departments as part of the overall corporate restructuring
- There was a perceived loss of primacy to other disciplines as key ideas (TQM, JIT, PBR, etc.) were generated outside marketing. By contrast, there was a general lack of innovation in marketing
- Marketing had not adapted to the new form of competition which pits networks rather than single companies against each other.

So what underlay this situation? Doyle (1995) suggested that firms of the 1960s–80s saw marketing as an autonomous function which was about such issues as segmentation and positioning. While these could exploit price elasticities between consumer segments by such stratagems as premium brands, thus capturing the 'consumer surplus', they were not real innovations, and as soon as an innovation occurred, for instance in reconfiguring the entire value chain in the way in which Direct Line did in the insurance industry, traditional marketing became secondary. Moreover, the need was for a much more integrationist perspective which saw marketing as just one part of the value chain, a value chain, what is more, which reached outside the firm to a network of suppliers and specialist agencies on hand to assist corporate decision-making. The winner in such a situation is the firm which has the best network, hence the great interest in recent years in supply chain management. Doyle (1995) suggested that this would mean externalization of specialist functions in marketing to other parts of the network as the costs of knowledge increased, with the result that marketing departments would be much smaller. Moreover, in the recession of the early 1990s the long-term commitment to marketing seemed to be waning, with less recruitment of brand managers and a decline in theme advertising as the need for short-term profitability became dominant and brands became tradeable assets.

CONCLUSIONS

In reflecting on marketing in Britain, there were early developments in merchanting to serve the staple industries of the First Industrial Revolution which, along with other factors, served to diminish that all-important link between the manufacturer and the customer that is central to modern marketing. The FMCG sector was an exception; indeed, the strength of British marketing, in so far as it has had strengths, has been in this sector. Outside the FMCG sector, the competitive capitalism of the late nineteenth and early twentieth centuries did not prove conducive to the rise of modern marketing, or even developments in marketing that kept pace with its main competitors, because there was no system of mass production or oligopoly in key industries to make marketing a key feature of firm strategy. Far too often there was too wide a range of products for effective marketing; too often there was no consolidation of separate units into anything like full integration; and too often there was dependence on promotions for short-term advantage, rather than long-term brand-building. Moreover, there was no sense of a professional function; rather, marketing was based on either hunch or intuition or personal experience by gifted entrepreneurs, who were then unable to make their knowledge explicit for those who came after them. For most of the nineteenth and twentieth centuries, management in many British industries, including the staples and intermediate goods, was seen as a production and cost problem, rather than a marketing problem, a situation which did not really change until the 1960s. As Supple (1974: 82) concluded, when evaluating British industry's investment strategy:

A more generalized, and possibly more persuasive, argument about investment strategy ... is that British entrepreneurs lacked marketing drive—and by implication, that lack was exposed and most aggravated at the very period (the late nineteenth century) when competition from newly industrializing nations was beginning to bite into overseas markets.

We would argue that Britain never did undergo what Fligstein (1993: 154) categorized as the period of sales and marketing conception of control which began in the United States in the 1920s, and which led the process of diversification in the search for new markets. This American process was associated with three factors: it was more pronounced in the technologically advanced industries; it was more likely to happen where the president of the firm had a sales or marketing background; and it often coincided with the elaboration of a divisionalized structure. None of these factors were strongly evident in Britain until the 1960s, explaining why, other than in the FMCG sector, marketing as a function was unimportant until the last quarter of the twentieth century. Nor did Britain have the socially negotiated framework which would have made the sales and marketing model logical and viable.

Of the main themes of the book, the two which relate most to marketing are those of externalization and professionalism. Externalization was and still is a key feature in most firms' approach to marketing. As for achieving professionalism, in terms of the institutional framework, arguably marketing has done so, but some such as Whittington and Whipp (1992) feel that the strength of professional ideology has been diminished by the rise of rival ideologies to that of markets, notably a resource-based view of the firm and a focus on efficiency and cost which has diminished the role of marketing as a dominant force in management.

11

The Practice of Management—Accounting and Finance

INTRODUCTION

Although we noted at the start of Chapter 9 that arguably the most important dimension of British management over the last two centuries has been the relationship between employers and their workforces, a matter of similar gravity was the extent to which firms developed financial control and information systems as essential elements in their internal planning and monitoring systems. Indeed, the two aspects were intrinsically linked, as we have noted in Chapters 3, 5, and 9, because the characteristics of British business helped to erect substantial obstacles in the way of financial planning and the use of such techniques as budgetary control. Of course, a variety of reasons can be adduced to explain why the latter failed to emerge to anything like the same extent as in the United States and Japan, providing further links with the market-cum-technological and institutional-cultural drivers that have featured so prominently in this book. It will also become clear that the chartered accountancy profession benefited enormously from our fourth theme, the slow transition towards professional management, in that they were seen as the most appropriate alternative people to recruit, given the generally low level of qualifications possessed by the managers that populated British business organizations. After establishing such a strong position in managerial hierarchies, this also laid the basis for our final evolutionary stage, namely, the emergence of financial capitalism (see The Managers, Chapter 1) after 1970, when City interests came to dominate the strategy and structure of especially the largest firms.

In addressing these issues, it will be important to differentiate between what we describe as internal (planning, control, and monitoring) and external (reporting and auditing) processes, with management accountants performing the former and chartered accountants the latter. This exercise will also help us to explain the relative rates of progress achieved by these two distinct groups, in that while financial and management accountancy were apparently evolving in tandem up to the late nineteenth century, thereafter it was mostly the chartered accountants who exerted more influence, becoming what Matthews, Anderson, and Edwards (1998) have described as *The Priesthood of Industry*. Although some (Roslender, Glover, and Kelly 2000) have warned that the influence of the accountancy profession might have peaked in the 1990s, it is still difficult to dispute

Anderson's claim (1985, 1987) that it has become the pre-eminent profession within British capitalist enterprise. Indeed, the nature of accounting in British business reflected the organizational forms that were adopted at various junctures, providing some stark insights into the links between these internal and external processes. The key issue would appear to have been the extent to which management preferred to utilize the expertise of financial accountants, rather than their management counterparts, given the reluctance of British business to internalize marketing and the labour control function, adopt mass production systems, and develop integrated management structures. This provides yet further insights into the main themes of the book, because the positions attained by different types of accountants were based on both the demand for their services at different points in time, as well as the inherent weaknesses in British management generally, especially in terms of training and qualifications. Studying accountants will also provide interesting insights into the nature of professionalism in Britain, especially as the chartered accountants competed with the management accountants over a range of status issues, leading to a bifurcation that has persisted into the twenty-first century.

ACCOUNTANCY AND INDUSTRIALIZATION

In a comprehensive overview of the history of financial accounting, Edwards (1989: 9) has identified four phases: the pre-capitalist era (4000 BC to AD 1000); commercial capitalism (1000 to 1760); industrial capitalism (1760–1830); and financial capitalism (1830 to date). While in terms of classifying managerial developments many might disagree with the start date of the last period, putting this perhaps 140 years later (see The 1980s and 1990s: Managerial Capitalism, Chapter 5), as far as accounting was concerned these phases indicate how techniques emerged to cope with the dictates of their respective times. In this context, it is vital to stress that the role of accounting is to provide accurate financial information that reflects the state of a concern at any given point in time. This information can take the form of either a balance sheet (financial reporting) or costing data in relation to a firm's actual operations (management accounting). It is also clear that up to 1900 there was often an overlap between the sources of these two types of information, a feature of the profession that persisted into the interwar era (Boyns 2005). Increasingly, though, from the 1880s financial reporting came to be performed by what were the more prestigious chartered accountants who operated mostly in private practices, while the costing function, where it existed at all, was generally conducted in-house by employees. As we go on to see, increasingly chartered accountants also started to infiltrate British business, often at the highest levels of management, reflecting important features of the managerial scene that need to be highlighted and analysed.

It was during Edwards' second period (specifically, the thirteenth and fourteenth centuries) that double-entry bookkeeping was developed in Italy (Lee

1994: 160). Although as we noted (see The Origins of Management, Chapter 1) Luca Pacioli, a Florentine friar, is credited with the first published book (in 1494) that explained this system, it is likely that North Italian bankers and merchants had been using double-entry bookkeeping for almost 200 years by that time (Witzel 2002: 170). The system spread slowly across much of Europe over the following centuries, often employed in response to the ever-present threat of fraud and theft. By the nineteenth century, though, especially in view of the substantial increase in fixed capital investment, considerable uncertainty existed over essential issues of accountancy. The vast majority of accountants at that time were involved either in low-level functions such as bookkeeping or insolvency work, indicating how both their status and general impact was limited. As Glynn (1994: 322–3) has also observed in relation to the mid-1840s railway legislation, few contemporaries were capable of understanding the stipulation that companies should produce 'full and true accounts'. One of the most fundamental problems was how to accommodate the fixed capital associated with modern capitalistic enterprise, and especially with regard to utilities like the railways, into a system that was designed by merchants to control liquidity (Pollard 1968: 248–9). It was equally difficult to define exactly what was meant by profit, while few business owners would have been capable of differentiating between management accounting and financial reporting. Crucially, as we noted in Chapter 3, most would have regarded accountants as mere bookkeepers, such was the reluctance of owner-managers to delegate responsibility to salaried managers or external advisors. Moreover, until quite recently historians would have agreed with Pollard's generalization (1968: 288) that the 'practice of using accounts as direct aids to management was not one of the achievements of the British industrial revolution'. Although Pollard (1968: 288) was willing to concede that some prominent manufacturers (e.g. Wedgwood, Boulton & Watt, and John Marshall) developed 'quite advanced and fairly accurate techniques', he approved of the earlier dictum issued by Solomons (1952: 17), that 'all signs point to a lack of interest among industrialists in the application of accounting to industrial processes'.

Thanks to much more exhaustive research by both British and American accounting historians, however, it is apparent that these views are no longer credible. Focusing mostly on the coal, iron and steel industries, the work of Fleischman and his collaborators (1990, 1992, 1993), and of what we refer to as the 'Cardiff School' (Edwards, Boyns, Anderson, and Matthews) has demonstrated graphically how accounting practice evolved rapidly in Britain up to the late nineteenth century. Indeed, as Boyns and Edwards (1997: 20–2) revealed, 'costing systems were fully integrated with the financial accounting systems', indicating how nineteenth-century managements were using these techniques as an important aid to their decision-making. Matthews, Boyns, and Edwards (2003: 48) have also revealed similarly impressive developments in the family-owned chemicals firm Albright & Wilson, extending the range of industries affected by this trend. Indeed, as Boyns (2005: 120) concludes from a recent survey of both secondary and archival sources, 'not only in key sectors such as coal and iron and steel, but also in engineering and chemicals, there is evidence of a development in cost calculation practices, usually in an on-going and evolutionary fashion prior to the First World War'. Although it is not yet possible to claim that either major industries like textiles or the vast majority of firms were as extensively affected as those covered to date by the 'Cardiff School', progress was clearly being made in this respect. These techniques were also being widely disseminated through the extensive informational networks which existed. Babbage's book on the *Economy of Machinery and Manufacture* (1832), had facilitated this process of dissemination, while much later in the century Garcke and Fells' *Factory Accounts* (1887) performed a similar function. Above all, though, it was as a result of empirical problem-solving that nineteenth-century managements devised appropriate accounting conventions which suited the needs of each individual business.

The work of the 'Cardiff School', as well as research conducted by Fleischman and Parker (1990, 1992), has significantly improved our knowledge of how management accounting especially was beginning to make an impact in British business from the late eighteenth century. It is important to stress, however, that critical accounting historians Hoskin and Macve (2000: 95, 109–10) dispute these findings, on the grounds that management accountancy techniques both at that time and even today provided neither a means of calculating human performance nor the kind of administrative coordination that is the hallmark of modern management. This distinct view of management accounting is predicated on the search for the link between generating knowledge and its direct application to business performance, especially at the level of human performance. It also relies heavily on Chandler's argument (1977) that administrative coordination fundamentally changed the nature of economic activity, giving rise to the *Visible Hand* of managerial control, as opposed to the invisible hand of market forces acting as the determinant of profits, prices, and wages. Boyns and Edwards (2000: 151–7), on the other hand, counter that inductive empiricism provides clear evidence of extensive interest in management accounting across some significant industries, supporting their claims that the old Solomons–Pollard orthodoxy lacks credibility. Many accounting and business historians would also agree that the deductive approach adopted by Hoskin and Macve (2000) fails to undermine this conclusion. In spite of the Cardiff School's findings, however, as we go on to see, management accounting became a much more marginal activity within British business than financial accounting, the rise of which was one of the most consistent features of the scene up to the late twentieth century.

Not only were new techniques appearing at that time but also both the number of accountants and the range of their services were expanding impressively. These trends can be explained by a variety of factors, but above all the increased adoption of the joint-stock company form could be regarded as by far the most significant (ICAEW 1966: 41–3). As we saw in Chapter 3, prior to the momentous series of Companies Acts of 1856–62 the railway sector had prompted the elaboration of new accounting practices, both in respect to costing and financial reporting (Gourvish 1973: 290). Moreover, the railways had been responsible for precipitating the reform of company law in 1844 and 1856, legislation that introduced new auditing and reporting conventions on all those firms that sought the sanctuary of limited liability. The consolidating Companies Act of 1862 has even been described as the 'accountants' friend' (Brown 1905, quoted in Stacey 1954: 37), given the central role they would play in auditing and liquidating the profusion of joint-stock companies that were created thereafter.

Having substantially extended their market from the traditional accountants' business of bookkeeping and insolvency, it is clear that from the 1860s opportunities for developing much closer links with the rest of the business community expanded exponentially. Admittedly, it was not until the Companies Act of 1900 that auditing was made compulsory, while it was 1947 before the law stipulated that this function had to be performed by a registered professional accountant. The adoption of joint-stock status also spread only slowly from the utility and banking sectors after 1862. Nevertheless, with the number of joint-stock companies increasing from 6,300 by 1880 to 63,000 in 1914, many arranged some form of auditing, the performance of which was mostly done by accountants working in private practices (Matthews, Anderson, and Edwards 1998: 35–6). As a growing proportion of these companies also sought quotations on either provincial or the London stock exchanges (Thomas 1973: 114–39; Cottrell 1980: 173–6), this provided accountants with yet another role in either valuing assets or presenting financial information to potential investors. One of the key reasons behind this trend, apart from legislative guidance, was 'the pervasive nature of fraud in Victorian business [which] helped to produce an environment conducive to the emergence of the professional auditor' (Matthews, Anderson, and Edwards 1998: 99). This reveals how the chartered accountant came to be accepted as a credible guarantor in British business, considerably strengthening the evolving relationship at a time when investors were searching for objective and reliable sources of information. Indeed, as well as auditing services, from the late nineteenth century accountants were used as consultants to other firms (Ferguson 2002: 23–6), initiating a source of income that was to expand enormously in the twentieth century. Accountants were especially in great demand during the intense merger waves of the late 1880s and at the turn of the century (Hannah 1983: 21–2), indicating how their market was expanding substantially up to the First World War. The case of Ferranti Ltd. in 1903 is indicative of the new-found status enjoyed by accountants, because when this family firm experienced severe liquidity difficulties as a result of the founder's reluctance to curb his engineering instincts, on behalf of the debentureholders Parr's Bank appointed two chartered accountants, A. W. Tait and Arthur Whittaker, to act as receiver-managers (Wilson 2000: 136–9).

Having demonstrated how the financial accountants were able to extend their influence over British business, at the same time it is vital to stress that management accountancy failed to make anything like the same impact. Although Melling (1980: 77) has observed how in some of the larger engineering firms a 'multirole supervisory system' was emerging from the 1880s, featuring foremen, rate-fixers, management accountants, and 'feed-and-speed' men, well into the mid-twentieth century workshop practices were still based on indirect control techniques. Indeed, as we stressed in Chapters 3 and 9, only from the 1940s did scientific management start to influence production strategies, significantly limiting the demand for management accountancy. Of course, as we have already noted, Boyns (2005: 120) has collected significant evidence to support the claim that cost calculation practices were evolving up to the First World War. Nevertheless, given the sluggish development of managerial coordination, even in the largest firms, it is difficult to avoid the conclusion that management accountancy was anything other than of marginal interest to the vast majority of firms. As Shadwell (1916: 375–6) asserted at that time, planning

is rarely done in a systematic way by British manufacturers. The number of works in which it is even attempted can be counted on one hand. Very often there is no planning at all; it is left to the operative and rule of thumb. Generally, there is some planning of a rough and ready kind, but some of the most famous works in the country are in such a state of chaos that the stuff seems to be turned out by accident.

On the other hand, given the enormous increase in popularity of the joint-stock company form, with its reporting, auditing, and insolvency implications, financial accountancy was making a much greater impact across British business (Armstrong 1984, 1987). As we see later, it was only once most of the large firms adopted the M-form after 1960 that financial planning infiltrated the business scene, while the contemporaneous introduction of standard costing led to clashes with trade unions over shop-floor control. Before we go on to examine these changes, however, it is necessary to assess the professionalization of accountancy and the impact this had on their status.

ASSOCIATIONS, DIVISIONS, AND ROLES

Having started the nineteenth century as one of the lowlier service trades, performing mostly bookkeeping and insolvency functions for both business in general and individuals, by the First World War it is apparent that accountants had become one of the essential features of a much-changed corporate scene. The emergence of capital-intensive industries like the railways and other utilities, the extension of joint-stock status to an increasing proportion of firms, especially after 1880, and the desire of investors for accurate and objective information, all fuelled this transformation, leading to the rapid increase in numbers of accountants and a move into areas like auditing, consultancy and even the management of other firms.

With this change in function and status, it was increasingly apparent to the accountants that in order to reinforce their reputation for probity they needed to project a professional image to potential and actual customers. This sentiment led in the 1850s and 1860s to the formation of a series of regional associations, the principal motivation behind which was 'to protect and regulate the provision of the specialist skills which, by the second half of the nineteenth century, were in growing demand' (Matthews, Anderson, and Edwards 1998: 61). In fact, 'accountancy exhibited many of the hallmarks of a profession long before the foundation of the societies', given the prominent role played by training and the growing acceptability of this occupation amongst the middle classes (Matthews, Anderson, and Edwards 1998: 30). Crucially, though, the objectives of the professional accountants' associations would appear to have been to exclude unsuitable functionaries as a means of projecting a certain image to the business community (Edwards 1989: 276–7).

The earliest accountancy associations appeared in Scotland (ICAEW 1966: p. xiii), where the term 'chartered accountant' arose out of the grant of a Royal Charter to the Society of Accountants in Edinburgh (in 1854) and the Glasgow Accountants and Actuaries (1855). Both of these bodies had been formed in 1853, reflecting the greater prominence of accountants in Scotland as essential elements in indigenous bankruptcy laws (Stacey 1954: 22). As Wilson (1999: 64–7) has also stressed, by establishing clear regulations concerning the length of training 'in articles' and the examination process to be completed, they provided a model that could be imitated south of the border. With this model in mind, and recognizing the growing demand for a credible accountancy service, during the 1870s a series of local associations were created in England. The first of these appeared in Liverpool and London (1870), followed by Manchester (1871), and Sheffield (1877), while in 1872 a Society of Accountants in England was also established. Crucially, in 1880 all of these bodies combined to form the Institute of Chartered Accountants in England and Wales (ICAEW), giving English accountants the same chartered status as their Scottish counterparts.

As we noted earlier, however, given the exclusive nature of the ICAEW's membership criteria—members had to serve five-years' articles in an accountant's office and pass the organization's examination—problems arose for those who were trained in either company or local authority offices. This resulted in the formation of the Society of Accountants and Auditors (SAA) in 1885, a body that as the Society of Incorporated Accountants and Auditors (SIAA) would in 1957 merge into the ICAEW. As Table 11.1 reveals, while never quite matching the ICAEW's size, and in spite of considerable criticism emanating from the ICAEW's mouthpiece, *Accountant*, SAA membership grew significantly up to the 1940s. Over that period, however, it was the ICAEW that continued to dominate in terms of both aggregate numbers and prestige (Matthews, Anderson, and Edwards 1998: 61–4), with 45 per cent of all UK-based accountants registered as members of a society in 1941.

While the festering division between the ICAEW and SAA reflected the worst aspects of professionalism, an even more distasteful conflict emerged just after the First World War when the management accountants started to consider applying for chartered status. While as we noted earlier Boyns and Edwards (1997: 20–2) claim that in the coal, iron and steel industries managements were employing integrated costing and financial accounting techniques to improve their decision-making, as far as the accountancy profession was concerned these

Table 11.1. Membership of the main accountancy bodies, 1881–1995

	ICAEW	SAA (SIAA from 1908)	ICAS #	ICWA (CIMA from 1986)	CAA ∧ (ACCA from 1939)
1881	1,185	—	285	—	—
1911	4,391	2,440	1,298	—	800
1921	5,642	3,360	1,788	372	700
1941	13,694	7,882	4,565	1,430	6,390
1961	35,600	*	6,928	7,387	11,006
1981	73,781	—	10,586	20,328	24,265
1995	109,233	—	14,016	41,634	47,230

Key:
— ICAS was a 1951 merger of the three Scottish societies formed in 1853–67; ∧—The CAA merged with the ACCA in 1941; *—SIAA merged with the chartered bodies in 1957; ICAEW—Institute of Chartered Accountants in England and Wales (1880); SAA—Society of Accountants and Auditors; SIAA—Society of Incorporated Accountants and Auditors (1908); ICAS—Institute of Chartered Accountants of Scotland (1951); ICWA—Institute of Cost and Works Accountants (1919); CIMA—Chartered Institute of Management Accountants (1986); CAA—Central Association of Accountants (1905); ACCA—Association of Certified and Corporate Accountants (1939).
Source: Matthews et al. (1998: 62, 284–5).

functions were to be considered as entirely separate. Moreover, the interest in management accounting owed more to 'systematic management' than to F. W. Taylor's scientific management, even though advanced firms like Hans Renold & Co. (Boyns 2001) and Willans & Robinson were demonstrating the possibilities in refined systems of cost control (Melling 1980: 77; Fitzgerald 1988: 48). The First World War undoubtedly accelerated this interest in such techniques, with Elbourne's *Factory Administration and Accounts* (1914) providing a textbook for those firms 'controlled' by the Ministry of Munitions from 1915. While Boyns (2005) has downplayed the role of the First World War, stressing the extent of cost calculation practices prior to that era, it is nevertheless interesting to note that arising out of these developments an Institute of Cost and Works Accountants (ICWA) was formed in 1919, indicating how this subsector of accountancy was beginning to develop greater strength. Ferguson (2002: 32–5) also reveals how an embryonic consultancy profession was offering advice on production efficiency and management accounting. Some of these consultants were also chartered accountants; indeed, there is abundant evidence to support the claim that many of the latter provided management accounting advice to industrial and commercial clients (Matthews, Anderson, and Edwards 1998: 112–19). This consequently helps to explain why both the ICAEW and SAA objected vigorously when in 1922 the ICWA sought chartered status.

While Matthews, Anderson, and Edwards (1998: 112–17) have defended the chartered accountants against the accusation of 'snobbery' in their attitudes towards management accountants, it is nevertheless true to note that in voicing their objections against granting the ICWA chartered status the ICAEW's annual report claimed that they were 'not engaged in professional work, but are employed in the service of traders' (Stacey 1954: 99). The ICWA was also prone to its own form of elitism, in admitting only those in senior industrial positions and excluding clerks. As a result, ICWA's membership grew sluggishly, reaching just 830 in 1931, or just 2.9 per cent of the 28,364 'costing and estimating clerks' registered in that year's census (Matthews, Anderson, and Edwards 1998: 66). Only after the Second World War did ICWA membership rise significantly, as the exigencies of that era revived interest in scientific management and encouraged British business to employ more management accountants.

It is consequently clear that while chartered accountancy was one of the oldest British professions, establishing by the First World War a wide reputation for probity and quality that was founded on extensive training and self-regulation, deep divisions had led to a bifurcation of interests with their management counterparts. While on the one hand ICAEW members mostly operated in private practices, offering their services to other businesses on a fee basis, those accountants employed directly by either industrial companies or governmental organizations were forced to resort to establishing their own societies as a means of imposing a set of professional standards. Apart from the inherently exclusionary nature of this activity, bifurcation also ran contrary to what Boyns and Edwards (1997: 20–2) described as the empirical combination of financial and cost accounting by many nineteenth century firms in the coal, iron and steel industries. It is too early in this analysis to assess whether this did much damage to British business, but one can only conclude that the division of interests limited substantially the integration of different accounting functions. On the other hand, as we now go on to see, specialization in the provision and development of accounting services did not prevent this profession from exerting an increasingly powerful influence over British business in general, a trend that hinged around the relationship between City of London financial institutions and the rest of the corporate world.

THE EMERGENCE OF FINANCIAL CAPITALISM

While the initial rise to prominence of chartered accountants was primarily linked to the auditing and reporting aspects of joint-stock company status, as well as insolvency work, arising from crucial changes in the corporate governance of British business over the course of the twentieth century this profession came to play an even more prominent role. As we see later, others have argued that the extensive use of chartered accountants in British business reflected inherent weaknesses in managerial training and qualifications (Handy 1987: 12; Barry 1989: 58). At the same time, given the changing ownership patterns in British business (Wilson 1995: 181–94), chartered accountants were often regarded as a 'safe pair of hands' by the institutional investors who by the 1970s had come to control the bulk of the equity floated on the London Stock Exchange. It is consequently vital to assess how the nature of corporate governance altered after the First World War, as a means of providing an even stronger platform for the chartered accountants as they sought to extend their influence over British business.

There is, of course, an enormous debate concerning the propensity of the City of London to support British business ventures (Wilson 1995: 119–32, 181–94), participating in which would distract us from our main concern of charting the changes in corporate governance. It is sufficient to say in this context that in spite of the growing proportion of London Stock Exchange activity that was classified as domestic over the course of the twentieth century (see Table 11.2), there remain deep suspicions concerning the preferences of what have been described as the 'gentlemanly capitalists' who dominated the City's activities (see The Banking Sector, Chapter 3; Cain and Hopkins 1993). As the highly influential Macmillan Committee on Finance and Industry noted in its 1931 report, the merchant banks could be reproached for 'being better informed on conditions in Latin America than in Lancashire or Scotland', concluding that 'in some respects the City is more highly organized to provide capital to foreign countries than to British industry' (quoted in Cain and Hopkins 1993*b*: 19). Crucially, the transformation in City activities can largely be explained by the traumas that struck the City between 1914 and 1945, most obviously two World Wars, the replacement of London by New York as the world's financial capital, severe international illiquidity and the deep recession following the Wall Street Crash of 1929. As Table 11.2 reveals, by 1939 the nominal value of non-UK securities quoted on the London Stock Exchange official list had fallen to 28.8 per cent of the total, compared to 59.1 per cent in 1913. Over the same period, if one combined UK financial operations, utility operations, and industrial and financial companies, by 1939 they accounted for 19.4 per cent of all shares traded, compared to 17.5 per cent in 1913. More importantly, as Michie (1999: 279–80) demonstrates, by 1939 the market values of these securities amounted to 34.7 per cent of the total, illustrating how the London Stock Exchange 'responded well to the changes forced upon it in the interwar years'.

Table 11.2. Nominal values of securities quoted on the London Stock Exchange Official List, 1913–80 (percentage of total)

	1913	1939	1970	1980
Non-UK	59.1	28.8	6.0	0.5
UK government	11.5	43.7	50.2	62.4
UK financial institutions	5.4	4.0	10.5	7.6
UK utilities	3.9	5.0	1.9	0.8
UK commercial and industrial	8.2	10.4	27.2	20.6
Total values (£million)	11,208	17,976	47,318	124,689*

* Apart from the categories listed by 1980, one should also remember that a further 5.5 per cent of the stocks quoted were in Eurobonds.
Source: Michie (1999).

While over the interwar era the balance of City activities moved slowly towards domestic investment, it was from the 1950s that this trend reached its climax. This claim is borne out by the evidence in Table 11.2, which reveals how shares in British financial institutions, utilities, and commercial and industrial operations had risen by 1970 to 39.6 per cent of the total quoted. In terms of the market value of securities quoted, the latter accounted for 69.6 per cent, compared to 16.6 per cent for the UK government (Michie 1999: 522), illustrating the central importance of British business to the development of a vibrant London Stock Exchange. Reader (1979: 160–82) has described this as 'the rise of the cult of the equity', given the greater propensity of both British business to sell voting stock to City institutions and the latter to purchase these investments.

As we noted in Chapter 5, however, it is doubtful whether these trends made much difference to the way in which British business was managed at the highest levels, at least until the 1970s. In the first place, even where there had been an extensive divorce between control and ownership, Quail (2000) has stressed how a system of proprietorial capitalism prevailed, with directors acting as agents of the shareholders and running the firm in a hierarchical fashion through a system of committees. As Hannah (1974*b*: 65–9) has also noted, this was 'the golden age of directorial power'; it was a period when those who sat on the board were trusted to take total charge of the proprietorial rights of all those who had bought shares in the enterprise. Even though corporate raiders like Charles Clore and Isaac Wolfson initiated the unprecedented step of bidding directly to shareholders, as opposed to negotiating a takeover with the incumbent board of directors, the market for corporate control remained highly conservative in style and nature (Roberts 1992: 183).

Running in parallel with this trend, of course, was the intense merger activity of the 1950s and 1960s (see Changing Corporate Governance, Chapter 5), with scale coming to be regarded as a defence against both intensifying competition and further takeover bids, and the City's leading financial institutions playing central roles in the process. One should add that because the regulatory framework remained extremely laissez-faire, giving management considerable control over strategy and structure as long as dividends were respectable, few mergers resulted in the promised synergistic benefits (Newbould 1970). For example, after absorbing its two largest rivals in 1967–8, under Arnold Weinstock as chief executive GEC became one of the most profitable firms in Britain, generating a substantial cash mountain. On the other hand, the firm failed to invest in high-tech ventures in semiconductors or consumer electronics, preferring the safer defence and capital equipment markets, as well as the accumulation of an enormous cash reserve. Although GEC's cash surplus was envied by many, its investment in bank accounts represented poor value for shareholders. At the same time, the late 1960s Labour government proved reluctant to impose new corporate governance regulations on business, resulting in the persistence of opaque accountability (Bowden and Gamble 2002). Lazonick and O'Sullivan (1997: 24–6) have also argued that, even though the market for corporate control promoted business diversification, capital market illiquidity and the slow growth of institutional investment prevented the effective external scrutiny of these activities.

Arising out of these trends was one of the most extensive transfers of business ownership in the last 200 years, as firms that had been dominated by either a single owner or a small coterie of entrepreneurs sold an increasing proportion of their equity to professional investors. This trend has already been described (see The 1980s and 1990s: Managerial Capitalism, Chapter 5), where it was noted that by the 1970s financial institutions (specifically, insurance companies, pension funds, and other financial operations) controlled well over one-half of the shares traded on the London Stock Exchange. As Zeitlin (1974: 1107) has argued with regard to American corporations, the alleged separation of ownership and control could well be described as a 'pseudofact', because all that had happened was a change in controlling interest from a small group of owners into the hands of an elite cadre of fund managers operating in the City of London. On the other hand, it is reasonable to use terms like financial capitalism to describe these trends in British business, because by the 1970s the City provided the nucleus of a new corporate class which dominated British business, working through a series of interlinking directorships that produced a 'national inter-corporate network, with financial and non-financial enterprise fully integrated' (Scott 1987: 180).

Not only did the financial institutions extend the range of services provided for business clients, but also representatives of the financial institutions were beginning to find places on their boards of directors. Indeed, in evaluating the extensive network of interlinking directorships Scott (1987: 60–1) has noted that financial institutions 'were pivotal points in loose groupings of industrial, trading and financial enterprises . . . act[ing], in effect, as proxies for the wider financial community; they act as the guardians of the interests of the hegemonic financials'. In a study of the fifty largest manufacturing companies in 1976, Utton (1982: 32) has revealed that thirty-two of their directors represented a clearing bank, while most large financial institutions were interlinked with each other (Whitley 1973: 622–9). This reveals how by the 1970s British business was beginning to resemble the system of financial capitalism that had emerged in the United States twenty years earlier (Fligstein 1993: 226).

The final major development in this context emerged after what has passed into the vernacular as the 'Big Bang' reforms of 1986. The most visible aspect of these changes was the introduction of computerized dealing, leading to the abandonment of the old trading floor of the Stock Exchange in favour of serried banks of computer screens that provided instant trading information (Thomas 1986: 162–3). Several longstanding regulations were also abolished, including the insistence on minimum commission rates, while the distinction between brokers and jobbers was terminated (Kay 1988: 144–7). Another important reform allowed Stock Exchange firms to be run by organizations which were not members of that institution, providing banks, insurance companies, and foreign investment houses (including the world's largest, Nomura from Japan and Merrill Lynch from the United States) with direct access to the market. As a result, not only were many City practices revolutionized by the 'Big Bang', it also precipitated a period of rapid expansion, leading to a 15-fold increase in trading volumes by 1995 (Weber 1999: 30–47).

The key trends arising out of these changes, however, would result in an even more radical transformation of the City and its nexus of power. In the first place, there was a massive rise in derivative trading, especially the development of financial futures and options, while the requirement for multinational companies to buy and sell in several currencies helped drive these changes. By the late 1980s, foreign exchange deals were worth $187 billion per day (Buckley 1992: 9), indicating how the City was reverting to the role it had played prior to 1914, in that its international activities were becoming much more important than its domestic (Cain and Hopkins 1993*b*: 293). The abolition of exchange controls in 1979 had been the first crucial step in this process (Michie 1999: 544), while the earlier enormous expansion of the eurodollar market had provided many firms with a larger role in international trading (Cain and Hopkins 1993: 292–3). City firms were consequently hiring much larger staffs to cope with this increased volume, with many broking firms more than doubling their workforce over the course of the 1980s, while the commercial banks opened substantial operations that soaked up huge amounts of capital. At the same time, as Augur (2000: 103–15) has outlined in great detail, a combination of managerial weaknesses, strategic errors, cultural inertia, and laissez-faire government undermined the ability of established City firms to exploit this business opportunity. Indeed, 'Big Bang' proved to be the opening chorus in what Augur (2000) describes as *The Death of Gentlemanly Capitalism*, precipitating a fundamental revision not only of City practices, but also the ownership and control of most sectors.

The institutional weaknesses inherent within the City would lead first to staggering financial losses, then to withdrawal from key markets that were soon swamped by American and other foreign financial institutions. By 2000, only two (Lazards and Rothschilds) of the top ten London-based merchant banks of 1983 were British-owned, all of the leading investment banks having been subsumed into mostly American-owned operations, while the top ten brokers of 1983 had all been through a similar metamorphosis. In the case of Barings' acquisition by ING, of course, weak supervision of the firm's Singapore office had resulted in losses of £869 million, leading directly to the collapse of a pillar of the City establishment (Fay 1996: 230–2). In general, though, the 'gentlemanly capitalists' had palpably failed to cope with the challenges and opportunities that the previous twenty years had offered, leading to an 'abject surrender' of enormous proportions (Augur 2000: 310).

ACCOUNTANTS AND BUSINESS

While there is much more that could be written about 'Big Bang' and its aftermath (Michie 1999: 569–95; Augur 2000: 307–43), it is clear that by the 1990s the City had changed markedly, especially in terms of the international orientation of its activities and the ownership of its leading institutions. At the same time, one should never forget the increasingly intimate relationship City institutions had forged with the rest of the British business community, both in terms of capital provision and interlinking directorships. Indeed, it is vital to consider the manner in which this relationship was manifested, and in particular the opportunities provided for accountants to infiltrate the higher echelons of British business. The market for corporate control that had first started to emerge in the 1950s had by the 1990s become a major feature of the City's portfolio, with ownership of most large-scale firms (see Table 5.1) having moved decisively from individuals to the powerful financial institutions. As Toms and Wright (2002: 106–17) have also demonstrated, the institutional shareholders that owned over 60 per cent of the equity quoted on the Stock Exchange were exerting a much stronger influence over management, with the rate at which these bodies voted at company meetings rising from 20 per cent in 1990 to 50 per cent by 1999. In response to some cavalier actions by boards of directors, as we saw in Chapter 5 new codes of practice were also introduced in the early 1990s, following the Cadbury and Greenbury recommendations (Charkham 1995: 248–344). Even though this failed to eliminate completely such questionable practices as insider trading and share price manipulation, a much more efficient and transparent system of corporate governance had evolved by the 1990s, instilling greater confidence in the investment system.

The transparency of corporate investment activities has been one of the biggest problems facing both financiers and potential shareholders ever since the first companies acts had been formulated. As we noted (see Introduction, Chapter 11), up to the interwar era considerable confusion surrounded such issues as calculating the true profitability of firms and revealing accurate information (Edwards 1989: 126–7). Even though compulsory external auditing was introduced in 1900 and further modifications to company law were introduced in 1928–9, it remained relatively easy for promoters and management to hide the real asset positions of their companies (Hannah 1974b: 69–71; Michie 1999: 264). More stringent regulations were fashioned after the Second World War, with an Act passed in 1947 to outlaw the formation and use of secret reserves, followed in 1948 by legislation that Hannah (1974a: 75) claims removed the informational constraint by insisting that managements should reveal the true asset and earning position of their firms. Maltby (2000: 31–60), on the other hand, while acknowledging the break from past traditions, has demonstrated that as a result of a powerful directors' lobby in favour of reduced disclosure, in practice the 1948 Companies Act failed to encourage greater transparency. It was not until the 1967, 1976, and 1981 Companies Acts had been enacted that investors were finally provided with a more complete picture of corporate finance, indicating how regulatory practices were slow to adapt to the changing ownership of British business (Edwards 1989: 211–12).

In spite of the sluggish nature of corporate accounting reform, as we also saw (see Introduction, Chapter 11) the chartered accountancy profession had benefited enormously from the surge in demand for their services, mostly following on from the conversion of many firms into joint-stock companies (Matthews, Anderson, and Edwards 1998: 89–112). The principal trend with which these members of the 'Cardiff School' are concerned, however, is the use and employment of accountants in business generally. In charting this trend, they have compiled Table 11.3, which indicates that in 1891 only 4 per cent of company directors in their sample of 541 firms were accountants. Of course, this ignores the extensive employment of accountants as advisors and consultants, not to mention their role in drawing up annual accounts, auditing, and liquidating firms. Nevertheless, it is apparent that in managerial terms one would conclude that by the 1890s this relationship remained embryonic. Over the course of the following 100 years, however, it is apparent from Table 11.3 that accountants came to play a highly significant role in the management of British business, with the proportion of companies in their sample having an accountant on the board rising to over 81 per cent.

The rise to prominence of accountants has been one of the most decisive trends in British business management over the last 150 years. In addition to their employment as directors, the aggregate number of accountants has also risen impressively, from almost 11,700 in 1911 to 198,490 in 1991, a 17-fold increase. In contrast, the legal profession has only grown threefold over that period, while engineering has experienced a ninefold rise. A further insight into their position can be found in the comparison with manufacturing employment: for every accountant in 1911, there were 633 manufacturing employees; by 1991, 'there were only 31 people making things for every one professional accountant adding up the figures' (Matthews, Anderson, and Edwards 1998: 72–3). Furthermore, only the United States has more practising accountants than the UK, while in terms of labour force per accountant the latter (at 198) far undercuts the former (427). The proportion of accountants that were employed in business, as opposed to private practice, had also altered dramatically, even amongst the ICAEW. Indeed, by the 1990s 55 per cent of the ICAEW membership worked in business, while the vast majority of Chartered Institute of Management Accountants (CIMA) members were similarly employed, indicating how British firms were increasingly keen to utilize this particular kind of expertise.

Table 11.3. Qualified accountants in company management, 1891–1991

	1891	1931	1971	1991
Companies in sample	541	340	322	324
Directors in sample	2,651	1,653	1,870	2,084
% of companies with accountant-director	4.0	19.1	65.8	81.2
% of chairmen who were accountants	0.8	4.6	13.6	20.7
% of managing directors who were accountants	0	2.6	13.8	19.3
% of company secretaries who were accountants	7.1	14.3	41.7	47.4
% of directors who were accountants	0.8	3.8	15.2	22.0

Source: Matthews et al. (1998: 125).

Having mentioned CIMA, it is also vital to explain in greater detail some of the key trends in the evolution of financial planning. As we noted (see Introduction, Chapter 11), for a variety of reasons the management accountants had struggled to gain a firm foothold within British business. In the first place, we noted (see Accountancy and Industrialization, Chapter 11) that even though the ICWA had been formed in 1919, the much more prestigious ICAEW blocked any moves this body made to gain chartered status, thereby undermining its drive for enhanced status. Consequently, as Table 11.1 indicates, while in 1961 there were 35,600 members of the ICAEW, only 7,387 had joined the ICWA, statistics that accurately reflect the relative levels of influence the two bodies exerted generally.

The second key issue relates to the demand for financial control and planning techniques, because as we explained in Chapter 9 labour management and control had for generations been delegated either to shop-floor supervisors or external agencies like the employers' federations that dominated the industrial relations scene until the 1980s. Furthermore, the limited application of mass-production techniques meant that the production of adequate costing information was rarely a major priority within British business. As Quail (2000) has also noted, the systems of personal or proprietorial capitalism that prevailed up to the 1960s preferred structures where directorial power was unmediated by senior management. After all, a system that required a level of day-to-day coordination, management, and delegation empowered those senior managers, creating a power structure that would undermine the proprietors or their representatives. One should also add that budgetary control not only integrates the enterprise and increases internal reflexivity, but also it undermines peremptory proprietorial management. This was the system that had taken over American business from the 1950s (Fligstein 1993: 226–9), by which time the M-form of organization had come to dominate the corporate sector and financial performance became the acid test for survival of the myriad range of subsidiaries operated by these large-scale firms. Of course, as Johnson and Kaplan (1987) have demonstrated, management accountancy had been extensively employed across American industry by the 1920s, largely because of the extensive use of either scientific or systematic management techniques. In Britain, on the other hand, Boyns (2005) has demonstrated how management accounting had yet to emerge to any significant extent during the 1920s. By the 1950s, however, management accountancy was being linked directly with budgetary control and financial planning on a much more extensive scale, providing a model that was soon to be exported across the Atlantic as British firms sought to tighten up in an area that had traditionally been neglected.

It was during the 1960s and 1970s that management accountancy made enormous progress in the UK, first through the adoption of standard costing across much of industry, and second as a result of the emergence of financial planning. Although standard costing had been used in American industry since the 1920s, little interest had been shown in this technique across British industry because of its links with scientific management. As we noted (see The 1940s and 1950s: Continuing Post-War Problems, Chapter 5), Granick's survey (1972) had been highly critical of British central company headquarters, given their relatively limited use of planning and financial controls, especially compared to American corporations. This is further illustrated by the example of Unilever, because when Cob Stenham took over as finance director in 1970 he stated that: 'The most pressing task was to install an effective management accounting system which laid more emphasis on monitoring profit forecasts. Unilever had almost no idea how to allocate resources, and there was little financial control' (Jones 2005: 522). If this was the case for what many regarded as one of Britain's most effectively managed firms, then it is difficult to imagine the level of effectiveness across the majority of firms. The preponderance of H-form structures had also mitigated against the introduction of American-style planning mechanisms, compounding the difficulties associated with the prevailing system of proprietorial capitalism. From the 1960s, however, Armstrong (1987) demonstrates graphically how the drive to modernize production, introduce scientific management, and gain greater control over labour resulted in a significant surge in the use of management accountants, often associated with computerization. At exactly the same time, with the M-form growing in popularity, financial planning and decision-making came into vogue, often as a result of visits from American management consultants, further increasing the need for management accountants. The Warwick survey of British business (Marginson et al. 1988) also revealed how by the 1980s line management had become heavily reliant on budgets and accounting control, while the personnel functions at divisional and HQ level became separated from, and reactive to, these developments.

Reflecting these trends, in 1986 the ICWA was renamed the CIMA, indicating how this group had gained comparable status to the ICAEW. Table 11.1 also demonstrates that while the ICAEW membership trebled between 1961 and 1995, by the end of that period CIMA was 5.6 times the size of its predecessor (the ICWA). Moreover, such has been the dramatic improvements in status associated with management accountancy, the two Institutes have initiated merger discussions as a first stage in harmonizing the training and qualification processes that have for so long been separated. This could well bring British accountancy back to the position noticed by Boyns and Edwards (1997: 20–2), in describing how in the early nineteenth century financial and management accountancy were evolving down the same track, even though there was a long period of divergence.

CONCLUSIONS

By the late twentieth century accounting in both of its main forms had clearly become major influences within British business generally, competing effectively to assert their comparability with other professions and ensuring that their techniques were employed extensively (Procter, Rowlinson, and Toms 1999). Roslender, Glover, and Kelly (2000: 208–10) have effectively argued that the accounting career could well have passed its peak, in terms of numbers and overall influence, while significant divisions between the lower levels of account-ants performing routine tasks and those at the top of the profession continue to undermine the need for cohesion in dealing with twenty-first-century challenges. Nevertheless, as we noted at the outset and building on Armstrong's contribution (1985, 1987) to this debate, by the late twentieth century accountants had become *The Priesthood of Industry* (Matthews, Anderson, and Edwards 1998), such was their control over key aspects of British managerial hierarchies. It is worth noting how this descriptive phrase was almost exactly the same as one devised by the leading interwar management authority, John Lee, who argued in favour of creating 'a priesthood in industry' capable of imposing a Christian style of management on the workforce (1922: 114–15, quoted in Perkin 1989: 304). As many authorities have demonstrated (Barry 1989), however, far from being a Christian influence, the growing power of accountants indicates how a profes-sional management cadre was slow to emerge in the UK, given that 'for many years [the accountancy qualification] has been the only serious professional preparation for would-be managers' (Handy 1988: 12). As the banks and finan-cial institutions 'moved more and more into the centre of the [corporate] networks' (Stanworth and Giddens 1975: 24), and ownership of British business was transferred to the City of London, this further enhanced the financial accountants' ability to strengthen their hold over decision-making.

Of course, there is a wider debate surrounding these trends related to the claims that, first, accountancy qualifications provide a highly unsuitable prepar-ation for management (Armstrong 1985), and second, this reinforced the short-termist nature of British business strategy (Clutterbuck and Crainer 1988). After all, with City institutions owning the bulk of the equity in Britain's major corporations, it was inevitable that they would impose their own disciplines on management, with financial accountants acting as their eyes and ears on the inside. On the other hand, given the paucity of British management training and the resistance from most managers to the need for greater professionalism, it seems hardly surprising that accountants, whether financial or management, came to play prominent roles within the evolving hierarchies. This was especially the case from the 1960s, when financial planning and decision-making finally became popular in British business, reinforcing the longer-term tendency to rely on *The Priesthood of Industry* (Matthews, Anderson, and Edwards 1998) for a wide range of services.

The chartered accountants especially, but more recently their management counterparts, consequently benefited enormously from the slow transition to-wards professionalism across British management generally, filling a gap that had been one of the most abiding characteristics of the business system since the nineteenth century. At the same time, one should stress that only since the 1970s has financial planning been adopted extensively in British firms, revealing how the influence of accountants on internal processes proved to be extremely limited for long periods. While up to that decade chartered accountants were becoming increasingly influential within the intercorporate networks, their roles were focused more on the external functions associated with reporting and auditing, rather than improving internal processes. Moreover, as they acted as the representatives of those financial institutions that by the 1970s owned the bulk of the equity traded in the City, their role was effectively to impose the short-termist strategies of financial capitalism on senior management. It is consequently a moot point whether British business benefited from having such a group operating at the heart of organizational hierarchies, even if more recently the management accountants have been able to impose more rigorous procedures and compensate for the allegedly baleful influences of their chartered counterparts. Overall, though, it is apparent that while in the United States senior managers are associated with the MBA and in Germany with engineering qualifications, the British cadre is dominated by accountants, bringing a form of professionalism to a community that in the past has lacked this essential element.

Part V

Conclusions and Reflections

12

Conclusions

As the conclusions are a time for reflection, we therefore spend a considerable amount of this final chapter reviewing the implications of the frames of reference that have been used throughout the book and the themes which subsume them. In addition, we also try to put changes in the managerial role and numbers into perspective, discuss some reflections about managerial capitalism, and what the past and the present have to say about the future. Although it is always difficult to bring a history right up to the present, because the events are too close and the interrelationships between the institution and its environment are too complex to obtain a clear perspective, it is important to address these issues. In this way, we can contribute directly to current debates about the nature and direction of management as it struggles to come to terms with a constantly changing environment.

Chapter 1 posited one frame of reference in the four managerial stages, representing a transition from the personal capitalism of the First Industrial Revolution to managerial capitalism. Whereas this was a single step in the comparator economies, in Britain there were intermediary periods of proprietorial capitalism and then a reaction to changing circumstances before managerial capitalism could be said to have emerged. But while the first three stages were essentially negative in explaining the British situation, it must be remembered that the British economy was substantially successful in generating reasonably high standards of living in comparative terms well into the post-Second World War period. If management was weaker than in other countries, this was only relative and did not prevent substantial British economic growth. It was not just economic growth; British society has always had great strengths, and if its institutions and values have come under criticism in this book in the context of industrial management, there were other contexts of tolerance, leadership, and political systems and organization that provided a stability and a generosity of spirit which was the envy of many other countries. Stage 4 has brought Britain back to an economic position equivalent to these other strengths which had seemed to be in danger of being lost. The stages, however, are not a model as such, merely a periodization of events. A further question, as to whether another, fifth, stage is emerging, is retained until the final section.

Chapter 2 set up two different frames of reference, or 'constructions' which provided the theoretical base for the book: the models of organizational growth and the drivers, or, rather, the restraining forces of change. It was from these that the four underpinning themes of the book were derived. As we put forward three models of organizational development derived from the academic literature, it is now time to review their contribution in explaining what we have identified as the key question of the book: 'The essence of the problem is once again attempting to understand why corporate management structures developed so impressively in countries like the USA, Germany and Japan, while in Britain relatively little progress was made in this respect' (Wilson 1995: 134).

The Chandler model, emphasizing market-cum-technological factors in an almost deterministic sense, has nevertheless been the dominant paradigm of organizational and industrial development. In particular, Chandler (1977, 1990) was able to identify the importance of management as the crucial factor of production in generating technological economies of scale, as well as developing and servicing markets. In pointing to the pivotal importance of a substantial central office management structure and staffing both in the development of organizations and the growth of management numbers, he provided a benchmark against which other business systems could be measured. However, as it was based on American experience, and while it has some relevance elsewhere, it does not fit as well for Britain, or indeed for Germany, Japan, and other industrial nations. In Britain, the dominance of the H-form as a federation of small companies, at a time when much organizational growth was taking place, meant that the central office staff structure was not directly associated with the growth in the size of organizations. Nevertheless, the transformation from H-forms to M-forms in the 1960s and 1970s was associated with a rapid overall growth in both the numbers of managers and a growth of central staffs.

The ideas developed by Popp, Toms, and Wilson (2003) are part of a paradigm that has enjoyed something of a revival in its relevance to British management. However, by its nature it is associated with heterarchy and external economies of scale, and with limited implications for the growth in management numbers. In the last two decades or so, indeed, it can be used to help explain the waves of delayering and outsourcing in large organizations, just as in earlier years it helps to explain why British management did not achieve the growth through organizational structure that other countries experienced.

The Fligstein (1993) model allows more flexibility in terms of country comparison in its explanation of the development of corporate structures, and thus of management. According to Fligstein (1993), it is in the nature of organizations that they will try to reduce competition by seeking to control the environment, and in the nature of the wider society that it will have concerns about this. British business did, indeed, try to control competition, rather successfully, but it took a long time for any social response to occur in Britain. Fligstein's argument reflects the successive domination of different functional groupings in American industrial development (controlling competition into the early twentieth century; manufacturing control up to the 1920s; sales and marketing control up to the 1950s; and finance control since then), and while this has some resonance in Britain, it is not itself an explanation for managerial growth in the British context.

As the synthesis developed in Chapter 2 helps to explain the counterbalancing forces in organizational growth, it is therefore valuable in helping to understand the broad trends. At the heart of our argument is a preference by British industrialists for externalization where possible, with a resulting lack of the managerial growth associated with internalization. These models, however, take us only so far, since they are dealing with organizations rather than with managers as such.

Nevertheless, the issues with which we have dealt are much wider than organizations; there is a need for considering the psychology, institutions, values, and power structure of British society as a whole. Here the drivers help us (see The 'Drivers' of Management Growth, Chapter 2). Britain had a mix of drivers which made it difficult to develop managerial capitalism in the same ways as the comparator countries which we examined in Chapter 4. The market-cum-technological group of drivers placed Britain initially in a positive, but later in a negative, light. It was the utilization of improved technologies, based on mechanical systems, and the production systems which went with them, which made possible the First Industrial Revolution. In association with these features, it was the development of a distribution system appropriate for small or relatively small companies which generated the demand and the means of serving it. But neither of these required a sophisticated managerial system, which was necessary at the next stage to operate the more advanced technologies and wider markets of the Second Industrial Revolution. The market-cum-technological drivers were no longer appropriate, path dependency was already established, and change became difficult. Similarly, the institutional-cultural drivers were predominantly negative for Britain. In the other countries, there were generally more conducive institutions and attitudes, managers were accorded a higher status, the state took a stronger role, and moreover, the institutions generally worked together. On the other hand, in Britain there was no such coherent institutional involvement in any of these areas. Business policy and practice as a group of drivers also emphasize British weaknesses in the way in which management developed and operated. However much market and institutional-cultural factors may have contributed to delays in the emergence of efficient management, internal structures, systems, and attitudes also bore a good deal of the responsibility. Here we are looking at the nature of personal and proprietorial capitalism and their dual tendency to externalize some (labour and marketing, for instance) decision-making, rather than delegate it to professional managers or retain total control over strategic management.

But the balance of drivers has changed a great deal in the recent past, as discussed in Figure 5.2. The market structure has changed to one where manufacturing is now less than 20 per cent of the economy (although it needs to be noted that the service sector was not notably more effective in developing managerial professionalization). In addition, open competition, change, and innovation are now the rule rather than the exception, and the move into European and global markets has changed the framework of trade. In relation to the institutional drivers, the political parties now all accept open market capitalism, the financial system has become primarily concerned with business performance, and both the general and the managerial educational and training systems have greatly improved the potential quality of management. Culturally, too, there has been great change. While attitudes towards manufacturing are still not strongly positive, that part of the economy is now much smaller; while being more evenly distributed, it does not contribute to the old North–South split. And although the financial elite in the City of London is still the dominant one in Britain, its focus is now much more on domestic issues, albeit with a heavy emphasis on short-term results. Moreover, attitudes towards management as a career have greatly improved compared to half a century ago. Finally, in relation to the operation of the firm, the focus on legitimacy rather than technical efficiency has now gone. In its place has been substituted shareholder capitalism, manifested by the share price, with little attention to other stakeholders. In relation to firm structure, the question is whether organizations are overmanaged, rather than undermanaged (Protherough and Pick 2002), although many would argue that leadership is still a rare management skill. Basic techniques have also improved, as has productivity in the last two decades. Most of these changes provide a better base for management as an organizational role, even if, and we reiterate this later, there is still room for improvement.

While the drivers are too numerous for detailed individual consideration, they can in large part be subsumed into the book's four main themes, to which we now turn in sequence.

THE PERSISTENCE OF PERSONAL AND PROPRIETORIAL CAPITALISM

Even though family capitalism has continued to be significant in many other countries, this theme was vitally important in its time, essentially up to the 1960s, but has now become relatively unimportant in Britain (Jones and Rose 1993; Church 1993). From the inception of limited liability in the 1850s, British firms employed the private limited company as a means of securing its benefits without the possible challenge to control associated with having external shareholders; for family members, indeed, the firm was a way of life, not just an organization (Owens 2002). For this reason, they did not tend to seek funds in the capital market, relying more on bank borrowing or fixed-interest securities, while within the company they were slow in adopting systems of delegation, even functional departmentalism. Rather, directors and senior managers involved themselves in day-to-day operations, sometimes at the expense of strategy. Quail (2000: 14) notes the strong tendency for committees of boards to carry out activities which in the United States and Germany would be performed by top professional management, that 'we can see from the survey of firm structure that top management was sparse or non-existent'. The result was smaller management teams and less separation of ownership and control. Britain was also unusual in that the personal-proprietorial phases continued well after the nineteenth century. As Guillén (1994: 210) notes: 'While professional managers were displacing founders and heirs from the top American and German corporations, British firms became even more dominated by family interests in the 1920s. The overriding concern was to maintain control rather than increase market share or exports.' This prevailing family dominance of even Britain's largest firms can be substantiated by referring to Hannah's data on the top 200 companies, which reveal that the proportion with owners on the board of directors in 1948 stood at 59 per cent, compared to 55 per cent in 1919 (Hannah 1980: 53). Moreover, there was still some continuation of this perspective up to the 1960s.

According to Chandler (1990), the economic costs of this style of control were high. As this prominent American business historian argued, in the new industries of the Second Industrial Revolution the period before the window of opportunity closed was brief. In many cases, the time between the initial commercialization of a new product or process and the introduction of Chandler's three-pronged investment strategy (see Introduction, Chapter 4) that determined the key players in an industry was little more than a decade. Crucially, while British entrepreneurs hesitated, Americans and Germans made the investments that permitted them to dominate British as well as international markets in the new industries. But the British approach also had an impact on the older industries, in that the efficiency limits of labour-intensity and externalization were reached and they became less competitive.

In its early days, proprietorial capitalism was also associated with limitations through a self-denying access to funds from financial institutions. Even when such access did occur through merger or floatation, it was associated with weak systems of governance in relation to the majority of shareholders. Directors acted on behalf of the owners, but without real internal controls or external accountability. As Hannah (1974b: 75) notes, this was 'the golden age of directorial power', when shareholders deferred to their influence over all aspects of the business. The ending of proprietorial capitalism in the 1960s and 1970s brought about not only managerial capitalism, but also the more immediate accountability which led to financial capitalism (Toms and Wright 2002).

Why was Britain so different? There is no single answer. Many of the drivers we have identified make some contribution, but psychology must have played a large part, comprised of a mixture of complacency based on previous success, risk and competition aversion, lack of strategic thinking, family self-regard, and the 'managers are born not made' syndrome. The net result was that managers did not emerge in Britain with the same authority, education and development, progression, or social status that they did in other countries. It did not, however, necessarily mean that Britain had noticeably fewer managers than other countries; an efficient plant in a large company would need a production manager, but several smaller plants producing the same output in total would also each require a production manager. Rather, the balance of managers between Britain and other countries is likely to have been different, with more production-oriented managers in Britain in a more labour-intensive context, but less staff managers.

The tradition of capturing external economies of scale by operating in dense industrial districts would also have meant that specialized skills like marketing and selling were only developed to a basic level in most sectors.

The problem became one of 'path dependency'—the tendency for past choices to mould the way an organization will act in the present and future, by creating specific core competencies or limiting the elaboration of managerial skills. Firms did not have strategies; rather, they responded opportunistically to market circumstances, mainly operating in limited product markets which tended to produce defensive organizational developments designed to protect existing vested interests, and benevolent (from the employers' point of view) labour markets. This short-term instrumentalism was a classic case of emergent, rather than planned strategies (Mintzberg 1996). Such contexts provided few incentives for managers to improve efficiency. Indeed, many British company policies were affected by, even dominated by, the past, well into the last quarter of the twentieth century, and arguably even now. There was something of a 'Catch 22' situation: without good managers, there was little capability for change; and without change, there was little chance of obtaining good managers. Even if the policies did have a certain short-term rationality, the long-term implications were devastating.

MANAGEMENT, ORGANIZATIONAL STRUCTURE, AND TRANSACTION COSTS

We have seen that this theme raises complex issues. On the one hand, there is the Chandlerian model of economies of scale generated by technological developments and the associated internalization of activities, resulting in the growth of size and complexity in organizations, or, for our purpose, managerial hierarchies. But while this has been the dominant paradigm for several decades and it still carries weight, more recently alternative models have appeared, as discussed (see Models of Organizational Growth, Chapter 2). But there was an even more full-bodied challenge that was certainly applicable to Britain, based on the concept of flexible specialization and the economies of externalization made available by industrial clusters and districts (Popp, Toms, and Wilson 2003). This argument looked to heterarchy as an alternative mode of organization to hierarchy, linking in with the work of Pettigrew and Fenton (2000). Porter (1990) has also utilized the cluster concept to identify sources of competitive advantage; indeed, he has recently recommended such an industrial framework as a possible future direction for British industry (Porter and Ketels 2003).

It is clear that this theme has in some senses gone full circle. Having used externalization extensively in the nineteenth and early twentieth centuries, the British economy moved in the second half of the twentieth century to internalize its activities, resulting in the emergence of classical managerial bureaucracies. But then the wheel turned again and the last fifteen years have seen the reassertion of the virtues of externalization under the name of outsourcing. As noted in

Chapter 5, the amount spent on outsourcing represents the largest category of expenditure in the MCA's income analysis. But while there are advantages in this form of organization, especially in satisfying the financial markets, there are also disadvantages if the organization does not maintain the knowledge and skills necessary to monitor the outsourcing. In fact, to go further, new forms of heterarchy are only efficient if they are underpinned by an effective management structure (Pettigrew and Fenton 2000). In some industries such as the railways, banking, posts and telegraphy, it is true, there was exploitation of internal economies from the mid nineteenth century (Popp, Toms, and Wilson 2003: 16), and these infrastructural industries provided external economies to manufacturing industry. Some large companies also utilized internal economies, mainly in the FMCG sector. Overall, though, the general orientation was towards externalization, with the third quarter of the twentieth century acting as a historical aberration that was soon overturned.

A major thrust of the book has been that externalization without any strategic vision carries severe disadvantages. The labour field was a particular example, with Anthony (1986: 1) arguing that management in Britain had refused to accept responsibility for the management of labour. On the other hand, to set against Anthony, Littler (1982: 143) would argue that a key factor was resistance to developing systems of managerial control. Such resistance came from foremen, groups of workers, organized and unorganized, and middle managers. Whatever be the case, this made it more difficult for effective management to emerge. In the traditional and craft industries, productivity tended to be increased through the efforts of manual workers rather than through the application of science or technology to industrial methods, or as a result of managerial methods of organization (McGivering, Matthews, and Scott 1960: 89). Managerial policies tended to be focused on cutting wages or increasing working hours, especially in industries such as coal where there was no time for sentiment. In the post-war period, although a major emphasis was placed on productivity, it proved less than easy to achieve for a range of reasons, mostly based on the power of tradition and a legacy of externalization.

But it was not just in the labour area that British business experienced problems. Some of the most insidious forms of externalization came in the various forms of anti-competitive practices, in which the state and the law colluded (Levine 1967). These not only had the direct effect of reducing competition and retaining the status quo, but also had such side effects as reducing the incentive for technical progress, organizational development, and managerial improvement. The intensity of associative anti-competitive activity was cyclical in nature, being not so great in periods of rising demand and prices as it was in periods of falling prices and slackening demand. But although this clearly suited the British entrepreneurial temperament, it was not alone; Germany had much stronger forms of anti-competitive behaviour, although these did not appear to impair its development of managerial structures, compared to the British scenario, while in the United States, trusts were widespread until the much earlier development of strong antitrust legislation.

Of course, some transactions costs were affected by forces largely outside the firm's control. In this context, the importance of diverse markets for companies, both at home and abroad and often bespoke, meant that there was less pressure to move to mass production than in the United States or Germany. This also held back marketing and made merchanting relatively more efficient (Broadberry and Marrison 2002). Penrose's argument (1959) that there is a managerial constraint on business growth must be relevant here. There was something of a self-reinforcing effect in not developing an efficient management cadre, which in turn affected the balance of transactions costs towards continued externalization. Moreover, as a result of proprietorial capitalism, Britain did not have the managerial coordination techniques necessary to reduce internal transactions costs.

SOCIAL ATTITUDES TOWARDS MANAGEMENT AND INDUSTRY

In the nineteenth century, the so-called grime of industry did not sit well with imperial grandeur or financial hegemony. As we saw in Chapter 6, the resulting low standing of management until the very recent past was a consequence of the strong social distinctions many contemporaries made between the two images. It is also important to recognize that the low standing of industry had some justification in reality. Rubinstein (1977: 605) has argued that it was actually much easier to make money in commerce, finance, and trade than in industry; that 'it is clear that the wealthy earned their fortunes disproportionately in commerce, finance and transport—that is, as merchants, bankers, shipowners, merchant bankers and stock and insurance brokers—rather than as manufacturers and industrialists'. Furthermore, it is important that within management production was the pariah, and indeed still is. Elsewhere, Rubinstein (1988) has argued that the drift to the South of the professions and commercial roles was logical in terms of a search for career security, as well as or rather than a search for status. We noted in Chapter 6 his comment that these provided a pull, rather than institutions or values providing a push, against industry. These factors help us remember that Britain in its basic attitudes and priorities was not really an industrial nation, but rather a commercial and trading economy. Thus, Britain's industrial retardation or decline did not automatically mean a decline in overall economic performance; other sectors could and arguably did compensate. Nevertheless, industrial life was uncertain not just within the social structure of the firm, but also externally in terms of competition, the trade cycle, and the lack of the kind of tariff protection for manufacturing industry that Britain's rivals enjoyed.

These perspectives had important consequences. At any given point in time, there was no shortage of voices decrying industrial retardation, educational inadequacy, or international competition. At the same time, the main elites in the South-East, the higher professions, the landed gentry, the pursuers of empire, and the financial markets were too satisfied with their own way of life to give support to any significant changes in national policy. The needs of industry, including those of management, were therefore given low priority in national policies. The state was not anti-capitalist, even under the Labour Party; rather, it was dominated for long periods by laissez-faire individualism. Supply-side management of the economy only became significant in the 1980s, replacing the macroeconomic focus of earlier periods (Shonfield 1958).

Another key issue was the lack of social status in which the management role was held, thus preventing the more gifted or more socially conscious of the nation's young from being interested in the occupation. This was compounded by the problem of relatively poor pay, at least by comparison with their counterparts in other countries (Granick 1972), as well as the likelihood of those in the traditional manufacturing industries having to work in what many regarded as an unfashionable part of Britain. While this situation was more pronounced in the manufacturing sector than the service sector, it could not be said of the latter either that there was an infrastructure leading to the development of professional management. Across the whole economy, management in the sense of being a professional administrator achieved a social recognition as a profession in the United States and Europe which it did not achieve in Britain; the same was also true to a considerable extent of engineering. In addition, internal issues of legitimacy and industrial democracy continued until the 1970s, exacerbating these external perspectives.

Again, this theme has seen a great deal of change, especially in Child's two non-technical roles (1969: 13), those of a system of authority and as an elite social grouping. Management has now achieved internal legitimacy, in the sense that as a system of authority it is no longer seriously challenged either by unions or by problems of legitimacy; the 'frontier of control', which we saw in Chapter 9 to be fiercely contested up to the 1970s, is no longer an issue. It has also achieved external legitimacy, in the sense that management is a socially acceptable role and career, so that it has become an identifiable elite social grouping. That status is now largely achieved by the bestowing of educational credibility through the MBA and other management-related qualifications (and by becoming the most popular undergraduate subject in the university system, even at Oxford), as well as by relaxing the social shibboleths associated with 'getting one's hands dirty by indulging in trade'. Indeed, managers as a group have benefited from the increasingly inequitable distribution of income in Britain, although their insecurity has also increased as a consequence of the greater liberalization of economic forces. At the same time, although management is a social group, it has not become a clearly defined interest group, being both too fragmented and lacking leadership. Thus, the fears of Burnham (1941) and others of a dominant managerial elite have not been realized in Britain, although more globally there is certainly concern about the power of big business.

THE SLOW TRANSITION TOWARDS PROFESSIONALISM

In what sense were British managers unprofessional? We have argued along two main lines. First, under proprietorial capitalism those higher up at board level were amateurs, chosen for their background and name, with a consequent lack of effective top management; while those at the bottom were narrow in their focus, undereducated, and socially insecure. Second, patterns of thought and action tended to be based not on systematic or scientific approaches, but on the rule of thumb, using the experience of a narrow function, without education or breadth.

While there were always salaried managers in British companies, until very late in the twentieth century the vast majority could not be called professional. In part, this was due to structural considerations. In the early days, before the emergence of M-form structures there was little need for managers in the professional sense, since most of the managerial functions were carried out either by family members or members of the directorial clique. There were fewer of them in the key planning and coordination roles in the M-form companies when the latter did emerge (Channon 1973), thus losing much of the rationale for having an M-form structure in the first place. Second, there were issues connected with the nature of the managerial labour market. Those managers who did exist, and at all levels of management, had been appointed and promoted by virtue of their performance in functional roles, usually having started in manual or clerical grades and having received little or no training or development as managers. There was little pre-selection in the role of manager and little mobility within management, whether interfunctional or interdivisional, not to mention between companies or geographical areas, partly because managers had few transferable skills and partly through lack of inclination. But arguably most problematic of all was that managers lacked legitimacy and authority, both being necessary characteristics of professionalism by its very nature.

This internal situation was exacerbated by a lack of a supportive institutional or educational framework until the last few decades. The institutional situation meant that there was no professional body for managers as managers, although there was a multiplicity of bodies representing the various functional roles of managers. It must be accepted, however, that management is too heterogeneous an occupation for any institution to expect to bring all managers under its roof. Similarly, there was a lack of an adequate educational framework for nascent managers, or for their development after being appointed. Moreover, there was no strong demand from industry for such a framework; indeed, when such a framework did emerge it is our contention that the major thrust from the demand side came from individual managers, not business. As we have argued in Chapter 8, professionalism must be about integration, not merely the skills of the individual. British management hierarchies tended not to be well integrated, either between functions or between levels. Production was particularly weak, because that was the main base of the practical, uneducated manager (Keeble 1992). British businessmen from the top to the bottom lacked the expertise, either from education or experience, to make the M-form work (Channon 1973; Quail 2000). As Levine (1967: 17) concluded: 'It appears that the Anglo-American and Anglo-German productivity differentials sprang primarily from the relative backwardness of British industrial technique.' Although he considered other possible factors, such as natural resource disadvantages, capital intensity, demand structure, and labour force differences, Levine (1967) felt that these did not outweigh the main concern about technique, which included management and management systems. Caves (1968) came to the same conclusion.

The second key dimension of professionalism involves a body of knowledge. While there is arguably still no fully accepted theory of management, would it have helped if Britain had developed a more structured theory of management? Littler (1982: 159) would argue positively on this point, using the concept of theory to incorporate ideology as well as technique when stating that 'it was possible for British employers to sweep the contractors away, but the absence of a systematic theory of management resulted in traditional foremen inheriting many of the powers and privileges of the contractors, and these foremen provided a rumbling resistance to Taylorism and bureaucratization right through the interwar period'. There was a general lack of a progressive industrializing ideology or vision; Bentham and Lyon Playfair in the nineteenth century and Urwick in the second quarter of the twentieth century found little support in industry or amongst the general public.

While Britain did have some significant thinkers and writers in the development of management, especially with regard to the humanistic literature that emerged from the 1920s (see Figure 2.1), they tend not to have received adequate recognition for their efforts. The main reason for this must surely be attributed to the momentum of industrial development having shifted to the United States by the early twentieth century, but a further reason is that they received little acclaim even in their homeland. Moreover, as British companies tended to be more secretive than their American counterparts, there was not the extent of development through discussion and sharing information that occurred in the United States (Outerbridge 1899). Of course, there were some major writers who were equal to their American counterparts in their contribution to the development of management as a subject. Amongst those who made major contributions which were recognized by the Americans were: Frederick Smith's *Workshop Management* (1878), Garcke and Fells' *Cost Accounting* (1887), Joseph Slater Lewis' *The Commercial Organisation of Factories* (1896), Alexander Hamilton Church's *The Science and Practice of Management* (1914) (even if by this time he had emigrated to the United States), Oliver Sheldon's *The Philosophy of Management* (1923), and Lyndall Urwick's wide range of books published over a considerable period of time. Thus, it was not that there was no intellectual curiosity and capability in the emerging subject of management. What Britain did not have until considerably later was journals in which people could write their views and expect them to be read and debated by their counterparts in other companies. Similarly, until the 1960s Britain lacked both a large body of consultants to spread the word, and with the exception of the limited outreach of the MRGs, networks that would help the dissemination process. Nor did its professional bodies provide a lead. And above all, industry showed little or no interest in developing a dialogue on this issue.

All this provided a recipe for a relatively ineffective cadre of non-professional managers that at the very least contributed to Britain's relative decline from about 1870 until the 1980s. Returning to Quail's concept (2002) of 'managerial capacity', first introduced in Chapter 2 to help explain American growth and structural change, Britain had neither the necessary human capital nor the ideological mindset. While it did have access to the American knowledge base, it did not make appropriate use of it.

More recently, though, Britain has moved towards the professionalization of its managers, even if it has still a long way to go. What are the signs of progress?

- Improving educational standards amongst managers
- Willingness to undertake CPD
- Although the issue of management as a profession is not a live one, managers are more willing to submit themselves to the requirements of one, that is, to the discipline of methods of training and the 'mastery of certain prescribed theoretical knowledge' (Urwick 1928)
- Moreover, the idea of management competencies is generally accepted and the national management standards are achieving some, if reluctant, acceptance
- A shortening time lag required to make improvements effective
- Acceptance that managers can be 'made' as well as 'born'
- The end of the cult of the amateur
- If not a pure science (indeed, some element of art is still relevant), it is accepted that management requires a knowledge base
- Management has achieved social and career credibility
- There has been a move away from managers starting their careers at shop-floor or clerical levels
- Whereas in the immediate post-war period the problem was with top managers, it is now with middle and lower managers (McGivering, Matthews, and Scott 1960; Granick 1962, 1972; Porter and Ketels 2003)
- Management has achieved the legitimacy of expertise in general, if not always as individuals

On the negative side, however, several factors need to be considered:

- Still only 30 per cent of managers have degrees or degree equivalents
- There is little evidence of the emergence of outstanding industrial leaders. Indeed, many of these leaders are outsiders from the management development system

Even once the idea and acceptability of professional management had taken hold, it took a generation for the concept to establish itself and for the new flow to replace the existing stock of managers. This raises the issue of the importance of time lags in management change, as well as those related to stock and flow. While the need for professional management was seen in the 1950s, the perceived need proved insufficient to overcome the institutional counter-pressures, resulting in a lag of thirty years before real changes occurred.

MANAGERIAL GROWTH AND CHANGE

Reflection is also required on two issues associated with managers which have emerged out of the book and to which we now turn, namely, how the role of the manager has changed, and the increase in the number and proportion of managers in the labour force. In the first instance, we compare the roles and status of managers in 1900 and 2000, while secondly it will be important to offer some explanation for the huge increase in numbers, especially after 1970.

In 1900, the manager still had an indistinct role somewhere between the employer and the workforce; certainly, it was not clearly understood by the wider public. The activity was rarely defined, but rather had emerged, like so much else in British management, from experiential development, being dependent as much on the person as the function; power was not so much delegated from above as accumulated in a piecemeal manner over time according to context and individual capabilities. There were few managers in comparison to the present; most were production-oriented, and there was little in the way of support from staff functions. Nor was there much support from systems or planning; these were areas of weakness compared to other countries. Crucially, rule of thumb was all too often the main focus of decision-making and problem-solving. The knowledge base of the manager was almost purely experiential; few managers read what literature was available, knowing little about other companies or even their own outside the department in which they worked. Nor was there a clear hierarchy in most British organizations; the plant was the main unit of operation and there was often only a small central office of emerging bureaucracy. There was no strong sense of ideological commitment in the sense of a set of values or a code of ethics. Legitimacy was, however, a problem, with little support from the owners of the business and a lack of professional credibility vis-á-vis the workforce. Accountability, in so far as it existed as a concept, was to the employer; the welfare considerations of managers were to come later, as were obligations to stakeholders. Perhaps the part of the role which has changed the least is that concerned with people; management styles differed, but in manufacturing the command and control approach was dominant.

It would be misleading to say that up to the 1960s there was an established career ladder or a managerial labour market; both of these terms assume general operational models involving significant numbers of managers which was not the case in 1900; each manager had a separate career and rarely moved from one company to another. Becoming a manager was for most a long, slow process and a culmination of success in lower level jobs; those with a more rapid appointment tended to be part of the owning family. Moreover, managers from the bottom found it difficult to rise above middle management. For the most part, managers did not interact in any professional capacity, except as part of the same company or cartel; there had as yet been no attempts to create any professional institution for managers (Brech 2002*a*). Nor was there any significant shared background in education or training; apart from primary school, indeed, most managers had little educational background. Female managers were almost unknown except in a few clearly defined fields such as retailing, textiles, and public houses.

By 2000, the role of the manager had changed substantially. There were many more managers, in a much wider range of functions, while an increasing proportion of the positions were held by women. The role was not only fully accepted by the wider society, but was held in considerable esteem and recognized as the key to economic success. The rule of thumb had been replaced by systems, many of them IT-led, with a range of performance indicators to measure different dimensions of achievement. Indeed, planning and especially control had become central to the manager's world. The knowledge base was much better established, although still far from making management into the science that early management thinkers had anticipated. The ideology had become assertive managerialism, with a more defined set of obligations to the organization, even if it was still curiously neutral in any ethical relation to the wider world, and especially in relation to people. While legitimacy was no longer a problem, though, there was still a weakness in relation to people.

Although considerably less than a majority of managers possessed degrees in 2000, the vast majority had undergone some training for their role. Many managers, indeed, had positively pushed for training as part of their commitment to their own career development. The MBA was popular amongst managers themselves and accepted by employers as a badge of merit (Thomson et al. 2001). The concept of manager was much wider than in 1900, with a generic component that had been largely absent; while the silo mentality was by no means obsolete, it was much less prevalent. Management traineeships were common, especially for graduates, although even in 2000 many managers started at the bottom. Merit was a much more important factor in success. Nevertheless, in 2000 as in 1900 and earlier, the general principles underlying the role could still be linked to Fayol (1916), even if his rationalistic approach was muddied by the more earthy perspective of Mintzberg (1973).

In comparing the situations in 1900 and 2000, implicitly we have also offered some explanation for what would seem to have been the inexorable increase in the numbers of managers (see Figure 1.7). Of course, while we discussed these issues (see Managers, Chapter 5), it is vital that some concluding comments are made on what is a grossly underresearched aspect of management history. Certainly, large organizations in 2005 have far less employees than they had in 1970, and probably considerably fewer managers, given the downsizing, delayering, and outsourcing that has taken place, to say nothing of the reduction in the strong central office hierarchies that Chandler (1977) saw as the key to managerial capitalism in the twentieth century. At the same time, while the renewed importance of heterarchy should enable decisions to be made by the market, rather than in managerial hierarchies, it is difficult to evaluate the impact on numbers. Modern value and supply chains still need managing, however elongated. On the other hand, we attribute a sizeable portion of growth to the extended nature of modern management; the concept of management has widened to include parts of the old supervisory and even blue-collar roles. Indeed, the term has become more elastic and even stretches to include train 'managers' who previously were called conductors, while it also covers administrative managerial roles such as office 'manager' which were previously primarily clerical and called chief clerks. But we accept that none of the historical models noted in Chapter 2 seem to provide a satisfactory explanation for the trend. We noted a considerable number of possible partial explanations (see Managers, Chapter 5), but no single convincing answer, although it must be supposed that the changes are associated with the logic of organizations. Far from computers taking over some of the planning, forecasting, and even controlling functions that might have been expected in a technocratic version of the 'Brave New World', the role of the manager and the computer have expanded side by side.

REFLECTIONS ON MANAGERIAL CAPITALISM AND THE FUTURE

The time has finally come to answer the 'big' question of why 'corporate management structures developed so impressively in countries like the USA, Germany and Japan, while in Britain relatively little progress was made in this respect' (Wilson 1995: 134). Chandler (1976: 47–8) offered three explanations for this conundrum: the size of the domestic market; the development and application of certain technologies; and different legal constraints. What we have argued in this book is that the issues were much broader, deeper, and more complex; they were linked to the nature of Britain as a society and need to take account of its values and its social and economic systems and priorities, manifested in its institutions and culture, as well as its business practices.

Moreover, our evidence illustrates that managerial capitalism and the modern capitalist corporation did not automatically or even logically evolve out of competitive market conditions such as those of the First Industrial Revolution; neither does modern management. Rather, it suggests the higher efficiency of oligopoly over competitive capitalism. As the British case also illustrates in the late 1960s, structure alone, even Chandlerian structure, was not enough; attitudes and skills were required in abundance. Again, whether structure followed strategy, rather than vice versa, was not by any means a predetermined issue, while this apparently deterministic relationship was not just a conundrum for the British; Servan-Schreiber (Quail 2002: 4) was speaking for all Europeans even in 1967 when he observed in America 'an art of organization that is still a mystery to us'. Nevertheless, by the end of the twentieth century Britain had made the transition

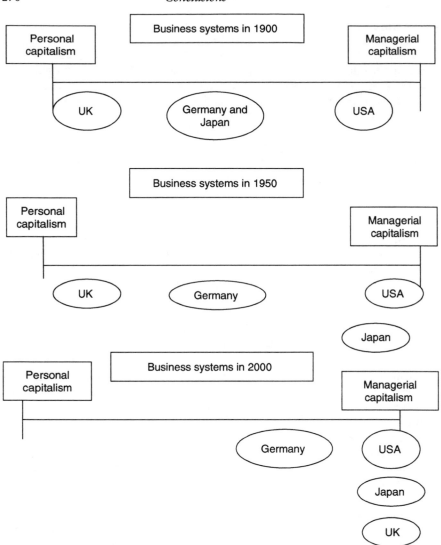

Figure 12.1. The transition to managerial capitalism

from personal to managerial capitalism, an issue that Figure 12.1 illustrates by positioning the four countries over the course of the century.

Whether managerial capitalism is destined to maintain the hegemony it achieved in the late twentieth century is another matter. One dimension is the way in which companies organize themselves. The economies of externalization are again becoming apparent, with a return to flexible specialization and the growth of extended supply chains and more ephemeral organizational structures based on projects, networks, and the management of knowledge. These are types of operations for which Britain seems to have a stronger capability compared with mass production, which exposed what Delmestri and Walgenbach (2005) saw as a British gap between technical and managerial competence, as well as an absence of trust in the short-term power relations of 'traditional' British industry (Fox 1974). Globalization has also asked new organizational questions, such as how best to structure multinational companies. Here, again, the issue of heterarchy has appeared as a feasible alternative to hierarchy, even if the research of Pettigrew and Fenton (2000) has demonstrated how the two systems now work together as a means of countering the deficiencies of the former. The rise of the joint venture, or what Dunning (1997) refers to as 'Alliance Capitalism', has also created a kaleidoscope effect that sees firms arranging manoeuvres with potential or actual rivals, leading to even further flux in the positions achieved by managers.

Within organizations the concept of hierarchy, with its massed battalions of 'organization men', has been undermined by successive rounds of delayering, outsourcing, and reductions in central staff roles, to the point where many managers are as insecure as blue-collar workers (Sampson 1995). While pronouncements in the 1980s and 1990s on the death of middle management may have been somewhat premature, the assumption of a lifelong corporate career in the same organization has certainly disappeared, even if some examples can still be found. The concept of the internal labour market is still less robust than in the United States, Germany, and Japan (Gospel 1992).

Another dimension of managerial capitalism is its continuity; here, very few British (as opposed to American, German, and Japanese) companies have maintained their identity and performance over any length of time. Unilever, Shell, and BP are arguably the only major British companies from the pre-war period. Some old companies have grown large to join them, for example Glaxo, and there has been the rapid rise of totally new companies like Vodafone. On the other hand, the corporate world no longer believes in continuity as a virtue; 'standing still' is seen as a recipe for disaster, leading to regular reorganizations or externalized moves to adapt to the changing environment.

Organizational change has been one dimension of the nature of managerial capitalism. A second has been the relationship between managers and owners, with the reassertion of ownership control, albeit in a different manifestation than in the days of personal and proprietorial capitalism. Sampson (2004), taking a societywide perspective, notes that there has been a decline in the power and influence of industry in Britain. The power of the City of London was always stronger, but is now even more forceful. The question to be asked is whether managerial capitalism has been replaced by financial capitalism, with control now moving back to the owners, or at least the intermediaries who represent them. One criterion is the extent to which short-run rather than long-run perspectives dominate, given that in Figure 5.2 financial institutions have been placed on the right-hand side of the diagram. Are the advantages of long-term planning and large-scale operations being lost almost as soon as they have been gained (Quail

2004)? Does the decline in the length of tenure of CEOs mean that managers do not have the security for assured decision-making? While these are certainly important issues, we would argue that on the one hand financial interests demand accountability for results and can certainly influence corporate strategy, at the same time they do not and cannot directly create strategy. That must be the role of the board, and since it is still composed of managers, it is still tenable to argue that managerial capitalism continues to be the crucial force in business decision-making.

Moreover, there is still a case for arguing that the M-form is the ultimate organizational structure for large companies. It is, of course, that framework within which modern corporate management emerged, with Whittington and Mayer (2000) suggesting that it is capable of evolving in a flexible manner. At present, there is no immediately obvious successor for large organizations, but there is a need for a more integrative approach to take up the new varieties of organizational form and interaction.

The last of our four managerial stages, covering the period since 1985, suggested reasonable grounds for optimism about the quantity and quality of managers, implying that an equilibrium might have been reached. But is there another stage discernible beyond the fourth? Is it likely, for instance, that the emergence of the knowledge age, or the fragmentation of organizations through outsourcing, or the widening of the concept of management to include it as a partial role performed further down the occupational ladder, will change the nature of management? Grey (1999) has certainly suggested that the boundary between managers and non-managed is becoming more fluid and perhaps even redundant. One dimension of this is that corporate restructuring has nullified one of the previously key distinctions between managers and workers, so that many managers are treated as a variable rather than a fixed cost. Moreover, while management always was a heterogeneous occupation, the gaps between its various levels seem to have been growing greater rather than coalescing into a consolidated professional grouping. Moreover, others would now argue that Britain is overmanaged (Protherough and Pick 2002), whereas our argument relating to a century or more ago was that Britain was undermanaged. On the whole, we do not think a further stage is likely, although the debates will doubtless continue; we believe that the future therefore promises a continuation of the deepening and widening process characteristic of our fourth stage.

Before concluding, we should note that in this debate we have assumed that professional management is a desirable end in itself, a view that does not go unchallenged. At the wider British level, Protherough and Pick (2002) would challenge it, while Sampson (2004) argues that the most effective managers are the outsiders, rather than those coming from within the new professional group. At both British and international levels, there are negative connotations in the way in which the concept of managerialism has been seen as a mode of governance and even domination. Thus, Enteman (1993) describes managerialism as an international ideology which has come to underpin the economic, social, and political systems of modern industrial societies, and in which 'societies are equivalent to the sum of the transactions of the practices of management'. Put into more explicit organizational terms, Fitzsimons (1999) describes managerialism as 'an elaboration of explicit standards and measures of performance in quantitative terms that set specific targets for personnel, and emphasis on economic rewards and sanctions, and a reconstruction of accountability relationships'. This issue, however, remains a debating point, with little balance having been achieved in both the arguments and positions taken by the various protagonists.

So at what point has management arrived as a grouping and where might it go in the future? We have noted the general tendency to assume that management is a professional cadre in Britain (Whittington and Mayer 2000; Porter and Ketels 2003). Going further, Perkin (1989: 25) argues that 'professionalism as an organizing principle has superseded class and that company management has become one of the two pivotal hierarchies of professional society'. Glover and Hughes (1996: 306) point further into the future with their concept of the professional-managerial class, noting the 'long march from amateurism in the vague direction of some sort of rather footloose technocracy'. All of these assume a degree of cohesion within management, a point we would dispute. Management as a group does not seem to be indicating any greater signs of cohesion; rather, the reverse is happening. There is no sense of management ever having acted in concert. We see management as and increasingly becoming such an all-encompassing activity as to deny any real identity, making fragmentation inevitable.

In a final look back, management in Britain has evolved a long way in the last century in terms of people, functions, and activities. In terms of people, by any standards there are many times more managers than at the turn of the previous century. Functionally, the initial dominance of production has disappeared, to be replaced by a flowering of staff functions, which in turn has been superseded by the hegemony of finance. In terms of activities, the manager has far more information, and indeed the processing of information has taken over from what used to be thought of as the key dimension of the manager's role, that of managing people. Moreover, the managerial role now involves much more fluidity and self-reflectivity than it did a century ago, while the context has changed considerably from being predominantly local to involvement in a global world. The inevitability of further change in the nature and structure of management and managers is perhaps the only constant. What we can see is that there will be continuing pressures to add value to all economic processes, and that the main obligation to achieve this will be placed on management. Certainly, without an effective, professional management cadre a modern economy cannot compete or grow. British management history attests to that truism.

Bibliography

AACP (Anglo-American Council on Productivity) *Reports* (1948–52). London: AACP.

Abbott, A. (1988). *The System of Professions: An Essay on the Division of Expert Labor.* Chicago, IL: University of Chicago Press.

Ackrill, M. (1993). 'Marketing in British Banking, 1945–80' in R. Tedlow and G. Jones (eds.), *The Rise and Fall of Mass Marketing.* London: Routledge.

—— and Hannah, L. (2001). *Barclays. The Business of Banking 1690–1996.* Cambridge: Cambridge University Press.

Acton Society Trust (1956). *Management Succession: The Recruitment, Selection and Promotion of Managers.* London: Acton Society Trust.

Ahlstrom, G. (1982). *Engineers and Industrial Growth: Higher Technical Education and the Engineering Profession During the Nineteenth and Early Twentieth Centuries: France, Germany, Sweden and England.* London: Croom Helm.

Aldcroft, D. H. (1992). *Education, Training and Economic Performance 1944 to 1990.* Manchester, UK: Manchester University Press.

Allred, B., Snow, C., and Miles, R. (1996). 'Characteristics of Managerial Careers in the Twenty-First Century', *Academy of Management Executive*, 10/4.

Anderson, G. (1976). *Victorian Clerks.* Manchester, UK: Manchester University Press.

Anthony, P. D. (1986). *The Foundation of Management.* London: Tavistock.

Armstrong, P. (1984). 'Competition between the Organizational Professions and the Evolution of Management Control Strategies' in K. Thompson (ed.), *Work, Employment and Unemployment: Perspectives on Work and Society.* Milton Keynes, UK: Open University Press.

—— (1985). 'Changing Management Control Strategies: The Role of Competition between Accounting and other Organisational Professions', *Accounting, Organisations, and Society*, 10/2.

—— (1987). 'The Rise of Accounting Controls in British Capitalist Enterprises', *Accounting, Organisations, and Society*, 12/5.

Aston Group (1976). D. Pugh and D. Hickson (eds.), *Organizational Structure in its Context.* Aldershot, UK: Gower.

Augur, P. (2000). *The Death of Gentlemanly Capitalism. The Rise and Fall of London's Investment Banks.* London: Penguin Books.

Babbage, C. (1832). *On the Economy of Machinery and Manufactures.* London: Charles Knight.

Barnett, C. (1986). *The Audit of War: The Illusion and Reality of Britain as a Great Nation.* London: Macmillan.

Barry, B. (1989). 'Management Education in Great Britain', in W. Byrt (ed.), *Management Education: An International Survey.* London: Routledge.

Baumol, W. (1959). *Business Behavior, Value, and Growth.* New York: Macmillan.

Bellm, A. (undated). *The History of the Chartered Institute of Marketing.* London: CIM.

Bendix, R. (1956). *Work and Authority in Industry.* New York: John Wiley & Sons.

Berle, A. and Means, G. (1932). *The Modern Corporation and Private Property.* New York: Macmillan.

Bernstein, J. (1995). 'Japanese Capitalism', in T. K. McCraw (ed.), *Creating Modern Capitalism*. Cambridge, MA: Harvard University Press.

Best, M. and Humphries, J. (1986). 'The City and Industrial Decline', in B. Elbaum and W. Lazonick (eds.), *The Decline of the British Economy.* Oxford: Clarendon Press.

Best, P. A. (1921), 'British and American Attitudes'. *Sales Promotion,* October.

Black, J. (2000). *Development of Professional Management in the Public Sector of the United Kingdom from 1855 to 1925: The Case of the Ordnance Factories*, Ph.D. dissertation, Open University.

Born, K. E. (1983). *International Banking in the Nineteenth and Twentieth Centuries.* London: Berg Publishers.

Bowden, S., Foreman-Peck, J., and Richardson, T. (2001). 'The Post-war Productivity Failure: Insights from Oxford (Cowley)'. *Business History,* 43/3.

—— and Gamble, A. (2002). 'Corporate Governance and Public Policy: "New" Initiatives by "Old" Labour to Reform Stakeholder Behaviour in the UK, 1956–1969', *Journal of Industrial History,* 5/1.

Bowie, J. (1930). *Education for Business Management.* Oxford: Oxford University Press.

Boyns, T. (2001). 'Hans and Charles Renold: Entrepreneurs in the Introduction of Scientific Management Techniques in Britain', *Management Decision,* 39.

—— (2005). 'Illuminating the Darkness: The Impacy of the First World War on Cost Calculations Practices in British firms', in J. C. Degos and S. Trébucq (eds.), *L'Enterprise, Le Chiffre et le Droit.* Bordeaux, France: Bordeaux University Press.

—— and Edwards, J. R. (1997). 'The Construction of Cost Accounting Systems in Britain to 1900: The Case of the Coal, Iron and Steel Industries', *Business History,* 39/3.

—— , —— (2000), 'Pluralistic Approaches to Knowing More: A Comment on Hoskin and Macve'. *The Accounting Historians Journal,* 27, 1.

—— and Matthews, M. (2001). 'Scientific Management in Britain and Comparisons with other Countries to 1939', A paper given at the Management History Research Group Workshop, Open University.

Brech, E. (2001). *Management in Britain.* Paper presented to management history workshop, Open University.

—— (2002*a*). *The Evolution of Modern Management,* Vol. 1. *The Concept and Gestation of Britain's Central Management Institute, 1902–1976.* Bristol, UK: Thoemmes Press.

—— (2002*b*). *The Evolution of Management History,* Vol. 2. *Productivity in Perspective, 1914–1974.* Bristol, UK: Thoemmes Press.

—— (2002*c*). *The Evolution of Modern Management,* Vol. 3. *The Evolution of Clerical, Office and Administrative Management in Britain, 1891–1978.* Bristol, UK: Thoemmes Press.

—— (2002*d*). *The Evolution of Modern Management,* Vol. 4. *A Century of Management-Related Literature, 1832–1939.* Bristol, UK: Thoemmes Press.

—— (2002*e*). *The Evolution of Modern Management,* Vol. 5. *Education, Training and Development for and in Management: Evolution and Acceptance in Britain, 1852–1979.* Bristol, UK: Thoemmes Press.

Broadberry, S. (1997). *The Productivity Race: British Manufacturing in International Perspective 1850–1990.* Cambridge: Cambridge University Press.

—— and Crafts, N. (1996). 'British Economic Policy and Industrial Performance in the Early Post-War Period', *Business History,* 38/4.

—— and Marrison, A. J. (2002). 'External Economies of Scale in the Lancashire Cotton Industry, 1900–1950', *Economic History Review,* 55/1.

Brown, J. A. C. (1954). *The Social Psychology of Industry.* Harmondsworth, UK: Penguin.

Brown, K. and Tamai, K. (2000). 'Labour Management in the Textile Industry', in D. Farnie, D. Jeremy, T. Nakaoka, J. F. Wilson, and T. Abe (eds.), *Regional Business Strategies: A Comparison of Lancashire and Kansai, 1890–1990*. London: Routledge.

Buckley, A. (1992), *Multinational Finance*. London, Routledge.

Burnham, J. (1941). *The Managerial Revolution*. London: Pitman.

Burns, T. and Stalker, G. (1961). *The Management of Innovation*. London: Tavistock.

Cain, P. J. and Hopkins, A. G. (1993*a*). *British Imperialism: Innovation and Expansion, 1688–1914*. London: Longman.

—— —— (1993*b*). *British Imperialism: Crisis and Deconstruction, 1914–1990*. London: Longman.

Capie, F. and Rodrik-Bali, G. (1982). 'Concentration in British Banking, 1870–1920', *Business History*, 24/2.

Carnevali, F. (2003). '"Malefactors and Honourable Men": The Making of Commercial Honesty in Nineteenth Century Industrial Birmingham', in J. F. Wilson and A. Popp (eds.), *Clusters and Networks in English Industrial Districts, 1750–1970*. Aldershot, UK: Ashgate.

Carter, G. R. (1913). *The Tendency Towards Industrial Combination*. London: Constable.

Cassis, Y. (1985). 'Management and Strategy in the English Joint Stock Banks, 1890–1914', *Business History*, 28/3.

—— (1994). *City Bankers, 1890–1914*. Cambridge: Cambridge University Press.

Casson, M. (1997). *Information and Organization: A New Perspective on the Theory of the Firm*. Oxford: Oxford University Press.

Caves, R. (1968). 'Market Organization, Performance and Public policy', in R. Caves (ed.), *Britain's Economic Prospects*. Washington, DC: The Brookings Institution.

—— (ed.) (1980). *Britain's Economic Performance*. Washington, DC: Brookings Institute.

CEML (Council for Excellence in Management and Leadership) (2002). *Managers and Leaders: Raising Our Game*. London: CEML.

Chance, W. (1930). 'The Selling of Glass', Presidential address to the Second Convention of the British Glass Industry, Buxton.

Chandler, A. D. (1962). *Strategy and Structure: Chapters in the History of the Industrial Enterprise*. Cambridge, MA: MIT Press

—— (1976). 'The Development of Modern Management Structure in the US and UK', in L. Hannah (ed.), *Management Strategy and Business Development*. London: Macmillan.

—— (1977). *The Visible Hand: The Managerial Revolution in American Business*. Cambridge, MA: Harvard University Press.

—— (1990). *Scale and Scope: The Dynamics of Industrial Capitalism*. Cambridge, MA: Harvard University Press.

—— Amatori, F., and Hikino, T. (1997). *Big Business and the Wealth of Nations*. Cambridge: Cambridge University Press.

Channon, D. (1973). *The Strategy and Structure of British Enterprise*. London: Macmillan.

Chapman, S. D. (1969). 'The Peels in the Early English Cotton Industry', *Business History*, 11/1.

—— (1984). *The Rise of Merchant Banking*. London: George Allen and Unwin.

—— (1992). *Merchant Enterprise in Britain: From the Industrial Revolution to World War I*. Cambridge: Cambridge University Press.

Charkham, J. (1995). *Keeping Good Company. A Study of Corporate Governance in Five Countries*. Oxford: Oxford University Press.

Checkland, S. G. (1983). *British Public Policy, 1776–1939.* Cambridge: Cambridge University Press.

Child, J. (1969). *British Management Thought.* London: George Allen and Unwin.

—— and Partridge, B. (1982). *Lost Managers: Supervisors in Industrial Society.* Cambridge: Cambridge University Press.

Church, R. (1993). 'The Family Firm in Industrial Capitalism: International Perspectives on Hypotheses and History', *Business History*, 35/4.

—— (1998). 'The History of Markets and Marketing: Perspectives and Possibilities', in J. Fink (ed.), *Business Records and Business History.* Aarhus, Denmark: Danish National Archives.

—— (1999). 'New Perspectives on the History of Products, Firms, Marketing and Consumers in Britain and the United States since the Mid-Nineteenth Century', *Economic History Review*, 52/3.

—— (2000*a*). 'Ossified or Dynamic? Structure, Markets and the Competitive Process in the British Business System of the Nineteenth Century', *Business History*, 42/1.

—— (2000*b*). 'Advertising Consumer Goods in Nineteenth Century Britain: Reinterpretations', *Economic History Review*, 53/4.

—— and Clark, C. (2000). 'The Origins of Competitive Advantage in the Marketing of Branded Packaged Consumer Goods: Coleman's and Reckitt's in Early Victorian Britain', *Journal of Industrial History*, 3/2.

Clark, C. (1951). *Conditions of Economic Progress.* London: Macmillan.

Clegg, H., Fox, A., and Thompson, A. (1964). *History of British Trade Unions since 1889*, Vol. 1. Oxford: Oxford University Press.

Clements, R. V. (1958). *Managers: A Study of Their Careers in Industry.* London: George Allen and Unwin.

Clutterbuck, D. and Crainer, S. (1988). *The Decline and Rise of British Industry.* London: Mercury Books.

Coase, R. (1937). 'The Nature of the Firm', *Economica*, 4.

Coleman, D. C. (1973). 'Gentlemen and Players', *Economic History Review*, 2/2.

—— (1987). 'Failings and Achievements: Some British Businesses, 1910–1980', *Business History*, 29/4.

Collins, M. (1991). *Banks and Industrial Finance in Britain, 1880–1939.* London: Macmillan.

—— (1994). 'Growth of the Firm in the Domestic Banking Sector', in M. W. Kirby and M. B. Rose (eds.), *Business Enterprise in Modern Britain.* London: Routledge.

—— and Baker, M. (2003). *Commercial Banks and Industrial Finance in England and Wales, 1860–1913.* Oxford: Oxford University Press.

Commons, J. R. (1909). 'American Shoemakers, 1648–1895', *Quarterly Journal of Economics*, 24, November. Reproduced in R. Rowan (ed.) (1972). *Readings in Labor Economics and Labor Relations.* Homewood, IL: Richard D. Irwin.

Connell, C. (2006). 'Shaping the Legal Environment for Business', *Business History*, 48/1.

Constable, J. and McCormick, R. (1987). *The Making of British Managers.* London: British Institute of Management.

Cookson, G. (2003). 'Quaker Networks and the Industrial Development of Darlington, 1780–1870', in J. F. Wilson and A. Popp (eds.), *Clusters and Networks in English Industrial Districts, 1750–1970.* London: Ashgate.

Copeman, G. (1955). *Leaders of British Industry.* London: Gee.

Corley, T. (1987). 'Consumer Marketing in Britain 1914–60', *Business History*, 29/2.

—— (1993). 'Marketing and Business History, in Theory and Practice', in R. Tedlow and G. Jones (eds.), *The Decline and Fall of Mass Marketing.* London: Routledge.

Cottrell, P. L. (1980). *Industrial Finance, 1830–1914*. London: Methuen.

Coulson-Thomas, C. and Coe, T. (1991). *The Flat Organisation: Philosophy and Practice*. London: British Institute of Management.

Crafts, N. (1991). 'Reversing Relative Economic Decline? The 1980s in Historical Perspective', *Oxford Review of Economic Policy*, 7/3.

—— and Woodward, N. (1992). 'The British Economy since 1945: Introduction and Overview', in N. Crafts and N. Woodward (eds.), *The British Economy since 1945*. Oxford: Oxford University Press.

Crockett, G. and Elias, P. (1984). 'British Managers: A Study of their Education, Training, Mobility and Earnings', *British Journal of Industrial Relations*, 22/1.

Crouzet, F. (1972). 'Introduction' to *Capital Formation in the Industrial Revolution*. London: Methuen.

—— (1985). *The First Industrialists*. Cambridge: Cambridge University Press.

Cully, M., Woodland, S., O'Reilly, A., and Dix, E. (1999), *Britain at Work*. London, Routledge.

Cyert, R. and March, J. (1963). *A Behavioral Theory of the Firm*. Englewood Cliffs, NJ: Prentice-Hall.

Daft, R. L. (1987). *Management*. New York: Dryden Press.

Davenport-Hines, R. P. T. (1984). *Dudley Docker: The Life and Times of a Trade Warrior*. Cambridge: Cambridge University Press.

—— (ed.) (1986). *Markets and Bagmen: Studies in the History of Marketing and British Industrial Performance 1830–1939*. Aldershot, UK: Gower.

Davis, L. (1966). 'The Capital Markets and Industrial Concentration: The US and the UK, a Comparative Study', *Economic History Review*, 19/2.

Delmestri, G. and Walgenbach, P. (2005). 'Mastering Techniques or Brokering Knowledge? Middle Managers in Germany, Great Britain and Italy', *Organization Studies*, 26/2.

Department of Industry (1977). *Industry, Education and Management: A Discussion Paper*. London: Department of Industry.

Devine, P. J. (1976). 'The Firm', 'Corporate Growth' and 'State Intervention in the Private Sector', in P. J. Devine, R. M. Jones, N. Lee, and W. J. Tyson (eds.), *An Introduction to Industrial Economics*. London: George Allen and Unwin.

Donkin, R. (2001). *Blood, Sweat and Tears—The Evolution of Work*. London: Texere.

Donovan, Lord (1968). *Royal Commission on Trade Unions and Employers' Associations*. Cmnd 3623. London: HMSO.

Doyle, P. (1995). 'Marketing in the New Millennium', *European Journal of Marketing*, 29/13.

Dubin, R. (1970). 'Management in Britain—Impressions of a Visiting Professor', *Journal of Management Studies*, 7/5.

Dunlop, J. T. (1958). *Industrial Relations Systems*. Carbondale, IL: University of Southern Illinois Press.

Dunning, J. (1958). *American Investment in British Manufacturing Industry*. London: George Allen and Unwin.

—— (1969). *The Role of American Investment in the British Economy*. London: Political and Economic Planning.

—— (1997*a*). 'US-owned Manufacturing Affiliates and the Transfer of Managerial Techniques', in M. Kipping and O. Bjarnar (eds.), *The Americanisation of European Business*. London: Routledge.

—— (1997*b*). *Alliance Capitalism and Global Business*. London: Routledge.

Dyas, G. P. and Thanheiser, H. T. (1976). *The Emerging European Enterprise.* London: Macmillan.

Edwardes, M. (1983). *Back from the Brink: An Apocalyptic Experience.* London: Collins.

Edwards, H. (1962). *Competition and Monopoly in the British Soap Industry.* Oxford: Clarendon Press.

Edwards, J. R. (1989). *A History of Financial Accounting.* London: Routledge.

—— and Newell, E. (1991). 'The Development of Industrial Cost and Management Accounting before 1850: A Survey of the Evidence', *Business History,* 33/4.

Elbaum, B. and Lazonick, W. (1986). 'An Institutional Perspective on British Decline', in B. Elbaum and W. Lazonick (eds.), *The Decline of the British Economy.* Oxford: Clarendon Press.

Elbourne, E. (1914). *Factory Administration and Accounts.* London: Longman Green.

Enteman, W. (1993). *Managerialism: The Emergence of a New Ideology.* Madison, WI: University of Wisconsin Press.

Erickson, C. (1959). *British Industrialists: Steel and Hosiery, 1850–1950.* Cambridge: Cambridge University Press.

Eriksson, P. (1999). 'The Process of Interprofessional Competition: A Case of Expertise and Politics', in D. Brownlie, M. Saren, R. Wensley, and R. Whittington (eds.), *Rethinking Marketing: Towards Critical Marketing Accounting.* London: Sage.

Fay, S. (1996). *The Collapse of Barings.* London: Richard Cohen Books.

Fayol, H. (1916/1949). *General and Industrial Management* (trans. C. Storrs). London: Pitman.

Fear, J. (1995). 'German Capitalism', in T. K. McCraw (ed.), *Creating Modern Capitalism.* Cambridge, MA: Harvard University Press.

Ferguson, M. (2001). 'Models of Management Education and Training: The Consultancy Approach', *Journal of Industrial History,* 4/1.

—— (2002). *The Rise of Professional Management Consulting in Britain.* Aldershot, UK: Ashgate.

Ferry, J. (1993). *The British Renaissance: How to Survive and Thrive Despite any Recession.* London: Heinemann.

Finniston, M. (1980). *Engineering our Future: Report of the Committee of Enquiry into the Engineering Profession.* Cmnd 7794. London: HMSO.

Fitzgerald, R. (1988). *British Labour Management and Industrial Welfare, 1846–1939.* London: Croom Helm.

—— (2000). 'The Competitive and Institutional Advantages of Holding Companies: British Business in the Inter-War Period', *Journal of Industrial History,* 3/2.

Fitzsimons, P. (1999). 'Managerialism', www.hr/ENCYCLOPEDIA/managerialism.htm

Flanders, A. (1970). *Management and Unions: The Theory and Reform of Industrial Relations.* London: Faber.

Fleischman, R. K. and Parker, L. D. (1990). 'Management Accounting Early in the British Industrial Revolution: The Carron Company, a Case Study', *Accounting and Business Research,* 20.

—— (1992). 'The Cost-Accounting Environment in the British Industrial Revolution Iron Industry', *Accounting, Business and Financial History,* 2.

Fligstein, N. (1991). *The Transformation of Corporate Control.* Cambridge, MA: Harvard University Press.

Florence, P. S. (1961). *Ownership, Control and Success of Large Companies: An Analysis of British Industrial structure and Policy 1936–1951.* London: Sweet and Maxwell.

—— (1972). *The Logic of British and American Industry.* London: Routledge and Kegan Paul.

Fox, A. (1974). *Power, Trust and Work Relations.* London: Faber.

Fraser, W. (1981). *The Coming of the Mass Market, 1859–1914.* London: Macmillan.

Freeland, R. F. (2001). *The Struggle for Control of the Modern Corporation. Organizational Change at General Motors, 1920s to the 1970s.* Cambridge: Cambridge University Press.

Froud, J., Johal, S., Leaver, A., and Williams, K. (2006), *Financialization and Strategy. Narrative and Numbers.* London, Routledge.

Fruin, M. W. (1992). *The Japanese Enterprise System.* Oxford: Oxford University Press.

Fullerton, R. (1988). 'How Modern is Modern Marketing? Marketing's Evolution and the Myth of the "Production Era" ', *Journal of Marketing,* 52/1.

Garcke, E. and Fells, J. M. (1887). *Factory Accounts.* London: Crosby, Lockwood & Son.

George, C. (1968). *The History of Management Thought.* Englewood Cliffs, NJ: Prentice-Hall.

Glover, I. (1999). 'British Management and British History: Assessing the Responsibility of Individuals for Economic Difficulties', *Contemporary British History,* 13/3.

—— and Hughes, M. (eds.) (1996). 'Towards a Professional Managerial Class?', in I. Glover and M. Hughes (eds.), *The Professional-Managerial Class: Contemporary British Management in the Pursuer Mode.* Aldershot, UK: Avebury Press.

Glynn, J. J. (1994). 'The Development of British Railway Accounting: 1800–1911', in R. H. Parker and B. S. Yamey (eds.), *Accounting History: Some British Contributions.* Oxford: Clarendon Press.

Goodall, F. (1986). 'Marketing Consumer Products Before 1914: Rowntrees and Elect Cocoa', in R. P. T. Davenport-Hines (ed.), *Markets and Bagmen: Studies in the History of Marketing and British Industrial Performance, 1830–1939.* Aldershot, UK: Gower.

Goodrich, C. (1920). *The Frontier of Control.* London: G. Bell and Sons.

Gordon, A. (1985). *Evolution of Labour Relations in Japan.* Cambridge, MA: Harvard University Press.

Gospel, H. F. (1983). 'Managerial Structures and Strategies: An Introduction', in H. F. Gospel and C. R. Littler (eds.), *Managerial Strategies and Industrial Relations.* London: Heinemann.

—— (1992). *Markets, Firms and the Management of Labour.* Cambridge: Cambridge University Press.

—— and Okayama, R. (1991). 'Industrial Training in Britain and Japan: An Overview', in H. F. Gospel (ed.), *Industrial Training and Technological Innovation.* London: Routledge.

Gourvish, T. R. (1972). *Mark Huish and the London & North Western Railway.* Leicester, UK: Leicester University Press.

—— (1973). 'A British Business Elite: The Chief Executive Managers of the Railway Industry, 1850–1922', *Business History Review,* 47/2.

—— (1987). 'British Business and the Transition to a Corporate Economy: Entrepreneurship and Management Structures', *Business History,* 29/4.

Granick, D. (1962). *The European Executive.* London: Weidenfeld and Nicholson.

—— (1972). *Managerial Comparisons of Four Developed Countries: France, Britain, United States and Russia.* Cambridge, MA: MIT Press.

Grant, R. (1998). *Contemporary Strategic Analysis.* Oxford: Blackwell Press.

Green, E. (1979). *A History of the Institute of Bankers, 1879–1979.* London: Methuen.

Grey, C. (1998). 'On Being a Professional in a Big Six Firm', *Accounting, Organizations and Society,* 23/5–6.

—— (1999). ' "We Are All Managers Now"; "We Always Were": On the Development and Demise of Management', *Journal of Management Studies,* 36/5.

Grey, C. (2005). *A Very Short, Fairly Interesting and Reasonably Cheap Book about Studying Organizations*. London: Sage.

Guillén, M. (1994). *Models of Management: Work Authority and Organization in a Comparative Perspective*. Chicago, IL: University of Chicago Press.

Hague, D. C. (1983). *The IRC: An Experiment in Industrial Intervention*. London: George Allen and Unwin.

Hamel, G. and Prahalad, C. (1994). *Competing for the Future*. Boston, MA: Harvard Business School Press.

Hampden-Turner, C. and Trompenaars, F. (1993). *The Seven Cultures of Capitalism: Value Systems for Creating Wealth in the United States, Britain, Japan, Germany, France, Sweden and the Netherlands*. London: Doubleday.

Handy, C. (1988). *The Making of Managers*. London: Manpower Services Commission.

Hannah, L. (1974*a*). 'Mergers in British Manufacturing Industry, 1880–1918', *Oxford Economic Papers*, 26.

—— (1974*b*). 'Takeover Bids in Britain Before 1950: An Exercise in Business "Prehistory" ', *Business History*, 16/1.

—— (1976). 'Business Development and Economic Structure in Britain since 1880', in L. Hannah (ed.), *Management Strategy and Business Development*. London: Macmillan.

—— (1980). 'Visible and Invisible Hands in Great Britain', in A. D. Chandler and H. Daems (eds.), *Managerial Hierarchies: Comparative Perspectives on the Rise of the Modern Industrial Enterprise*. Cambridge, MA: Harvard University Press.

—— (1983). *The Rise of the Corporate Economy*, 2nd edn. London: Methuen.

Hardy, L. (1987). *Successful Business Strategy: How to Win in the Market-Place*. London: Kogan Page.

Harvey, C. and Press, J. (1989). 'Overseas Investment and the Professional Advance of British Mining Engineers, 1851–1914', *Economic History Review*, 42/1.

Hedlund, G. (1986). 'The Hypermodern MNC—a Heterarchy?', *Human Resource Management*, 25.

Hicks, M. (2004). 'The Recruitment and Selection of Young Managers by British Business 1930–2000', Oxford, D.Phil.

Hickson, D. and Pugh, D. (1995). *Management Worldwide*. Harmondsworth, UK: Penguin.

Hilton, A. (1987). *City Within a State. A Portrait of Britain's Financial World*. London: I. B. Taurus.

Hirschmeier, J. and Yui, T. (1975). *The Development of Japanese Business, 1600–1973*. London: George Allen and Unwin.

Hofstede, G. (1980). *Culture's Consequences: International Differences in Work-Related Values*. London: Sage.

Holmes, A. R. and Green, E. (1986). *Midland: 150 Years of Banking Business*. Oxford: Oxford University Press.

Hoskin, K. W. and Macve, R. H. (2000). 'Knowing More as Knowing Less? Alternative Histories of Cost and Management Accounting in the US and the UK', *Accounting Historians Journal*, 27/1.

Hounshell, D. (1984). *From the American System to Mass Production, 1800–1932*. Baltimore, MD: Johns Hopkins University Press.

Howe, A. (1984). *Cotton Masters, 1830–1860*. Oxford: Oxford University Press.

Huczynski, A. (1993). *Management Gurus: What Makes Them and How to Become One*. London: Routledge.

Huselid, M. (1995). 'The Impact of Human Resource Management Practices on Turnover, Productivity and Corporate Financial Performance', *Academy of Management Journal*, 40/1.

ICAEW (1966). *The History of the Institute of Chartered Accountants in England and Wales, 1880–1965*. London: Heinemann.

James, H. (1990). 'The German Experience and the Myth of British Cultural Exceptionalism', in B. Collins and K. Robbins (eds.), *British Culture and Economic Decline*. London: Weidenfeld and Nicolson.

Jefferys, J. B. (1954). *Retail Trading in Britain, 1850–1950*. Cambridge: Cambridge University Press.

Johnson, H. T. and Kaplan, R. S. (1987). *Relevance Lost: The Rise and Fall of Management Accounting*. Boston, MA: Harvard University Press.

Jones, G. (2005). *Renewing Unilever: Transformation and Tradition*. Oxford: Oxford University Press.

—— and Rose, M. (1993). 'Family Capitalism', *Business History*, 35/4.

Kay, W. (1988). 'Big Bang and After', in R. Heller (ed.), *The Complete Guide to Modern Management*. London: Harrap.

Keeble, S. (1992). *The Ability to Manage*. Manchester, UK: Manchester University Press.

Keenoy, T. (1985). *Invitation to Industrial relations*. Oxford: Basil Blackwell.

Keep, E. and Mayhew, K. (2001). *Globalization, Models of Competitive Advantage and Skills*. Research Paper No. 22, ESRC Centre on Skills, Knowledge and Organisational Performance (SKOPE).

—— and Westwood, A. (2003). *Can the UK Learn to Manage?* ESRC Centre on Skills, Knowledge and Organisational Performance (SKOPE).

Keith, R. (1960). 'The Marketing Revolution', *Journal of Marketing*, 24/1.

Kempner, T. (1984), 'Education for Management in Five Countries: Myth and Reality', *Journal of General Management*. Winter.

Kennedy, W. P. (1987). *Industrial Structure, Capital Markets and the Origins of British Economic Decline*. Cambridge: Cambridge University Press.

—— and Payne, P. (1976). 'Directions for Future Research', in L. Hannah (ed.), *Management Strategy and Business Development*. London: Macmillan.

Kieser, A. (1997). 'Rhetoric and Myth in Management Fashion', *Organization*, 4/1.

Kim, S. (1999). 'The Rise of Multiunit Firms in US Manufacturing', *Explorations in Economic History*, 36/4.

Kindleberger, C. (1964). *Economic Growth in France and Britain 1851–1950*. Cambridge, MA: Harvard University Press.

Kipping, M. (1999). 'American Management Consultancy Companies in Western Europe, 1920 to 1990: Products, Reputation and Relationships', *Business History Review*, 73/2.

—— and Tiratsoo, N. (eds.) (2002). *Americanization in Twentieth Century Europe: Business, Culture, Politics*, 2 vols. Lille, NY: Lille University Press.

Kirby, M. W. (1981), *The Decline of British Economic Power since 1870*, London, Allen & Unwin.

Kirby, M. W. (2003). *Operational Research in War and Peace: The British Experience from the 1930s to 1970*. London: Imperial College Press.

Kocka, J. (1978). 'Entrepreneurs and Managers in German Industrialisation', in P. Mathias and M. M. Postan (eds.), *The Cambridge Economic History of Europe*, VII, Part 1. Cambridge: Cambridge University Press.

Kocka, J. (1980). 'The Rise of the Modern Industrial Enterprise in Germany', in A. D. Chandler and H. Daems (eds.), *Managerial Hierarchies: Comparative Perspectives on the Rise of the Modern Industrial Enterprise.* Cambridge, MA: Harvard University Press.

Kransdorff, A. (1998). *Corporate Amnesia: Keeping Know-how in the Company.* Oxford: Butterworth-Heinemann.

Landes, D. (1969). *The Unbound Prometheus.* Cambridge: Cambridge University Press.

Langlois, R. and Robertson, P. (1995). *Firms, Markets and Economic Change: A Dynamic Theory of Business Institutions.* London: Routledge.

Lazonick, W. (1990). *Competitive Advantage on the Shop Floor.* Cambridge, MA: Harvard University Press.

—— and O'Sullivan, M. (1997). 'Finance and Industrial Development. Part 1: The United States and the United Kingdom', *Financial History Review,* 4/2.

Lee, C. (1990). 'Corporate Behaviour in Theory and History. II: The Historian's Perspective', *Business History,* 32/2.

Lee, G. A. (1994). 'The Oldest European Account Book: A Florentine Bank Ledger of 1211', in R. H. Parker and B. S. Yamey (eds.), *Accounting History: Some British Contributions.* Oxford: Clarendon Press.

Lee, J. (1921). *Management: A Study in Industrial Organisation.* London: Pitman.

—— (ed.) (1928). *Dictionary of Industrial Administration.* London: Pitman.

Levine, A. L. (1967). *Industrial Retardation in Britain.* London: Weidenfeld and Nicholson.

Lewin, K. (1951). *Field Theory in Social Science.* London: Harper.

Lewis, J. S. (1896). *The Commercial Organisation of Factories.* London: Spon and Chamberlain.

—— (1899a). 'Works Management for the Maximum of Production. I. Organisation as a Factor of Output', *Engineering Magazine,* 18.

—— (1899b). 'Works Management for the Maximum of Production. II. The Labour Factor in the Intensification of Output', *Engineering Magazine,* 18.

—— (1899c). 'Works Management for the Maximum of Production. III. Commercial Aspect of the Problem of New Process', *Engineering Magazine,* 18.

Litterer, J. (1986). *The Emergence of Systematic Management as Shown by the Literature of Management from 1870 to 1900.* New York: Garland Publishing.

Littler, C. (1982). *The Development of the Labour Process in Capitalist Societies.* London: Heinemann.

—— (1983). 'A Comparative Analysis of Managerial Structures and Strategies', in H. F. Gospel and C. R. Littler (eds.), *Managerial Strategies and Industrial Relations.* London: Heinemann.

Locke, R. (1984). *The End of the Practical Man: Entrepreneurship and Higher Education in Germany, France and Great Britain, 1880–1940.* Greenwich, CT: JAI Press.

—— (1989). *Management and Higher Education since 1940: The Influence of America and Japan on West Germany, Great Britain and France.* Cambridge: Cambridge University Press.

—— (1996). *The Collapse of the American Management Mystique.* Oxford: Oxford University Press.

Mabey, C. (2005). *Management Development Works: The Evidence.* London: Chartered Management Institute.

—— and Ramirez, M. (2004). *Developing Managers: A European Perspective.* London: Chartered Management Institute.

MacGregor, D. H. (1906). *Industrial Combination.* Cambridge: George Bell & Sons.

Macrosty, H. W. (1907). *The Trust Movement in British Industry: A Study of Business Organisation.* London: Longman.

McGivering, I., Matthews, D., and Scott, W. (1960). *Management in Britain.* Liverpool, UK: Liverpool University Press.

McKendrick, N. (1960). 'Josiah Wedgwood: An Eighteenth Century Entrepreneur in Salesmanship and Marketing Techniques', *Economic History Review*, 12/3.

—— Brewer, J., and Plumb, J. (1982). *The Birth of a Consumer Society.* Bloomington, IN: Indiana University Press.

McKenna, C. D. (2006). *The World's Newest Profession: Management Consultancy in the Twentieth Century.* Cambridge: Cambridge University Press.

McKenna, R. (1991). 'Marketing Is Everything', *Harvard Business Review*, 69/1.

McKinlay, A. (1991). 'A Certain Short-Sightedness: Metalworking, Innovation, and Apprenticeship, 1897–1939', in H. F. Gospel (ed.), *Industrial Training and Technological Change.* London: Routledge.

—— and Zeitlin, J. (1989). 'The Meanings of Managerial Prerogative: Industrial Relations and the Organization of Work in British Engineering, 1880–1939', *Business History*, 31/2.

Maltby, J. (2000). 'Was the 1947 Companies Act a Response to a National Crisis?', *Accounting History*, 5/2.

Mangham, I. and Silver, M. (1986). *Management Training: Context and Practice.* London: Economic and Social Research Council.

Mannari, H. (1974). *Japanese Business Leaders.* Tokyo: Tokyo University Press.

Mansfield, R. and Poole, M. (1991). *British Management in the Thatcher Years.* London: British Institute of Management.

Marginson, P., Armstrong, P., Edwards, P., and Purcell, J. (1988). 'The Control of Industrial Relations in a Large Company: Initial Analysis of the Second Company-Level Industrial Relations Survey', Warwick Papers in Industrial Relations, 45.

Marris, R. (1964). *The Economic Theory of Managerial Capitalism.* London: Macmillan.

—— (1998). *Managerial Capitalism in Retrospect.* London: Macmillan.

Marrison, A. J. (1996). *British Business and Protection, 1903–1932.* Oxford: Oxford University Press.

Marshall, A. (1890). *Principles of Economics.* London: Macmillan.

—— (1919). *Industry and Trade.* London: Macmillan.

Martin, R. and Moores, B. (1985). *Management Structures and Techniques.* London: Philip Allan.

Matthews, D., Anderson, M., and Edwards, J. (1998). *The Priesthood of Industry: The Rise of the Professional Accountant in British Management.* Oxford: Oxford University Press.

—— Boyns, T., and Edwards, J. R. (2003). 'Chandlerian Image or Mirror Image? Managerial and Accounting Control in the Chemical Industry: The Case of Albright & Wilson, c.1892 to c.1923', *Business History*, 43/4.

Melling, J. (1980). 'Non-Commissioned Officers: British Employers and Their Supervisory Workers, 1880–1920', *Social History*, 6/3.

Mercer, D. (1996). 'Marketing Practices in the 1990s', A paper given to the Marketing Educators Group.

Michie, R. C. (1999). *The London Stock Exchange. A History.* Oxford: Oxford University Press.

Mintzberg, H. (1973). *The Nature of Managerial Work.* New York: Harper and Row.

—— (1996). *The Strategy Process: Concepts, Contexts and Cases.* New Jersey, NJ: Prentice-Hall.

Miyamoto, M. (1986). 'Emergence of National Market and Commercial Activities in Tokugawa Japan, with Special Reference to the Development of the Rice Market', *Osaka Economic Papers*, 36/1–2.

Monsen, R. and Downs, A. (1965). 'A Theory of Large Managerial Firms', *Journal of Political Economy*, 73/3

Morikawa, H. (1975). 'Management Structure and Control Devices for Diversified Zaibatsu Business', in K. Nakagawa (ed.), *The Strategy and Structure of Big Business*. Tokyo: Tokyo University Press.

—— (1992). *Zaibatsu*. Tokyo: Tokyo University Press.

Musson, A. (1978). *The Growth of British Industry*. London: Batsford.

Myers, C. (1921). *Mind and Work*. London: University of London Press.

—— (1926). *Industrial Psychology in Great Britain*. London: Cape.

—— and Welch, H. (1932). *Ten Years of Industrial Psychology*. London: Pitman.

Nakagawa, K. (1975). 'Strategy and Structure in Japanese Business', in K. Nakagawa (ed.), *The Strategy and Structure of Big Business*. Tokyo: Tokyo University Press.

NEDO (National Economic Development Office) (1979). *The UK's Performance in Export Markets*, Discussion Paper No. 6. London: NEDO.

Nelson, R. L. and Winter, S. G. (1982). *An Evolutionary Theory of Economic Change*. Cambridge, MA: Belknap Press.

Newbould, G. D. (1970). *Management and Merger Activity*. London: Guthstead.

Newton, L. (1998). 'English Banking Concentration and Internationalisation: Contemporary Debate, 1880–1920', in S. Kinsey and L. Newton (eds.), *International Banking in an Age of Transition. Globalisation, Automation, Banks and their Archives*. Aldershot, UK: Ashgate.

Nicholas, S. (1984). 'The Overseas Marketing Performance of British Industry, 1870–1914', *Economic History Review*, 2nd ser., 37/2.

Niven, M. (1967). *Personnel Management, 1913–63*. London: Institute of Personnel Management.

Olson, M. (1982), *The Rise and Decline of Nations Economic Growth, Stagflation and Social Rigidities*. New Haven, Yale University Press.

Outerbridge, A. E. (1899). 'The Policy of Secretiveness in Industrial Work', *Engineering Magazine*, 18.

Owens, A. (2002), 'Inheritance and the Life-cycle of Family Firms'. *Business History*, 44, 1.

Patterson, M., West, M., Lawthorn, R., and Nickell, S. (1997). *Impact of People Management Practices on Business Performance*. London: Institute of Personnel and Development.

Payne, P. L. (1984). 'Family Business in Britain: An Historical and Analytical Survey', in A. Okochi and S. Yasuoka (eds.), *Family Business in the Era of Industrial Growth*. Tokyo: Tokyo University Press.

—— (1988). *British Entrepreneurship in the Nineteenth Century*, 2nd edn. London: Macmillan.

—— (1990), 'Entrepreneurship and British Economic Decline', in B. Collins and K. Robbins (eds.), *British Culture and Economic Decline*. London, Wiedenfeld.

Penrose, E. (1959 and 1980, 2nd edn.). *Theory of the Growth of the Firm*. Oxford: Blackwell.

PEP (Political and Economic Planning) (1966). *Attitudes in British Industry*. Harmondsworth, UK: Pelican.

Perkin, H. (1987). 'Professionalism, Property and English Society since 1880', Stenton Lecture, University of Reading.

—— (1989). *The Rise of Professional Society*. London: Routledge.

Perren, L. (2000). *Management and Leadership in the UK Professions: An Analysis of Survey Results*. London: Council for Excellence in Management and Leadership.

—— Davis, M., Kroessin, R., and Hannon, P. (2001), *Mapping of Management and Leadership Development Provisions for SMEs.* CEML.

Pettigrew, A. and Fenton, P. (2000). *The Innovating Organization.* London: Sage.

Platt, D. (1972). *Latin America and British Trade 1806–1914.* London: Macmillan.

Piore, M., and Sabel, C. (1984), *The Second Industrial Divide: Possibilities for Prosperity.* London Basic Books.

Pollard, S. (1968). *The Genesis of Modern Management.* Harmondsworth, UK: Penguin.

—— (1989). *Britain's Prime and Britain's Decline: The British Economy, 1870–1914.* London: Edward Arnold.

—— (1992). *The Development of the British Economy, 1914–1990.* London: Edward Arnold.

Poole, M., Mansfield, R., and Mendes, P. (2001). *Two Decades of Management.* London: Institute of Management.

Popp, A. (2001). *Business Structure, Business Culture and the Industrial District. The Potteries, c.1850–1914.* Aldershot, UK: Ashgate.

—— Toms, S., and Wilson, J. F. (2003). 'Strategy, Governance and Industrial Organization: Historical Perspectives on the Dynamics of Industrial Clustering in England', Nottingham University Business School Discussion Paper.

Porter, M. (1980). *Competitive Strategy: Techniques for Analyzing Industries and Competitors.* New York: Free Press.

—— (1990). *The Competitive Advantage of Nations.* New York: Free Press.

—— and Ketels, C. (2003). *UK Competitiveness: Moving to the Next Stage.* DTI Economics paper No. 3. London: Department of Trade and Industry.

Prais, S. J. (1976). *The Evolution of Giant Firms in Britain.* Cambridge: Cambridge University Press.

Procter, S., Rowlinson, M., and Toms, S. (1999). 'The M-form Enterprise and Scientific Management: Exploring the Relationship between Organizational Structure and the Management of Labour', Nottingham University Business School Discussion Paper.

Protherough, R. and Pick, J. (2002). *Managing Britannia: Culture and Management in Modern Britain.* Exeter, UK: Imprint Academic.

Pumphrey, A. (1959). 'The Introduction of Industrialists into the British Peerage: A Study in Adaptation of a Social Institution', *American Historical Review,* 65.

Purcell, J. and Sisson, K. (1983). 'Strategies and Practice in the Management of Industrial Relations', in G. S. Bain (ed.), *Industrial Relations in Britain.* Oxford: Blackwell.

Quail, J. (2000). 'The Proprietorial Theory of the Firm and Its Consequences', *Journal of Industrial History,* 3/1.

—— (2002). 'Visible Hands and Visible Handles: Understanding the Managerial Revolution in the UK', *Journal of Industrial History,* 5/2.

—— (2004). 'The Revolution in the Managerial Revolution—Contingency and Outcomes in the UK 1965 to 1990', Paper given to the Management History Research Group Workshop, University of Nottingham.

Reader, W. J. (1970). *Imperial Chemical Industries,* Vol. I, *The Forerunners 1870–1926.* Oxford: Oxford University Press.

Robbins, Lord (1963). *Report of the Committee on Higher Education.* Cmnd 2154. London: HMSO.

Roberts, D. (1979). *Paternalism in Early Victorian England.* London: Croom Helm.

Roberts, R. (1984). 'The Administrative Origins of Industrial Diplomacy: An Aspect of Government-Industry Relations, 1929–1935', in J. Turner (ed.), *Businessmen and Politics. Studies of Business Activity in British Politics, 1900–1945.* London: Heinemann.

Roberts, R. (1992). 'Regulatory Responses to the Rise of the Market for Corporate Control in Britain in the 1950s', *Business History*, 34/1.

Robinson, A. (1934). 'The Problem of Management and the Size of the Firm', *Economic Journal*, 44.

Robinson, J. (1933). *The Economics of Imperfect Competition*. London: Macmillan.

Roethlisberger, F. and Dickson, W. (1966). *Management and the Worker*. Cambridge, MA: Harvard University Press.

Roll, E. (1968). *An Early Experiment in Industrial Organisation*. London: Frank Cass.

Roslender, R., Glover, I., and Kelly, M. (2000). 'Future Imperfect? The Uncertain Prospects of the British Accountant', in I. Glover and M. Hughes (eds.), *Professions at Bay. Control and Encouragement of Ingenuity in British Management*. Aldershot, UK: Ashgate.

Rostow, W. W. (1960). *The Stages of Economic Growth*. Cambridge: Cambridge University Press.

Routh, G. (1980, 2nd edn.). *Occupation and Pay in Great Britain*. Cambridge: Cambridge University Press.

Rubinstein, W. D. (1977). 'The Victorian Middle Classes: Wealth, Occupation and Geography', *Economic History Review*, 2nd ser., 30/1.

—— (1981). *Men of Property: The Very Wealthy in Britain since the Industrial Revolution*. London: Croom Helm.

—— (1988). 'Social Class, Social Attitudes and British Business Life', *Oxford Review of Economic Policy*, 4/1.

—— (1994). *Capitalism, Culture and Decline in Britain, 1750–1990*. London: Routledge.

Sampson, A. (1995). *Company Man*. London: HarperCollins.

—— (2004). *Who Runs This Place?* London: John Murray.

Sanderson, M. (1972). *Education and Economic Decline in Britain*. Cambridge: Cambridge University Press.

Scarbrough, H. (1998). 'The Unmaking of Management? Change and Continuity in British Management in the 1990s', *Human Relations*, 51/6.

Schmitz, C. (1993). *The Growth of Big Business in the United States and Western Europe, 1850–1939*. Cambridge: Cambridge University Press.

Schoenhof, J. (1892). *The Economy of High Wages: An Inquiry into the Cause of High Wages and Their Effect on Methods and Cost of Production*. New York: G. P. Putnams.

Scott, J. (1987). 'Inter-Corporate Structure in Britain, the United States and Japan', *Shoken Keizai*, 160.

—— (1997). *Corporate Business and Capitalist Classes*. Oxford: Oxford University Press.

Scranton, P. (1991). 'A Review of *Scale and Scope*', *Technology and Culture*, 32.

—— (1997). *Endless Novelty. Specialty Production and American Industrialization, 1865–1925*. Princeton, NJ: Princeton University Press.

Shadwell, A. (1916). 'The Welfare of Factory Workers', *The Edinburgh Review*, October.

Sheldon, O. (1923). *The Philosophy of Management*. London: Pitman.

—— (1925). 'Policy and Policy-Making', *Harvard Business Review*, 4/1.

Shenlav, Y. (1999). *Manufacturing Rationality; The Engineering Foundations of the Managerial Revolution*. Oxford: Oxford University Press.

Shonfield, A. (1958). *British Economic Policy since the War*. Harmondsworth, UK: Penguin.

Simon, H. (1960). *Administrative Behavior*, 2nd edn. New York: Macmillan.

Singleton, J. (2002). 'British Engineering and the New Zealand Market, 1945–60', *Business History*, 44/4.

Slichter, S. (1919). 'The Management of Labor', *Journal of Political Economy*, 27.

Smith, A. (1776). *The Wealth of Nations*.

Smith, F. (1878). *Workshop Management*. London: Wyman and Sons.

Solomons, D. (1952). 'The Historical Development of Costing', in D. Solomons (ed.), *Studies in Costing*. London: Pitman.

Sraffa, P. (1926). 'The Law of Returns Under Competitive Conditions', *Economic Journal*.

Stacey, N. A. H. (1954). *English Accountancy. A Study in Social and Economic History, 1800–1954*. London: Gee.

Stanworth, P. and Giddens, A. (1975). 'The Modern Corporate Economy: Interlocking Directorships in Britain, 1906–1970', *Sociological Review*, 23.

Storey, J. (2001). 'Human Resource Management Today: Assessment', in J. Storey (ed.), *Human Resource Management: A Critical Text*, 2nd edn. London: Thomson Learning.

Supple, B. (1974). 'Aspects of Private Investment Strategy in Britain', in H. Daems and H. Van der Wee (eds.), *The Rise of Managerial Capitalism*. The Hague, the Netherlands: Nijhoff Press.

Taylor, F. W. (1903). *Scientific Management*. New York: Harper.

Tedlow, R. (1993). 'The Fourth Phase of Marketing: Marketing History and the Business World Today', in R. Tedlow and G. Jones (eds.), *The Rise and Fall of Mass Marketing*. London: Routledge.

Teece, D., Pisano, G., and Sheun, A. (1997). 'Dynamic Capabilities and Strategic Management', *Strategic Management Journal*, 18/7.

Thomas, W. A. (1973). *The Provincial Stock Exchanges*. London: Frank Cass.

—— (1978). *The Finance of British Industry, 1918–1976*. London: Methuen.

—— (1986). *The Big Bang*. London: Philip Allan.

Thompson, F. (2001). *Gentrification and the Enterprise Culture: Britain 1780–1980*. Oxford: Oxford University Press.

Thomson, A., Storey, J., Mabey, C., Gray, C., Farmer, E., and Thomson, R. (1997). *A Portrait of Management Development*. London: Institute of Management.

—— Mabey, C., Storey, J., Gray, C., and Iles, P. (2001). *Changing Patterns of Management Development*. Oxford: Blackwell.

—— (2001). 'The Case for Management History', *Accounting, Business and Financial History*, 11/2.

—— and Wilson, J. F. (2006), 'British Management History: Stages and Paradigms', paper presented to the New Zealand Business History Society conference.

Tilly, R. (1974). 'The Growth of Large-Scale Enterprise in Germany since the Middle of the Nineteenth Century', in H. Daems and H. Van Der Wee (eds.), *The Rise of Managerial Capitalism*. Leuven, Belgium: Leuven Press.

Tiratsoo, N. (1999). ' "Cinderellas at the Ball": Production Managers in British Manufacturing, 1945–80', *Contemporary British History*, 13/3.

—— Edwards, R., and Wilson, J. F. (2003). 'Shaping the Content of Business Education in Great Britain, 1945–90: Production Engineers, Accountants and Shifting Definitions of "Relevance" ', in R. P. Amdam, R. Kvalshaugen, and E. Larsen (eds.), *Inside the Business Schools. The Content of European Business Education*. Copenhagen Business School Press.

Toms, S. and Wilson, J. (2003). 'Scale, Scope and Accountability: Towards a New Paradigm of British Business History', *Business History*, 45/1.

—— and Wright, M. (2002). 'Corporate Governance, Strategy and Structure in British Business History, 1950–2000', *Business History*, 44/3.

—— —— (2005). 'Divergence and Convergence Within Anglo-American Corporate Governance Systems: Evidence from the US and UK, 1950–2000', *Business History*, 47/2.

Towne, H. R. (1885). 'The Engineer as Economist', *Transactions of the American Society of Mechanical Engineers*, 7.

Ure, A. (1835). *Philosophy of Manufacturers*. London: Charles Knight.

Urwick, L. (1928). 'Principles of Direction and Control', in J. Lee (ed.), *Dictionary of Industrial Administration*. London: Pitman.

—— and Brech, E. (1945–8). *The Making of Scientific Management*, 3 vols. London: Pitman.

Utton, M. A. (1982). *The Political Economy of Big Business*. London: Martin Robertson.

Veblen, T. (1899). *The Theory of the Leisure Class*. London: George Allen and Unwin.

Wallace, K. (2003). 'J & P Coats Ltd. A Study in Organization', Paisley Ph.D.

Walshe, J. G. (1991). 'Industrial Organisation and Competition Policy', in N. Crafts and N. Woodward (eds.), *The British Economy since 1945*. Oxford: Oxford University Press.

Wardley, P. (1991). 'The Anatomy of Big Business: Aspects of Corporate Development in the Twentieth Century', *Business History*, 33/2.

—— (1999). 'The Emergence of Big Business: The Largest Corporate Employers of Labour in the United Kingdom, Germany and the United States, c. 1907', *Business History*, 41/4.

—— (2000). 'The Commercial Banking Industry and its Part in the Emergence and Consolidation of the Corporate Economy in Britain Before 1940', *Journal of Industrial History*, 3/2.

Weber, B. (1999). 'Next Generation Trading in Futures Markets', *Journal of Management Information Systems*, 16/2.

Wengenroth, U. (1997). 'Germany: Competition Abroad—Co-operation at Home, 1870–1900', in A. D. Chandler, F. Amatori, and T. Hikino (eds.), *Big Business and the Wealth of Nations*. Cambridge: Cambridge University Press.

Whitley, R.D. (1973), 'Commonalities and Connections among Directors of Large Financial Institutions', *Sociological Review*, 21, 4.

—— (1999), *Divergent Capitalisms: The Social Structuring and Change of Business Systems*. Oxford: Oxford University Press.

—— Thomas, A., and Marceau, J. (1981). *Masters of Business? Business Schools and Business Graduates in Britain and France*. London: Tavistock Publications.

Whittington, R. and Whipp, R. (1992). 'Professional Ideology and Marketing Implementation', *European Journal of Marketing*, 26/1.

—— and Mayer, M. (2000). *The European Corporation. Strategy, Structure and Social Science*. Oxford: Oxford University Press.

Whyte, W. H. (1956). *The Organization Man*. New York: Anchor.

Wiener, M. (1981). *English Culture and the Decline of the Industrial Spirit*. Harmondsworth, UK: Penguin.

Wilkins, M. (1986). 'Japanese Multinational Enterprise Before 1914', *Business History Review*, 60.

Williams, K. (2004). 'Corporate Governance and Disappointment', paper given to a seminar at Queen Mary College London on 'Managers and business history'.

Williams, S. (2002). *Characteristics of the Management Population in the UK: Overview Report*. London: Council for Excellence in Management and Leadership.

Williamson, O. (1964). *The Economics of Discretionary Behavior: Managerial Objectives in a Theory of the Firm*. Englewood Cliffs, NJ: Prentice-Hall.

—— (1970). *Corporate Control and Business Behavior*. Englewood Cliffs, NJ: Prentice-Hall.

—— (1975). *Markets and Hierarchies: Analysis of Antitrust Implications*. New York: Free Press.

Willmott, H. (1999). 'On the Idolisation of Markets and the Denigration of Marketeers: Some Critical Reflections on a Professional Paradox', in D. Brownlie, M. Saren, R. Wensley, and R.Whittington (eds.), *Rethinking Marketing: Towards Critical Marketing Accounting*. London: Sage.

Wilson, C. (1954). *The History of Unilever*, 2 vols. London: Cassell.

—— (1968). *Unilever 1945–1965: Challenge and Response in the Post-war Industrial Revolution*. London: Cassell.

Wilson, J. F. (1992). *'The Manchester Experiment'. A History of Manchester Business School, 1965–1990*. London: Paul Chapman Publishing.

—— (1995). *British Business History, 1720–1994*. Manchester, UK: Manchester University Press.

—— (2000). *Ferranti. A History*, Vol. 1. *Building a Family Business, 1882–1975*. Lancaster, UK: Carnegie Publishing.

—— (2006), *Ferranti. A History*, Vol. 2. *From Family Firm to Multinational, 1975–1987*. Lancaster, UK: Carnegie Publishing.

—— and Nishizawa, T. (1999). 'Management Education in Japan and the United Kingdom: Regional Dimensions', in D. Farnie, D. Jeremy, T. Nakaoka, T. Abe, and J. F. Wilson (eds.), *Regional Business Strategies: A Comparison of Lancashire and Kansai, 1890–1990*. London: Routledge.

—— and Popp, A. (eds.) (2003). *Clusters and Networks in English Industrial Districts, 1750–1970*. Aldershot, UK: Ashgate.

Wilson, R. G. (1999). 'Office Workers, Business Elites and the Disappearance of the "Ladder of Success" in Edwardian Glasgow', *Scottish Economic & Social History*, 19.

Witzel, M. (2002). *Builders and Dreamers: The Making and Meaning of Management*. London: Pearson Education.

Woodward, J. (1958). *Management and Technology*. London: HMSO.

—— (1965). *Industrial Organization: Theory and Practice*. Oxford: Oxford University Press.

Wren, D. A. (1994). *The Evolution of Management Thought*, 4th edn. New York: John Wiley & Sons.

Wright, M., Robbie, K., Chiplin, B., and Albrighton, M. (2000). 'The Development of an Organisational Innovation: Management Buy-Outs in the UK, 1980–97', *Business History*, 42/4.

Wrigley, J. (1986). 'Technical Education and Industry in the Nineteenth Century', in B. Elbaum and W. Lazonick (eds.), *The Decline of the British Economy*. Oxford: Clarendon Press.

Yamamura, K. (1978). 'A Re-Examination of Entrepreneurship in Meiji Japan (1868–1912)', *Economic History Review*, 21.

Yamazaki, H. (1989). 'Mitsui Bussan During the 1920s', in A. Teichova, M. Levy-Leboyer, and H. Nussbaum (eds.), *Historical Studies in International Corporate Business*. Cambridge: Cambridge University Press.

Young, A. K. (1979). *The Soga Shosha: Japan's Multinational Trading Companies*. Colorado, CO: Westview Press.

Yui, T. (1988). 'Development, Organisation and Business Strategy of Industrial Enterprises in Japan (1915–1935)', *Japanese Yearbook on Business History*, 5.

Zeitlin, J. (1983) 'The Labour Strategies of British Engineering Employers, 1890–1922', in H. F. Gospel and C. R. Littler (eds.), *Managerial Strategies and Industrial Relations*. London: Heinemann.

Zeitlin, M. (1974). 'Corporate Ownership and Control: The Large Corporation and the Capitalist Class', *American Journal of Sociology*, 79.

Index